OUT OF OPTIONS

This book tackles an area of adolescent behavior that presents a significant challenge for parents, teachers, and professionals the world over. Although much has been written on the topic of adolescent suicide, we see continued high rates throughout industrialized nations. The overlap between suicidal behaviors and other forms of serious risk-taking is a relatively new avenue of research and gives insight into the motivations of some adolescents. The cognitive model developed and evaluated in this book provides further insight into the progression from early problems faced by young people to the serious outcomes of suicide and risk-taking. The model allows us to suggest points of intervention for young people and to demonstrate that, although there are overlapping features between suicidal and risk-taking behaviors, attempts to intervene would target different problem areas for suicidal adolescents than for risk-taking adolescents.

Kate Sofronoff is currently a Lecturer in Clinical Psychology in the School of Psychology at the University of Queensland, Brisbane, Australia. She completed a Ph.D. in clinical psychology in 1998 in the area of adolescent suicide and risk-taking. Prior to undertaking studies in psychology, she worked as a high school teacher for 10 years, so she has considerable experience working with adolescents. Dr. Sofronoff is continuing to pursue research interests in the area of adolescent behavior as well as in other areas of clinical psychology.

Len Dalgliesh is a Senior Lecturer in Judgement and Decision Making in the School of Psychology at the University of Queensland. From 1981 to 1988, he was a Lecturer in the Department of Social Work, where his interest in child protection decision making developed. He has given many keynote talks, conference presentations, and workshops on risk assessment and decision making. He is currently preparing a book, *Risk and Decisions in Child Protection*. He is on the editorial board of *Child Abuse Review*.

Robert Kosky, M.D., is Emeritus Professor of Child Psychiatry at the University of Adelaide. He has written extensively in the areas of youth suicide, delinquency, and early intervention. He was Chair of the National Collaborating Centres for the child and adolescent component of the Australian Government's National Survey of Mental Health and Wellbeing.

CAMBRIDGE STUDIES IN CHILD AND ADOLESCENT HEALTH

Steering Committee:

Klaus Hurrelmann, *University of Bielefeld, Germany*
Candace Curric, *University of Edinburgh, United Kingdom*
Vivian B. Rasmussen, *WHO Regional Office for Europe, Copenhagen, Denmark*
John Schulenberg, *University of Michigan*

The ISCAH series publishes books on the health and disease status of children, adolescents, and young adults and on intervention strategies in medicine, psychology, sociology, public health, and political science. The series is supported by the international research network Health Behavior in School Children (HBSC) and is sponsored by the World Health Organization (WHO) Regional Office for Europe.

In this series:

Diabetic Adolescents and Their Families, Inge Seiffge-Krenke
How Children Learn to Be Healthy, Barbara J. Tinsley
Gender Differences at Puberty, Chris Hayward

OUT OF OPTIONS

A Cognitive Model of Adolescent Suicide and Risk-Taking

KATE SOFRONOFF

University of Queensland

LEN DALGLIESH

University of Queensland

ROBERT KOSKY

University of Adelaide

PUBLISHED BY THE PRESS SYNDICATE OF THE UNIVERSITY OF CAMBRIDGE
The Pitt Building, Trumpington Street, Cambridge, United Kingdom

CAMBRIDGE UNIVERSITY PRESS
The Edinburgh Building, Cambridge CB2 2RU, UK
40 West 20th Street, New York, NY 10011-4211, USA
477 Williamstown Road, Port Melbourne, VIC 3207, Australia
Ruiz de Alarcón 13, 28014 Madrid, Spain
Dock House, The Waterfront, Cape Town 8001, South Africa

http://www.cambridge.org

First published 2005

Printed in the United States of America

Typefaces ITC Stone Serif 9.5/15 pt. and ITC Symbol   *System* LaTeX 2_ε [TB]

A catalog record for this book is available from the British Library.

Library of Congress Cataloging in Publication Data
Sofronoff, Kate.
Out of options : suicide and risk-taking in adolescents : a cogitive model / Kate Sofronoff,
Lenard Dalgliesh, Robert Koskey.
p.   cm. – (International studies on child and adolescent health)
Includes bibliographical references and index.
ISBN 0-521-81238-0
1. Teenagers – Suicidal behavior.   2. Suicide – Prevention.   3. Risk-taking (Psychology)
in adolescence.   I. Dalgliesh, Lenard.   II. Koskey, Robert.   III. Title.   IV. Series.
HV6546.S59   2004
362.28′0835 – dc22   2004043425

ISBN 0 521 81238 0 hardback

We dedicate this book to the many young people who helped us by talking to us so openly at difficult times in their lives and by answering questionnaires that were undoubtedly tedious for them. Many of these young people espoused a hope that by helping us they would in some way be helping other adolescents. Although we know that movement in this area is slow, there are currently projects and interventions in progress that may see this help eventuate for some young people.

Special thanks must also go to Kate Lilley, whose work in proofreading and editing made the final draft of this manuscript possible.

Contents

CONTENTS

AN EVALUATION OF THE S/RT MODEL

IMPLICATIONS FOR TREATMENT

CONTENTS

Preface

This book focuses on one aspect of youth suicide prevention – the role of cognitive mediators in the suicide process in young people. We have written it because the topics we investigated may contribute to practical interventions to prevent suicide in young people.

Most current suicide prevention programs are educational in nature. They try to give young people knowledge about where to go for services and how to recognize symptoms in themselves and their peers. This is a reasonable approach, since one of the barriers to young people's accessing adequate care, and one of the causes of delays in treatment, is the lack of this information (Sawyer, Kosky, & Graetz, 2000).

However, even with this knowledge, it is not clear whether a young person who is seriously suicidal and in a crisis can utilize it to avoid the adverse outcome. To do so requires appropriate cognitive skills, the ability to work out what is important and what is not, and the capacity to apply the knowledge to solve the looming problems. We have focused on this point in the suicidal process. We have tried to assess whether there are cognitive skills that are deficient in suicidal young people and, if so, whether any clear implications for clinical programs in suicide prevention flow from this.

For a previous work, one of us sat in on juvenile court hearings to listen to the stories of the young people who faced the courts (Sofronoff, 1999). Another of us surveyed young people who were in detention centers (Kosky, Sawyer, and Gowland, 1990). We were both struck by the evident similarities between young people who take serious risks and those who were seriously suicidal. Serious risk-taking youths often end up in the juvenile justice system. Seriously suicidal youths often end up in the mental health system. Both have potentially fatal outcomes.

Our clinical impressions and research findings about young people in the criminal justice system have, of course, been noted by others, notably Lewis (1988). Taking as our focus the processes that lead to these adverse outcomes, we have tried, in this book, to measure the differences and similarities in the cognitive capacities involved in the decisions made by young people who are attracted to suicide or risk-taking. Again, we have done this with a view to developing a practical approach to suicide prevention.

We begin the book with an overview of risk factors in suicide and risk-taking youth. Then we follow with a qualitative comparison of young people who do not exhibit suicidal or risk-taking tendencies with those who are suicidal or risk takers. We then use the findings from these comparisons to derive a hypothesis about the cognitive skills of young people who make up the target groups.

We attempt to fit these findings into a model of suicide in which we posit cognitive processes as mediators between pathological emotional states and adverse outcomes. From this we develop a number of practical suggestions in relation to prevention. Of course, we are not yet in a position to be able to test these possibilities insofar as they can prevent suicide; that would require further research and perhaps other people to follow up our ideas.

Introduction

There are many different definitions of suicide, and it is important for us to define from the outset what we mean by suicide and attempted suicide. Durkheim (1951), in his important contribution to the taxonomy of suicide, "Le Suicide," defined suicide as follows:

> All cases of death resulting directly or indirectly from a positive or negative act of the victim himself which he knows will produce this result, whereas an attempt is an act thus defined but falling short of the actual death. (p. 44)

It is this definition that we use in this book. In particular, we should note that when we talk about "attempted" suicide, we are talking about failed suicide. In other words, the young people in this book who make up the categories involving attempted suicide were drawn from hospital populations. Their suicidal act had resulted in damage to themselves to the extent that they required medical treatment, even though this damage fell short of actual death. Since it is not possible to use young people who have completed suicide in research of this type, those who have failed in the suicide attempt are the closest we can come to a group who have not survived the tragedy of suicide.

1

The definition proposed by Durkheim has proved useful for purposes of communication among workers in the field and for gathering statistics. It forms the basis of the national statistics available from most countries. However, it has its limitations. Although it alludes to intention by including "knowing the result of the act," it says nothing about the processes that bring a person to this point.

There have been other definitions of suicide that have alluded to process or to the way in which suicide may develop in a person. Shneidman (1985) provided a definition that regards suicide as an act undertaken by those suffering from a complex and painful condition to which suicide is a solution:

> suicide is a conscious act of self-annihilation best understood as a multidimensional malaise in a needful individual who defines an issue for which suicide is perceived as the best solution. (p. 203)

This definition implies a link between suicide and problem-solving deficits. It is this link that we propose to investigate in this book. We contend that some adolescents who make a suicide attempt are doing so in a maladaptive effort to solve their problems. This is by no means an original idea and has been proposed by a number of other investigators. Many of them have followed up this view with significant work, which we mention in the body of this book (McLaughlin, Miller, & Warwick, 1996; Strosahl, Chiles, & Linehan, 1992).

The idea that problem solving is a component of adolescent suicide has many implications. If suicide is seen as a solution to complex personal problems, then the issue is opened up to involve the impact of modern youth culture on young people. We note that in the past two decades, music, television, and film have dealt with the issue of youth suicide, and some at least seem to have made suicide more

2

acceptable as a solution to life's problems, particularly among adolescents. For instance, *Dead Poets Society*, an immensely popular film, has a young character commit suicide when he feels thwarted by his father's ambitions for him.

Why is suicide a particular problem of youth? How young are children when they perceive the finality of death? According to most of the research findings, children of about the age of 9 years understand death in a way familiar to most adults, although there is obviously great variation among children. Certainly, suicide seems rare before the age of 12 years. Quinnet (1987) suggests that younger suicide attempters are less capable of perceiving the finality of suicide and therefore more likely to see suicide as an immediate, short-term solution to their problems. With their lack of conception of finality, they think that if this fails to work, some other solutions can be tried in the future. Paradoxically, when suicide attempts are made by children, the acts are unusually violent in nature, with hanging and running into traffic figuring prominently and with a high likelihood of this being a fatal act (Kosky, 1982).

There is a change in suicide patterns after puberty. There is a rapid rise in the prevalence of suicide after a person reaches the age of 13 years. The prevalence rates peak around the age of 25 years. In this respect, suicide appears to be a developmental problem. The use of substances for poison increases as a method, although hanging and firearms are also prominent causes. There are so many things changing in adolescence, it is hard to know what might be contributing to the increasing prevalence rates for suicide. It seems unlikely that the biological processes of puberty have a specific association. The single study that looked at this issue showed that it was more likely that increasing suicide rates between the ages of 12 and 18 were due to psychosocial determinants rather than biological ones (Zubrick, Kosky, & Silburn, 1987).

Adolescent Development

Adolescence is a significant period in human biological and psychosocial development. In addition to the onset of puberty, adolescents struggle with the critical tasks that accompany the transition from childhood to adulthood. These include the establishment of an individual identity, the formulation of goals and future direction, and the move away from dependency on family and caregivers toward independence (Austrian, 2002). This transition and the factors that measure or affect its success have been a subject for intensive psychological theory and research. The most recent theory identifies three overlapping stages in the progression through adolescence: young, middle, and older adolescence (Austrian, 2002).

Puberty is perceived to be the most influential factor in young adolescence (ages 12–14). Young people are preoccupied with bodily appearance and the need to conform with an undefined code of normalcy. They adopt conformity and peer compliance as defenses against rejection and disapproval. Self-esteem is largely dependent on peer acceptance, and an emerging emotional distance from parents ensues.

In middle adolescence (14–16 years), peers remain influential in the development of interpersonal and social skills. Parental dependence fluctuates. Adolescent youth in this stage are also characterized by fluctuations in elation, irritability, moodiness, and depression that arises from biological changes or out of conflict between individual value systems and conformity to social mores. The search for identity and autonomy is further complicated by decisions regarding risk-taking and sexual behaviors. These decisions are usually foreshadowed by experimentation with alcohol and sometimes other substance use and the formation of tentatively intimate relationships. Growth in self-esteem usually stems from "successes" in these social aspects as well as from athletic or academic achievement.

Older adolescence (16–19 years) is distinguished by the capacity for consideration of the consequences of decisions and behavior. The ability to make these decisions is bolstered by the increased confidence and independence associated with obtaining a driver's licence and reaching the legal drinking age (in some countries). Successful negotiation of these issues through positive decision making results in personal and vocational skills being crystallized into young people who can find a place in society that combines individuals' own value systems and their sexual and occupational self-identities. From this position, they approach adulthood and attempt to formulate a meaning of life.

Despite entrenched opinion about the vicissitudes of adolescence, most people do not experience turmoil or psychological disturbances during the developmental processes of adolescence (Offer, Schonert-Reichl, & Boxer, 1996). Most young people enter adulthood confident in their new identity (Austrian, 2002). However, Erikson raised a point of caution. He highlighted the possibility of the development of a "negative identity," in which young people struggle with an inability to bring these developmental issues together and instead experience a sense of chronic role diffusion; they seem to choose to be "nobody," "someone bad," or even "dead" (Austrian, 2002).

Adolescents and Suicide

Attention has been focused on the problem of suicide in adolescents on a worldwide basis. Overall, most countries are reporting a rise in the rates of suicide among young people aged 15–25 years. The highest increases have been reported in the developed Western nations, although this may be an artifact produced by more thorough health-recording methods available in those countries. Nevertheless, the rises can be clearly seen in the statistics provided by UNICEF (1993) and presented here in Figure 1.

Despite the alarming growth patterns illustrated here, the literature devoted specifically to adolescent suicide is relatively limited to epidemiology and there are still many unknown causes. For example, the role of hopelessness as a factor in adolescent suicide and attempted suicide is still unclear. The relative weight to be attached to adverse family factors, social pressures such as school pressures, thwarted ambition, experience of loss, experience of abuse, and the many other factors that have been implied as contributing to youth suicide is still unclear.

The increase in youth suicide is dominated by young male suicides. Some of these young men can only be described as model citizens. Connell (1972) pointed out that many of the young schoolchildren who attempted suicide were successful, well behaved, and highly regarded young people. However, some also come from the population that comes into contact with the criminal justice system and are likely to be aggressive, to engage in serious risk-taking behavior, and to present difficult management problems. Suicidal young people may not be catered to by available health services.

For both of these groups, the spotting of suicidal tendencies presents difficulties. For the former well-regarded group, it is often difficult for parents, friends, teachers, and others to accept that such adolescents have any problems. For them, their difficulties may be overlooked and they may do nothing to draw attention to their personal struggles. For the aggressive risk-taking youth, their personal problems may be buried underneath acting-out aggressive behaviors. In these cases, it is difficult to reach the world of turmoil that they are experiencing.

The upshot of the problem of identifying presuicidal youth is apparent in a study conducted in Norway. Of 99 boys and 30 girls who committed suicide, only 24% had ever accessed treatment for

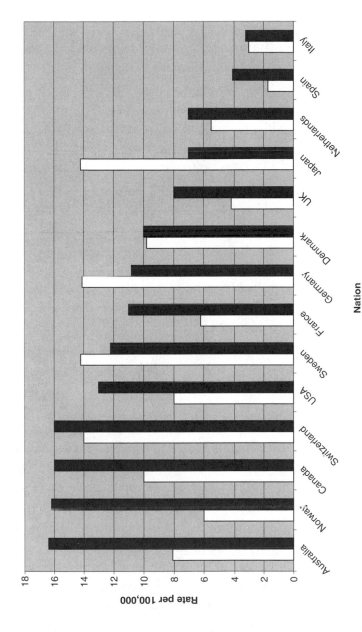

Figure 1. Rates of suicide per 100,000 for 15- to 24-year-olds in 1970 (☐) and 1987–1990 (■) for 14 industrialized nations.

7

emotional or behavioral problems (Groholt et al., 1997). There are many examples like this from other parts of the world. This has led to the proposition that although suicide risk increases with age for adolescent males, treatment decreases (Piacentini et al., 1995).

The failure of adolescents to access services or for those services to pick up on the suicidal feelings present in some adolescents gives the development of prevention programs a sense of urgency. There is a dearth of controlled studies on treatment modalities for suicidal young people (Rudd, 2000). Risk-taking behaviors can be positively correlated with suicidal behaviors (Woods et al., 1997). We explore the nature of this link in this book.

That some such link between suicide and risk-taking should exist is not surprising, for risk-taking behaviors fall comfortably within the definitions of both Durkheim and Schneidman that we quoted earlier. Self-harm can occur through risk-taking such as driving while intoxicated, driving at high speed, binge drinking, and substance abuse as well as engaging in risky sexual and eating behaviors. At least one way of seeing these risk-taking behaviors is that they are forms of self-murder.

Although the absence of a manifest intention to cause immediate death is often relied on to exclude risk-taking behaviors from the spectrum of suicidal acts, both sets of behaviors have a central factor in common: Each is deliberately calculated to involve the risk of death and each may in fact have a fatal outcome. In this sense they conform to the definition of Durkheim. Serious forms of risk-taking behavior may differ from suicidal behavior only because the intention to cause death is not made explicit. The usual failure to clearly indicate intention tends to confound coronial inquiries, which may lead to misclassification of cause of death, for instance, of fatal motor vehicle accidents (Kosky, 1982).

As to the processes involved, there are evident similarities between the psychological and social factors considered as markers in suicide and serious risk-taking. When one of us attended the children's court, it was very apparent that in a large number of the cases observed, the background factors of dysfunctional families, parental psychopathology, abuse, significant negative life events, and suicidal behavior were present in the stories that the young people brought to court. They were strikingly like the 18 children who were among the first suicidal young people to be systematically described in the scientific literature. These children were reported to be disturbed, depressed, and aggressive (Bender & Schilder, 1937).

The question we address in this book is this: Given the links between suicidal and risk-taking young people, do they have cognitive deficits, and, if so, are they the same ones or are they different?

An area long fraught with difficulty is the prediction of suicidal behavior. A distinguished authority (Litman, 1996) has said that, despite the current wealth of literature and research effort devoted to the topic,

> we can pick out individuals and groups who are more vulnerable to suicide than other individuals and groups, but we cannot predict which individual will commit suicide or when. (p. 3)

One aim of this book is to look at possible similarities and differences in the populations encompassed by suicide and risk-taking behaviors and to draw that information together as a model of suicidal and risk-taking behavior. This model would show how adolescents progress to these extreme behaviors. These pathways will show those variables that are significant mediators between early indications of risk and the later adverse behaviors. If it is possible to produce such a model and to justify it through empirical data, then it will provide opportunities to predict the potential for adverse behavioral outcomes, thereby increasing the opportunities for early interventions to prevent these outcomes.

1 Adolescent Suicide: An Overview of the Epidemiology

Epidemiology

Epidemiological studies indicate that suicide is a leading cause of death among adolescents throughout the industrialized world. The rate of suicide among adolescents increased dramatically over the last part of the 20th century, and this increase is of the greatest concern to the community. In the United States of America, the overall rate of suicide has remained steady but the mean age of those committing suicide has decreased. The rate at which young people commit suicide has risen dramatically (see Table 1). This trend is mirrored in Australia, where the overall rate of suicide for 15- to 24-year-olds is 16.4 per 100,000, among the highest in the industrialized world (UNICEF, 1993).

Age and Gender

The suicide rate among male adolescents, aged 15–19 years, is particularly alarming. In Australia, the Australian Bureau of Statistics

Table 1 U.S. Suicide rates per 100,000 of population by age groups, between 1957 and 1987

Year	Ages 15–19	Ages 20–24	Ages 15–24
1957	2.5	5.8	4.0
1987	10.3	15.3	12.9
% change	+312	+163	+222

Source: From *Vital Statistics of the United States* (annual mortality summaries), U.S. Department of Health and Human Services, Hyattsville, MD: National Center for Health Statistics (in Lester & Yang, 1998).

(1995) reported a fourfold increase between 1960 and 1995 in suicides for young males. In 1960, 50 males between the ages of 15 and 24 committed suicide, representing a rate of 6.8 per 100,000 of the general population. By 1994 this had increased to 384, or a rate of 27 per 100,000. Female suicides are significantly less common than male suicides (approximately 1:5; Leslie, Stein, & Rotheram-Borus, 2002).

These trends are seen across the world. Figures 1.1 through 1.5 illustrate both the gender discrepancy in suicide and the increase in

	5-14yrs	15-24	25-34	35-44	45-54	55-64	65-74	75+
Total	1.3	26.7	25.1	14.8	14.7	13.3	17	13.6
Male	1.1	39.1	44	24.9	21.5	23.3	29.1	29.2
Female	1.5	14.3	7.2	5.1	7.9	3.4	6.2	4.5

Figure 1.1. Suicide rates (per 100,000) by gender and age, New Zealand, 1996.

12

	5-14yrs	15-24	25-34	35-44	45-54	55-64	65-74	75+
◆ Total	0.2	14.6	18.7	15.9	14.7	13.7	11.8	16
■ Male	0.3	23.1	31	24.8	21.7	21.3	18.5	26.8
▲ Female	0	6.1	6.4	7	7.7	6	5	5.2

Figure 1.2. Suicide rates (per 100,000) by gender and age, Australia, 1995.

adolescent rates in a selection of countries. The statistics are the most recent available and were obtained from the World Health Organization, Geneva, 2000.

Adolescent males with substance abuse and conduct disorders have been established as major contributors to the rise in suicide rates among young people (Litman & Farberow, 1986; Wunderlich et al., 2001). In the United States there is also ready access to guns, which may be even greater than usual, for young people with this combination of behavioral problems. Guns are involved in 60%

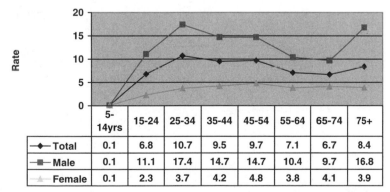

	5-14yrs	15-24	25-34	35-44	45-54	55-64	65-74	75+
◆ Total	0.1	6.8	10.7	9.5	9.7	7.1	6.7	8.4
■ Male	0.1	11.1	17.4	14.7	14.7	10.4	9.7	16.8
▲ Female	0.1	2.3	3.7	4.2	4.8	3.8	4.1	3.9

Figure 1.3. Suicide rates (per 100,000) by gender and age, United Kingdom, 1997.

13

Figure 1.4. Suicide rates (per 100,000) by gender and age, U.S.A., 1997.

of the suicides in the U.S.A. These troubled American youths are extremely difficult for mental health services to deal with, and they tend to "fall through the cracks" in terms of orthodox treatment facilities.

Although suicide risk for younger males increases with age, the chances for treatment may decrease (Piacentini et al., 1995). This

Figure 1.5. Suicide rates (per 100,000) by gender and age, Japan, 1997.

paradoxical trend may be related to higher rates of conduct disorder and substance abuse found among older male adolescents, which seem to reduce the likelihood of seeking assistance or of receiving it from wary service providers. In addition, these conditions usually carry low levels of compliance with treatment (Weiner, Abraham, & Lyons, 2001). Similarly, adolescents who exhibit conduct disorder or who have substance abuse problems are often neglected in research because they are difficult to access, difficult to deal with on a consistent basis for research projects, and taxing on the emotions of research staff. For instance, an exhaustive follow-up study of juveniles in detention centers could only locate 50% of these youths after their release (Kosky, Sawyer, & Fotheringham, 1996), and such an attrition rate is not uncommon among these young people in research studies that require the subject's cooperation over time (Lewis et al., 1994).

Rates of attempted suicide are much greater than rates of actual suicide. About 1 in 200 females and about 1 in 500 males aged 15–24 years attempt suicide each year, compared with an actual suicide rate of about 1 in 20,000 for females and 1 in 5,000 for males of the same age in Australia (Davis & Kosky, 1991). Furthermore, it has been found that a previous suicide attempt puts a person at significantly greater risk for future attempts as well as for completed suicide. King et al. (1995) found that 18% of adolescents hospitalized after an attempted suicide tried to commit suicide again within 6 months.

Up to 60% of high school students who attempt suicide have experienced times when they had thoughts about suicide prior to the attempt (Lewinsohn, Rohde, & Seeley, 1996). It may be that suicidal ideation predicts future suicidal behavior. Unfortunately, there is also evidence that increased suicidal ideation actually decreases the likelihood that the adolescent will seek help (Carlton & Deane, 2000). The studies in this book look closely at suicide attempters and adolescents with depressive symptomatology who may consider suicide as a way of overcoming their problems.

2 Risk and Predisposing Factors in Adolescent Suicide

Introduction

It is commonly accepted that there are risk factors and personal vulnerabilities that make a person more likely to attempt suicide or to commit suicide. These factors include sociocultural and individual influences. Durkheim (1897) considered social and cultural factors to be the major influence on suicidal behavior. In fictional literature, such as Shakespeare's story of Romeo and Juliet, the stress of personal relationships was often foregrounded as a powerful influence. Freud also considered suicide to be a psychological act, with personal problems and sociocultural pressures, such as school expectations, contributing to the outcome. The literature continues to debate the relative importance of individual, psychiatric, and environmental stressors in explaining suicidal behavior; the following review highlights the complexity of the interrelationships among these factors.

Environmental Variables

STRESSFUL LIFE EVENTS

Stressful life events or recent family difficulties have been found to precede most adolescent suicide attempts. The most common problems that occur in the weeks before an adolescent suicide or suicide attempt include relationship breakups, interpersonal conflict, and difficulties with discipline and the law (Shaffer & Piacentini, 1994). Unresolved conflict within the family and a lack of closeness between family members are also commonly reported (Kosky, Silburn, & Zubrick, 1990b; Watt & Sharp, 2001). This implies that many suicidal adolescents do not feel supported by their family when they feel at their most vulnerable.

Disciplinary crises, for instance in school or with the law, were found to have occurred as immediate precursors in 36% of 30 children aged 12–15 years who committed suicide in the U.K. (Shaffer, 1974). Such crises along with those caused by separation or loss occurred in all but 2 of 53 completed adolescent suicides in Norway (Marttunen et al., 1994). A second study limited to 19 female suicides aged 13–22 years revealed similar results, with interpersonal difficulties of this sort preceding the suicide in all but one case (Marttunen et al., 1995). These findings are hardly surprising since it is usually supposed that any act as serious and desperate as self-destruction must surely follow a personal crisis. The question is why the adolescent chose suicide as a solution to this problem. Similar situations are borne by almost all teenagers in the course of their schooling and life. What made suicide the only option?

Suicidal adolescents tend to experience a period of escalating problems that start with the onset of puberty (Hoberman & Garfinkel, 1988) or simply with increasing age (Zubrick et al., 1987). A study that compared adolescent suicide attempters with depressed adolescents

18

and a control group found that the suicidal group had experienced more negative life events in the previous year than either of the other two groups (de Wilde et al., 1992). These negative events, however, were not seen to have been the cause of the suicide attempt; Hoberman and Garfinkel (1988) point out that although it is true that some form of stress precedes most suicides, the stressors themselves are common life events for all adolescents. We know that adolescence, particularly middle and later adolescence, is likely to be a time of stress for many adolescents with respect to conflict with parents, mood disturbance, and participation in risk activities (Arnett, 1999).

FAMILY DYSFUNCTION

Other research has emphasized the role of actual family dynamics in adolescent suicide. Suicide attempters have described feeling that their families were unsupportive and stressful. They typically described them as lacking closeness, having high conflict, and exhibiting poor control (Asarnow, Carlson, & Guthrie, 1987; Kosky, 1983; Kosky, Silburn, & Zubrick, 1986).

One problem in attempting to address the problem of the relationship between an adolescent's suicidal behavior and his or her family is the possible bias in self-reports. Current mental state may result in distortions in the perception of life events. It may also be that the adolescent's psychiatric problems have caused the family difficulties that he or she complains about. Asarnow (1992) found that higher levels of depression and low levels of family closeness were correlated with suicidal behavior in a group of 6- to 13-year-old psychiatric inpatients. These findings suggest that family problems, stressful life events, and psychological factors interact in the process of suicidal behavior.

A lack of closeness between family members can be a major contributing factor in the development of depression (DiFilippo &

Overholser, 2000). Garrison et al. (1990), however, found that only 21% to 36% of the variance in depressive symptom scores could be explained by a lack of intimacy within the family. Demographic, family, and life event data failed to offer insight into the additional causes of depression. This suggests that the development of depression is complex and is likely to have multiple causes.

The results of these studies provide an insight into the kinds of background factors that may place young people at greater risk of developing depression and other psychological problems, and how these factors may further interact to increase this risk. These studies suggest that undesirable life events and a lack of closeness between family members are potentially associated with an increase in thoughts about suicide.

INTERPERSONAL INTERACTIONS

Relationship breakdowns and disciplinary crises were found to be major contributors to suicide in a study of 120 completed adolescent suicides (Gould et al., 1996). The factors examined included socioeconomic status (SES), parent–child relationships, severe physical punishment, parental psychopathology including history of suicide and criminal activity, stressful life events, school or work problems, and psychiatric diagnoses. It is most important to note that the found stressors existed within the context of symptoms of psychiatric problems. Gould et al. (1996) concluded that once they had adjusted for the presence of the adolescent's psychiatric disorder, the only other problem that contributed to adolescent suicide was adverse parental involvement with the police. This was a psychological autopsy study, however, and therefore used post-mortem data.

The findings from studies looking at environmental factors are mixed. Kienhorst et al. (1990) concluded from their study that psychological factors such as depression and self-concept increase suicidal behaviors in adolescents more than sociodemographic variables such as gender and parental divorce. A second study, however, found that both depression and low levels of social support from the family increase adolescent vulnerability to suicidal behaviors (Lewinsohn, Rohde, & Seeley, 1993).

FAMILY INTERACTIONS

The families of suicidal adolescents may tend to avoid conflict more than the average family. Mitchell and Rosenthal (1992), however, found that although these families did avoid conflict, they were no more overprotective or overinvolved with their child than the families of nonsuicidal adolescents. Conflict avoidance within the family might explain why suicidal adolescents feel isolated, alienated, and powerless. It may be that low family support and poor conflict resolution within the family make it more likely that an adolescent will show poor problem-solving skills and increased levels of hopelessness. A vulnerability to psychiatric problems would place these adolescents at even greater risk of developing suicidal behaviors.

It is often suggested that parental divorce may increase an adolescent's vulnerability to suicide. Gould et al. (1998) found that, in general, parental divorce increased suicide risk only if the mother had psychiatric problems or the father had been in trouble with the police. The study also assessed the indirect effect of separation or divorce on suicide through increased risk of mood disorders, disruptive disorders, and substance abuse. Only substance abuse was more common in divorced or separated families, and this was only significant if the father had a history of criminal behavior. It would therefore appear unlikely that parental divorce or separation can explain the dramatic increase in adolescent suicide. There does, however, appear to be a connection between divorce or separation and parental psychiatric disorders, and these problems are frequently found in the backgrounds of suicidal adolescents.

It is also important to take into account the difficulties associated with studying life events and family problems in relation to suicidal behavior. The current mental state or personality profile of the adolescent may influence his or her impression of particular life events, or even create an environment where negative events are more likely to occur. In other words, it is necessary to consider the importance of life events within the context in which they occur and to gather other information to try to understand the development of these events. It is also the case that in many of these studies the information is collected after the suicide has occurred, and the fact that a family member has committed suicide may influence the memories that individuals have about past events. It is also possible that the inconsistent findings seen in these studies are caused partly by the differences in the populations that researchers choose to study, and the varied approaches adopted by these researchers. Different studies not only measure different factors but also use varying methods of studying these factors.

In summary, the literature points to the fact that the adolescent's environment and family may play a role in the development of suicide risk and should be included in any model of adolescent suicidal behavior. It also seems fairly certain that a stressful life event such as relationship breakdown, problems with discipline, or some other significant stressor will act as the immediate trigger for the act. The literature also suggests that these problems often coexist with psychiatric disorders, and that it is the combination and interaction of these factors that produces suicidal behavior. Unfortunately, these environmental and family problems that predispose children and adolescents to depression, substance abuse, or behavioral problems will probably still be present in the background after the young person has developed problems.

Intrinsic Factors

The personal traits that make it more likely a child will develop some form of psychiatric problem in adolescence interact with stressful life events and environmental circumstances. Some of these traits are distinctly individual, such as gender and genetic disposition, but others could also be seen as stressful life events or family factors, such as abuse as a child or a family history of psychiatric problems. Intrinsic factors are defined here as those factors that may have existed and influenced the child over time and thereby become an intrinsic part of the adolescent's character.

GENDER

Many studies have stressed the fact that gender is a risk factor for both major depression and suicide attempts. Adolescent girls are much more likely than boys to be depressed, have thoughts about suicide, and to attempt suicide. Adolescent boys, on the other hand, are more likely to complete suicide. King et al. (1993) found that approximately five times as many boys as girls in the 15- to 24-year-old age group will commit suicide; however, 1 in 10 girls and 1 in 25 boys are likely to report a suicide attempt (Lewinsohn et al., 1996). The fact that these findings are self-reported may distort the differences between the genders, as girls may be more willing to admit a suicide attempt than boys.

It is likely that there are also gender differences in the combination of disorders that occur during adolescence and the level of risk for the adolescent that accompanies these combinations (Wichstrom & Rossow, 2002). Typically, boys display symptoms of substance abuse and conduct disorder while girls show symptoms of depression and anxiety (Leslie et al., 2002). However, findings are once again mixed. Andrews and Lewinsohn (1992), for example, found that boys who suffered from an anxiety disorder were at an increased risk for suicide but girls were not. Some studies suggest that males and females are equally likely to attempt suicide, especially if they use alcohol or drugs (Hollis, 1996), and that the gender bias disappears with increasing age (Wunderlich et al., 2001). Unfortunately, males frequently attempt suicide by means such as using firearms and hanging that are more likely to prove fatal (Wichstrom & Rossow, 2002; Wunderlich et al., 2001).

The information gained from this literature is important because it indicates the types of psychological disorders we might expect to see in girls and boys who have been exposed to the risk factors and background variables discussed in this review. We can conclude that although girls will more commonly exhibit depressive symptomatology and will attempt suicide, boys more commonly display conduct problems and their suicidal behavior is such that death is more likely to result before any help is accessed through mental health services. It is imperative, therefore, to engage those adolescent males who participate in risk behaviors before they reach the stage of attempting suicide.

SEXUALITY

Though lacking in depth and longevity, there is significant research to foreground young people who are gay or bisexual as being at special risk of attempting suicide (Leslie et al., 2002). A recent study performed by D'Augelli, Hershberger, and Pilkington (2001) on lesbian, gay, and bisexual (LGB) youths confirmed this association between suicidality and sexual orientation: 42% had sometimes or often thought of suicide and one third (33%) reported at least one suicide attempt. In a population-based study of Minnesota public schools, 28% of gay or bisexual males and only 4% of heterosexual males reported a past suicide attempt. The results for females, though less convincing, showed a similar discrepancy, with 21% of lesbian or bisexual females and 15% of heterosexual females reporting an attempt (Remafedi et al., 1998). Garofolo et al. (1999) also concluded that sexual orientation had an independent association with suicide attempts for male youths. Psychological autopsies of adolescent suicides do not support higher rates of suicide among homosexual young people, and the figures reported are not significantly greater than community surveys. It may be, however, that there are somewhat different risk factors operating for this population.

Research is now directed toward the predicting factors for this "special risk" group. In many cases, risk factors outlined in this book are exacerbated for LGB youths. These youths are more likely to suffer from a lack of support from social networks and an increased risk of negative health behaviors, and they are more likely to experience victimization, threats, and ejection from their homes (Leslie et al., 2002). Generally, suicidal LGB youths acknowledged a relationship between their suicidal ideation or suicide attempts and their sexual orientation (D'Augnelli et al., 2001). Most suicide attempts followed awareness of same-sex feelings and preceded disclosure of sexual orientation to others. A test for correlation with negative parental response to youths' sexual orientation found that of suicide attempters in a sample of LGB youths, 48% perceived their father and 28% their mother as being rejecting or intolerant compared with 28% and 19% for nonattempters (D'Augnelli et al., 2001).

McDaniel, Purcell, and D'Augelli (2001) emphasized the limitations associated with studying this particular demographic. Apart from the small sample sizes created by a relatively low prevalence of both suicide and homosexuality, one must take into account the fact that sexual identity is still developing in adolescence. The common reluctance among young people toward disclosure creates results that are skewed toward youths who are comfortable with their sexuality. However, movement toward greater community acceptance and removal of discriminatory laws may alter these dynamics of reluctant disclosure and perceived rejection. It is possible that an individual's masking of development of same-sex preferences may affect current postmortem analyses by hiding this as a reason for suicide. It is also the case that definitions and measures for sexual behaviors and orientation have yet to be standardized.

FAMILY HISTORY OF PSYCHIATRIC ILLNESS

Brent (1995) suggests that parental psychological problems such as depression, substance abuse, and criminal and antisocial behavior can cause problems for children in several ways. The children are not only more likely to suffer from the same disorders but also to grow up in an environment that puts them at greater suicide risk. This suggestion is supported by the fact that psychological problems have been found in the parents of adolescents who have committed suicide, even when these adolescents appeared to be free of such disorders themselves (Brent et al., 1993b).

Psychological problems in divorced parents may also increase the risk of adolescent suicide. Children of divorced families are only at greater risk of attempting suicide than those from intact families if their parents have psychological or criminal problems (Gould et al., 1998). In addition to this, it seems to be the case that divorced mothers are more likely to suffer from mood disorders.

EXPERIENCES OF ABUSE AS A CHILD

It has been widely suggested that suicide attempters and depressed adolescents are much more likely than nonsuicidal adolescents to have experienced sexual or physical abuse. We know that research continues to show depression as a significant psychological consequence to sexual abuse (Pillay & Schoubben-Hesk, 2001).

Silverman, Reinherz, and Giaconia (1996) examined the relationship between the experience of physical and sexual abuse as a child and the later development of psychological problems. The results strongly indicated that young adults who had experienced physical or sexual abuse were at risk for developing major depression, posttraumatic stress disorder, antisocial behavior, substance abuse disorder, suicidal ideation, and suicide attempts. A large number of these adolescents showed symptoms of two or more psychiatric disorders. At age 21, one in four had made a suicide attempt.

These findings have been supported more recently in a study by Wunderlich et al. (2001), who also found an elevated rate of sexual abuse and related posttraumatic stress disorder among female adolescents who had attempted suicide.

GENETIC PREDISPOSITION

Many studies show support for the idea that some people are genetically vulnerable to developing disorders such as depression (Winokur, 1991). Genetic factors may increase the likelihood that depression will develop by making an individual more sensitive to the depressive aspects of stressful life events.

There may be independent genetic influences for suicide that are independent of depression or linked to depressive disorders (Kety, 1990). To take this information a step further, Pandey et al. (1995) looked at the possibility of a biological marker for suicidal behavior. They reasoned that since most suicide victims suffer from a disorder such as depression, schizophrenia, or alcohol dependence, and since abnormal neurotransmitter functioning is implicated in these disorders, then it might be important to assess biological factors in suicide. The study found that abnormal seratonergic mechanisms (platelet 5-HT$_{2A}$ receptors) were found in suicidal patients. They found a higher incidence of these platelet receptors even if the patients did

27

not have a psychiatric disorder, and they suggested that this may be genetically determined.

Mitterauer (1990) also examined the possibility that genetic heredity plays a role in suicide and that this role is independent of the common mental disorders. This was a postmortem study using 6,704 patients from which there were 161 suicides. The author concluded that genetic factors play a role in suicide and that this role is above and beyond the role of affective disorders such as depression. Similar findings were reported in a study that looked at adolescent suicide victims (Brent et al., 1996). The researchers found that suicidal behavior appeared to be transmitted within families independent of a broad range of psychiatric conditions, including both Axis I and Axis II disorders (American Psychiatric Association, *Diagnostic and Statistical Manual of Mental Disorders*, 4th ed., 1994). It was also suggested that these adolescents were more likely to display aggressive behaviors. As stated earlier, many of the young males who commit suicide do belong to peer groups in which aggressive behavior is common.

In summary, the literature suggests that factors such as stressful life events, family dysfunction, gender, sexuality, family history of psychiatric illness, abuse as a child, and genetic predisposition, whether combined or isolated, can make a young person more vulnerable to the kinds of symptoms and behaviors that are commonly seen in suicidal individuals. Therefore, these symptoms and behaviors might be seen as risk factors for the development of psychological disorders even though it is not possible to predict what these disorders might be. However, these factors alone do not predict psychological problems or suicidal behaviors, so we must look further in order to understand the progression toward suicidal behaviors.

Although these family and individual factors are often shown to be present in the histories of suicide victims, they are also present in the backgrounds of many young people who do not attempt suicide.

Beautrais, Joyce, and Mulder (1997) suggested that these factors might precipitate suicide in those individuals who are vulnerable to suicidal behavior. However, to be vulnerable to suicidal behavior, one must usually be predisposed to or vulnerable to one of the psychiatric disorders that most commonly precede or accompany suicidal behavior. These are reviewed in the next chapter.

3 Emotional Problems and Adolescent Suicide

The literature now almost universally accepts that individuals who complete or attempt suicide are likely to be suffering from a mental disorder (Mazza & Reynolds, 2001). Lewinsohn et al. (1996) examined adolescents who had attempted suicide and found that 100% of the boys and 94% of the girls had a diagnosable mental disorder. This was a large prospective study using data collected from 1,709 high school students who were assessed on several occasions across a 10-year period from 1985. The researchers were, therefore, able to monitor psychiatric problems associated with suicide before the suicide attempt was made. In other studies, suicidal adolescents have not been prediagnosed and it is more difficult to be certain of the relationship between psychiatric disorders and suicide. The evidence that is available, however, is compelling.

Of 53 adolescent suicides in Finland, all but 3 were diagnosed with a psychiatric disorder (Marttunen, Aro, & Lonnqvist, 1992). Fifty-one percent were diagnosed with depressive disorders, 26% with alcohol abuse or dependence, 21% with adjustment disorder, 17% with conduct disorder or antisocial personality disorder, and 6% (three cases) with schizophrenia. Antisocial behavior during the year preceding the suicide was reported for 45% of the boys and 33% of the girls. In 78% of these cases, a diagnosis of alcohol abuse or depression was also present.

Depressive Disorder

Among the general population of adolescents, the prevalence of depressive disorder (as defined by DSM-IV criteria) is about 5% (males 4.8% and females 4.9%) according to the Survey of Mental Health and Well-Being of Australians (Sawyer, Arney, & Baghurst, 2000). Depression is the most common mental disorder associated with suicidal behavior in adolescents (Kelly, Cornelius, & Lynch, 2002). A review of seven epidemiological studies of attempted suicide found that depression was strongly associated with suicide. Across studies, past and current mood disorder was seen as a consistent risk factor for attempted suicide in both males and females. Overall, these studies found depressive disorder in 35% to 76% of suicidal adolescents (Brent, 1995).

The most powerful predictor of future suicidal behavior, other than a previous suicide attempt, is affective illness. This is particularly so when the illness is chronic, severe, or recurrent, or when the illness occurred in the presence of problems such as conduct disorder or substance abuse (Brent et al., 1993b; Kelly et al., 2002). A follow-up study of 100 adolescents who had been admitted to an adolescent psychiatric inpatient unit found that adolescents who engaged in suicidal behavior within 6 months of leaving the hospital were more likely to have chronic symptoms of depression than those who were not suicidal (King et al., 1995). More recent findings are consistent and, in addition, include substance use and risk-taking behaviors as risk factors (Stewart et al., 2001).

Adolescents who attempt suicide are far more likely to have a history of depressive illness than adolescents who do not attempt suicide. A group of high-risk preadolescents and young adolescent psychiatric inpatients was followed for a 6- to 8-year period. Those adolescents who had a history of thinking about suicide and had made a suicide attempt during the follow-up period were found to be seven times more likely to be suffering from depression than similar adolescents who had not attempted suicide (Pfeffer et al., 1991).

Depressive disorder seems to be stronger than sociodemographic factors in predicting eventual suicide. In a community sample of approximately 10,000 adolescents, depression or a mental disorder was the correct classification for 73% of those who attempted suicide and 85% of nonattempters (Kienhorst et al., 1991).

Adolescents who have attempted suicide are more likely to make a subsequent attempt if they are depressed. The relative effects of psychiatric disorders, social adjustment problems, and stressful life events on the risk of a repeat suicide attempt were examined in a group of high-risk preadolescent and young adolescent psychiatric inpatients (Pfeffer et al., 1993). Fifty percent of the suicide attempters made repeat attempts. Poor social adjustment just before the suicide attempt was the most consistent problem facing those adolescents who attempted suicide on a second occasion. These adolescents were 3.5 times more likely to have a mood disorder than those who did not attempt suicide again. This finding reinforces the suggestion that a history of suicide attempts increases the risk for future attempts.

There is some suggestion in the literature that an early development of depression is a special risk factor for suicide. A study of adolescent psychiatric inpatients found that the suicidal adolescents had suffered onset of depression at an earlier age and self-rated their depression as more severe than the nonsuicidal adolescents (Brent et al., 1990). This finding is consistent with that of Brent et al. (1993b) who suggested that a patient with early onset depression complicated by behavioral problems or substance abuse is particularly at risk for suicide. This may be a result of chronic social impairment caused by these problems.

A review of eight psychological autopsy studies of adolescent suicides found that over 90% of the subjects had suffered from at least one major mental disorder (Brent, 1995). Although depression is the most common psychiatric problem seen in suicidal adolescents, it frequently coexists with other risk factors. There is strong evidence to suggest that other factors will increase the risk for suicidal behavior in the presence of a depressive disorder. An autopsy study found that 70% of adolescents who had committed suicide had a psychiatric profile that involved several coexisting disorders (Shaffer et al., 1996). Alcohol use, depression, and family dysfunction are common coexisting problems in patients who report having thoughts about suicide or display suicidal behaviors. King et al. (1993) found that depression plus family dysfunction was most likely to predict the presence of thoughts about suicide, but that alcohol consumption plus perceived family dysfunction predicted the presence and severity of suicidal behaviors.

An adolescent is at particular risk of attempting suicide if he or she has both depression and disruptive behavior disorders or substance abuse. Lewinsohn et al. (1996) found that half of all subjects who committed suicide suffered from a mood disorder alone or from a mood disorder combined with disruptive and alcohol or substance abuse disorders. They concluded that a limited range of diagnoses most commonly characterizes adolescent suicides. These adolescents usually have a mood disorder that may coexist with conduct or substance abuse problems.

Kovacs, Goldston, and Gatsonis (1993) conducted a longitudinal study with two samples of children who were aged 8–13 years at the beginning of the study. Of these children, 142 had a diagnosis of depression and 49 had a psychiatric diagnosis other than depression. Eighty-seven suicide attempts were made during the study. Of these attempts, 50 (57.5%) were made during a severe episode of depression; a further 14 attempts were made by children who had both depression and conduct or substance abuse disorders, and another 9 suffered from other disorders with depressed mood. The study found, therefore, that 73 of 87 attempts (83.9%) occurred in the context of a mental disorder with depressive components.

Depression, conduct disorders, and substance abuse are often found in the family members of adolescents who are suicidal. Rao et al. (1993) conducted a longitudinal study with assessments made in childhood or adolescence and adulthood. Seven of the subjects committed suicide during the course of the study. All seven persons suffered depression, five had a family history of depression, four had a family history of alcohol abuse, and one had a family history of behavioral disorders. One of the male suicides and two of the female suicides died by ingesting an overdose of antidepressant medication.

Although the findings outlined herein emphasize the importance of depression, it is also important not to fall into the trap of looking for the best single predictor of suicide. Although depression is often present in people who commit suicide, it is not a perfect predictor, and it is not the only influence on suicidal behavior. Not all depressed adolescents attempt or even contemplate suicide. In fact, some adolescents who attempt suicide do not report feeling any depressive symptoms (Kosky et al., 1986). This has led researchers to look for factors other than depression that may place an adolescent at increased risk of attempting suicide. There are several other factors that predict suicidal behavior in both the presence and absence of depression.

Bipolar Disorder

Bipolar disorder is not as prevalent as single-episode major depression. It occurs in 0.4% to 1.5% of the population (DSM-IV, 1994) and is not a common focus of research with suicidal adolescents. However, several studies have found higher rates of suicide attempts in adolescents diagnosed with bipolar disorder compared with adolescents diagnosed with a major depressive disorder alone (Cornelius, Kirisci, & Tarter, 2001; Kelly et al., 2002; Lewinsohn, Klein, & Seeley, 1995).

Conduct Disorder, Substance Abuse, and the Issue of Comorbidity

Conduct disorder and substance abuse are the other most common disorders associated with suicidal behavior. Children and adolescents with depression differ from adults in that they frequently also display symptoms of anxiety or conduct disorder (Cantwell & Baker, 1991). Craighead (1991) emphasized the importance of recognizing such mixed disorders when dealing with adolescent depression. He pointed out that males who were diagnosed as depressed and conduct disordered were more likely to become victims of violent death, to become substance abusers, or to engage in criminal activity than those who were suffering from depression alone.

Although depression is a major predictor of suicidal behavior, adolescents who also have conduct or substance use disorder are at higher risk of suicide. A combination of these diagnoses is a more powerful predictor of suicidal behavior than a diagnosis of depression alone (Kelly et al., 2001, 2002; Weiner, Abraham, & Lyons, 2001). In a study by Kovacs et al. (1993), it was found that young male adolescents with a history of mood disorders were three times more likely to attempt suicide if they also were diagnosed with conduct or substance use disorder. A study conducted by Kelly et al. (2002) found that, after the effects of depression were controlled for, the rate of conduct disorder was twice as high in participants who attempted suicide than in those who did not exhibit suicidal behavior.

Some research findings suggest that conduct problems may be a better predictor of suicidal behavior than depressive illness. In a 3-year longitudinal study, Myers et al. (1991) evaluated childhood depression in psychiatric inpatients and outpatients who were 7–17 years of age. The researchers found that the strongest predictor of suicidality was conduct problems followed by a diagnosis of depression. However, they also pointed out that the majority of the youths with conduct problems also had a diagnosis of major depression. They concluded that the relative risks of depression and conduct problems could not be determined. Life stress and parental psychiatric problems were slightly more common in the suicidal youths but were not significant predictors of suicide in this study.

In a sample of hospitalized adolescents, it was found that those diagnosed with conduct disorder were more suicidal and less depressed than those diagnosed with a major affective disorder (Apter et al., 1988). While depression is usually associated with suicidal behavior in adolescents, conduct disorder frequently coexists with this depression (Trautman et al., 1991).

An adolescent may present in a clinic situation as angry and hostile, in a manner typical of conduct disorder, and yet a more probing interview may reveal that he or she is deeply troubled and depressed. Lehnert, Overholser, and Spirito (1994) conducted a study comparing 104 adolescents who had been admitted to the hospital following a suicide attempt with 323 high school students who had never made a suicide attempt. The assessed items included internalized, externalized, and expressed anger; impulse control; self-image; and depression. Suicidal adolescents were found to be more likely to

37

experience aggressive outbursts and to have reduced impulse control. Adolescents who internalized their anger were at increased risk for depression and hopelessness.

Adolescents who abuse alcohol are likely to have been exposed to long-term stressful processes and to have an accumulation of stress. Marttunen et al. (1994) compared the recent life stressors for suicidal adolescents diagnosed with depression only, and the stressors of suicidal adolescents diagnosed with alcohol abuse with or without a coexisting depression. Difficulties regarding discipline or the law were relatively common in the alcohol abuse group, as were financial and employment difficulties. Similarly, a relationship breakdown prior to the suicide was common. In all but one case the suicide took place while the adolescent was intoxicated. The depressed group was more likely to have experienced interpersonal conflict and physical illness. The results suggest that not only are there observable behavioral differences among adolescents at risk for suicide but also that their vulnerability to various psychosocial stressors may depend on their psychiatric diagnosis.

When the alcohol abuse group was examined to compare gender differences, the results suggested that depression, a prior suicide attempt, and a previous psychiatric history were more common in female suicides (Marttunen et al., 1995). It was also found that alcohol abuse was almost as high among females as males and a high proportion of the females committed suicide while intoxicated.

The Role of Alcohol in Suicidal Behavior

In a study of completed suicide in children and adolescents, very few of the suicides showed any sign of preparation; most of them seemed to be the result of impulsive behavior (Hoberman & Garfinkel, 1988). Many of the young people were intoxicated, and the authors suggested that this may have reduced their ability to make rational judgments about their current life circumstances. Alcohol may alter the reactions of adolescents to stressful life events. King et al. (1993) found that the severity of suicidal behavior in a group of depressed girls increased with higher levels of alcohol consumption but was not related to the severity of their depression. This is a very important finding with serious implications for treatment.

Some people use alcohol to cope with feelings of anger, depression, loneliness, anxiety, or guilt, and they believe that alcohol enhances their social behavior despite evidence to the contrary. A sample of psychiatric patients reported drinking in response to unpleasant emotions. They experienced behavioral, social, and medical problems when intoxicated and tended to engage in risk behaviors when drunk (McKay et al., 1992).

There is some evidence that there are gender differences in the pattern of alcohol consumption among depressed adolescents. King et al. (1995) found that many adolescents in a severely disturbed inpatient group had a combination of depression and substance abuse. Several factors distinguished the depressed girls also suffering from alcohol abuse from boys with the same diagnoses. The girls became depressed at an earlier age, and it was suggested that the alcohol abuse probably developed as the girls used alcohol to regulate their depressed mood. These girls exhibited more severe social maladjustment than girls with a diagnosis of depression alone. There were likely to be conduct problems, early involvement with boys, and impairment in school performance. Boys with a comorbid alcohol abuse and depression tended to be older, to show conduct disorder, and to have impaired school performance.

A high proportion of girls commit suicide while under the influence of alcohol. Marttunen et al. (1995) found that alcohol abuse in completed suicides at 21% was almost as high among females as among males. These results indicate the importance of alcohol-related problems in youth suicide among both males and females. Adolescents who committed suicide and who had abused alcohol were likely to have suffered rather different psychosocial stressors in the weeks preceding their suicide (Marttunen et al., 1994). They were more likely to have discipline problems, relationship breakdowns, an increased number of stressors, and poor parental support. These results gave an indication of the generally poor social setting in which these adolescents, with their already marked social deficits, were struggling.

In the state of Queensland, Australia, alcohol was detected by postmortem in 39% of suicides during 1990–1992. This rate was similar for both rural and urban populations and was slightly higher for males than for females (Cantor & Slater, 1997).

The findings in these studies make it obvious that the role of alcohol in suicidal behavior is significant. Other questions including an estimation of the impact and effects of alcohol on problem solving and decision making are further discussed later in this book.

Personality Disorder

Some research shows a link between personality disorder and suicidal behavior in adolescents (Brent et al., 1993a; Mazza & Reynolds, 2001). Brent et al. (1993a) found that adolescents who attempted suicide were likely to have shown emerging signs of a personality disorder, and in particular traits of borderline personality. Since recurrent suicidal behavior, gestures, or threats is one of the diagnostic criteria for borderline personality disorder (DSM-IV, 1994), this is not a surprising finding. Although it is by no means the case that the majority of suicide attempts are made by adolescents with such a personality disorder, most of the research focus in suicide is on Axis 1 disorders (mental disorders); further research may be warranted in the area of personality disorders.

Schizophrenia

Several "psychological autopsy" studies point to the fact that a small percentage of completed suicides among adolescents have a prior diagnosis of schizophrenia (Hoberman & Garfinkel, 1988; Marttunen et al., 1992). Because it is not possible to retrieve data concerning the immediate mental status at time of death, it cannot be known how many completed suicides were in the early stages of schizophrenia and were undiagnosed. There is a strong case for early active intervention in psychoses that, if implemented effectively, may reduce suicide levels among young people who are in the early phases of a psychotic disorder (Power et al., 2003). This may be a point of some significance in suicide prevention, as a reduction in the duration of undiagnosed and untreated psychosis and prompt effective treatment intervention may be able to reduce suicide rates among members of this group (Edwards & McGorry, 2002).

Panic Disorder

Individuals with substance abuse who also had panic disorder are more likely to have attempted suicide than those who did not suffer from panic disorder (Norton et al., 1993). Andrews and Lewinsohn (1992), however, found no association between panic disorder and attempted suicide in their study. Anxiety disorders such as panic disorder are frequently found to coexist with depression. It may be this link with depression rather than the panic disorder itself that increases suicide risk. Beautrais, Joyce, and Mulder (1996) also found that anxiety disorders did not increase suicide risk when the risk from coexisting disorders was taken into account.

In summary, it seems fair to conclude from this body of literature that while depressive disorders have a significant role to play in adolescent suicidal behavior, there are other disorders that interact with depression or act independently. In practical terms, it is often the case that these disorders have not actually been diagnosed.

Overall, the major psychiatric influences on suicidal behavior would seem to be depressive disorders, conduct disorder or behavior problems, and substance abuse or dependence. Any one of the disorders – depression, conduct disorder, or substance abuse disorder – may place an adolescent at risk for suicidal behavior, but a combination of these disorders creates a serious increase in that risk. Any model of suicidal behavior has to include these disorders or sets of symptoms. Both conduct disorder and substance abuse are discussed at greater length in Chapter 6.

4 Adolescent Suicide: Cognitive Variables

Although we can identify adolescents in the community who, through a combination of environmental factors and individual factors, are at risk of suicide when placed in a situation of stress, we still do not have a complete picture of the process leading to the act of self-destruction. It is necessary to understand the relationship between the emotional and cognitive processes that allow adolescents to reach the belief that death is the best solution available to them. The following review looks at the cognitive factors most commonly associated with suicide risk in adolescence. They include the concepts of hopelessness, problem solving, coping, and protective factors.

Hopelessness

The role of hopelessness in adolescent suicide is based on the suggestion that how a person thinks about his or her future when depressed is more likely to influence outcomes toward suicidal behavior than feeling states (Beck, 1963, 1967). Although there was some support for this theory in research conducted with adult suicide attempters, the research using adolescents appears to be much less consistent. Rotheram-Borus and Trautman (1988) found that in a group of adolescent Hispanic and black girls, neither hopelessness nor depression predicted suicidal intent. The authors suggested that hopelessness might be a symptom of depression in adolescents rather than an independent cognitive factor predicting suicidal behavior. They also pointed out that hopelessness might not be a good predictor of suicidal intent among minority adolescents.

Cole (1989) found that mood was a more important predictor of suicide than hopelessness, especially for boys. After the effects of mood were controlled for, hopelessness did not lead to an increase in suicidal behavior. Brent et al. (1990) also found that hopelessness did not predict which adolescents would attempt suicide, and they concluded that it may not play as important a role in adolescent suicidal behavior as it appears to do in adult suicide. Spirito, Overholser, and Hart (1991) found that hopelessness failed to predict suicide attempts; however, Pinto and Whisman (1996) found that hopelessness was more common in adolescents who had thoughts about suicide than in those that attempted suicide.

Despite or perhaps because of the equivocal nature of the findings related to hopelessness and adolescent suicide, research has continued to flourish in the area. Rudd, Rajab, and Dahm (1994) used two groups – suicide attempters ($n = 43$) and suicide ideators ($n = 57$) – to test a model suggesting that hopelessness bridged the gap between stressful life events and suicidal thoughts. They suggested that this relationship would be moderated by problem-solving appraisal (a self-rating of one's ability to solve problems). Although the age range of 18–37 years indicates that this was largely an adult rather than an adolescent study, the method used is of interest, as are the findings. The items measured included stress, hopelessness, problem solving, and suicide ideation. Unlike earlier studies, negative life stress predicted neither hopelessness nor thoughts about suicide. Problem-solving appraisal, however, was highly predictive of both hopelessness and suicide thoughts in both groups. Those people who thought they had poor problem-solving skills were more likely to feel hopeless and to think about suicide. Rudd et al. (1994) concluded that their model of suicidal behavior should be expanded to include problem-solving appraisal. Interestingly, although the differences were small and not significant, hopelessness scores were higher for the suicide ideation group than for the suicide attempters.

As hopelessness has been conceptualized as a general set or attitude to problems, there may be a degree of overlap between problem-solving appraisal and hopelessness. Once again, these results have to be clarified and the model tested on adolescents. Certainly, the methods used in the Rudd et al. study were effective and aspects of it will be used to evaluate focal variables in this book.

More recently, Goldston et al. (2001) reached a similar view that the predictive capacity of hopelessness may be due to the strong relationship between hopelessness and depression. Their study found that hopelessness did not predict later suicide attempts after depression was controlled for.

Problem Solving

There have been relatively few studies that have dealt directly with the problem-solving capacity of suicidal and depressed adolescents. Orbach, Rosenheim, and Hary (1987) conducted a study with children aged 6–12 years. This study examined the inflexible thoughts (cognitive inflexibility) that suicidal children might have about death. The children were asked to come up with alternative ideas about given situations. Although this may be a narrow measure of cognitive inflexibility, it has been found to be associated with suicidal behavior. The suicidal children were compared with chronically

45

ill and normal children, and the results indicated that suicidal children were less able to generate alternative attitudes toward life and death than the other children. The authors concluded that suicidal children show an attraction toward death that other children do not show.

An adolescent who has inadequate social skills will have difficulty building close relationships with his or her family and peers. Poor problem-solving skills may lead an adolescent to social isolation and increase his or her vulnerability to suicidal behavior. An important study conducted with an adolescent population looked at the issue of social problem solving (Sadowski & Kelley, 1993). The researchers compared problem solving, hopelessness, and depression in adolescent suicide attempters, nonsuicidal psychiatric adolescent patients, and normal adolescents. The suicide attempters displayed much poorer social problem-solving skills than the other adolescents. The suicide attempters rated their problem-solving ability lower than did the other groups. Both the suicide attempters and the psychiatrically disturbed groups reported poorer problem-solving skills than the normal control group. This study did not find a significant relationship between hopelessness and suicidality.

Adolescents who experience a number of stressful life events may resort to suicide because they are unable to generate alternate solutions to their problems. In an important adult study, Schotte and Clum (1987) proposed a diathesis–stress model of suicidal behavior that suggested that rigid thought processes might increase the likelihood of suicide following a stressful life event. This model suggests that some people have a reduced ability to engage in divergent or flexible thinking and cannot generate effective alternative solutions when faced with stressful situations. The model further suggests that this inability leads to a state of hopelessness that increases vulnerability for suicidal behavior. Suicidal ideators were able to come up with less than half as many potential solutions to interpersonal problems

46

selected from their own lives than the depressed but nonsuicidal controls. They were also more likely to suggest that the solutions would be ineffective. These suicide ideators reported a higher level of life stress, and this level of stress significantly correlated with the measures of hopelessness and suicide intent.

Rudd et al. (1994), in the previously mentioned study, aimed to replicate this study by using a clinical sample. They found that problem-solving appraisal predicted both hopelessness and suicidal thoughts. The age of the participants (18–37 years) again leaves unanswered the question of the validity of the constructs with an adolescent population.

Hopelessness and Problem Solving

Hopelessness might be the link between problem solving and suicidal behavior. Dixon, Heppner, and Rudd (1994) suggested that problem-solving appraisal, problem-solving skills, or a combination of the two are associated with an increase in levels of hopelessness and thoughts about suicide. They reanalyzed the data used by Rudd et al. (1994) and showed a direct link between hopelessness and suicidal thoughts, and an indirect link (by way of hopelessness) between problem-solving appraisal and suicide intent. Since hopelessness appears to be less consistently linked to suicidal behavior in young people, these links still need to be tested with adolescents. The studies presented in this book aim to test whether hopelessness can discriminate between different groups of adolescents. The role of hopelessness in mediating between depression, conduct problems, substance abuse, and suicidal behavior is also assessed.

A study by McLaughlin et al. (1996) compared three groups of adolescents on measures of depression, hopelessness, suicidal intent, reasons for self-harm, and a single problem-solving item (whether the adolescents thought that taking an overdose would solve their problems). The groups were composed of adolescents who had engaged in deliberate self-harming behaviors ($n = 51$), as well as school controls ($n = 37$) and clinic controls ($n = 32$). The self-harm group of adolescents showed higher levels of hopelessness, and many of them felt unable to generate solutions to their problems. The authors suggested that the exhaustion of one's problem-solving ability might be associated with the cognitive state of hopelessness:

> [There is] a difficulty in generating solutions to problems, leading to a state where one feels there is no way out of a stressful situation. This in turn may lead to the use of maladaptive problem-solving techniques such as self-harm. (p. 524)

The study took a narrow rather than a comprehensive measure of problem solving. The adolescents were simply asked to respond to a question; their ability to generate solutions to problems was not tested directly. Problem-solving appraisal was not assessed, although it may predict both hopelessness and suicidal ideation.

Adolescents' problem solving appraisal may be as important as their actual problem solving skills. Marton et al. (1993) examined social problem solving, social understanding, and social self-evaluation in depressed adolescents. The adolescents were given photographs of five problematic situations with peers and were asked to describe the problem, generate solutions, select the best solution, and describe the possible consequences. The depressed adolescents were able to assess interpersonal problems and provide solutions but tended to think that the consequences of the outcomes of their solutions would be poor. The authors concluded that the depressed adolescents had problems with assessing the effectiveness of their own problem-solving solving ability.

A combination of ineffective problem solving and poor social adjustment is often found in suicidal adolescents. Poor social adjustment may reflect a deficit in interpersonal problem solving. Brent et al. (1993a) attempted to explain the relationship between personality disorder and suicidality as a function of poor social and problem-solving skills. They suggested that early onset chronic affective illness might predispose an individual to cognitive distortion, poor social skills, and personality disorders. Pfeffer et al. (1993) also claimed that the strongest risk factor for a repeat suicide attempt was impairment in social adjustment just before the suicide attempt.

Coping Strategies

Several studies have investigated the relationship between coping strategies and adolescent suicidal behavior. Asarnow et al. (1987) found that adolescents with suicidal thoughts were much less likely to generate active coping strategies than nonsuicidal adolescents. Brightman (1990) found that adolescents with more severe depression were less likely to use coping strategies. In effect, these young people were susceptible to learned helplessness following failure. Cole (1989) investigated coping beliefs in relation to depression and suicide in a group of delinquent boys. He concluded that a failure to believe in one's own self-efficacy and the ability to cope is a greater risk factor for suicide than hopelessness, especially for boys. These concepts sound remarkably similar to those described by Rudd et al. (1994) as a deficit in problem-solving appraisal. That is, the adolescent either does not believe that he or she is capable of generating solutions to problems or believes that the solutions are likely to fail. In another sense, this is a hopelessness related to one's ability to manage (problem solve) one's current life circumstances, which is a more specific hopelessness than the all-encompassing construct.

It does seem that hopelessness, problem solving, and poor coping are interrelated concepts that are often seen in individuals who display suicidal behaviors. Lewinsohn et al. (1993) also found that inadequate coping skills increased vulnerability to a suicide attempt even after the effects of depression were controlled for. Dixon, Heppner, and Anderson (1991) suggested that impaired coping (described as suicidal thoughts and a feeling of hopelessness) is a function of current stress and a belief that one cannot solve one's problems. Once again, this definition is remarkably similar to problem-solving appraisal. This explanation, however, is in line with the diathesis–stress model discussed in the following section, but it has yet to be validated with an adolescent clinical population.

It has been suggested that adolescents who use social isolation as a coping strategy might be more vulnerable to suicidal behaviors. Spirito et al. (1996) conducted a study by using five groups of adolescents: medically hospitalized suicide attempters, psychiatrically hospitalized suicide attempters, psychiatrically hospitalized suicidal ideators, nonsuicidal psychiatric patients, and a group of high school controls. The participants were assessed for coping strategies and depression. It was expected that suicide attempters would choose social isolation as a coping strategy more often than the other groups, but this was not the case. Social isolation appeared to be an equally popular coping strategy for all of the adolescent groups with psychiatric problems. The researchers also expected the suicidal children to be able to come up with fewer active coping strategies than the other groups, but this proved not to be the case. This inconsistency may be accounted for by the fact that the use of specific problem-solving strategies (active coping strategies) or attitudes to problem solving were not measured directly. In addition, the participants were not asked to generate their own coping strategies; instead, strategies were selected from a list of 10 and rated as to whether they would be used or not. An approach requiring adolescents to think of their own strategies might have highlighted differences between the groups.

In summary, although the idea that suicidal adolescents might lack the coping strategies to deal with life's problems is appealing, not all of the research findings support this hypothesis. This seems to be due to the overlap between measures such as problem-solving appraisal and hopelessness. Problem solving represents only one positive aspect of coping, and hopelessness represents just one negative aspect.

Protective Factors

Identifying maladaptive characteristics that might predict suicidal behavior has been the favored approach in suicide research. The question of whether suicidal persons actually lack important adaptive characteristics that protect others against suicidal behaviors has been marginalized. Linehan et al. (1983) approached suicidal behavior from a cognitive-behavioral viewpoint and suggested that the belief system of a suicidal person might be different from that of a nonsuicidal individual. They suggested that there are many life-oriented beliefs and expectations that may argue against attempting suicide.

The aim of their study was to compare suicidal and nonsuicidal people on a measure of beliefs and expectations hypothesized to protect against suicidal behaviors. They developed the Reasons for Living Scale (RFL), which encompassed six reasons for living factors: survival and coping beliefs, responsibility to family, child-related concerns, fear of suicide, fear of social disapproval, and moral objections. Two studies were conducted with the RFL. One study used participants from the general population and the second study used clinical populations. The results indicated that, in both populations, suicidal persons differed from nonsuicidal persons in the degree to which they attached importance to life-oriented beliefs and expectancies, which are protective factors against suicidal behavior. Participants who were currently suicidal, as well as those who had made a prior attempt, re-ported fewer important reasons for living than did participants with no history of suicide. This was not true of the participants who suffered from other psychiatric problems.

Connell and Meyer (1991) used the RFL with 205 undergraduate students categorized into four groups – never suicidal, brief suicidal ideation, serious suicidal ideation, and parasuicidal. The students were also assessed for depression and hopelessness. Those students who had experienced thoughts about suicide or were suicidal were less likely to consider survival and coping beliefs, responsibility to family, and moral objections to be reasons for not committing suicide. It was also found that students with higher levels of depression and hopelessness were at greater risk of suicidal behavior.

Westefeld, Cardin, and Deaton (1992) carried out two studies in order to develop and then evaluate a measure of suicidal risk in ado-lescent college students based on the RFL. The six factors identified were survival and coping beliefs; college and future-related concerns; moral objections; responsibility to family and friends; fear of suicide; and fear of social disapproval. In Study 2 by Westefeld et al., another sample of 208 college students responded to the 46-item inventory produced in Study 1. These students also completed the Beck Depres-sion Inventory (BDI; Beck, 1961) and a Suicidal Risk Questionnaire (SRQ) developed by the authors that asked the students to self-report on their current, past, and future risk of suicide. The results indi-cated some strong similarities between student responses and the responses from the Linehan et al. (1983) study. It was found that the survival and coping beliefs, fear of suicide, fear of social disap-proval, and moral objections subscales were very similar. The major differences found were that there was no scale equivalent to child-related concerns but there was a scale that included responsibility to friends as well as to family. The authors concluded that, in this age group, friends assume a position of major importance. Once again this is in keeping with what we know about adolescent development (Austrian, 2002).

The other analyses using the BDI and SRQ indicated that the RFL is useful in predicting the level of risk of suicide in an undergraduate population. Westefeld et al. recommended that the scale be used in conjunction with other assessment tools but suggested that the RFL does provide a unique perspective of suicide risk by measuring protective factors. A further study of the RFL–Adolescent version (Gutierrez et al., 2000) added support for the utility of the measure as well as for the approach of focusing on protective factors against suicidal behavior. Gutierrez et al. (2000) found that the measure not only differentiated between groups of suicidal and nonsuicidal adolescents but also yielded valuable information about levels of optimism, peer acceptance, and support and alliance with family. The authors noted that this level of information is clinically more useful than noting that an adolescent has an elevated hopelessness score.

Affect Dysregulation

Affect dysregulation is defined as the inability to cope with heightened levels of emotion, whereas affect regulation is the method used by a person to change or reduce emotional arousal. A study by Zlotnick et al. (1997) examined the relationship between affect dysregulation and self-destructive behaviors in suicidal adolescents. The aim of the study was to see if measures of affect regulation and measures of self-destructive and risk-taking behaviors could differentiate between adolescents who think about suicide and those that attempt suicide. The findings reported in this study are similar to those reported in the problem-solving and coping strategies literatures, and they point to the fact that suicidal adolescents, for whatever background reasons, are less able to deal with the problems they may encounter than are other adolescents. This supports the idea that suicide attempters may have both problem-solving and emotional difficulties.

In summary, the literature suggests that there is evidence of strong links between hopelessness, problem-solving, protective factors, and suicidal behavior. Although the concept of coping is appealing, there is considerable overlap among coping, problem-solving appraisal, and hopelessness that makes the research findings difficult to interpret. The inconsistent results for coping strategies suggest that further research is required to clarify the construct. The construct of affect dysregulation is also conceptually linked with problem solving, hopelessness, and deficits in protective factors. It is evident that adolescents who engage in suicidal behaviors are likely to be in the grip of strong unpleasant emotions with which they feel they cannot cope. The more pressing question that arises is which cognitive process might produce strategies that the suicidal adolescent could use in stressful situations in the future. The model developed in this book considers hopelessness, problem solving, decision making, and protective factors as possible mediators among depression, conduct problems, substance abuse, and suicidal behaviors.

Conclusions

A majority of studies indicate that suicide attempts commonly occur in conjunction with a "mental" disorder. Depression, conduct problems, and substance-related disorders frequently precede suicidal behavior. The disorders that place adolescents at risk for suicidal behavior may also reduce their ability to think positively. Alternatively, it may be the case that these deficits were in existence before the disorder appeared. Although it may not be possible to determine which came first, we can suggest that, when these adolescents experience a negative life event, they may be unable to generate a positive problem-solving approach, they have few effective coping strategies, and suicide appears as the best solution. Alternatively, a suicide attempt may be the only solution these adolescents can generate to reduce the emotional pain they are experiencing.

In many instances, it seems that the decision to commit suicide has not been carefully planned or even thought through. Some studies have suggested that not all suicide attempters are aware of the consequences of their actions and seem to be acting impulsively, while intoxicated, or both. Those cognitive variables that vary between disturbed adolescents who do attempt suicide and those who do not need to be explored in greater detail.

From the literature reviewed in the preceding chapters, several variables must be considered as background factors or vulnerabilities that place a child at risk of developing dysfunctional behavior patterns or psychological problems. These risk factors include the following:

- **Stressful life events**
- **Family dysfunction**
- **Gender**
- **Family history of psychopathology**
- **Abuse as a child**
- **Genetic predisposition**

The dysfunctional behavior patterns and likely psychological problems include these:

- **Conduct problems**
- **Substance-related problems**
- **Depressive symptomatology**

By the time that an adolescent shows symptoms of the afore-mentioned problems, there are likely to be emotional and cognitive difficulties that become apparent when the adolescent is faced with a stressful situation. The best supported and empirically documented of these in terms of suicidal behavior are these:

- **Problem-solving deficits**
- **Hopelessness**
- **Deficits in protective factors**

A model of adolescent suicide based on the literature reviewed so far, therefore, would consider the aforementioned constructs as essential components. It is important to note, however, that this would only represent a partial model. The following chapters continue with a further literature review to include those adolescents engaged in risk-taking behaviors, including behaviors that could be termed delinquent. The model is then extended to include constructs that arise as a result of this literature review.

The review in the preceding chapters has focused mainly on those adolescents recognized as being at risk because they are depressed. There is also a body of literature concerned with adolescent risk-taking behavior, but, on the whole, these adolescents are not widely recognized as being depressed. However, the delinquent, risk-taking and conduct problem adolescents are demonstrating a similar or greater risk of suicide. The aim of this book is to develop a model that incorporates both groups and identifies the mediating influences in their progression toward suicidal behavior. The next chapters address the current literature dealing with adolescent risk-taking behaviors. The full model is presented and discussed in Chapter 8.

ADOLESCENT RISK-TAKING

5 Adolescent Risk-Taking: An Overview

While suicide among adolescents is a distressing problem, it is not generally the leading cause of death among adolescents. In most industrialized countries of the world, this dubious honor goes to accidents. In the United States, accidental injury accounts for 55 per 100,000 deaths of 15- to 19-year-olds compared with 11.4 per 100,000 for suicide. In 1998, for white males (15–19 years old), the statistic for which accidental injury caused death was 70.3 per 100,000; it was 122.6 per 100,000 for black males (Center for Disease Control and Prevention, 2001). In 1997 in Australia, the figure for accidental death was 40 per 100,000 for 12- to 24-year-olds, compared with 14.6 per 100,000 for suicide for 15- to 25-year-olds (Moon, Meyer, & Grau, 1999).

It is a common belief that adolescent risk-taking behavior plays a significant role in many accidents, particularly motor vehicle accidents. For instance, 55% of adolescent deaths are attributable to motor vehicle accidents and at least half of those involve a blood alcohol level in excess of .10 (Irwin & Millstein, 1992). This indicates a willingness to risk injury to self and others as well as to ignore the legal consequences of drinking and driving. Although adolescent

risk-taking increases accidental injury, other forms of physical recklessness such as involvement with smoking, drug use, and delinquency have also been shown to be associated with depressive symptomatology and suicidal ideation (Clark et al., 1990). Similar findings
were reported in Australia from the child and adolescent component
of The National Survey of Mental Health and Wellbeing (Patton &
Moon, 2000; Sawyer et al., 2000).

National arrest rates provide a measure of adolescent risk-taking
behavior resulting in incarceration in juvenile detention centers. In
Australia the arrest rate for juveniles is 1% of adolescents aged 13–17
years (Mukherjee, 1985). Most arrested juveniles do not go to court
and fewer still are incarcerated. Of 13,912 charges brought before
the Children's Court of Queensland in 1994, only 870 young people
received a sentence of detention (Mukherjee et al., 1997). This represents an overall rate of incarceration of about 15 per 100,000 adolescents (a similar prevalence rate to adolescent suicide in Australia).

The literature concerned with adolescent suicide tends to focus
on risk factors such as psychopathology, family factors, negative environmental factors, and mediating cognitive variables. In contrast
to this practical approach, the literature concerned with adolescent
risk-taking is generally theory based. One of the central aims of this
book is to see if adolescents who engage in risk-taking behavior share
common risk factors and cognitive deficits with adolescents who attempt suicide. Some adolescents who are suicidal and some who are
risk takers report similar psychological problems, have destructive
thought processes, and seem to carry similar predisposing factors. It
may be that these two groups form a population of adolescents who
engage in both suicidal and risk-taking behaviors.

For the purposes of this book, risk-taking behavior means deliberate behaviors in which the outcomes are uncertain and from which
there is a possibility of identifiable and serious, possibly fatal, injury.
These behaviors could cause physical harm to the participant or

others. They would include drinking alcohol and driving, driving at high speed, using illicit drugs carelessly, exhibiting aggressive behavior toward others, and, in certain circumstances, engaging in unprotected sexual activity. They also include behaviors that are antisocial and could result in serious legal consequences (shoplifting, serious vandalism, assault, theft, and drug dealing).

Despite the concentration on theoretical models, the literature devoted to risk-taking behavior among adolescents is diverse. Some studies suggest that risk-taking is a form of adolescent sensation seeking. This drive produces a failure to think of things from other points of view and to weigh up the consequences of alternative behaviors. Arnett (1990) concluded that sensation seeking and egocentrism do contribute to reckless behavior among adolescents, in particular to the tendency of some adolescent girls to have sex without taking care about contraception.

Adolescents who take risks may have poor skills for decision making. Gordon (1990) examined the area of adolescent use of contraception and concluded that adolescent girls who become pregnant because they fail to use contraceptives have difficulty creating alternative solutions to problems, in evaluating alternatives, in taking a long view of consequences, and in reasoning about chance and probability. A study that examined adolescent contraceptive use found that intelligent adolescents were more likely to make good decisions. Adolescents who had difficulty seeing things from the perspective of another person (that is, they were inclined to egocentrism) made poor decisions (Green, Johnson, & Kaplan, 1992).

Behavioral studies in the area of HIV–AIDS and risky sexual behavior among adolescents have thrown some light on the issue of risk-taking in young people. In a self-report survey of 7,699 adolescents in the U.S.A., in which the mean age was 17 years, almost 60% reported having experienced sexual intercourse and 52.5% reported having their first sexual experience before the age of 16. Almost

20% reported that emotional or physical coercion had been used to force sexual intercourse against their wishes, and 30.5% reported that drugs or alcohol were involved in their sexual experience. Eighteen percent reported having had six or more partners and a further 26.5% reported having had between three and five partners (Downey & Landrey, 1997). The authors concluded that early sexual activity, multiple partners, and the use of alcohol and drugs in sexual encounters were indicators of sexual risk-taking behavior and that this level of risk-taking may be more common than expected or even normal. Unfortunately, the study did not comment on the use of adequate protection against sexually transmitted diseases or pregnancy.

Smoking and drinking is another area of risk-taking. Adolescents who engage in these behaviors consistently overestimate the percentage of their peers who do the same (Gibbons & Gerrard, 1994 cited in Gibbons, Helweg-Larson, & Gerrard, 1995). This is known as the false-consensus effect. The false-consensus effect normalizes the behavior in question, leading to preparedness to engage in the activity at some time in the future (Gibbons et al., 1995). Use of alcohol and illicit drugs in adolescents in the 12- to 25-year age range maybe a manifestation of sensation seeking and egocentrism (Arnett, 1992). Gibbons et al. (1995) suggest that these activities serve to enhance self-image in the face of peer pressure during adolescence. Jessor (1992) suggests that we consider what an adolescent may have to gain by engaging in risk behaviors.

Risk-taking in adolescence is increasingly being viewed as a normal part of the developmental process of "growing up." A modest degree of risk-taking in adolescence is frequently considered normal and may be associated with positive psychological characteristics. Shedler and Block (1990) assessed the prevalence of risk-taking behaviors in a sample of 18-year-olds. They found that these adolescents could be grouped into three categories: abstainers (29%) had never tried any type of drug; experimenters (36%) had tried marijuana a few times; frequent users (20%) used marijuana once a week or more and had tried at least one other drug. They found that these three groups displayed very different psychological characteristics. The abstainers tended to be tense, anxious, overcontrolled, and socially isolated with poor social skills. The frequent users tended to be troubled, withdrawn, and unhappy, and they tended to engage in antisocial behaviors. The experimenters tended to be socially competent, cheerful, and energetic, and they displayed higher levels of self-satisfaction. This suggests that a willingness to engage in some risk-taking behavior may be a normal and healthy part of adolescent development.

Differing Perspectives on Adolescent Risk-Taking

There are a number of organic causes that can lead to an increase in risk-taking behavior. Brain injury may lead to problems with controlling inappropriate behavior or an inability to regulate behavior adequately. Attention deficit hyperactivity disorder may cause problems with impulse control. Although this book cannot provide a detailed review of all possible organic or psychological causes of this type of behavior, it is nonetheless important to note that these causes should not be overlooked when one is dealing with young people engaged in these types of behaviors.

SENSATION SEEKING AND EGOCENTRISM

The developmental perspective on adolescent risk-taking describes the behaviors in terms of sensation seeking and adolescent egocentricity (Arnett, 1992). This theory suggests that some adolescents are more prone to behaving impulsively by seeking out intense and varied activities, and to having a large appetite for experience. Egocentrism is characterized by two dimensions, the imaginary audience and the cognitive distortion known as the personal fable. The imaginary audience implies that adolescents feel themselves to be under constant scrutiny from their peers and believe that their own lives are unique and exceptional. The personal fable refers to the adolescents' belief in their own invulnerability or the tendency to believe that unpleasant consequences will not happen to them even though they may occur to others (Elkind, 1967, 1985).

It has been suggested that adolescents are egocentric and seek attention because they may not yet have developed the ability to use abstract reasoning or to correctly estimate the likelihood of an outcome. Arnett (1992) maintains that adolescents are poor at making judgments and are susceptible to assessing probability without reference to base rates or do so on the basis of stereotypical beliefs. A common stereotypical belief is the "gambler's fallacy" that, after a run of red in roulette, for example, one should bet black in order to win. "Availability" is the belief that the easier it is to imagine something happening, the more likely it is to occur. However, these shortcomings (common heuristics and biases) also apply to adults, and Arnett does not provide any evidence that adolescents rely on them any more than adults do. Fischhoff, Bostrum, and Quadrel (2000) suggest that we are all too heavily reliant on heuristics and biases and need to better understand our limitations as risk assessors.

PROBLEM BEHAVIOR THEORY

Problem behavior theory dismisses the notion of sensation seeking and egocentrism, although it does not discount the influence of family, peers, and other environmental factors in its "psychosocial approach" (Jessor, 1992). Jessor maintained that both positive and negative outcomes of risk behavior should be considered. That is, we need to consider what an adolescent has to gain from a risk experience, rather than emphasizing the potential costs alone. He continued to point out that many behaviors such as drinking alcohol, using drugs, driving in a risky manner, and engaging in early sexual activity can be seen as important to an adolescent in gaining peer acceptance or establishing autonomy. This would appear as an extreme outcome of development through adolescence (Austrian, 2002). The theory considers personal and situational factors and identifies risk factors (unstable family environment, poverty, models for deviant behavior, and low self-esteem) and protective factors (cohesive family, conventional peer models, intolerance of deviance, and involvement in conventional activities). This approach looks at how the individual interacts with the situation and considers the role of the risk and protective factors in decision making.

Jessor (1992) pointed out that research has shown adolescent risk behaviors to be functional, purposive, instrumental, and goal directed. These goals are often important to adolescent development and include the promotion of peer acceptance and the establishment of autonomy. He suggested that the term "risk-taking" should only be used to describe behaviors for which there is a conscious awareness of the risk or danger involved and a deliberate seeking for the thrill that issues from the uncertainty of beating the odds.

Jessor also addressed the issue of whether risk behaviors vary between individuals so that they cluster or form a risk behavior syndrome; that is, are there specific behaviors that go together to suggest a young person is at greater risk of continued risk-taking? He concluded that the empirical evidence supports the existence of organized patterns of adolescent risk behaviors. In an earlier study, it was found that the same underlying risk factors could account for an adolescent being involved in alcohol misuse, marijuana use, delinquency, or sexual precocity (Donovan & Jessor, 1985).

DECISION MAKING

Assessment of risk has long been the focus of a large body of literature dealing with decision making and judgments made in uncertain situations. More recently, risk assessment has been used to help us understand adolescent risk-taking. Decision theory suggests that the decision to engage in risk behavior is rational if that decision reflects the values and beliefs of the decision maker (Beyth-Marom et al., 1993). Thus individuals can make different decisions because they have different values and beliefs. Adolescents may engage in more risk behaviors than adults do because they place different values on the outcomes and consequences.

Decision theory outlines five steps to be taken in making a rational decision: (1) identify possible options; (2) identify possible consequences ensuing from each option; (3) evaluate the desirability of each consequence; (4) make an assessment of the likelihood of each consequence occurring; and (5) combine these steps according to a logical decision rule (Beyth-Marom et al., 1993). Using the structure of decision theory, some researchers have tested previously accepted opinions that adolescents show poorer decision-making skills than adults do.

EMPIRICAL STUDIES

Decision-making theory suggests that adolescents who undertake risk behaviors do so because they believe that the benefits of the behavior outweigh the risks and negative consequences. Lavery et al. (1993) conducted a study with a group of adolescents who had been referred to a community counseling clinic for a range of problems including truancy, running away, delinquency, depression, and family conflict. The goal of the study was to assess the relationship between risk involvement and problem behavior personality and to examine the role of adolescent egocentrism in risk-taking. They found that egocentric adolescents engaged in no more risk-taking behavior than other adolescents and that they were equally able to assess the risks of a given situation. Adolescents who were involved in high levels of risk behavior were more likely to have a conduct disorder or to be delinquent. These findings add support to the problem behavior theory of risk-taking proposed by Jessor and Jessor (1975). The adolescents who engaged in risk behaviors perceived the benefits of those behaviors more positively, which also offers some support for a decision-making model of risk-taking.

Some researchers question whether adolescents are able to judge which behaviors are risky and how well they are able to assess the outcomes of those behaviors. A study that explored these questions asked adolescents to nominate four behaviors that they considered risky and to rate their positive and negative thoughts about each behavior (Moore & Gullone, 1996). The results indicated that these adolescents nominated very similar risk behaviors to those considered socially as risky. The behaviors included criminal activity, drug use, alcohol use, dangerous driving, unprotected sexual activity, and so on. The adolescents were capable of generating both positive and negative outcomes of the behaviors, indicating that they were well aware of the risks involved in the behaviors. Although the authors concluded that the adolescents did not have a clear or coherent reason for engaging in the risk activities other than a very broad category of "pleasure," increased peer acceptance was rated as a significant positive outcome associated with smoking. This study found that adolescents tend to focus on the positive outcomes when making a decision about engaging in risk behaviors.

There are six commonly held beliefs about the decision-making capabilities of adolescents: Adolescents are not capable of competent decision making; adolescents take more risks than adults; adolescents do not sufficiently consider consequences; adolescents think that they are invulnerable; adolescents let emotions rule their choices; adolescents rely heavily on peer information and attitudes when making decisions about risk behavior. Furby and Beyth-Marom (1992) reviewed the literature on the role of these beliefs in adolescent decision making. They concluded that there is a lack of empirical evidence on the issue of adolescent risk-taking and that this reflects the dearth of information about how adolescents perceive the options and possible consequences that they face. Questions that have to be addressed include which options adolescents consider, how well they assess the probability of the possible consequences, and how important those consequences are to them.

It is often suggested that adolescents indulge in risk behavior because they believe they are invulnerable to negative outcomes. Beyth-Marom et al. (1993) used decision theory to compare the ability of adolescents and adults to anticipate the possible consequences of risk behavior. The results did not support the idea that adolescents feel invulnerable. The adolescents in this study generated very similar consequences to those of the adults.

Other studies by this group of researchers have found that adolescents are capable of evaluating the negative outcomes of risk behaviors. Quadrel, Fischhoff, and Davis (1993) found that both adults and adolescents use slightly biased decision-making processes in estimating the likelihood of risk and that it was adults rather than adolescents who saw themselves as less at risk than others. When adults and adolescents were asked what they knew about specified risk behaviors, they gave very similar responses. These results indicate little support for the theory put forward by Arnett (1992) that explains adolescent risk-taking in terms of developmental shortcomings. The results also indicate a need to examine why adolescents continue to engage in risk behaviors when it appears that they are aware of the negative consequences and do recognize that they are as likely as anyone else to suffer from them.

On the other hand, the literature on teenage pregnancy and contraception suggests that adolescents who become pregnant have difficulty engaging in formal operational reasoning (Gordon, 1990). Formal operational reasoning involves generating or envisioning alternatives, engaging in perspective taking, evaluating alternatives, and reasoning about chance and probability. Namerow, Lawton, and Philliber (1987) found that adolescents were poor at assessing the probability of getting pregnant, and that the contraceptive decisions of these adolescents were more closely related to the perceived risk of pregnancy than to actual risks. However, even Arnett (1992) concedes that it is now widely accepted that not all adults are able to use formal operational reasoning and those who can use it do not do so all of the time.

These studies tend to reflect support for the problem behavior theory of Jessor (1992) that risk-taking behavior is an interaction between psychological and social variables and that individuals tend to engage in a number of risk behaviors rather than just one. The results of these studies also suggest that adolescents are aware of the consequences of engaging in these behaviors, do not show a sense of invulnerability, and in general do not show a more deficient decision-making style than adults. If this is the case, we are still left with the question of why they continue to engage in risk behaviors. The perspective of behavioral decision theory as outlined in the previous section would seem to be a useful paradigm within which to address this question. It is also important to find out if adolescents in clinical populations (depressed, conduct disordered, and suicidal adolescents) are as capable of generating consequences for risk behaviors as are normal adolescents.

The theory proposed by Jessor describes situational factors as playing an important role in the decision to engage in risk behaviors. These factors, including both family and environmental influences, are the same as those we have shown to be predisposing factors to adolescent suicidal behavior. The risk factors and predisposing variables associated with suicidal behaviors also occur in the backgrounds of young people who engage in risk-taking behaviors.

69

6 Risk and Predisposing Factors in Adolescent Risk-Taking

The studies outlined later in the book refer to adolescents who are described as exhibiting problem behaviors or conduct disorder. Adolescents with these problems invariably engage in higher than normal levels of risk-taking. We examine the factors that predispose these adolescents to risk-taking.

Environmental Variables

FAMILY DYSFUNCTION

If adolescents feel supported by their families, they are less likely to engage in risk-taking behavior. A study that looked at perceived quality of support found that adolescents with either emotional or behavioral problems were four times more likely to report a lack of family support than students without these problems (Garnefski & Diekstra, 1997). Those adolescents with both emotional and behavioral problems were eight times as likely to feel unsupported by their families. Students who indicated a lack of support from more than one system (family, school, or peers) were also likely to have more problems.

These results suggest that similar background problems and family risk factors are involved in the development of both emotional and behavioral problems. These factors may include family dysfunction and real or perceived life stressors.

The development of problem behavior has been linked with the same background factors as suicidal behavior (see Chapter 3). A study into family risk factors for adolescent suicide concluded that family dysfunction is likely to be a nonspecific risk factor for the development of psychopathology in children (Wagner, 1997). Wagner's review article suggests that various family experiences such as divorce or separation, parental depression, and abuse are risk factors for a broad spectrum of child behavior problems and psychiatric disorders. Research on specific child and adolescent disorders has also found striking similarities in risk factors across disorders.

Consistent, emotionally positive, and supportive family relationships may act as a protective factor against risk-taking behavior. A longitudinal study, which assessed the impact of family factors on adolescent risk-taking behaviors, concluded that adolescents were more likely to become involved in risk activities if they came from loose-knit families with poor problem-solving skills (Fisher & Feldman, 1998). These adolescents are more likely to be influenced by friends and other adults than by their families.

PEER INFLUENCE

Peer influence contributes to adolescent risk-taking behavior. It has been found that members of a peer group exhibit similar behaviors at a similar rate (Donovan, Jessor, & Jessor, 1983). There is, however, a strong family factor in the way that an adolescent becomes susceptible to peer influence. The more time that adolescents spend with their parents, the less they are influenced by their peers (Kandel & Andrews, 1987). Parents also have more influence over an adolescent's decision to engage in risk behaviors than peers, but peers have more influence over the continuation of risk-taking behaviors (Tremblay et al., 1995). Other studies have suggested that coercive family relations and poor parental monitoring allow adolescents to form associations with risk-taking peer groups (Patterson & Bank, 1989; Patterson & Dishion, 1985; Patterson, Reid, & Dishion, 1992).

These studies suggest that environmental factors, either family or peer group but most likely a complex interaction of both, provide part of the explanation for the progression toward serious and continued risk-taking behavior by adolescents. However, there is no simple explanation or single model to illustrate the reasons for these behaviors. As with suicidal behavior, it is necessary to look further and explore other variables that interact with environmental influences to more clearly explain the increasing incidence of adolescent risk-taking. Certainly, once an adolescent is found to be regularly engaging in risk-taking behaviors, the issue of peer influence should be considered; for this reason peer influence is a variable that should be included in any model of adolescent risk-taking.

Intrinsic Factors

GENDER

Some recent studies challenge the popularly held belief that males engage in more risk-taking behaviors than females. Shapiro et al. (1998) found that older females (17–21 years) reported engaging in very similar risk behaviors and at similar rates to males. The authors concluded that the results supported the suggestion that females drink, smoke, and engage in behaviors such as drinking and driving at high speed as frequently as males. They also found that these adolescents were able to give reasons for their risk-taking and suggested that this finding was contrary to the widely held belief that risk-taking is "mindless" or merely "sensation seeking."

FAMILY HISTORY OF PSYCHIATRIC ILLNESS

The links between parental and adolescent psychological disorders suggest that these problems are transmitted through environmental factors (Brent, 1995). Several studies have indicated that a father's criminal history increases the risk of aggressive and delinquent behavior in adolescent males (Gould et al., 1998). This in turn is likely to indicate a higher than normal level of risk-taking behavior.

EXPERIENCES OF ABUSE AS A CHILD

The study by Silverman et al. (1996) indicated that children who have suffered either physical or sexual abuse were at risk for developing a range of pathologies, including antisocial behavior and drug abuse or dependence. Garnefski and Diekstra (1997) looked at gender differences in adolescents who had suffered childhood sexual abuse. They found that the pattern of problem behaviors exhibited by sexually abused boys was different from the pattern exhibited by girls. Sexually abused boys were more likely to exhibit multiple problems, and these were likely to include aggressive or criminal behavior and addiction-risk behavior as well as increased suicidality.

GENETIC PREDISPOSITION

Frick and Jackson (1993) suggested that a predisposition to antisocial behavior is genetically transmitted from parent to child. They suggested that this predisposition in the parent leads to dysfunctional family environments, and that this predisposition in the child leads to antisocial behavior. They further suggested that this model explains the link between family factors and childhood and adolescent antisocial behavior. In support of their model, the authors reviewed literature to indicate the intergenerational links in antisocial behaviors found in adoption and twin studies of children referred for conduct problems.

In a study of adopted children, it was found that 30% of biological mothers and fathers of the children referred for conduct problems were diagnosed with antisocial personality disorder; this is a similar rate to that found in family history studies (35% to 46% across studies). None of the adoptive parents with conduct disordered children had antisocial disorder. This suggests that the problem is more one of genetics rather than of problem parenting (Jarey & Stewart, 1985).

SEXUALITY

Lesbian, gay and bisexual (LGB) youths have been identified as showing significantly higher participation in health risk behaviors than heterosexual youths. Rosario, Hunter, and Gwadz (1997) found that 93% of LGB females and 89% of males from a sample recruited from New York City gay-focused organizations reported having used an illegal or illicit substance. Sixty-seven percent of females and 59% of males reported the use of an illicit drug. Hallucinogens, inhalants, and cocaine had been sampled by at least one in five LGB youths. Only 26% of females and 8% of males reported using a psychotherapeutic drug. Since Rosario et al. found that the lifetime prevalence rate was higher than that reported by national samples of presumably heterosexual youths (6.4:1 for females and 4.4:1 for males), they concluded that LGB youths were at risk for substance abuse. Self-identifying LGB youths showed a higher proportionate risk for suicide, victimization, sexual risk behaviors, and multiple substance use. LGB youths were more likely to report engaging in and initiating risk behaviors at an earlier age than their peers (Faulkner & Cranston, 1998; Garofalo et al., 1998).

These differences in health risks among LGB youths were probably mediated by victimization at school: Combined LGB status with high at-school victimization resulted in the highest levels of health risk behaviors. LGB youths demonstrated higher levels of substance use, suicidality, and sexual risk behaviors than their victimized heterosexual peers. The levels of these behaviors for LGB youths reporting low levels of victimization were approximately equal to their heterosexual peers (Bontempo & D'Augelli, 2002).

It is apparent that the type of pathology a young person develops (depression, conduct problems, or substance abuse) and the type of behavior exhibited (suicidal, aggressive, or risk-taking) depends on a complex interaction of both individual and environmental factors. It seems fair to say, however, that remarkably similar factors can lead to different forms of pathology and different forms of behavior.

Psychiatric Correlates of Adolescent Risk-Taking

SUBSTANCE ABUSE

Both suicidal and risk-taking behaviors are commonly associated with alcohol and drug use. However, risk-taking is more likely to be associated with substance abuse than with an affective disorder (Clark et al., 1990).

Many adolescents use alcohol in response to unpleasant emotions such as anger, depression, and loneliness. A study of adolescent psychiatric patients who engaged in risk behaviors when drunk found that these subjects later regretted their actions. The adolescents who reported the greatest alcohol-related problems believed that alcohol would improve their social abilities. These adolescents continued to believe that alcohol improved their social behavior despite also reporting frequent problems with parents, friends, and girlfriends or boyfriends when they were drinking (McKay et al., 1992).

Adolescent drug use may interfere with the development of protective factors such as effective coping strategies and social skills that normally assist in effective functioning. A longitudinal study that examined the impact of adolescent drug use found that it

76

increased delinquency at each of the developmental stages for both male and female participants (Brook et al., 1996). This suggests that drug abuse can have short- and long-term influences on the development of criminal behaviors. This supports the findings of Stacy and Newcomb (1995) that drug use in adolescence is a significant predictor of adult criminality.

CONDUCT DISORDER

Among the general population of adolescents, the prevalence of conduct disorder using DSM-IV criteria is about 2.4% (males 3.8% and females 1%) according to the survey of the Mental Health and Wellbeing of Australians (Sawyer et al., 2000). Delinquent behavior occurred among 6.2% of adolescents (males 6.4% and females 5.9%). Many risk-taking behaviors incorporate a measure of illegality such as drinking alcohol and driving at high speed, stealing cars and joyriding, vandalizing, shoplifting, physically aggressive behavior, and so on. It is, therefore, not surprising that an overlap exists between the youths apprehended for these behaviors and those diagnosed as conduct disordered or described as delinquent. Naturally, not all of the youths engaged in risk-taking behaviors have received a diagnosis of conduct disorder. This is largely because the services that they are likely to encounter are justice and welfare services rather than health services.

The criteria for a diagnosis of conduct disorder (DSM-IV, 1994) require that a degree of severity be met. The pattern of behavior must be ongoing and must impair the young person's ability to function effectively at school, at home, in the community, or at work. Aggressive behaviors, directed toward other people or animals, are included. The young person may, for example, engage in bullying or threatening behavior, physical intimidation, use of a weapon, cruelty to people or animals, coercion including sexual coercion, or direct confrontation while attempting theft. Other classes of behavior involving destruction of property may occur. Acts of deceitfulness and theft are included. In more general terms, young people with conduct disorder frequently violate rules such as being absent from school, running away from home, ignoring parental restrictions, and so on.

In summary, we know that adolescents with a diagnosis of substance abuse or conduct disorder comorbid with a diagnosis of depression are at increased risk of suicidal behavior. However, many of the young people engaged in serious delinquent or risk-taking behavior may not be assessed for depression, and therefore their increased suicidal risk is not considered.

7 Adolescent Risk-Taking: Cognitive Variables

Problem Solving

The literature pertaining to the problem-solving capacity of adolescents is generally focused on conduct disordered or delinquent populations. As stated previously, there is considerable overlap between adolescents who engage in risk-taking behavior and those who have been diagnosed with conduct disorder or termed delinquent. It is therefore fair to assume, for the purposes of this book, that the majority of adolescents included within these populations would also engage in risk behaviors.

Many aggressive adolescents and those with a conduct disorder demonstrate problem-solving deficits. Lochman and Lampron (1986) were interested in the problem-solving characteristics of aggressive and nonaggressive boys. They used means–ends stories containing a problematic interpersonal situation and a conclusion in which the problem no longer existed. The children were asked to provide the middle of the story and later to give any alternative solutions they could generate. The aggressive boys generated fewer verbally assertive solutions to problems, instead showing a preference for actively aggressive solutions.

Social goals may vary in different adolescents. Aggressive adolescents might value control and hostility but place a low value on their interactions with peers and their feelings about those peers. Lochman, Wayland, and White (1993) conducted a study in which they examined the relationship between social goals such as dominance, revenge, avoidance, and affiliation in terms of social problem solving. They found that the boys who valued dominance and revenge had little regard for affiliation. They also had a wide range of delinquent, substance, and behavioral difficulties. They found that the social goals of aggressive adolescents were clearly different from those of their nonaggressive peers.

Social problem solving is the ability to overcome difficulties in the formation and maintenance of social relationships. Adolescents with conduct problems show poorer social problem-solving ability than both depressed and normal control adolescents. Joffe et al. (1990) found that adolescents with conduct disorder had problems with generating the relevant steps to a social goal. They had difficulties with anticipating obstacles to be dealt with in the pursuit of a social goal, and they were much less capable of coming up with assertive verbal responses in difficult social situations. The authors suggest that these adolescents do not perceive obstacles to their solutions. Taken in conjunction with the finding that boys with a conduct disorder are more likely to act aggressively when they act impulsively (Dodge & Newman, 1981), it is conceivable that these boys become frustrated when they encounter obstacles. If they are not able to generate and consider other responses, then aggressive acting-out behavior may appear to be the only option.

It has been suggested that although depressed young people and those with conduct disorder both suffer from interpersonal problem-solving deficits, these deficits are different at different ages.

Aggressive and depressed children exhibit problems at all stages of information processing in social situations, and both groups tend to distort the meaning of what they see and hear (Dodge, 1993). Aggressive adolescents attend to supposedly hostile acts directed toward them (often leading to hostile attributions and retaliatory aggression). Depressed adolescents attend to failure, loss, and negative self-reference (Dodge & Newman, 1981).

It has also been found that both aggressive and depressed adolescents have a reduced ability to understand the emotions or reasoning of other people (i.e., perspective taking). This means that these adolescents often misunderstand the intentions of others and are likely to infer hostile intent. This effect is known as "hostile attributional bias" in many studies (Dodge et al., 1990). However, whereas the aggressive adolescents retaliate with aggression to the perceived hostility of others, the depressed adolescents blame themselves. Once the adolescents have developed a mental picture of a situation, they then consider possible behavioral responses. With increasing age, aggressive adolescents may come to generate as many responses as their nonaggressive peers, but the quality of those responses are poor. Aggressive adolescents are more likely to generate responses that are verbally coercive, physically aggressive, or irrelevant to the task or situation.

There is a discrepancy in the literature between problem-solving deficits and problem-solving distortions. A deficit implies the lack of a skill, for example in the number or relevance of solutions generated. A distortion refers to a misperception or misappraisal, such as underestimating one's problem-solving ability or attributing hostile intentions when none exist.

A study by Pont (1995) showed that adolescents with emotional and behavioral problems were able to generate a similar number of solutions to adolescents without these problems, but that the quality of their solutions was poorer. The problem group showed evidence of impulsivity and a lack of clear planning, and their solutions were more aggressive and problematic than those of adolescents without emotional and behavioral problems. These results indicated that there were both deficits and distortions occurring in the problem-solving approaches of this sample of boys.

These findings suggest that it is important to access information about deficits as well as distortions, and we address this in the studies reported in this book by using several different measures of problem solving. It is also important that we assess the quality of solutions (relevant versus irrelevant), since allowing any solution irrespective of usefulness to be counted does not give a meaningful indication of the adolescent's problem-solving ability.

Hopelessness

Children and adolescents with high levels of hopelessness display a defiant attitude, are hurtful to themselves and others, and exhibit socially inappropriate behaviors. They are more likely to express anger openly and aggressively and perceive their families as unsupportive. They are also more likely to experience a range of negative emotions including shame, fear, guilt, and hostility. These young people are likely to engage in socially inappropriate behaviors and are more likely to break the law (Kashani et al., 1997).

Adolescents who engage in antisocial behaviors generally come to the attention of the authorities at some stage. Since legal and disciplinary problems are one of the major life events reported by suicidal adolescents, it is important to be aware that many of these young people may also be experiencing high levels of hopelessness. Adolescents with a diagnosis of depression and adolescents with a diagnosis of conduct disorder report similar levels of depression and hopelessness (Kempton et al., 1994). Therefore, clinicians faced with an adolescent diagnosis of conduct disorder should check for the presence of both depression and hopelessness.

Protective Factors

Protective factors decrease the likelihood of an adolescent engaging in problem behaviors, while risk factors increase the likelihood of these behaviors occurring. Jessor et al. (1995) identified seven protective factors: positive orientation to school; positive orientation to health; intolerant attitude to deviance; positive relations with adults; perception of strong social controls or sanctions for transgressions; awareness of friends who model conventional behavior; and actual involvement in prosocial behavior. They also identified six risk factors: low expectations for success; low self-esteem; a general sense of hopelessness about life; awareness of friends who model involvement in problem behaviors; a greater orientation toward friends than parents; and poor school achievement or school dropout.

These psychosocial protective factors appear to play both a direct role and a moderating role in problem behavior. Adolescents with high protection scores exhibited fewer problem behaviors. The protective factors reduced problem behaviors even if the adolescent was exposed to a number of risk factors. This is an important finding that demonstrates the similarity of the role of protective factors in both problem behavior and suicidal behavior (Jessor et al., 1995).

The Effects of Alcohol and Stress on Problem Solving and Decision Making

The review of substance abuse in Chapter 6 indicates the important role that alcohol plays in risk-taking behaviors. What is still unknown is the role that alcohol might play in decreasing an adolescent's ability to engage in effective problem solving and decision making. The studies reviewed indicate that conduct disordered and delinquent adolescents are likely to exhibit problem-solving deficits. A question of interest is whether this deficit is likely to be exacerbated by alcohol consumption.

The discussion of the relationship of alcohol and suicide also indicates that it is an important variable to be considered with the suicidal population. Once again the literature indicates that these adolescents exhibit problem-solving deficits. Are these deficits also likely to be exacerbated by alcohol consumption? It is considered important to include the role of alcohol in a model of suicidal and risk-taking behavior and to endeavor to assess the effects of alcohol on problem solving and decision making.

A second variable clearly important in adolescent suicide is stress. An extensive body of literature indicates that a stressful situation, usually interpersonal loss or conflict or a disciplinary crisis, often precedes suicide. Young people engaged in risk-taking who are in trouble with the law are also more likely to have experienced interpersonal loss or conflict and disciplinary crises. The question of interest is the effect of stress on the adolescent's ability to engage in effective problem solving and decision making. Once again it is important to include the role of stress in a model of adolescent suicidal and risk-taking behavior.

A PILOT STUDY

A preliminary study using university undergraduates was conducted to evaluate the effect of alcohol and stress on problem solving and decision making (Sofronoff, 1999). Student volunteers were randomly allocated to one of four conditions: alcohol, stress, alcohol plus stress, and a comparison group. Under these conditions, the students completed self-report measures of problem solving and decision making.

Results indicated that those students in the two alcohol groups performed at a significantly lower standard on the problem-solving measures than the comparison group. Specifically, they produced more irrelevant and aggressive responses to problem situations. These students also indicated that they would engage in significantly more risk activities than the comparison group. The participants in the stress condition also produced fewer relevant solutions to problems, showed a less positive attitude toward problem solving, indicated they would engage in more risk activities, and showed a level of underconfidence in their knowledge of risk activities.

Tentative conclusions drawn from these findings suggest that both alcohol and stress do have a deleterious effect on problem solving and decision making. Since we found this effect with highly functioning university students, it does not seem unreasonable to suggest that similar effects would occur with those adolescents already showing deficits in problem solving and decision making.

An Overlap Between Suicidal and Risk-Taking Adolescents

One study, which looked for predictors of suicidal behavior in adolescents who had a current or past diagnosis of major depressive disorder, found that conduct problems were a stronger predictor of suicidality than depression. Those adolescents who had both depression and a conduct disorder were at the greatest risk for suicidal behavior (Myers et al., 1991). A further illustration of the high risk factor of this combination of disorders is the increasing incidence of death in custody among young offenders. Bearing this in mind, we find it becomes more important to include this risk-taking population in a study of adolescent suicide.

Many adolescents exhibit risk-taking behaviors more clearly than they exhibit the classic symptoms of depression or suicidal ideation. Woods et al. (1997) suggested that a suicide attempt would be associated with other risk and problem behaviors. They compared 288 adolescents who reported having made a suicide attempt. The results indicated that there were significant relationships between a suicide attempt and female gender, poor class standing, lack of seat belt and helmet use, and multiple substance use, including substance use before driving and use before sexual activity. Suicide attempts were also associated with histories of fighting, gun use, sexually transmitted diseases, and same-gender sexual experiences. The strongest relationships included cigarette use, alcohol use, marijuana use, other drug use, aggressive behavior, substance use before sexual activity, and carrying a gun. This study supports the suggestion that risk-taking and problem behaviors as defined by Jessor (see Chapter 5) are related to suicide attempts.

Rohde, Mace, and Seeley (1997) conducted a study to evaluate the correlates of suicidal behavior in a population of adolescents in a juvenile detention center. They pointed out that the adolescents in question were considered delinquent and that this term is a legal term used to describe a child or adolescent who has committed a criminal offense. They went on to point out that the term also overlaps considerably with the psychiatric diagnosis of conduct disorder. Once again, the population being described includes those adolescents considered as risk takers.

The results indicated a higher rate of suicide attempts and suicidal ideation among adolescent risk takers. Rates of suicidal behavior were particularly high among the girls, with 50% reporting suicidal ideation and 40% reporting a past suicide attempt. The authors concluded that overall this population (both male and female) has rates of suicidal behavior comparable with psychiatric inpatients, and they suggested that psychiatric care should be delivered accordingly. These findings are very similar to those of Kosky, Sawyer, and Gowland (1990), who found that youths in a detention center had significantly higher rates of depression than a community sample did.

Conclusions

While there are a number of theories about why adolescents engage in risk-taking behavior, it is not usually suggested that they are engaging in a form of suicidal behavior. However, the major correlates of this type of behavior suggest they are likely to be at risk of suicide. The combination of substance abuse, conduct disorder, and cognitive deficits such as problem solving, hopelessness, possible faulty decision making, and a lack of protective factors may simply carry these adolescents to the same end by a different path.

While one group of adolescents presents with internalizing symptoms such as depression, the other group, who may also be depressed, exhibits externalizing behaviors such as recklessness, aggressiveness, or risk behaviors. Risk behaviors may precede later suicidal behavior or be part of a suicidal behavior complex.

It would seem warranted to compare this group of adolescents with the depressed and suicidal adolescents in an attempt to clarify the extent of their similarities and differences.

It is our intention, with the studies presented in this book, to access six different groups of adolescents. They include the following:

- **Depressed adolescents** (depressed group)
- **Adolescents engaged in minor problem behaviors, including school or family problems, truancy, and alcohol and drug use, with no legal ramifications** (problem behavior group)

- **Adolescents who have attempted suicide and have been hospitalized** (suicide group)
- **Adolescents who have engaged in risk-taking behaviors that have resulted in legal consequences** (risk-taking group)
- **Adolescents who have attempted suicide and have also engaged in risk-taking behaviors** (suicide and risk-taking combined group)
- **Adolescents with no history of depression, conduct problems, substance use problems, risk-taking, or suicide attempts** (comparison group)

Following the literature review presented in preceding chapters, there are some additions to be made to the first stage of the suicide model briefly outlined at the end of Chapter 4. It was decided to include both conduct problems and substance use problems under the single group of problem behaviors as suggested by Jessor (1992). The work of the decision theorists also provides a useful paradigm within which to access information about the decision-making ability and attitude toward risk of both risk takers and suicidal adolescents. It is hypothesized that decision making may be a mediator between problem behaviors and serious risk-taking and suicidal behavior.

As illustrated, problem solving, hopelessness, protective factors, and decision making are the four constructs that may mediate between psychopathology (depression, conduct disorder, and substance abuse) and suicidal or risk-taking behavior. The operationalization of these constructs and the actual measures to be used are fully outlined in Chapter 9.

A MODEL OF SUICIDE AND RISK-TAKING

8 An Integrated Model of Suicide and Risk-Taking

Introduction

This integrative chapter aims to present the Suicide and Risk-Taking (S/RT) model developed from our review of the extant literature and to provide the theoretical basis for that model. The chapter begins with a review of how the model was derived, an explanation of how it differs from a similar model proposed in the literature, and an outline of the component parts of the model. We then briefly revisit the literature concerned with the major factors associated with suicide and risk-taking included in the model in order to provide a rationale for the structure of the model. The chapter proceeds to outline a theoretical framework to explain the way in which the proposed mediating variables, problem solving, hopelessness, protective factors, and decision making are hypothesized to work in suicidal and risk-taking behaviors.

An Earlier Model

In a review article, Yang and Clum (1996) suggested that early environmental factors are linked to suicidal behavior by means of the mediating influence of cognitive factors. In order to reach their conclusion, Yang and Clum examined evidence from other studies to show links between (a) cognitive deficits and suicidal behavior, (b) early environmental factors and cognitive deficits, and (c) early environmental factors and suicidal behavior. They proposed the model of suicidal behavior shown as Figure 8.1.

This model proposes that early negative life events form a background to suicidal behavior, but the exhibition of this behavior is determined by several cognitive factors acting as mediators. These factors include low self-esteem, external locus of control, field dependence, poor problem-solving skills, and hopelessness.

Our S/RT model (Figure 8.2) differs from that put forward by Yang and Clum (1996) in several ways. It draws from two bodies of literature, both the literature of adolescent suicide and the literature of adolescent risk-taking behavior. We have tried to take into consideration a progression from early environmental risk factors to psychopathology, either in the form of depressive symptomatology or, alternatively, behavior problems and substance abuse problems. In order to understand the development of these problem behaviors in individuals, we propose a S/RT model whereby cognitive factors (problem solving, hopelessness, deficits in protective factors, and decision making) mediate between psychopathology and suicidal or risk-taking behavior rather than the usual understanding that links environmental factors directly to suicidal or risk-taking behaviors.

We have also taken into account the fact that environmental factors predispose individuals to psychopathology (depression and

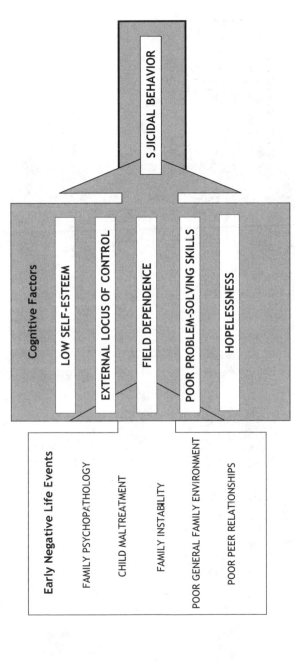

Figure 8.1. A proposed model of suicidal behavior (Yang & Clum, 1996).

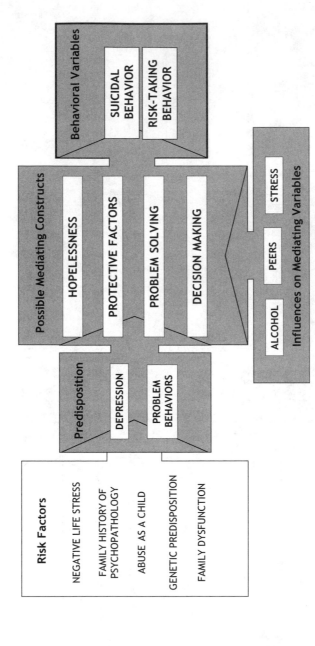

Figure 8.2. A model of suicidal and risk-taking behaviors.

problem behaviors). However, the psychopathology is then linked to suicidal and risk-taking behavior by means of the mediating influence of cognitive factors.

The literature reviewed in earlier chapters examined environmental and individual factors found to be related to suicidal behavior, and it reviewed environmental and individual factors found to be related to risk-taking behaviors. This review led to the conclusion that these risk factors occur as forerunners to psychopathology or in the context of current psychopathology.

The earlier literature reviews also examined links between psychopathology and suicidal or risk-taking behaviors. The links between psychopathology and cognitive deficits and between cognitive deficits and suicidal and risk-taking behavior were reviewed. Links included in the model are covered in the preceding literature reviews. Therefore, although interacting background factors may predispose an individual to develop psychopathology, it seems more likely that it is the nature of the psychopathology that predisposes that individual to suicidal behaviors or risk-taking behaviors.

The S/RT Model

The S/RT model (Figure 8.2) starts with the antecedent variables or risk factors that feature in the backgrounds of many adolescents who later engage in either suicidal or risk-taking behaviors. These variables include negative life stress, family conflict, abuse as a child, family psychopathology, genetic predisposition, and gender. The S/RT model suggests that these risk factors and environmental or individual variables create a vulnerability for these young people to develop psychopathology such as depression, conduct problems, and substance abuse problems.

The central section of the S/RT model proposes that adolescents with these psychopathologies show increased evidence of particular cognitive deficits. Problem-solving deficits, hopelessness, fewer protective factors, and poor or impulsive decision-making are proposed as possible mediating variables. The central section of the S/RT model also suggests that these deficits may be exacerbated by alcohol or drug use and by current stressful events. Problem behaviors and risk-taking behaviors may also be affected by peer influence. The S/RT model proposes, therefore, that problem solving, hopelessness, protective factors, and decision making are cognitive constructs that are possible mediating variables among depressive symptoms, conduct problems, substance abuse, and the behavioral outcomes of risk-taking and suicidal behaviors.

In addition to testing whether or not the identified cognitive variables do function as mediators between psychopathology and the negative behavioral outcomes (suicide and risk-taking), we also examine why some adolescents continue to make risk decisions and continue to engage in risk-taking behaviors over time. We look at the reasoning processes associated with decision making across different groups of adolescents, using the decision theory paradigm to assess decision making in risk situations. We were interested in whether these young people appreciated the risks involved in their actions. If they did, as Furby and Beyth-Marom (1992) and Quadrel et al. (1993) have suggested, why did they decide to keep taking those risks?

A Rationale for the S/RT Model

RISK FACTORS FOR SUICIDE AND RISK-TAKING

Many of the reviewed studies revealed common factors in the backgrounds of adolescents presenting with different problems, including depression, conduct problems, suicidal behaviors, and risk-taking behaviors. These factors include negative life stress (de Wilde et al., 1992; Marttunen et al., 1994, 1995; Tarrant & Woon, 1995), abuse as a child (Brent, 1995; de Wilde et al., 1992; Silverman et al., 1996), family history of psychopathology (Brent et al., 1993b; Brent, 1995; Kosky et al., 1990a; Tarrant & Woon, 1995), family dysfunction (Adams, Overholser, & Lehnert, 1994; Kosky et al., 1990b), and genetic predisposition (Brent et al., 1996; Frick & Jackson, 1993). A significant effect of gender has been found. More females than males report depressive symptomatology, and more males than females report conduct problems (Craighead, 1991; King et al., 1993; Kovacs et al., 1993; Lewinsohn et al., 1993). More females attempt suicide and more males complete suicide (Lewinsohn et al., 1996; Ohberg et al., 1996).

PSYCHOPATHOLOGY, SUICIDE, AND RISK-TAKING

The link between depression and suicide is well established (see Chapter 3). However, the alternative link to suicidal behavior by means of conduct disorder and substance abuse is also becoming increasingly well documented (see Chapter 3). Many recent studies have found that almost all cases of suicide and suicide attempts show previous psychopathology (Lewinsohn et al., 1996). It has also been suggested that other risk-taking behaviors such as smoking, engaging in physical fights, not using a seat belt, and carrying a weapon are also likely to be associated with suicidal behaviors (Kann et al., 1996; Woods et al., 1997). Moreover, these behaviors are also likely to be associated with psychopathology.

MEDIATING VARIABLES, SUICIDE, AND RISK-TAKING

Our earlier survey of the literature has identified several possible factors that could mediate between psychopathology and suicidal or risk-taking behaviors. These factors may determine the particular outcome in individual cases (see Chapter 4 and Chapter 7). Several studies support the suggestion that a possible mediating variable may be problem solving. It is possible that problem solving may be useful in differentiating among depressed adolescents, those with conduct problems, and normal adolescents (Dodge, 1993; Joffe et al., 1990; Rotheram-Borus et al., 1990; Sadowski & Kelley, 1993; Schotte & Clum, 1987; Slaby & Guerra, 1988). Hopelessness has been suggested as a mediating variable between current stress and suicidal behavior in an adult sample (Rudd et al., 1994). The decision theory paradigm attempts to explain how adolescents engaging in risk behaviors make their decisions. In this sense, decision making must be considered a potential mediating schema (Beyth-Marom et al., 1993; Furby & Beyth-Marom, 1992). The availability of working protective factors for suicidal behaviors and for risk-taking also represents a potential mediating factor (Jessor, 1992; Linehan et al., 1983). Our research aimed to elucidate the roles of these potential or likely variables in either suicide or risk-taking. There could be different mediators for different populations of at-risk adolescents.

It was also necessary to assess the problem-solving and decision-making factors in conjunction with other variables likely to influence them – peer pressure, alcohol use, and current stress. Alcohol use and current stress are commonly identified as contributing to suicidal and risk-taking behaviors. Peer influence can be seen as a contributing factor in many instances of risk-taking, but it could also be a factor in suicidal behavior as has been suggested following the deaths of certain popular entertainers. There were reports of suicides by fans following the death of silent-film star Rudolph Valentino in the 1920s (Murphy, 1996). In 1994, mental health professionals feared an eruption of copy cat suicides following the suicide of grunge idol Kurt Cobain. As such, the media were encouraged to refrain from sensationalised reporting of the event and state and national health services were emphatically publicized (Jobes et al., 1996). Cluster suicides in Plano, Texas in the mid-80s clearly illustrated the combined effect of media sensation and peer-influence (Phillips, 1986).

Problem-Solving and Decision-Making Deficits in Suicidal Behavior

The literature reviewed in earlier chapters found very little in the way of theoretical explanation for the role of mediating variables in the suicidal trajectory. A major source of interest in our research, however, is the impact of strong emotion or affect on the suggested mediating variables of problem-solving and decision-making abilities. It has been found that emotional states, both positive and negative, can affect a diverse array of decision and problem-solving tasks. To date, the majority of studies have focused on positive mood influences (Isen & Geva, 1987; Isen & Means, 1983; Lewinsohn & Mano, 1991). However, several researchers have concentrated their efforts on the effects of depression and negative affect on problem solving and decision making (Conway & Giannopoulos, 1993; Hartlage et al., 1993; Hertel & Rude, 1991; Ingram, 1990; Mano, 1992; Wright & Bower, 1992). From this research, two competing theories have arisen to explain the reason for the apparent and consistent deficits found in memory and problem-solving among these subjects.

COGNITIVE CAPACITY
Several research groups have suggested that depression somehow causes a reduction in the cognitive capacity an individual has to work with. This hypothesis was first introduced by Hasher and Zacks (1979). It was later refined to suggest that the extent of capacity reduction is directly related to the severity of depression (Hasher et al., 1985). These researchers maintained that depression should most severely constrain performance when the task is difficult and requires

effort. Easy tasks should not be affected because they require little cognitive capacity. In terms of a causal mechanism for this hypothesis, dopaminergic dysfunction may interfere with effortful cognitive processes (those requiring greater cognitive capacity) but leave automatic processes relatively intact (Roy-Byrne et al., 1986). However, in a series of three experiments with college undergraduates, researchers were unable to find any significant differences between depressed and nondepressed participants in their ability to recall information presented (Hasher et al., 1985).

One reason for this may have been the use in this experiment of an undergraduate population with a rather low criterion level for depression (a score above 7, with a mean of 12 on the Beck Depression Inventory, or BDI) which would generally indicate the absence rather than presence of depressive symptomatology. In this type of population, for whom recalling information is a central part of routine daily activity, it may be necessary to have more severe levels of depression to find evidence of interference with this type of task.

A second problem may be that high or low levels of arousal may cause reduced cognitive capacity and consequent impairment of performance on tasks needing effortful processing. The basis for this suggestion is the Yerkes–Dodson law (1908), which construes performance as an inverted U-shaped function of arousal. Kahneman (1973) also supports the belief that performance varies as a function of arousal. He maintains, however, that the effects of high and low arousal are caused by different mechanisms. Low arousal results in a lack of motivation while high arousal causes a narrowing of attentional focus, thereby restricting the range of cues to which an individual is capable of attending.

NARROWING OF ATTENTIONAL FOCUS

An alternative hypothesis to explain the negative effect of depression on decision making argues that total cognitive capacity is not reduced but that depressed people focus on task-irrelevant thoughts. This results in impaired performance on effortful tasks (Hartlage et al., 1993). Several studies have illustrated that emotional states produce a narrowing of attentional focus (Conway & Giannopoulos, 1993; Mano, 1992; Wright & Bower, 1992). Ingram (1984a; 1984b; 1990) suggested that available cognitive capacity is occupied with depression-related or self-related information. Subjects who had an induced negative mood and who were presented with unfavorable self-related feedback recalled more of that feedback than subjects who had a positive mood induced in them. It seems that people with negative moods give more weight to, or focus more attention on, negative material than do those who have a positive outlook.

Mano (1992) conducted a study to assess the effects of displeasure on judgments, evaluations, and gambles made during a naturally occurring distressing situation. He found that subjects under distress adopted simpler decision rules and expressed more polarized judgments. He also found that distressed subjects were more likely to take a risk than controls (they were willing to pay more for the same lottery).

Applying these study findings to the naturally occurring situation, we find that it seems reasonable to suppose that depressed people will focus on self-related or depression-related cues and will, therefore, show deficits in cognitive processes that require cognitive effort. Such deficits may be compounded when several emotional disorders are combined, such as depression, conduct disorder, and substance abuse. If an individual is not capable of engaging in deep or effortful processing of all the information relevant to his or her particular problem, it is likely that the decision made will show evidence of impulsivity. That is to say, simpler decision rules will be used, fewer cues will be attended to, and more polarized or extreme judgments will be made (Mano, 1992).

Dysphoric subjects also made less use of relevant information in an evaluative task than nondysphoric subjects did, even though the task was highly structured (Conway & Giannopoulos, 1993). From the research gathered to date, it would seem that this mode of decision making is characteristic of both suicidal and risk-taking adolescents.

Problem-Solving and Decision-Making Deficits in Risk-Taking

Adolescents do not appear to believe that they are invulnerable or indestructible. They are as capable as their adult counterparts of assessing the risks and consequences of a variety of risk behaviors commonly associated with adolescence. They were also found to be very similar to adults in their ability to judge the probability of adverse outcomes occurring for themselves and others (Beyth-Marom et al., 1993; Quadrel et al., 1993). These studies suggest that when adolescents choose to engage in risk behaviors they are as aware of the possible consequences as adults are. However, we are still left with the question as to why some adolescents continue to choose to engage in serious risk behaviors.

NARROWING OF ATTENTIONAL FOCUS

One possibility is that the individual who chooses to engage in risk behaviors is like an individual engaged in problem solving while in a state of depression or stress. There may be a narrowing of his or her attentional focus caused by the anticipation of the activity. This may lead to a situation in which simpler decision making strategies are used and attention is paid to fewer cues. A study by Benthin, Slovic, and Severson (1993) found evidence to support the hypothesis that perception and assessment of risk differs depending on whether the subject engages in the activity he or she is assessing or not. Adolescents who had engaged in the behaviors they were assessing for risk, when compared with adolescents who had not engaged in the activities, reported a greater confidence in their knowledge of the risks involved (this knowledge may or may not have been accurate). They also reported less fear of the risks, greater benefits than risks associated with the activity, less seriousness of effects, greater peer pressure to engage in the activity, more personal control over the risks, less ability to avoid engaging in the activity, and a higher perceived participation rate by peers. This finding could support the suggestion that when an individual is actually involved in making a decision to engage in a risk activity, the level of arousal is such that he or she is using simpler decision rules and attending to fewer cues (Mano, 1992).

REGRET THEORY

A theoretical basis for minimizing loss in decision making may be found in the literature dealing with decision making under uncertainty. Regret theory (Bell, 1983, 1985) suggests that risk preference and decisions involving risk can be understood in terms of a person's desire to avoid the unpleasant psychological consequences of making a wrong choice (Larrick, 1993). In contrast to subjective expected utility (SEU) theory, regret theory suggests that individuals do not simply combine probabilities and outcomes to reach an overall value for a decision (SEU). Instead, they compare the outcome of an action with the outcomes that might have occurred if they had made different decisions. They then choose the action that minimizes regret. For example, the odds of winning the Lotto are extremely remote, but an individual would experience intense regret if he or she failed to play on an occasion when he or she would have won. Therefore, many individuals participate to minimize regret.

It would seem possible to apply this formulation to the types of decisions made by adolescents who engage in risk-taking behavior. Beyth-Marom et al. (1993) point to the fact that it is important when one is assessing adolescent attitude toward risk to assess the consequences for them of *not* engaging in risk behavior. An assessment of the costs and benefits of the perceived consequences of both engaging in and not engaging in a risk behavior could serve to illustrate the decision processes involved in taking risks that to many may appear to be inordinate and unnecessary. Regret theory would suggest that adolescents know the risks involved in their behaviors but are willing to take them because they wish to avoid the feeling of regret produced by not taking, and successfully negotiating, a risk.

JUDGMENT AND CONFIDENCE

Bell (1983, 1985) also suggests that a willingness to take risks is associated with a higher level of self-esteem and confidence. This may, in fact, be the case with risk-taking adolescents. However, a contrary explanation is that their self-esteem is tied to their willingness to engage in risk-taking behavior or to be part of a risk-taking peer group. If this is the case, then the decision to engage in the behavior may indicate a lack of self-esteem and a low level of decision making. Quadrel et al. (1993) found, in a test of general knowledge about the consequences of risk behavior, that a group of high-risk adolescents (delinquents) were much more confident of the accuracy of their knowledge, when they were in fact wrong, than either low-risk adolescents or adults.

Beyth-Marom et al. (1993) conducted a study to examine whether risk takers see different consequences for risk behaviors when they are compared with adolescents who engage in few risk behaviors. The results showed very similar responses for the two groups. However, one noticeable difference was that the risk takers produced fewer consequences for the risk behaviors. The authors concluded that these

104

adolescents do not work as hard or as effectively at generating possible consequences as the nonrisk group. Certainly it is necessary to assess whether these high-risk adolescents view their own risk-taking behavior in the same light as they view hypothetical situations.

It may be the case that in situations in which the adolescents have had actual experience (where presumably nothing bad has occurred), they are overconfident in their knowledge and, by inference, their ability to cope. This would then fit with Bell's theory that a willingness to take risks is associated with a higher self-esteem. Things go wrong for these adolescents when their judgment is poor and they end up in trouble or, worse still, in jail or a detention center. They have obviously made a wrong decision, self-esteem decreases, problem-solving deficits come into play, and they may suffer depression; at this point they are at risk of suicidal behavior. If one were to interview adolescents who have engaged in risk behaviors and to ask them to describe the costs and benefits of engaging in or not engaging in the behavior at the time the decision was made, then we may be closer to comprehending the assessment of such risks.

Conclusions

The studies undertaken by Borst and Noam (1993), Dodge (1993), and Rotheram-Borus and Trautman (1988) all indicate that there are at least two quite distinct groups of adolescents at risk for suicidal behavior. One group exhibits depressive symptomatology and the other group presents with conduct disorder and aggression. Both groups show deficits in problem solving and decision making. However, these deficits are different for each group, as are the types of behaviors they engage in and the symptomatology they display. It should also be the case that embedded in the problem-solving and decision-making deficits are differing attitudes toward, and perceptions of, risk and risk-taking behavior. Following from this, it is also likely that decision-making processes may be different. For example, there may be different reasons for making particular decisions, the costs and benefits may be perceived differently, or the costs of not engaging in behavior may be significant. It is important to clarify the distinctions between these groups, both for purposes of recognition or diagnosis and because intervention programs would have different points of emphasis.

Our task from here is twofold. First, we need to establish whether our formulation of the interrelationships between variables presented is valid – whether, in fact, the variables that we suggest (problem solving, hopelessness, protective factors, and decision making) demonstrate significant mediation between psychopathology such as depression, symptoms such as conduct problems and substance problems, and later outcome behaviors such as suicide attempts and serious risk-taking. Second, we need to establish whether our formulation is clinically useful. That is, are these identified variables actual deficits in identifiable at risk populations, and can we use them in a clinically useful manner so that, by correcting them, we create a means to intervene before suicide is attempted?

AN EVALUATION OF THE S/RT MODEL

9 Depressed and Problem Behavior Adolescents

So far, the literature reviewed suggests that depressed adolescents and risk-taking adolescents differ from normal adolescents in their problem-solving, risk-assessment, and decision-making capacity. The S/RT model described in Figure 8.2 suggests that early risk factors are precursors to the development of psychopathology such as depression and problem behaviors (conduct disorder and substance abuse problems). Alcohol, stress, and peer pressure may exacerbate these deficits, while protective factors may offer stability to young people in this situation.

This chapter and the next two describe research that shows empirical support for the S/RT model in three distinct ways. This chapter checks that depressive symptomatology and problem behaviors relate to the mediating constructs: problem solving, hopelessness, protective factors, and decision making. Chapter 10 checks that these mediating constructs relate to suicidal behavior and risk-taking behavior. Chapter 11 tests whether these constructs do mediate between depression and problem behaviors on one side and suicidal behavior and risk-taking behavior on the other.

The S/RT model aims to demonstrate links between cognitive constructs and behavioral outcomes. In previous research and in the literature, adolescents are often grouped by terms such as "depressed," "problem behaviour," "risk takers," and "suicidal." The design used to test the links in the S/RT model uses these groups. Adolescents can also be measured according to their depressive symptoms, problem behaviors, risk-taking behaviors, and suicidal behaviors. Broadly speaking, we note that depressive symptomatology and problem behaviors are like independent variables; suicidal and risk-taking behaviors are like dependent variables. The mediating constructs of the S/RT model operate between the independent and dependent variables. Thus, our research used both between-group comparisons and multiple regression (using variables to predict outcomes) to test the links in the S/RT model. To do this we used some measures of the constructs from the literature, and we developed some of our own.

The independent variables in the model are depression and problem behaviors, and the questionnaires measuring these constructs were used to form groups for this study. Depressive symptomatology is measured by the BDI (Beck, 1978). Scores on the BDI range from 0 to 63. Although these scores do not allow a diagnosis of depression, they do indicate the level of depressive symptomatology.

The measures used to assign participants to the problem behavior group included the Substance Use Scale, which asked individuals to indicate any substances they used, how frequently they used them, the quantities used, and whether they considered that they abused either alcohol or drugs. The scale was developed for use in this research. Other indicators of problem behaviors included self-report or teacher–parent report of behaviors such as being truant, staying out late, having arguments at home, or experiencing problems at school. It was also possible to identify potential participants for this group from responses to the Perception of Risk Scale (Benthin et al., 1993), which asked participants to indicate the activities they had participated in within the past 6 months and how frequently.

The dependent variables for the model encompass constructs of suicidal behavior, risk-taking behavior, and suicidal and risk-taking behavior combined. They are used to define group membership in the study reported in Chapter 11.

Participants were assigned to the suicide group if they had made one or more suicide attempts that had resulted in hospitalization. The measure of suicidal behavior was the Suicide Behavior Scale (SBS) developed for use in these studies. Participants were assigned to the risk-taking group if they had engaged in risk-taking behavior such that they had served time in a detention center or performed community service. They must never have made a suicide attempt of any kind and risk-taking was measured by the Risk-Taking Behavior Scale (RTBS) developed for use in these studies. The suicide and risk-taking combined group was made up of participants who fulfilled criteria for both suicide and risk-taking; that is, they had made a suicide attempt resulting in hospitalization and had engaged in behavior that had resulted in legal consequences and the combined behavior was measured by the SBS and the RTBS combined.

Each of the proposed mediating variables is a cognitive construct and is discussed in Chapters 5 and 8. These are problem solving, hopelessness, protective factors, and decision making. Problem solving was measured with a range of variables. The first measure of problem-solving appraisal was the Problem Orientation Scale (POS) from the Social Problem-Solving Inventory (SPSI; D'Zurilla & Nezu, 1990) and a measure of appraisal of solutions generated from the Social Situations Analysis Test (Connolly, 1988). The next measures of problem solving involved the ability to generate relevant solutions to social or interpersonal problems. The two measures used were the

111

Means–Ends Problem-Solving Test (Platt & Spivack, 1975) and the Social Situations Analysis Test (Connolly, 1988). Two scores were taken
from these tests – the number of relevant solutions generated and the
number of irrelevant or aggressive solutions generated. The final measure of problem solving was the use of identifiable problem-solving
strategies, and this was measured by the Problem-Solving Scale (PS)
from the SPSI (D'Zurilla & Nezu, 1990). Taken together, four variables
were obtained to evaluate the problem-solving skills and deficits of
the different groups of adolescents. This allowed for a more detailed
assessment of both similarities and differences than those undertaken
in earlier studies.

Hopelessness was measured with the Beck Hopelessness Scale
(Beck et al., 1974). This is a single scale with multiple items. It was expected that hopelessness would only be pertinent in the second study
in which the suicidal adolescents took part, but it was used as a measure in both studies. The construct of protective factors was measured
by the College Reasons for Living Scale (College RFL; Linehan et al.,
1983; Westefeld et al., 1992). This measure was included because it
gives an indication of some of the adaptive beliefs and expectations
that protect against suicidal and risk behaviors (Linehan et al., 1983).
It has also been found (Strosahl et al., 1992) that the Survival and
Coping Beliefs subscale of the RFL is more effective in discriminating
suicide attempters from nonsuicidal psychiatric patients and suicide
ideators than hopelessness. It was also expected that this construct
would only be relevant in the study that accessed adolescents who
had attempted suicide (reported in Chapter 10), but it was used as a
measure in this study for comparison purposes.

The final construct, decision making, was measured within the
framework of risk assessment. This was done because the types of decisions of interest in this book are decisions made in and about risk
situations. In a task based on the work of Beyth-Marom et al. (1993)

112

and Quadrel et al. (1993), participants were given three hypothetical situations (riding with a drunk driver, taking an unknown drug at a party, and being truant from school). They were then asked whether they would actually take part in the activity and to state the reasons for their decisions. For each situation they were given different outcomes. One such outcome was called the False Alarm situation, a no-harm outcome for an activity from which the participant abstained. Participants were then asked to write down the costs and benefits under these circumstances.

Prior use of this task by Sofronoff (1999) showed, by means of a content analysis, that the costs for the False Alarm scenario fell into two categories: the negative reactions of peers and the regret of missing the fun of the activity. Their responses were scored by use of the importance score (0–4) with which the adolescent had rated them. The total of the importance score for the two categories was termed the response to the False Alarm situation.

Data Collected

We obtained data on three groups of adolescents, namely a depressed group, a problem behavior group, and a comparison group. The study compares adolescents who show current symptoms of depression or problem behaviors with nondepressed adolescents with no problem behaviors to see if they vary on measures of the cognitive variables – problem solving, hopelessness, protective factors, and decision making. The variables used are presented in Table 2. The risk factors that predispose young people toward both depression and problem behaviors have already occurred in the lives of these adolescents, and the study does not attempt to look for evidence of these predisposing factors. We accept that they have had their effect.

Table 2 Measures taken and details of group allocation

Measures of constructs (Independent and dependent)	Source
Beck Depression Inventory	Beck (1978)
Substance Use Questionnaire	Constructed for this research
Perception of Risk Scale	Benthin et al. (1993)
Suicide Behavior Scale	Constructed for this research
Risk-Taking Behavior Scale	Constructed for this research

Measures of mediating constructs

Beck Hopelessness Scale	Beck et al. (1974)
Reasons for Living Scale	Westefeld et al. (1992)
Means–Ends Problem-Solving Test	Platt & Spivack (1975)
No. of relevant solutions	
No. of irrelevant or aggressive solutions	
Social Situations Analysis Test	Connolly (1988)
No. of relevant solutions	
No. of irrelevant or aggressive solutions	
Appraisal of solutions	
Social Problem-Solving Inventory	D'Zurilla and Nezu (1990)
Problem Orientation Scale	
Problem-Solving Scale	
Risky decision making	Constructed for this research
No. of risky decisions	
False Alarm response	Constructed for this research
Regret	
Peer influence	

Groups	Criteria
Depressed adolescents: $n = 21$ (17 females, 4 males)	BDI score > 16; no suicide attempt or ideation; no antidepressant medication. Mean BDI $= 21$, $SD = 5.0$. Mean no. of risky activities $= 4.7$, $SD = 2.1$. Mean substance abuse $= 0$, $SD = 0$ (0,1).

114

Groups	Criteria
Problem behavior adolescents: $n = 19$ (6 females, 13 males)	Self-reported participation in aggressive and risky behaviors as included on Perception of Risk Scale (Benthin et al., 1993). Reports by others (psychologist or parent) of problem behaviors, or self-report or other report of substance abuse. Mean BDI $= 8$, $SD = 5.7$. Mean no. of risky activities $= 6.7$, $SD = 2.5$. Mean substance abuse $= .42$, $SD = 0.51$ (0,1).
Comparison adolescents: $n = 18$ (9 females, 9 males)	Selected to be comparable in age, gender, and educational level with other groups. Mean BDI $= 4.0$, $SD = 3.54$ Mean no. of risky activities $= 2.66$, $SD = 2.11$. Mean substance abuse $= 0$, $SD = 0$ (0,1).

Method

PARTICIPANTS

The participants in the depressed group ($n = 21$) and in the problem behavior group ($n = 19$) were recruited from an undergraduate population at a university and from psychologists and psychiatrists in private practice. Adolescents in the comparison group ($n = 18$) were recruited from the same undergraduate population and from the community. They were comparable in age, gender, and educational level with the young people in the other two groups. The participants were between 16 and 21 years of age.

MATERIALS AND PROCEDURE

Table 2 provides a list of measures collected from the participants along with the criteria used for group assignment. All participants completed the BDI (Beck, 1978) and a questionnaire pertaining to substance use (including alcohol use) that was developed specifically for these studies. Participants completed some of the measures as a means of ensuring correct group allocation. The participants were administered the battery of questionnaires individually, and this took between $1\frac{1}{4}$ and $1\frac{1}{2}$ hours.

Results

The main question was whether there would be a relationship between the independent constructs and the mediating constructs as depicted in the S/RT model. Since we "measured" the independent constructs by allocating participants into groups, that is, depressed, problem behavior, and comparison, an analysis testing for differences among the three groups on the measured mediating variables will address the research questions. There are nine mediating variables and we expect correlations between them. To take into account these correlations, we performed a discriminant analysis not only to test for the differences between the means of the groups on each mediating variable but also to show the pattern of group differences with the mediating variables as a set. We performed all analyses by using SPSS (Statistical Package for the Social Sciences, Version 10). The results of these analyses appear in Table 3.

An advantage of discriminant analysis is that it provides a way to represent the multivariate differences among the groups. There were two significant functions. The first function ($\chi^2 = 110.06$, $df = 18$, $p < .0001$) separated the depressed group from the other two groups, with the depressed group endorsing significantly lower scores

116

Table 3 Means, standard deviations, Univariate F ratios, F-to-remove statistics, and structure coefficients

	Group			Univariate F ratio $df = (2, 55)$	F-to-remove $df = (2, 46)$	Structure coefficients	
	Depressed	Problem behavior	Comparison			F_1	F_2
Hopelessness	7.48 (4.9)	3.00 (2.4)	2.17 (3.1)	12.04***	0.31	−.40	−.03
Reasons for living	42.14 (7.3)	48.74 (5.4)	46.00 (9.1)	4.06**	1.51	.19	.19
Relevant solutions	11.29 (2.8)	10.95 (2.5)	14.50 (4.2)	6.85***	0.63	.18	−.35
Irrelevant solutions	1.48$_a$ (1.8)	3.95$_b$ (1.9)	1.44$_a$ (1.3)	8.09***	1.59*	−.12	.44
POS	43.0$_a$ (20.2)	85.4$_b$ (18.3)	93.6$_b$ (11.9)	48.66***	17.39***	.79	.06
PS	80.62 (22.0)	94.05 (17.2)	105.88 (16.5)	8.71***	0.81	.32	−.14
Positive resp. to solutions	2.66$_a$ (1.3)	3.57$_b$ (1.2)	4.50$_b$ (.7)	13.63***	2.98**	.40	−.19
No. of risky decisions	0.43 (.7)	1.42 (.7)	0.11 (.3)	20.49***	0.99	.06	.76
Resp. to False Alarm situation	3 76$_a$ (3.7)	8.26$_b$ (4.3)	0.56$_c$ (.8)	25.01***	5.13***	−.05	.84

Notes: Standard deviations are given in parentheses.

a,b,c Subscripts are used to indicate results of a Tukey honestly significant difference comparison.

Means in the same row that do not share subscripts differ at $p < .05$

* With transformed data, $F(2, 46) = 3.44$, $p < .05$; ** $p < .05$; *** $p < .001$.

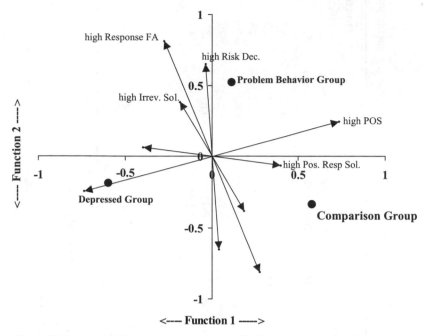

Figure 9.1. A plot of the group centroids for the three groups, showing the separation of the groups by the mediating variables on the discriminant functions (FA = false alarm). POS. = Problem Orientation Scale; Pos. Resp. Sol. = Positive Response to Solutions; Risk Dec. = Decisions taken to engage in hypothetical risk activities; Irrev. Sol. = Number of irrelevant or aggressive solutions to problems.

on two measures of problem-solving appraisal, that is, the POS and the number of positive responses to solutions generated. The squared canonical correlation for this function of 54% indicates a very strong effect.

The second function ($\chi^2 = 42.08$, $df = 8$, $p < .0001$) separated the problem behavior group from the other two groups, with the problem behavior group having a high value placed on regret and negative reactions of peers in response to the False Alarm situation, a high number of decisions taken to engage in hypothetical risk activities, and a high number of irrelevant or aggressive solutions to problems (Means–Ends Problem-Solving Test and Social Situations Analysis Test). The squared canonical correlation for this function was 32% and shows a strong effect.

Figure 9.1 shows the plot of the three group centroids on the two discriminant functions. To graphically show the role the variables play in separating the groups, we plot the variables by using coordinates given by the structure coefficients. The depressed group is clearly at the low end of the POS variable and positive response to solutions. The problem behavior group is clearly high on their response to False Alarm situations, the number of risk decisions endorsed, and the number of irrelevant solutions they generated.

Discussion

This chapter set out to test the relationship between the mediating constructs of problem solving, hopelessness, protective factors, and decision making and the dependent constructs of depression and problem behavior in the S/RT model. It was necessary to operationalize and measure these constructs. Three groups were selected for the study, encompassing depressed, problem behavior, and comparison individuals. Each group was measured on a range of variables reflecting the mediating constructs. The discussion first focuses on the differences between the groups for each of the mediating constructs in turn.

PROBLEM SOLVING
Problem solving was operationalized as both appraisal of problem-solving skills and actual problem-solving skills. The appraisal of problem solving was measured by the POS from the SPSI (D'Zurilla & Nezu, 1990) and the number of positive responses to solutions generated on the Social Situations Analysis Test (Connolly, 1988).

Actual problem-solving skills were measured by the PS from the SPSI (D'Zurilla & Nezu, 1990), the number of relevant solutions generated on the Means–Ends Problem-Solving Test and the Social Situations Analysis Test, and the number of irrelevant or aggressive solutions generated on the Means–Ends Problem-Solving Test and the Social Situations Analysis Test.

These measures were each successful, from the univariate F ratios, in differentiating between groups, which lends support to the suggestion that problem solving may be an important mediating construct as proposed by the S/RT model shown in Figure 8.2. However, when the correlations among the variables are taken into account, a simpler picture emerges. From the discriminant analysis, the measures of problem-solving appraisal uniquely differentiated the depressed group from the problem behavior group and the comparison group, while the number of irrelevant or aggressive solutions generated uniquely separated the problem behavior group from the other two groups.

The analyses also found, as expected, that the problem behavior group produced more irrelevant or aggressive solutions to problems (actual problem-solving skills). From an anecdotal point of view, the researcher (Kate Sofronoff) observed these adolescents during the process of gathering the data. It became apparent to her that they tended to write down the first responses that came into their heads. This was often either an aggressive or an irrelevant response. Then they reflected on these answers and came up with more acceptable responses. It may be that in a real situation, when under stress, or under the influence of drugs, alcohol, or peers, these adolescents would not take the extra time to reflect and come to a more acceptable conclusion. They may simply act on their initial thoughts. In other instances, the researcher noted that some adolescents were able to generate only one or two solutions to problems and after this they tended to offer irrelevant and aggressive suggestions.

Beyth-Marom et al. (1993) also found that in a delinquent population only a few solutions were generated. This finding was important because it underlined the value of actually examining the quality of the solutions offered. If only the number of solutions had been used as in the study by Pont (1995), reviewed in Chapter 8, then no significant differences would have been found between groups. On the PS, a measure of the adolescent's knowledge of actual problem-solving skills, the mean for the depressed group was lower than that for the other two groups. This was not expected since the literature suggests that depressed adolescents are capable of finding solutions to problems. The effect is not strong enough to suggest meaningful conclusions, and it was no longer significant when correlation with other variables was taken into account (F-to-remove statistic). However, it will be interesting to see if this finding is replicated with the adolescents who have attempted suicide, as reported in the following chapter.

The results of analyses also demonstrated, as expected, that the depressed group would score significantly lower on the POS from the SPSI; that is, they demonstrate negative and avoidant responses when asked about dealing with problem situations. They also endorse fewer positive responses to their own solutions to problems (appraisal of problem-solving skills); this is demonstrated by an ability to generate a solution to a problem but then a statement to the effect that this solution would not work for them. It is important to note that this result was very strong despite the fact that these adolescents had not received a diagnosis of clinical depression, had not been prescribed antidepressant medication, and at the time of their participation were functioning apparently normally. This finding lends support to the suggestion in the literature (e.g., Rudd et al., 1994) that, when depressed, adolescents doubt their ability to solve problems even when they are actually doing so. They believe that the solutions they generate are unlikely to produce a good outcome, and they say that even though these solutions may work for others they would not work for them (Schotte & Clum, 1987). This finding lends further support to the suggestion (Rudd et al., 1994) that problem-solving appraisal is more important than actual problem solving as a predictor of future pathology.

DECISION MAKING

Decision making was operationalized in the context of risk assessment and was measured by the number of hypothetical risk decisions the adolescents said they would make. These decisions were then further studied when adolescents were asked about the costs of a decision *not* to engage in a risk activity when there are no negative consequences, a False Alarm situation. These costs concerned either negative reactions from peers or regret at missing out on the fun. The data analysis, including both regret and negative reactions of peers, found similar differences between the groups for both measures. For this reason the two costs of a False Alarm situation were pooled to get the total response of the adolescent to the False Alarm situation. There is a very high correlation, .74, between the response to the False Alarm situation and the number of high-risk decisions endorsed. This explains why only the response to the False Alarm situation was significant on the F-to-remove statistic and the number of risk decisions was not significant.

Figure 9.1 shows these two variables clearly distinguishing the problem behavior group from the other two groups. What this means is that the problem behavior group decides to engage in more risk activities and also associates more costs with the False Alarm situations (not engaging in a risk activity when the outcome is neutral). It is also very interesting that the problem behavior group differed so strongly on regret and perceived negative reactions of peers. This shows a mechanism by which peer influence affects risk-taking behavior and suggests that it may be a mediating variable. We return to this point and its implication for therapy in later chapters.

This study also demonstrated that the adolescent participants, regardless of whether they engaged in the risk activity or not, were able to outline the consequences of engaging in a risk activity. This supports earlier findings (Beyth-Marom et al., 1993; Quadrel et al., 1993) that adolescents are aware of the consequences associated with risk activities and do not believe themselves to be invulnerable. What we are moving toward in this study is a clearer understanding of the seemingly paradoxical finding that, although these adolescents are aware of the consequences of their decisions to engage in risk behaviors, they nonetheless continue to decide to do so.

The result of this analysis leads to the suggestion that, in a risk situation where an adolescent does not know the outcome, as in any real-life risk situation, those who are prone to take risks are strongly influenced by a combination of peer influence or a need to be with peers and a strong feeling that they will regret missing the fun if they do not engage in the activity. It would seem that this combination of factors outweighs any fear of consequences, which is the deterrent endorsed by adolescents unwilling to engage in risk activities.

HOPELESSNESS

The Beck Hopelessness Scale measured the mediating construct of hopelessness. Univariately, the depressed group had the highest hopelessness mean score. However, these differences were not significant when the correlations among the variables were taken into account. This is not to say, however, that it will not prove to be a useful mediating variable in the next study when the data from suicidal adolescents are analyzed. The construct of protective factors was also measured by a single instrument, the College RFL (Westefeld et al., 1992). Univariately, the depressed group had lower reasons for living scores than the problem behavior group. Again, these differences were not significant when the correlations among the variables were taken into account. It was not expected that these variables would differentiate between nonsuicidal groups.

In summary, the results show that adolescents with depressive symptomatology, a correlate of suicide, can be discriminated from other adolescents on measures of problem-solving appraisal. They describe a negative orientation to the task of problem solving, and, when they do generate solutions to problem situations, they rate these solutions as unlikely to be effective.

Adolescents with conduct and substance abuse problems (problem behaviors) can be discriminated from other adolescents by their tendency to generate more aggressive and irrelevant solutions to problems, by their willingness to accept risk by deciding to engage in risk behavior, and by their unwillingness to experience regret at missing out and negative reactions from their peers.

10 Suicide Attempters and Risk Takers

In this chapter we turn our focus to the outcome behaviors – suicidal behaviors and serious risk-taking. This research tests whether these behaviors are related to the mediating constructs in our S/RT model (Figure 8.2). One of our aims was to find whether the cognitive mediating constructs might be useful as potential indicators of a trajectory toward suicidal behavior. If we can identify common deficits in the cognition of suicidal young people, it may be possible to target preventative programs more effectively in order to remediate these deficits. The same reasoning applies to serious risk-taking behaviors. The strategy is to compare suicidal and risk-taking adolescents with each other and with a comparison group of adolescents who do not show these behaviors.

Method

PARTICIPANTS AND GROUP ALLOCATION
All participation was voluntary and all participants received 20 dollars for their time. There were no indigenous Australians in these

groups. Participants in the groups were recruited from a variety of sources: through consultant referral from a hospital; through referral from social workers in Juvenile Justice; through referral from psychologists and psychiatrists in private practice; and from a shelter for homeless youth.

Adolescents were interviewed individually, and they generally completed the questionnaires in a session of $1^1/_2$ hours. In the course of data collection, it became apparent that several of the adolescents were unable to read and write and could not understand the questions even when they were read to them. These adolescents were paid for their time but data from them were not included in the analyses. There were six participants who were excluded on this basis.

SUICIDE ATTEMPTER GROUP

These participants were selected on the basis of the individual having made a suicide attempt serious enough to have warranted treatment from a doctor or nurse. Adolescents were excluded from this group if they had also been in trouble with the police and as a result spent time in a detention center or received a Community Service Order. There were 15 young people, 4 males and 11 females, in this group aged from 15 to 21 years (mean age 17.7 years). Table 5 (shown in the Results section) reports the means for this group on the SBS, where $0 =$ have never contemplated nor attempted suicide and $10 =$ have made more than two severe suicide attempts. Participants were also asked this question: "Would you ever consider suicide to be a realistic solution to your problems?" Table 4 also reports the proportion who responded "yes" to this question as well as the means for the RTBS, Substance Use Questionnaire, and the BDI. These variables were used as screening variables for checking the allocation to groups.

126

Table 4 Means, standard deviations, and *F* ratios for screening measures

	Group				
	Suicide attempters	Suicide attempters + risk takers	Risk takers	Comparison	$F(3, 61)$
SBS	6.47$_a$	7.40$_a$	0.61$_b$	0.59$_b$	65.3**
	(2.53)	(2.75)	(0.50)	(0.51)	
Suicide as option	0.40$_a$	0.73$_b$	0.28$_{ab}$	0	3.93[1]
(yes or no)	(0.51)	(0.46)	(0.46)	(0)	
RTBS	2.07$_b$	8.27$_a$	7.94$_a$	3.47$_b$	32.55**
	(2.34)	(2.15)	(2.13)	(2.15)	
Risky activities	5.53	10.13	6.72	2.76	17.04**
	(2.90)	(3.50)	(3.12)	(2.17)	
Substance Use	0.07$_a$	0.67$_b$	0.44$_{a,b}$	0	7.15[2]
Questionnaire	(0.26)	(0.49)	(0.51)	(0)	
BDI	21.47$_{ab}$	28.73$_b$	16.83$_a$	4.53$_c$	12.74**
	(11.40)	(14.30)	(13.40)	(3.84)	

Notes: Standard deviations are given in parentheses. Means in the same row that do not share subscripts differ at $p < .05$ in Tukey's honestly significant difference comparison.

[1] Comparison group is not included in analysis of variance; $F(2, 45) = 3.93, p = .027$.

[2] Comparison group is not included in analysis of variance; $F(2, 45) = 7.15, p = .002$.

** $p < .001$.

SERIOUS RISK-TAKER GROUP

These participants were selected on the basis of the individual having exhibited behavior that had resulted in their breaking the law in a way sufficient to cause them to be before a court and to be detained in a detention center or to have been sentenced to time spent in community service. There were 18 young people, 15 males and 3 females, in this group aged from 15 to 20 years (mean age 17.3 years). Table 4 reports the means for the screening variables.

127

SUICIDE ATTEMPTERS AND RISK TAKERS COMBINED GROUP
Participants in this group were selected on the basis of a suicide attempt for which they had received hospital attention as well as behavior serious enough to result in time spent in a detention center or in community service. There were 15 young people, 9 males and 6 females, in this group aged from 14 to 21 years (mean age 17.13 years). Table 4 reports the means for the screening variables for this group.

COMPARISON GROUP
The comparison group was recruited so as to be comparable in age and educational level with the other groups. These individuals ranged in age from 16 to 20 years (mean age 18.35 years), and there were 18 participants – 9 males and 9 females. Half of these participants were recruited from a shelter for homeless youth and the rest were either high school students or university undergraduates. Table 4 reports the means of the screening variables for this group.

MATERIALS AND PROCEDURES
The materials used were identical to those in the first study. Table 2 (Chapter 9) shows the variables measured. The measures were administered to each participant individually in order to maximize full completion and to ensure that participants took a break if they appeared tired or bored.

Results

The main question was whether there would be a relationship between the mediating constructs and the independent constructs as depicted in the S/RT model. Consistent with the data analytic approach taken in Chapter 10, a discriminant analysis was used to test for differences between the four groups of adolescents on the nine correlated mediating variables. We performed all analyses by using SPSS (Version 10).

Table 5 reports the means and standard deviations for each mediating variable for each group together with the F-to-remove statistic and the structure coefficients. The univariate F ratio for each mediating variable was significant at $p < .001$ (not shown in Table 5). As explained in Chapter 9, it is the F-to-remove statistic that indicates the unique contribution of a variable to the separation between the groups after all the other variables have been taken into account.

Using this statistic, we see that there are significant differences between the groups on the RFL; the number of relevant solutions generated; the positive response to solutions; and the number of risk decisions endorsed. The use of identifiable problem-solving strategies, measured by the PS of the SPSI, was significant at $p = .07$. Given that the variable's structure coefficient was relatively high on the second discriminant function, 0.63, it was decided to include this variable in the interpretation of the second discriminant function. While problem orientation (problem-solving appraisal) also has a high structure coefficient on the second function, it was not included in the interpretation because it has a small F-to-remove statistic.

While the comparison between the means for each variable is useful and interesting, it does not show the pattern of differences across variables. The discriminant analysis yielded three significant discriminant functions. As a way to enhance interpretation by showing what variables most clearly separate the groups, an orthogonal varimax rotation was done (Tabachnick & Fidell, 2001).

The first discriminant function, $\chi^2(27) = 117.0$, $p < .0001$, separated the comparison group from the other three groups and the depressed group from the other two groups, with the comparison group endorsing significantly higher scores on a measure of actual problem-solving skills, the number of relevant solutions, a measure

Table 5 Means, standard deviations, F-to-remove statistics, and structure coefficients

	Group				F-to-remove $df = (2, 46)$	Rotated structure coefficients		
	Suicide attempters	Suicide + risk takers	Risk takers	Comparison		F_1	F_2	F_3
Hopelessness	6.80 (5.19)	10.87 (5.66)	7.22 (4.82)	2.24 (2.91)	1.08	−0.11	−0.26	0.46
Reasons for living	28.53$_a$ (14.41)	27.40$_a$ (12.74)	44.39$_b$ (12.01)	53.00$_b$ (5.65)	4.27**	0.03	0.84	0.02
Relevant solutions	9.40$_a$ (3.87)	7.73$_a$ (4.06)	6.39$_a$ (2.99)	15.06$_b$ (3.90)	4.79**	0.66	−0.04	−0.26
Irrelevant solutions	4.00 (2.62)	4.40 (3.04)	4.83 (2.66)	2.00 (1.66)	1.17	−0.32	0.00	0.09
POS	49.73 (25.75)	41.47 (21.08)	65.00 (24.03)	91.00 (12.15)	0.91	0.17	0.61	−0.16
PS	71.47$_a$ (23.24)	62.73$_{ab}$ (21.93)	90.06$_{bc}$ (23.18)	106.12$_c$ (17.24)	2.52	0.02	0.63	−0.17
Positive resp. to solutions	2.00$_a$ (1.41)	2.20$_a$ (1.37)	1.89$_a$ (1.81)	4.65$_b$ (0.61)	3.18*	0.62	0.18	0.10
No. of risky decisions	0.53$_{a,b}$ (0.92)	1.53$_c$ (0.83)	1.11$_{b,c}$ (0.83)	0.12$_a$ (0.33)	3.66**	−0.16	−0.03	0.74
Resp. to False Alarm situation	2.33 (1.68)	3.00 (1.51)	2.72 (1.67)	0.65 (1.54)	0.97	−0.30	−0.12	0.23

Notes: Standard deviations are given in parentheses. Means in the same row that do not share subscripts differ at $p < .05$ in Tukey's honestly significant difference comparison.

* $p < .05$; ** $p < .01$.

Figure 10.1. A plot of the group centroids for the four groups, showing the separation of the groups by the significant mediating variables on the first and second discriminant functions. RFL = Reasons for Living Scale; Rel. Sol. = Number of Relevent Solutions; Pos. Resp. Sol. = Positive Response to Solutions; PS = Problem-Solving Scale.

of appraisal of problem-solving skill, and the number of positive responses to solutions generated. The squared canonical correlation for this function of 72% indicates a very strong effect.

The second discriminant function, $\chi^2(16) = 44.6, p < .0001$, separates the two suicide attempter groups from the risk-taking and comparison groups, with the two suicide attempter groups scoring significantly lower on the RFL and the PS of the SPSI. The squared canonical correlation for this function of 39% indicates a strong effect. Figure 10.1 shows the group centroids with respect to the first and second discriminant function. It also shows differences between the groups, but it especially shows the closeness of the two suicide attempter groups on the mediating variables that define the first two discriminant functions.

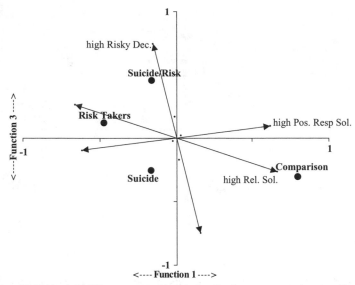

Figure 10.2. A plot of the group centroids for the four groups, showing the separation of the groups by the significant mediating variables on the first and third discriminant functions. Risky Dec. = Decisions taken to engage in hypothetical risk activities; Rel. Sol. = Number of Relevant Solutions; Pos. Resp. Sol. = Positive Response to Solutions.

The third discriminant function, $\chi^2(7) = 16.6$, $p < .05$, splits the two suicide attempter groups in terms of the number of risk decisions endorsed, with the combined suicide and risk-taking group significantly higher on this variable. This function separates both groups of risk takers from the suicide attempter and comparison groups. The squared canonical correlation for this function of 25% indicates a moderate effect. Figure 10.2 shows the group centroids with respect to the first and third discriminant functions.

Discussion

The purpose of the study was to test the relationship between the mediating constructs (problem solving, hopelessness, protective factors, and decision making) and the independent or outcome constructs (suicidal and risk-taking behavior) in the S/RT model. The results indicate that there are different combinations of mediating variables that clearly differentiate suicidal and risk-taking behavior. Of importance was the clear demonstration that there are adolescents who not only have high levels of risk-taking behavior but also attempt suicide.

The adolescents who engage in serious risk-taking activities split quite clearly into a group of individuals who were also suicidal and depressive and a group of them who were not suicidal, although their mean score on the BDI was higher than that of the comparison group (see Table 4). This finding suggests that there are a significant number of risk takers also likely to engage in suicidal behaviors and develop depressive symptomatology.

It is also important to note that this suicide and risk-taking combined group displays more extreme scores on all scales than the other groups (see Tables 3, 4, and 5). This means that they endorse items to suggest that both their suicidal behaviors as well as their risk-taking behaviors are more extreme than either the suicide group or the risk-taking group. This is consistent with much research that has found comorbidity to suggest greater risk of suicide (Lewinsohn et al., 1996) and also research suggesting that aggressive and delinquent youths are affectively as well as behaviorally disturbed (Kosky et al., 1990a).

The findings from this study are not consistent with research that suggests that risk-taking adolescents are not depressed (Gonzalez et al., 1994). This only seems to be the case if the behaviors are "minor" in comparison with the risk-taking behavior of the two groups in this study. When adolescents with problem behaviors are the focus rather than serious risk takers, as in Chapter 9, the levels of depressive symptomatology in the adolescents are more similar to the comparison group than they are to the depressed group.

PROBLEM SOLVING

The discussion now focuses on the differences between the groups on the nine variables measuring the mediating constructs of the S/RT model. As in Chapter 9, problem-solving was operationalized as both appraisal of problem-solving skills and actual problem-solving skills. Appraisal of problem-solving was measured by the POS from the SPSI and the number of positive responses to solutions generated on the Social Situations Analysis Test; see Table 2 for the list of measures. Actual problem-solving skills were measured by the PS, the use of identifiable problem-solving strategies from the SPSI, the number of relevant solutions generated on the Means–Ends Problem-Solving Test and the Social Situations Analysis Test, and the number of irrelevant or aggressive solutions generated on the Means–Ends Problem-Solving Test and the Social Situations Analysis Test. While each these measures differentiated between the four groups using the univariate F ratios, the variables with the stronger, unique effect were the number of positive responses to solutions, the number of relevant solutions, and the PS. This adds further to the support from the previous study for problem solving as a mediating construct between psychopathology and suicide and risk-taking behavior as proposed in the S/RT model.

We expected that the suicide and risk-taking groups would generate fewer relevant solutions to problems than the comparison group, and this was clearly supported. These groups also had a lower positive response to solutions, which was not expected. Figure 10.1 shows these results clearly, as these two variables contribute most strongly to the first discriminant function.

These results are interesting because even though the problems in the Social Situations Analysis Test and Means–Ends Problem-Solving Test were perhaps not strongly related to the personal issues relevant to these particular adolescents, it is obvious that their

134

ability to generate alternatives and solutions and appraise them is impaired.

One might extrapolate from this result the possibility that when faced with a personal crisis, these adolescents will show a tendency to produce an even narrower band of alternative solutions (Mano, 1992). Many of these adolescents stated that they saw suicide as a possible option in solving their problems (see Table 1). If the option of suicide is seen as realistic and the adolescent is unable to generate other alternatives or appraise solutions, then the act of suicide becomes more understandable. The suicide attempt is likely to occur whenever a problem situation appears too difficult. This is consistent with the suggestion of Strosahl et al. (1992) that, for these adolescents, a suicide attempt may represent both an effort at problem solving and an expression of distress.

When we look at the responses on the PS, the use of identifiable problem-solving strategies, there were significant differences between the two groups containing suicide attempters and the risk-takers and the comparison group. Figure 10.1 shows how this variable contributes to the second discriminant function in separating the groups. The low scores obtained on this scale by the suicide groups suggest that not only do these adolescents feel that they cannot solve problems but they are also lacking in the skills and strategies required to solve problems. This was not the case for the depressed group described in Chapter 9, and it suggests that as behavior becomes more extreme the options narrow and any belief in the possibility of a solution to a problem, even in the hypothetical sense, is seen as too difficult and effortful a task to undertake.

This finding, although not expected, adds further to the profile of a depressed adolescent with little faith in his or her ability to solve even minor problems and an apparent lack of knowledge about how best to tackle a problem situation.

DECISION MAKING

The decision-making construct was operationalized as the number of risk decisions the adolescents said they would make given two hypothetical situations (riding with a drunk driver and taking an unknown drug at a party). We also measured their response to the False Alarm situation, which is a decision *not* to engage in a risk activity when there are no negative consequences. The content analysis of participants' responses to the False Alarm situation confirmed that the two main costs were negative reactions from peers or regret at missing out, and the importance rating was used to calculate the score on this variable. While there was a significant univariate F ratio for the response to False Alarm situation, it was not significant when other variables were taken into account. Inspection of Table 5 shows that the comparison group has a lower mean score than the other three groups.

However, the content analysis found that the individuals in the suicide Attempter and risk-taking combined group, instead of stating benefits associated with these activities, tended to say that they did not care about the consequences. This was a new reason and had not been evident in the comparison between depressive and problem behavior adolescents; nor was it present in the content analyses of the same task by Sofronoff (1999).

Conversations during the testing of the risk-taking groups with the researcher provided some examples of this reason. Some of these adolescents had been in trouble with the police, and this had become a way of life. Some felt that they would die young anyway and so taking risks was not of concern. One 15-year-old stated that, after an overdose when he had been hospitalized, he had received the best care and attention from nursing staff that he could recall ever receiving in his young life. He also said that, for him, this had been a positive aspect of a supposedly bad outcome from the drug use.

136

This information adds to the understanding of why these adolescents, who obviously are aware of the consequences of engaging in risk activities, continue to take risks. The presence of this reason may explain why the suicide and risk-taking combined group did not differ from the risk-taking group or the suicide attempter group on the numerical score for the response to the False Alarm situation, since the test scale did not include an "importance value."

As expected, there were differences between the groups on the number of risk decisions endorsed. Figure 10.2 shows that this variable clearly separates the suicide and risk-taking combined group from the suicide group. Both risk-taking groups were significantly higher than the comparison group on this measure.

PROTECTIVE FACTORS

The construct of protective factors was operationalized by the College RFL (Westefeld et al., 1992). Figure 10.1 shows that this variable is strong in differentiating the suicidal groups from the nonsuicidal groups. This scale is useful in that it looks at suicide from a different perspective. It asks the adolescents to indicate what would stop them from attempting suicide if they were contemplating it. The results indicate quite clearly that those adolescents who have at some time attempted suicide, even though they are not currently suicidal, place a low value on beliefs that would prevent adolescents from attempting suicide if they were to consider it.

This finding suggests that RFL (Westefeld et al., 1992) may constitute a valuable predicting measure to use with adolescents believed to be at risk of suicidal behaviors. The findings in this study are consistent with results from other studies using the RFL (outlined in Chapter 5) and indicate its value with an adolescent population other than university or college undergraduates. The RFL may prove to be important as a mediating variable between depressive symptomatology and suicidal behavior.

137

HOPELESSNESS

Hopelessness was operationalized and measured by the Beck Hopelessness Scale (Beck et al., 1974). Although the univariate F statistic indicated that scores on the Beck Hopelessness Scale were significant, $F(3, 61) = 9.07$, $p < .0001$, the F-to-remove statistic, which indicates the unique contribution of the variable when all other variables are removed, was not significant. This tends to suggest that although suicidal and risk-taking adolescents did endorse more items on the scale than the comparison group, there are other variables related to hopelessness that more clearly differentiate them. This is discussed more fully in Chapter 11 when the model is assessed as a whole.

In summary, the results of this study indicate that adolescents who engage in suicidal behaviors can be discriminated from risk-taking adolescents and from "normal" adolescents on measures of problem solving, both in terms of attitude toward problem solving and actual problem-solving skills. They can be further discriminated by their responses on the College RFL. They have decreased capacity to approach problems positively but also to engage in positive strategies, and they place low value on reasons for living.

Adolescents who engage in risk-taking behaviors can be discriminated from other adolescents by their willingness to accept risk and by their decision making. They were also found to exhibit poor problem solving and to hold a belief that their solutions to problems would not work.

The group exhibiting combined suicidal and risk-taking behaviors was more extreme on all measures.

It was expected that the variables measured would discriminate between groups even more clearly than in the comparison between depressed and problem behavior adolescents. The reason for this expectation was that the adolescents participating in this study were expected to exhibit more severe deficits. When the means are compared with the earlier studies, this was found to be the case. However, it was still not so easy to discriminate between the three suicide and risk-taking groups because the adolescents in these groups all tended to show a similar degree of impairment.

The next chapter brings the results from these two studies together and provides direct tests of the extent to which the variables mediate between depression and problem behaviors on the one side and suicidal and risk-taking behavior on the other.

11 The Impact of Cognitive Variables as Mediators

The research reported in Chapters 9 and 10 aimed at demonstrating the relationship between the cognitive constructs in the S/RT model and depressive symptoms and problem behaviors (Chapter 9), and the cognitive constructs and suicide and risk-taking behaviors (Chapter 10). The research used between-group comparisons to demonstrate the relationships. The data analyses reported in this chapter directly test whether the nine cognitive variables mediate between depressive symptomatology and problem behaviors on the one hand and suicide and risk-taking behavior on the other. It uses path analysis to do this.

An advantage of the group comparison approach is that, by looking at the mean scores of the groups across the nine cognitive variables and the screening variables, we can make a cross-study comparison. There were three groups in the first set of analyses (Chapter 9) and four groups in the second set (Chapter 10). There was a comparison group in each study. The results from these two comparison groups can be pooled since a discriminant analysis found they were not significantly different from each other.

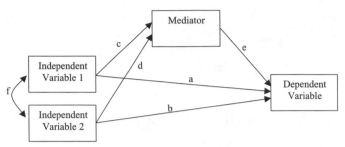

Figure 11.1. Path diagram for the effect of the mediator with two independent variables.

Path analysis (see Figure 11.1) is an extension of multiple regression that allows one to simultaneously assess the relative importance of two or more independent variables while testing for the influence of a mediating variable.

All the paths, direct and indirect, can be tested for statistical significance. Structural equation model programs such as EQS (Chou & Bentler, 1995) perform this analysis and test the paths for significance. They also calculate the amount of variance in the dependent variable accounted for by the independent variables and the mediator. We present the results of three sets of path analyses. The first set has suicidal behavior as the dependent variable, and depression and problem behaviors as independent variables for each of the nine mediating variables. The second set has risk-taking behavior as the dependent variable, and the third set has suicidal and risk-taking behaviors combined as the dependent variable.

The data being used in the path analyses are those presented in Chapter 10 ($N = 66$). These were the only participants who actually engaged in the behavior measured with the dependent variables, that is, suicidal behavior, serious risk-taking behavior, and suicidal and risk-taking behavior combined. The adolescents who took part in the earlier research (Chapter 9) exhibited symptoms of the two independent variables, that is, depressive symptomatology and problem behaviors, but had not made a suicide attempt or engaged in risk-taking to a level serious enough to have suffered legal consequences. Therefore, while Chapter 9 allows for an examination of variables associated with suicidal and risk-taking behavior and allows for components of the model to be examined, it is only the data from Chapter 10 that can be used to test the mediational ability of the proposed mediating variables.

The Paths to Suicidal Behavior

A path model (Figure 11.1) was fitted for each proposed mediator. These mediators were problem-solving appraisal measured by the POS of the SPSI (D'Zurilla & Nezu, 1990) and the positive response to solutions from the Social Situations Analysis Test (Connolly, et al., 1992), problem-solving skills measured by the PS of the SPSI, number of relevant solutions generated and number of irrelevant or aggressive solutions generated (Means–Ends Problem-Solving Test and Social Situations Analysis Test), hopelessness measured by the Beck Hopelessness Scale (Beck et al., 1974), protective factors measured by the College RFL (Westefeld et al., 1992), and decision making measured by the number of risk decisions participants were willing to make during the assessment and responses on the False Alarm scenario. The dependent variable was the score on the SBS. The independent variables were the BDI scores and a composite score of behavior problems formed by averaging the standardized scores on the number of risk activities (Perception of Risk Scale, Benthin et al., 1993) and the Substance Use Scale.

For the nine path models fitted, each accounted for a different amount of the variance of the SBS, the dependent variable. The mean amount of variance accounted for was 38%, with the lowest at 34.4% and the highest at 51.4%. All are highly statistically different from

143

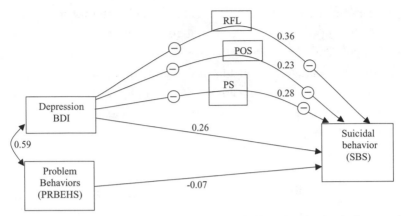

Figure 11.2. An illustration of the mediating variables, showing both direct and indirect effects of depressive and problem behaviors on suicidal behavior. A minus sign on an indirect path indicates a negative relationship between two variables.

zero. These are substantial amounts of the variance of suicidal behavior to account for.

Three of the cognitive variables had statistically significant mediating effects. Figure 11.2 shows them and the magnitudes of the direct and indirect effects. The curved line through the mediator indicates the amount of mediation and is the product of the paths from the BDI scores to the mediator and from the mediator to SBS scores. The three indirect effects from depression to suicidal behavior, the paths through the mediators, are all positive and significant at $p <$ .008, and they are larger than the average direct effect from depression to suicidal behavior. None of the direct or indirect paths from problem behaviors was significant. The magnitude of the paths takes into account the relatively high correlation (.59) between depression and problem behaviors. The direct effect of 0.26 indicates that the higher the (depression) BDI score, the higher the (suicide) SBS score.

Problem solving is an important mediator, both in the form of skills and negative problem-solving appraisal. The POS is a measure of problem-solving appraisal and the PS is a measure of actual problem-solving skills and strategies that the adolescents indicate they are able to use. The other important mediator is the Survival and Coping Behavior subscales of the RFL. Low problem-solving skills (PS) or negative problem-solving appraisal (POS) or low reasons for living appear to increase the likelihood of suicidal behavior. High depression (BDI) scores are associated with low reasons for living and with low problem-solving skills and negative appraisal of problem-solving ability. A low score on these three mediators is associated with higher levels of suicidal behavior as demonstrated in higher SBS scores. An inspection of the items on the Survival and Coping Behavior subscales of the RFL shows that some of the items are close in meaning to problem-solving appraisal, such as "I believe I can cope with my problems" and "I have confidence in my ability to deal with problems."

The Paths to Risk-Taking Behavior

A set of path models such as that of Figure 11.1 was fitted for each of the nine mediators, with the dependent variable being the score on the RTBS. Four of the cognitive variables were significant mediators between depression and problem behaviors and risk-taking behavior. For the nine path models fitted, each accounted for a different amount of the variance of RTBS, the dependent variable. The mean amount of variance accounted for was 37%, with the lowest at 33.3% and the highest at 45.1%. All are highly statistically different from zero. These are substantial amounts of the variance of risk-taking behavior to account for. Figure 11.3 shows the magnitude of the direct and indirect effects (amount of mediation) for these four cognitive variables.

The direct effects of depression and problem behaviors clearly show that depression does not have a direct effect on risk-taking

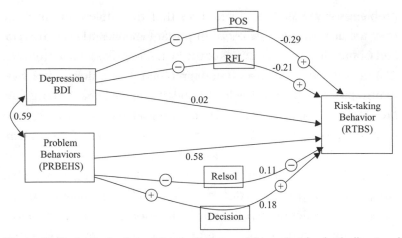

Figure 11.3. An illustration of the mediating variables, showing both direct and indirect effects of depressive and problem behaviors on risk-taking behavior. A minus or plus sign on an indirect path indicates a negative or positive relationship, respectively, between two variables. Relsol = relevant solutions.

behavior. It is not surprising that the measure of problem behaviors does have a direct effect on risk-taking behavior, such that the higher the problem behavior, the higher the risk-taking behavior.

There is an interesting pattern with the four significant mediators, with some positive and negative indirect effects. Problem-solving skills, as measured by the number of relevant solutions generated, and decision making, the number of risk decisions that participants were willing to make, exert an influence on risk-taking behavior. High scores on problem behavior are associated with a lower number of relevant solutions; low scores on this mediator are associated with a high RTBS score. Thus, having good problem-solving skills appears to reduce the effect of high problem behaviors. A high score on problem behaviors is associated with a high score on the number of risk decisions, and a high score on this mediator is associated with a high RTBS score. Thus, a tendency to make risk decisions increases the effect of problem behaviors on serious risk-taking measured by the RTBS.

However, the path analyses show that there are two mediators, reasons for living and appraisal of problem solving (POS), between depression and risk-taking behavior with negative indirect effects. Depression is linked to risk-taking behavior in an interesting way. The negative indirect effect means that a high score on the BDI is associated with a low RFL score and a low RFL score is associated with a low RTBS score. There is a similar interpretation for positive appraisal of problem solving (POS). The more depressed the person, the lower his or her positive appraisal of problem solving; the lower the problem-solving appraisal, the lower the risk-taking behavior. Thus, a high score on depression acts to lower risk-taking by means of a low score on the RFL or a low score on positive appraisal of problem solving.

The Paths to Risk-Taking and Suicidal Behaviors

A set of path models such as that of Figure 11.1 was fitted for each of the nine mediators, with the independent variable being the average of the standardized score on the RTBS and the standardized score on the SBS. The reason for including the combined score was to find out the important mediators for those adolescents who engage in both behaviors. While one might expect that the findings from this set of path analyses should be like the "average" of the patterns shown in Figures 11.2 and 11.3, the results were more complex than this (see Figure 11.4).

Four of the cognitive variables were significant mediators between depression and problem behaviors and risk-taking and suicidal behavior. For the nine path models fitted, each accounted for a different amount of the variance of suicidal and risk-taking behavior combined, which was the dependent variable. The mean amount of variance accounted for was 52.6%, with the lowest at 51% and the

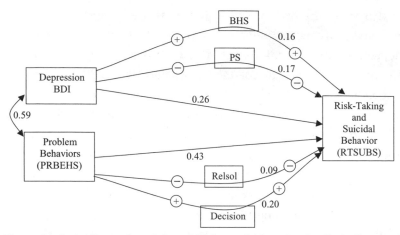

Figure 11.4. An illustration of the mediating variables, showing both direct and indirect effects of depressive and problem behaviors on risk-taking and suicidal behavior. A minus or plus sign on an indirect path indicates a negative or a positive relationship, respectively, between two variables. Relsol = relevant solutions; BHS = Beck Hopelessness Scale.

highest at 56%. All are highly statistically different from zero. These are substantial amounts of the variance of risk-taking and suicidal behavior to account for. Both depression and problem behaviors have a direct effect on risk-taking and suicidal behavior, with problem behavior having the larger effect.

In the separate path models for suicidal behavior and risk-taking behavior (Figures 11.2 and 11.3), appraisal of problem solving was a significant mediator. When the focus is on the combination of serious risk-taking and suicidal behavior, hopelessness is a significant mediator from depression to risk-taking and suicidal behavior. A high score on the BDI is associated with a high score on hopelessness, and a high score on hopelessness is associated with a high score on risk-taking and suicidal behavior. Problem behavior indirectly influences risk-taking and suicidal behavior by way of decision making. A high score on problem behaviors is associated with a high score on the number of risk decisions, and a high score on this mediator is associated with a high risk-taking and suicide behavior score.

The problem-solving skills variable is again an important mediator. Two measures of problem-solving skills, the number of relevant solutions generated and the PS of the SPSI, influence risk-taking and suicidal behavior differently. For the PS, a high score on the BDI is associated with a low score on problem solving and a low score on problem solving is associated with a high score on risk-taking and suicidal behavior. For the number of relevant solutions generated, a high score on problem behaviors is associated with a low score on the number of relevant solutions, and a low score on this mediator is associated with a high score on risk-taking and suicidal behavior. This result may be a reflection of the different ways data were collected for these two variables. The PS score is a scaled score from a questionnaire passively filled out, whereas the number of relevant solutions generated is from a task in which participants actively generate solutions. Depression may impair performance on the questionnaire, whereas problem behaviors may impair performance on actively generating responses.

Conclusions

The research and data analyses reported in this and the previous two chapters show detailed support for the S/RT model. The cognitive constructs of problem solving, decision making, hopelessness, and protective factors are strongly related to both depressive symptoms and problem behaviors and to the outcome constructs of suicidal and risk-taking behavior. The path analyses reported in this chapter added to our understanding by finding which of these cognitive variables are mediators. These analyses have added to our understanding of the fine-grained differences between groups shown in

Tables 4 and 5. For example, the results reported in Chapter 9 show that the response to False Alarm situations clearly differentiated the problem behavior group from the depressed and comparison groups. Thus, motivations for taking risk decisions, regret at missing out, and the negative reactions of peers are important, even when there are no differences in the number of risk decisions taken.

Figures 11.2, 11.3, and 11.4 show how negative appraisal of problem solving and lower reasons for living increase the effect of depression on suicidal behavior, whereas for risk-taking behavior the effect is to make the relationship between depression and risk-taking behavior negative. The effect of these two mediators depends on the "target outcome behavior." These two cognitive mediators work with depression so that if adolescents are depressed and have low scores on them, then the tendency is toward high suicidal behavior but lower risk-taking behavior. On the other hand, if adolescents are not depressed and have high scores on the POS (problem-solving appraisal) and RFL, then the tendency is toward higher risk-taking behavior but lower suicidal behavior.

Problem-solving skills is also an important mediator and works differently depending on whether the target outcome behavior is suicidal behavior, risk-taking behavior, or the combination of these behaviors. Deficits in problem-solving skills together with high problem behaviors or high depression increase the tendency for each of the target outcome behaviors.

Hopelessness mediates between depression and combined suicidal and risk-taking behavior and adds to the effect of depression on this combined target behavior. It is particularly interesting to find that hopelessness is not supported as a mediator between depressive symptomatology alone and suicidal behavior. This may account for the inconsistent findings regarding the efficacy of hopelessness as a mediator in adolescent suicidal behavior in the literature reviewed earlier. The results may simply depend on the populations that were accessed. Those adolescents who made up the suicide–risk-taking group were more seriously disordered than any other group, both in terms of the number of deficits they exhibited and in terms of the severity of those deficits. This finding supports literature that has suggested comorbidity increases the risk of suicide (Lewinsohn et al., 1995), but it also extends these findings by illustrating how this risk is affected through the cognitive mediating variables reported in this chapter.

It is also interesting to find that the construct of decision making was useful as a mediator between problem behaviors and risk-taking and suicide–risk-taking behaviors. This is a construct that has not previously been used with suicidal adolescents. Its use in this research has extended the work completed by the Fischhoff group (Beyth-Marom et al., 1993; Quadrel et al., 1993) with adolescent delinquents and risk takers. It has illustrated not only that these adolescents take risks with their lives but also that they are aware that they are doing so and have reasons that they can articulate. As suggested by Furby and Beyth-Marom (1992), these reasons have more to do with the loss anticipated from *not* engaging in the activities than from any actual benefits, although peer influence is also a major factor and the risk-taking adolescents do endorse more benefits from engaging in the risk activities than do the non-risk-taking adolescents.

IMPLICATIONS FOR TREATMENT

12 Clinical Implications: The Development of Problem Solving

So far, we can summarize our findings as follows: We found that both suicidal and risk-taking young people demonstrated cognitive deficits. In meeting challenging problems, they generated only a narrow range of options as possible solutions and their capacity to develop alternative solutions was impaired. Furthermore, the options they did generate were likely to be irrelevant for the solution of the problem or were likely to be aggressive responses to the challenge. Neither suicidal nor serious risk-taking adolescents seemed to care about the consequences of the choices they made. Risk takers were more influenced by their perception of likely reactions from their peers and suicidal adolescents were not protected by beliefs that life had value.

Suicidal adolescents demonstrated less confidence in their ability to solve problems correctly or in the likely success of the solutions they generated than either risk takers or asymptomatic adolescents. In fact, when put to the test, they were less able to solve hypothetical problems than were normal adolescents. They lacked the skills and strategies required to reach workable solutions.

Such cognitive deficits in adolescents may make them vulnerable to developing a single all-encompassing solution when they are dealing with a challenging problem. Their solution may not be an adaptive one. Suicide, as a simple solution, becomes a possibility when the individual fails to generate other solutions or when the individual does not have confidence that any other solution is workable.

Risk-taking adolescents also showed deficits in their ability to generate solutions. They produced more irrelevant and aggressive responses than normal adolescents. These young risk takers were willing to take a risk with their future in order to remain connected to their peer group. Despite this, they espoused beliefs that they valued their lives. Thus their solutions or decisions were gambles against the odds of staying connected to the peer group while risking their future.

What are the clinical implications of these findings? The cognitive skills we identified, or deficits in them, are factors mediating on the one hand between depressed and suicidal states of feeling, and, on the other, between conduct disordered behavioral states and serious risk-taking behaviors. Therefore, they are points for potential interventions to prevent suicide and self-destructive behaviors in adolescents. If prevention interventions are to be developed for vulnerable young people, it is worthwhile to consider how these cognitive skills develop, in humans, and where and how deficits might occur in them.

The Development of Problem-Solving Skills

One way of defining problem solving is that it is the capacity to create potential mental solutions to problems in order to effect changes in a state of affairs, currently existing, toward a more desirable condition (Meadows, 1993). To do this, mental processes generate a range of potential solutions. The effectiveness of these possible solutions to bring about the desired change is first judged mentally in a hypothetical form. The one judged most likely to be effective or workable as a hypothesis is then applied in practice. Other solutions are tried if this one fails. The most effective solution is stored in memory for future use. Noneffective solutions are discarded.

The cognitive processes involved in this process of problem solving develop in the human brain from an early age. The main groundwork for the organization of problem-solving cognitions occurs during infancy. The five processes involved are the development of the capacity to symbolize, the mental capacity to control emotions, the development of a moral sense, the capacity for verbal conceptual memory, and the capacity to maintain constancy in behavior (Sardonoff, 1989).

SYMBOLIZATION

According to Piaget (1968), the ability to create symbols occurs between the ages of 15 and 24 months. During this time, infants move from dealing with objects in their minds that are unmodified versions of the real object, to playing with these mental images. This involves giving the original image new meanings. Once this occurs, symbols can be developed.

The development of the capacity for symbolization depends on the emergence of the abilities to recognize similarities and differences between objects. It also depends on the capacity to displace meaning from one object to another. Because of the measure of delay involved when holding images in the mind, there is the opportunity for these images to be influenced by feelings arising from needs, desires, and moods. For instance, Klein has suggested that one powerful need in infants is for them to protect the primary caregiver from self-generated (infant) aggressive urges (Hinshelwood, 1991, p. 216). The infant mentally displaces such urges symbolically onto the breast during feeding, and they are manifest in crying and tantrums when the feeding breast is removed.

Disturbances in the mother–infant relationship, inconsistent responses to the baby's sounds and gestures, and aggression or lack of affection may disturb the development of the capacity for symbolization or come to reside in the symbols themselves and disturb later relationships. Interventions in the perinatal period to ensure psychological and social well-being may be an effective early intervention. Fonagy and his colleagues have described the value of the development of meaningful narratives about one's life as providing resilience for mothers and babies (Fonagy et al., 1994).

MEMORY

The capacity to memorize underlies the ability to solve problems. The cognitive organization of memory occurs in infancy and childhood and develops with the progress of intelligence as a whole. Intelligent thought is built up as a progressive transformation of mental activity that becomes steadily more adaptive to the environment, giving increasing mastery over the self and more controlled management of environmental experiences.

According to Piaget's (1968) schema of mental development, the earliest infantile mental activities are based on reflex actions to environmental stimuli. This sensorimotor stage persists as an important modality until around 2 years of age. A preoperational stage follows, in which thinking occurs; although intuitive thoughts also begin to develop, thinking at this stage is mostly action orientated. This stage lasts until about 7 years of age. From then until the beginning of adolescence, thought processes become dominated by concrete operations that are built on the capacity to deal in a formal way with logical categories, classes, and rules.

During adolescence, the capacity to think ahead develops much more fully. The young person can use this skill to try out various hypotheses as potential solutions to problems and problem-solving skills can be more fruitfully employed. These processes do not develop in isolation. Piaget (1968) emphasized that the processes of mental development are a "basic unity," from

> the construction of the practical universe by infantile sensorimotor intelligence, ... to the reconstruction of the world by the hypothetico-deductive thinking of the adolescent, via the knowledge of the concrete world derived from the systems of operations of middle childhood. (p. 69)

Memory, as a system, stores information during this learning process and brings it back into consciousness when it is needed. Memory function depends on the ability to give close attention to pattern recognition. The capacity for selective attention can be impaired as a result of immature development of the higher executive functions of the brain, as in attention deficit hyperactive disorder (ADHD; Barkley, 1997). Individuals with this impairment may experience problems learning and retaining new material, and this may affect the orderly development of mental processes.

Memory has short- and long-term faculties that are probably distinct processes. Short-term memory may be mainly contained in an electronic state in the brain, whereas long-term memory may depend on the structural integrity and function of the hippocampus area. This long-term memory is better developed in humans than in the nonhuman higher species of animals. Structural damage to these areas of the brain can interfere with the development of long-term memory capacity. Typically, this occurs during fetal development or at birth, as in fetal alcohol or drug syndromes, or is acquired through injury or infection. The role of alcohol in producing later memory and other cognitive deficits requires greater consideration, especially among socially disadvantaged mothers and indigenous populations (Hunter, 1993).

Memory is strongly affected by events and is susceptible to feeling states, suggestions, bodily sensations, and the general condition of other cerebral functions. It is therefore a dynamic construct and subject to modifications and distortions over time. A child's memory may be particularly unstable (Leichtman, Ceci, & Morse, 1997) and will be made more so by adverse historical events (Anthony, 1983).

Adolescence includes rapid physical changes, which are accompanied by corresponding changes in the mental map of the body. There is intensification of interest in the self, rather than others, and there is intensification of old and new personal relationships. New figures are sought for bonding, and these to some extent replace the primarily bonded parent figures. Such transitions are complex, and successful passage through them is dependent on a consistent facilitating environment and good physical health.

These changes in adolescence are accompanied by increased introspective thinking. The broadening of problem-solving scenarios and the capacity to develop new types of solutions based on the acquisition of a wider range of new and memorized knowledge is a part of the developing hypothetico-deductive thinking patterns. These thinking processes allow for testing possible solutions in a virtual (mental image) situation rather than in a real setting. When accompanied by these new thinking capacities, adolescent experimentation in imagined life and in real life should promote a deeper understanding of the consequences of an individual's own actions.

MORAL REASONING

Adolescents should be able to demonstrate an ability to solve problems with an understanding of the possible consequences to self and others. Such moral reasoning begins in the home, and the development of a moral sense begins in infancy.

At first, the infant and child adheres to the moral rules laid down by the parents, who represent a higher authority. This adherence is motivated by the infantile wish to placate and to please the parents. The responses to moral problems based on these external rules are all or nothing, black or white. The parents need to maintain fair, firm, and consistent limits on the child's behavior so the child can begin to socialize within his or her limits.

As the child grows, he or she experiences wider influences from socialization beyond the parent–child triadic complex. This may include contact with other adults and children in child-care situations, extended family members, and other families. Wider influence leads to the sharing of perspectives from which arises a desire for cooperation. These developments reach their fruition at about the time the child is ready for school. At this time, children should be able to play together, share, compromise, and cooperate. All-or-nothing responses are inappropriate in a social, school situation.

A socializing child needs to develop working solutions to the problems of sharing on a day-to-day basis. School now becomes an important source for learning these skills, but it does not replace the parents' authority. In these circumstances, the child needs the capacity to develop reciprocal relationships among his or her peers. Ideally such relationships will be based on mutual respect, rather than on unilateral attempts to placate peers, or to draw admiration from them out of fear of loss of their companionship, as would be the case at an earlier period of development.

By about the eighth year of life, moral decision making develops. Moral decision making is guided by a sense of internalized guilt rather than by obedience to parental rules. At this stage, the child has developed mental images of the external parental rules and of what behavior is expected of him or her by parents, peers, and the social structure of school. The construct of acceptable behavior becomes governed by the internal rules controlled by guilt. Thus, the individual should reflect on actions that reduce his or her feelings of guilt in order to make "right" decisions in the absence of the peer group, parents, or explicit social rules.

Advanced capabilities, such as remembering, planning, categorizing, evoking of memory, and abstract testing of solutions, reach maturity during adolescence. These cognitive developments enhance problem-solving skills and become central to formulating effective solutions. Skills such as literacy, numeracy, and general knowledge about the world extend the individual's capacity to broaden the basis of his or her potential solutions. These skills allow exposure to the previous experience of others that is contained in texts and in visual and aural images, thereby further enhancing the capacity to solve new problems. Failure to develop these skills limits options and approaches for problem solving in the future.

DEVELOPMENTAL INTELLIGENCE

Since every person has different innate capacities and different individual experiences during his or her development, each person's capacity to solve problems will be different. As a result, some people will be handicapped in problem solving compared with others because their innate capacities will be relatively deficient or their relative experiences limited to a nonfacilitating environment. This does not mean that they cannot learn new skills.

The nature of genetic variations contributes to expectations of a wide range of cognitive development across the population. We see this range in the typical bell-shaped curve of scores measured by standard cognitive assessment instruments such as the Wechsler Intelligence Scale for Children (WISC). Slow or limited development of the cognitive phenotype in some individuals compared with others in the same population may be a result of genetic variations or chromosome anomalies, such as found in Down's syndrome.

Some facets of cognitive development might be weaknesses in certain situations, but strengths in others. For example, ADHD may be a considerable disadvantage in the classroom, where rule breaking and distractibility are unacceptable, but, on a battlefield or in sport, such apparent weaknesses may become strengths and, in the former case, add to the survival value of the group (Barkley, 1997).

A further domain of difficulty with problem-solving development occurs when education and life experiences fail to provide the knowledge with which problems can be solved effectively. The development of numeracy, literacy, and general knowledge provides the foundations for the memory of concepts. This creates possibilities for a wide range of potential solutions to challenges. In the absence of skills in these areas, and the failure to build up a bank of knowledge of potential solutions, the capacity to generate solutions will be greatly restricted and will tend to be self-referential rather than based on the wider experience of others. Solutions will tend be repetitive without reference to the problem, because they will be based on a few, personalized pieces of knowledge, special to the individual, that have become highly valued.

CONSTANCY OF EMOTIONS

Inadequate early nurturing may reduce the degree of stimulation that is required to acquire a broad-based experience of the real world. These negative experiences intensify emotions by increasing frustration and rage (Bowlby, 1988). Such feeling states can disrupt the acquisition of problem-solving developmental patterns. For instance, prolonged experiences of inadequate nurturing may persistently narrow options and direct solutions down pathways of aggression. This disrupted thinking style was evident in the conduct disordered adolescents we considered earlier.

Inadequate early socialization experiences may also restrict the range of alternative solutions available to the individual when the

163

problems to be solved have a social dimension: The development of independence in response to rules may be inadequately internalized. This may leave an individual more than usually dependent on the approval of peers or sensitive to rejection from the peer group.

CONSTANCY OF BEHAVIOR

If rules are inconsistent from the very beginning and the limits provided by parents and others on behavior are unclear or ambivalent, the developing child will fail to internalize a consistent set of rules and therefore will not develop constancy of behavior when left to his or her own resources. Instead, as the child comes into adolescence, loosening ties with his or her parents and in the face of different external values, the child's behavior will become increasingly erratic.

A vicious circle may develop in these circumstances: The development of morals will be hampered by behavioral inconstancy. Sharing, compromising with peers, cooperative behavior, and the capacity to stick with tasks will also all be adversely affected by behavioral inconstancy. A heightened desire for attention from peers and fear of losing their respect will replace the more adaptive development of mutual respect among others. Thus, problems will tend be solved in a way that will reflect these fears and needs, rather than a steady sense of right and wrong or a desire for mutual adaptability. We have identified aspects of this vicious circle. Those adolescents trapped in this negative pattern need to be identified and given skills to extract themselves so that their development and maturation can progress on a more positive footing.

13 Clinical Implications: Intervention and Resilience Building

Specific attempts to improve adolescent problem-solving capacities can be approached on two different levels. The first level is a universal intervention across a population. This would aim to increase personal resilience to developing depression and conduct disorder among the individuals in that population. The advantage of such programs is that they help a wide range of young people, not specifically those who are at risk. However, this may also represent a gross misallocation of resources since they target many adolescents who may neither need nor benefit from the intervention.

The second approach involves selective interventions, targeted at children who are already symptomatic, with a view to preventing the outcomes of suicide and risk-taking. These programs target resources on identified at risk individuals, thereby conserving them. However, there may be negative long-term consequences for a group of young people so specifically identified and perhaps labeled.

A brief review of some currently available programs may indicate ones that could be usefully employed to prevent suicide and risk-taking in a predisposed adolescent through the modification of cognitive variables either during the individual's development or once he or she has been identified as being at risk.

Programs to Improve Problem-Solving Skills

There are several programs that have been developed to improve problem solving by training children in this skill. One example of this type of program is the Problem Solving for Life Program (PSLP). The purpose of this program is to enhance problem-solving skills in young people. The PSLP requires that high school students work in groups. In one of the activities, students are provided with puzzle pieces that have positive or negative phrases written on them. Each group then decides where the puzzle fits on a poster. On a positive poster, there is movement from the problem toward thinking ("it's a challenge, at least try"), to feeling ("good feelings, excitement"), to doing ("relaxing, thinking clearly, possible alternatives"), leading ultimately to an effective solution. In a similar way, on the negative poster unhelpful thoughts lead to negative feelings and a poor solution outcome. It is made clear that not all problems have solutions and coping with doubt is seen to be a positive outcome (Spence & Sheffield, 2000).

The PSLP also provides information about where to go for support when problems seem unmanageable. This is an important aspect of any program making a universal intervention. Despite the best intentions of the program, some children will be better at the work than others. Some will still have difficulty in solving problems. For these children, it is important that real-life information is available when their problem-solving skills fail to meet the challenge.

Earlier, we saw that many young people who identified themselves as having mental health problems did not obtain help. A lot of these young people feel they can manage the problems themselves.

These apparently "self-managing" young people may only generate restricted solutions to their problems and may not see potentially helpful alternative solutions. Improving the problem-solving skills of these young people through such programs may lay the foundations for the development of a wider range of possible solutions, including asking for help.

Another program for training in problem solving applied on a universal scale is the I Can Problem Solve Program (ICPS). This is an interpersonal cognitive program for children. The ICPS was designed to teach children to think in ways that will help them to resolve interpersonal problems successfully. This program is aimed at children in preschool or primary school and was designed to improve children's behavior through cooperation.

The intervention elements include teaching problem-solving vocabulary ("might–maybe, why–because") and thinking skills ("listen, concentrate, consider") that are needed in approaching a problem. The program also directly teaches problem-solving skills and strategies ("causes, possible solutions, consequences, choice") and techniques for avoiding negative outcomes ("upset, aggression, withdrawal, impulsivity").

Unusual among universal preventive programs in mental health, the ICPS has been evaluated. The results are encouraging given the complexities of field research and evaluations in this area. Behavior and coping skills improved among the test children, and these effects were generally lasting (Shure, 1996).

Challenging Outdoor Programs

Programs with a broader approach place volunteers in challenging real-life situations, somewhat outside their usual experience and knowledge. Wilderness challenge programs are the most well known of these programs. They occur in many different forms, from scouts, through army cadets, to outward-bound challenge programs. Wilderness adventures, residential and adventure camps, tall-mast sailing, summer camps during the school breaks, and many other variations of these out-of-school programs have become a traditional part of the experiences offered to young people throughout the U.S.A. and other parts of the world. They are regarded as having a formative influence on an earlier generation of young Americans (Goodman & Stoehr, 1978). Such programs remain significant for many young people across the world, and outdoor pursuits have often been built into school curricula.

The School Culture

The general culture of a school is a powerful influence on the improvement of problem-solving capacity (Oeser, 1960). School is a prime place for the acquisition of knowledge and represents society in miniature. Three figures stand out as playing a critical role in the development of the child's capacity to deal with the challenges thrown up by life. They are the mother, the father, and the teacher. If these figures are experienced as nurturing, loving, benevolent, and wise, and if they are devoted to maintaining the self-esteem and integrity of the child, then the child will most likely grow up able to effectively regulate his or her own behavior in the context of the society. If these figures are experienced as punitive, denying, and frustrating, then the child is either likely to grow up having a submissive, passive set of attitudes or to be rebellious and destructive.

Children attend formal school at around 5 to 6 years of age. Most have learned to understand rules by this time and have learned to cooperate in play with their peers. In the formal setting of the school, a child's learning is affected by the qualities of the teacher. This includes both his or her human qualities and the professional skills that the teacher brings to the classroom. Good schools have committed teachers. Committed teachers are able to encourage children to do well with their academic work, help develop their intellectual skills, and encourage them to progress socially in the presence of their peers (Rutter, 1983). The school culture offers an important avenue for developing problem-solving skills, decision-making abilities, and beliefs to improve resilience.

In the classroom, interest in learning is generated and sustained by social interactions between the children as much as between the child and the teacher. The teacher's professional skills should allow him or her to present material in a way that is easily assimilated yet challenging and motivating to the child. As the child progresses through school, the child gains in literacy, numeracy, and general knowledge, and these skills form the basis for his or her future capacity to solve problems effectively.

Some children, for a variety of social and personal reasons, miss out on education. This means they miss out on acquiring many of the skills necessary to solve problems in an effective and adaptive way. Some learn maladaptive methods on the street. There has been recent and belated recognition of how much of a disadvantage this can be to young people in today's society.

One example is mathematics. Robert Moses, who in Mississippi in the 1960s was a leader in the struggle for civil rights for African Americans, has since considered that the civil rights legislation was not, by itself, sufficient to make people free, if they do not have the skills to compete with others and to access their citizenship. He thought these skills were mainly learned at school and that most African-American children were at an educational disadvantage compared with white middle-class children. In particular, they lacked mathematical skills (Jetter, 1993).

Moses aimed to improve problem-solving skills through the Algebra Project. Algebraic concepts require a sense of the direction of things that allows greater application to everyday problems than simple arithmetic. Algebra Project students learned to think by tackling algebraic problems that arise in everyday life, such as negotiating an underground railway system. These types of activities are drawn as directional models, written down and talked about, and then translated into mathematical language and put into symbols. Algebra Project students puzzle away with these in order to ask the right questions and chart out a variety of solutions.

Literacy has a similar, perhaps even more apparent, role in problem solving. Greater flexibility in problem solving is created by greater use of word descriptions. Words allow for subtle variations in considering the personal impact of experiences. Limitations in the vocabulary possessed by an individual restrict the way experiences can be understood or interpreted, and this limits the possibility of thoughtful responses to problems.

As well, words enable reading, and reading, opens the way to the problem-solving activities of past thinkers. Inability to access past literature and to reference the thinking of other people that is held in books (now also on the Internet) denies an individual access to the rich variety of solutions that others have previously tried. Formal literacy instruction in schools and special encouragement to read at home are keys to opening these avenues for the developing child.

There is a direct relationship between poor vocabulary and poor literacy skills and heightened risk for conduct disorders and criminal behavior (Walsh, 1991). However, few programs have been developed for young people with emotional and behavioral problems that are aimed at increasing their literacy skills, apart from the special school curricula for "developmentally delayed" children.

Improving Problem Solving in Symptomatic Adolescents

Programs to improve problem-solving skills for adolescents with depression, conduct disorders, suicidal behavior, or risk-taking behaviors have not been a strong focus of activity in mental health. However, there are some important exceptions.

DEPRESSION

A preventive program for depression is the Penn optimism program developed by Seligman and colleagues at Pennsylvania State University USA in 1990 (Jaycox, Reivich, Gillham & Seligman, 1994). This program has been widely used in a number of variations. Games, comic strips, and role play are utilized to help children develop the link between thoughts and thinking styles and to encourage recognition of pessimistic thoughts. The aim is to replace the pessimistic thoughts with optimistic ones and to create children who have developed a sense of mastery, no matter what the situation. In one variant the children have contact with the program for 2 hours per week during the 12 weeks of school time.

Cognitive behavior therapy interventions and treatment with antidepressant medications have been subject to evaluation and have had components that have proved effective as clinical interventions against depression. Problem-solving techniques have rarely been used (National Health and Medical Research Council of Australia, 1999).

SUICIDE

There have been many programs aimed at youth suicide prevention. Universal prevention programs have aimed to ameliorate the effects of individual risk factors, family risk factors, community risk factors, and those coming from the culture of home and school. Most universal programs have used educational approaches included in the school curriculum. These involve education about suicide, its symptoms, and its prevention, and they give directions for accessing treatment facilities. These programs are usually delivered in the classroom in the context of the health curriculum.

Most of the selective suicide prevention programs are aimed at individuals who have evidence of depressive symptoms or who have made suicidal gestures. These programs usually involve some form of cognitive behavior therapy and are generally combined with other forms of behavioral therapy, such as relaxation therapy or social skills programs. Other programs involve active follow-up for young people who have threatened or attempted suicide.

The Centers for Disease Control and Prevention in the United States of America reviewed 27 youth suicide prevention programs in 1992. None addressed issues of possible deficits in problem solving or decision making among the target groups of adolescents (Centers for Disease Control, 1994). A national stock take of early intervention programs for the mental health of young people operating in Australia in 1999 identified only one program that was specifically directed toward improving problem-solving capacities in young people. This was the Penn optimism program that was employed for prevention of depression in adolescents (Davis et al., 1999).

While it is not possible to do justice here to the huge range of youth suicide prevention projects that have been developed across the world in recent years, a careful examination of the written accounts of these programs shows that few of the universal programs, or of the more selective programs, have been directly aimed at developing problem-solving skills in adolescents (Kosky et al., 1999; National Health and Medical Research Council of Australia, 1999).

172

CONDUCT DISORDERS AND SERIOUS
RISK-TAKING ADOLESCENTS

Marshall and Watt have made an extensive review of 21 programs that were specifically developed for children and adolescents with conduct disorders. They found that 14 of the programs had been adequately evaluated. Of the evaluated programs, 3 involved developing problem-solving skills as part of their interventions (Marshall & Watt, 1999). We briefly describe these programs.

One was a selective intervention aimed at children aged 10–12 years who were identified by teacher and peer ratings as underachieving and disruptive. Students ($N = 100$) were randomly assigned by classroom to the intervention group and to a control group. The intervention occurred in groups of six students and occupied two 1-hour sessions twice weekly over 12 weeks. The content included assertiveness and social skills training taught through games, role play, and interpersonal problem solving. The intervention group displayed improved interpersonal problem-solving ability and assertiveness, and increased popularity was noted in the intervention group immediately after the program and again at 1-year follow-up (Rotheram, 1982).

Another program was aimed at children aged 9 to 10 years who exhibited conduct disorders and aggression. Students ($N = 52$) were randomly assigned to the intervention group or to a control group. The intervention was school based and consisted of 26 individual sessions for 30 minutes plus 8 small group sessions. The content of the intervention included a cognitive behavioral program intended to inhibit distorted social perceptions in order to improve social problem solving. There was a decrease in aggression and improved peer relationships among the intervention group immediately and at 1-year follow-up (Lockman et al., 1993).

In another program, the Earl's Court social skills group, 40 aggressive and disruptive students aged 6 to 12 years were randomly assigned to the intervention group or to a control group. The intervention occurred over one school term and included two 1-hour sessions per week for 12 to 15 weeks in groups of 6 students. The content of the intervention included social commentary programs with skills taught in problem solving, learning to recognize feelings, using self-control, listening, and following instructions. At 3 months there were fewer aggressive behaviors and better social problem-solving skills in the intervention group (Pepler, King, & Byrd, 1991).

The Rochester Social Problem Solving Program has been evaluated in Australia with students enrolled in primary schools. This program consists of social skills training and is based on the principle that children who have problems with their relationships are at increased risk for emotional and behavioral problems. The program was taught to children enrolled in Years 3 and 4 (aged about 8 years). The classroom teachers taught the program during school hours over a 20-week period. The program is based on cognitive therapy principles that aim to provide children with skills for recognizing feelings in themselves and others, generating a range of solutions to interpersonal problems, and understanding the consequences of their actions.

Intervention children had more positive relationships with their peers than children who did not participate in the program. However, this improvement was not maintained at 1-year follow-up. The investigators have suggested more actively including parents as a possible ways of improving the program (Sawyer et al., 1997).

SERIOUS RISK-TAKING

There have been a variety of programs devised for serious risk-taking young people, but few had been evaluated. McLaren (1992), who reviewed a wide range of these programs, considered that most programs did not seem to have any long-term effect and few had been shown to be effective at all. She concluded that, of the many programs available for seriously delinquent youth, wilderness adventure programs probably were the most effective. They gave some participants greater confidence in their capacity to overcome challenges and to find new solutions to old problems.

In the drug and alcohol field, there are a number of nonmedication prevention programs described that may be effective in reducing alcohol and drug intake among adolescents. One of these is the ALERT program (Ellickson, Bell, & McGuigan, 1993). This is the largest intervention for the prevention of drug use that has been evaluated to date. A randomized, controlled trial of 6,527 school children participated in the evaluation. The intervention consisted of eight curriculum-based sessions in Year 7 (age about 12 years) with three booster sessions in Year 8. The interventions targeted social attitudes toward drug use and were designed to promote positive attitudes and skills to help young people resist peer pressures to use drugs.

The evaluation showed modest reductions in alcohol, marijuana, and tobacco use, but these reductions were not sustained in the long run. The findings suggested that better results could be obtained when peer leaders were used to reinforce the interventions.

Clinical Interventions

Standard therapeutic modalities for children and adolescents with emotional and behavioral problems usually involve some problem-solving component, even if this is not specifically acknowledged. The three most widely used psychological therapeutic modalities are cognitive behavior therapy, family therapy, and dynamic psychotherapy.

Cognitive behavior therapy programs typically involve multiple components. These include self-evaluation, cognitive restructuring, activity scheduling, relaxation training, social skills training, and interpersonal problem-solving training. Techniques include problem identification, generation of alternative solutions, prediction of consequences of choices, and selection of the most appropriate strategies for problem resolution. This is the most specifically problem-solving clinical approach.

In clinical practice, cognitive behavior therapy is typically conducted on an individual basis and the composition of the program is usually tailored to individual needs. There are six published controlled studies of the effectiveness of cognitive behavior therapy in the treatment of adolescents who were diagnosed with depressive disorder or depressive symptoms. All report a significantly better outcome in the group receiving cognitive behavior therapy than in the control group (National Health and Medical Research Council, 1997, p. 71).

Family therapy is based on the assumption that psychological problems appearing in the young person are, at least in part, the result of broader disturbances in family. Family therapy is aimed at improving relationships and communications within the family. Some family therapy modalities are focused on solving day-to-day interaction problems that confront the family relationships. In this model, the aim is to get the family to work together as a group, cooperating and compromising in order to generate more potential solutions and to reach more effective answers to the problems they confront.

Group therapy for adolescents, once a common approach at all levels of multidisciplinary mental health activity, is now rarely used in clinical practice. This is perhaps a pity because, if it can be shown to be an effective preventative intervention, it has obvious cost benefits over individual casework. It involves a group of disorganized young people coming together under supervision and learning from each other and from therapeutic relationships formed among themselves and with their therapist. In terms of our model of cognitive mediators, group therapy would be best for working on expanding possible solutions to problems and increasing the repertoire of positive and adaptive reactions that are available to the young person. The processes involved in dynamic group therapy for adolescents have been well described by Evans (1998).

Dynamic psychotherapy is derived from the principles that underpin psychoanalysis, in particular, the presence of unconscious drives that influence behavior and decision making. It aims to allow the individual to change these influences so as to reach more realistic and effective solutions, uncontaminated by fixations on old maladaptive ones (neuroses). It therefore involves the rational examination of conscious and unconscious conflicts.

The purpose of dynamic psychotherapy for young people is to help them increase their capacity for mature decision making. Within the therapeutic relationship, problems are identified and solutions for them are sought. In recent developments of this form of psychotherapy, the idea of narratives that underlie the constancy of the understanding of self has been developed as a major focus. It seems that meaningful narratives about one's personal, remembered experiences protect esteem and shield against the development of negative relationships with others (Fonagy et al., 1994).

There are no controlled trials of the treatment of depression or conduct disorder in young people by dynamic psychotherapy. There have been many positive case reports, and these are readily available in the literature. This form of therapy is intensive and usually long term, although brief interventions have been developed based on the same principles. The intensity of the treatment, its length, and its cost have been seen as a disadvantage.

Leaving aside specific problem-solving approaches, we should note that there are other important forms of treatment apart from psychological and social ones. In particular, there may be an important role for medication in individual cases. The selective sero-tonin reuptake inhibitors (SSRIs) such as fluoxetine have proven effective in adults with depressive disorders, and although there is some controversy about their effectiveness and safety in young people, there are strong clinical impressions that these medications may be effective in reducing depressive symptoms in adolescents. They carry side effects and complications that both clinician and patient need to understand.

Lithium, carbemazepine, and sodium valporate may also have useful roles to play, particularly in the treatment of bipolar affective disorder in young people. Some clinicians have reported that these drugs may also be useful in moderating behavioral inconstancy in young people. No controlled studies exist to determine whether these clinical observations are correct, and these medications also have adverse effects.

However, it may be that medication is necessary in order for the young person to fully utilize the psychological and psychosocial interventions in an effective way. Depression slows down cognition and limits concentration. Psychosis scrambles thoughts. In neither case will an affected young person be able to effectively utilize problem-solving approaches. An effective clinician will find the optimal balance between these interventions.

Conclusion

Our findings suggest that problem solving is impaired in young people who progress from depression to suicide and from conduct disorders to serious risk-taking behavior. Our findings also suggest that young people who develop depression and conduct disorders already have some impairment in their capacity to solve problems. Currently these deficits appear to be overlooked in the development of prevention programs for suicide and serious risk-taking behaviors among young people.

It is possible to see problem-solving interventions as being useful at two levels. First, interventions can be developed prior to the onset of emotional or behavioral disorders as a means of preventing these disorders from developing. Second, interventions could be made after the onset of depression or conduct disorder as a means of preventing the serious outcomes of suicidal behavior and risk-taking behavior. Of course, interventions with a problem-solving focus would not be the be-all and end-all of interventions that could, or should, be conducted, but they may be a powerful addition to the range of intervention programs for the mental health of young people.

The Epidemiological Catchment Area study has indicated quite clearly that depressive disorders first become manifest in adolescence. Therefore, problem-solving interventions for the prevention of depression have to be aimed at late primary and early high school students. Conduct disorders seem to have an even earlier first manifestation, possibly around the middle of the primary school years (Rey, 1992). Prevention programs for conduct disorders therefore have to be aimed at primary school students.

Apart from the timing of problem-solving interventions, thought has to be given to the components of such programs. Reference to Table 5 shows the problem-solving deficits present in conduct disordered, depressed, suicidal, and risk-taking young people as demonstrated in our studies. Programs have to be developed that address each of these points.

Components of the programs should, therefore, enable the individuals who participate to generate a wider range of potential solutions to problems, to generate solutions that are more relevant to the problem, to generate less aggressive responses, to select solutions after consideration of their consequences, and to create solutions that actually work. The programs should impart confidence that the solutions generated can work. Self-governed solutions should be valued over those that are developed for the sake of making one look good in the eyes of peers. The programs should also encourage positive attitudes that value life.

This raises a lot of questions about how to approach this. In this book we have tried to generate these questions rather than to provide the answers. Now we require those with expertise in the development of programs that focus on problem-solving skills to come forward and develop interventions that take the Suicide and Risk-Taking model into account. Then the long process of testing them in the field will commence. Despite this enormous task, the work will be addressing one of the major concerns of our global community – the emotional life of our young people.

References

Adams, D.M., Overholser, J.C., & Lehnert, K.L. (1994). Perceived family functioning and adolescent suicidal behavior. *Journal of the American Academy of Child and Adolescent Psychiatry, 32*, 1–6.

American Psychiatric Association. (1994). *Diagnostic and Statistical Manual* (4th Edition). Washington DC: Author.

Andrews, G., Hall, W., Teeson, M., & Henderson, S. (1999). *The Mental Health of Australians.* Canberra, Austalia: Commonwealth Department of Health and Aged Care.

Andrews, J.A., & Lewinsohn, P.M. (1992). Suicidal attempts among older adolescents: Prevalence and co-occurrence with psychiatric disorders. *Journal of the American Academy of Child and Adolescent Psychiatry, 31*, 655–662.

Anthony, E.J. (1983). An introduction to the psychology and psychopathology of change. In E.J. Anthony and C. Chiland (Eds.), *The child in his family: Children and their parents in a changing world.* New York: John Wiley & Sons.

Apter, A., Bleich, A., Plutchik, R., Mendelsohn, S., & Tyano, S. (1988). Suicidal behavior, depression, and conduct disorder in hospitalized adolescents. *Journal of the American Academy of Child and Adolescent Psychiatry, 27*, 696–699.

Arnett, J. (1990). Contraceptive use, sensation seeking, and adolescent egocentrism. *Journal of Youth and Adolescence, 19*, 171–180.

Arnett, J. (1992). Reckless behavior in adolescence: A developmental perspective. *Developmental Review, 12*, 339–373.

REFERENCES

Arnett, J. (1999). Adolescent storm and stress, reconsidered. *American Psychologist, 54*(5), 317–326.

Asarnow, J.R. (1992). Suicidal ideation and attempts during middle childhood: Associations with perceived family stress and depression among child psychiatric inpatients. *Journal of Clinical Child Psychology, 21*, 35–40.

Asarnow, J.R., Carlson, G.A., & Guthrie, D. (1987). Coping strategies, self-perceptions, hopelessness, and perceived family environments in depressed and suicidal children. *Journal of Consulting and Clinical Psychology, 55*, 361–366.

Australian Bureau of Statistics. (1995). *Cause of death – Australia, 1994* (Catalogue No. 3303.0). Australian Government Publishing Services.

Austrian, S.G. (2002). Adolescence. In S.G. Austrian (Ed.), *Developmental Theories Through the Life Cycle* (pp. 123–180). New York: Columbia University Press.

Barkley, R.A. (1997). *ADHD and the nature of self-control.* New York: Guilford Press.

Baron, R.M., & Kenny, D.A. (1986). The moderator-mediator variable distinction in social psychological research: Conceptual, strategic, and statistical considerations. *Journal of Personality and Social Psychology, 31*, 1173–1182.

Beautrais, A.L., Joyce, P.R., & Mulder, R.T. (1997). Precipitating factors and life events in serious suicide attempts among youths aged 13 through 24 years. *Journal of the American Academy of Child and Adolescent Psychiatry, 36*, 1543–1551.

Beautrais, A.L., Joyce, P.R., & Mulder, R.T. (1996). Risk factors for serious suicide attempts among youths aged 13 through 24 years. *Journal of the American Academy of Child and Adolescent Psychiatry, 35*, 1174–1182.

Beck, A.T. (1961). A systematic investigation of depression. *Comprehensive Psychiatry, 2*, 163–170.

Beck, A.T. (1963). Thinking and depression. *Archives of General Psychiatry, 9*, 324–333.

Beck, A.T. (1967). *Depression: Clinical, experimental and theoretical aspects.* New York: Hoebner Medical Division, Harper and Row.

Beck, A.T. (1978). *Depression inventory.* Philadelphia: Center for Cognitive Therapy.

Beck, A.T., Brown, G., Berchick, R.J., & Stewart, B.L. (1990). Relationship between hopelessness and ultimate suicide: A replication with psychiatric outpatients. *American Journal of Psychiatry, 147*, 190–195.

182

Beck, A.T., Kovacs, M., & Weissman, A. (1975). Hopelessness and suicidal behaviour: An Overview. *Journal of the American Medical Association, 234,* 1146–1149.

Beck, A.T., Weissman, A., Lester, D., & Trexler, L. (1974). The measurement of pessimism: The Hopelessness Scale. *Journal of Consulting and Clinical Psychology, 42,* 861–865.

Bell, D.E. (1983). Risk premiums for decision regret. *Management Science, 29,* 1156–1166.

Bell, D.E. (1985). Putting a premium on regret. *Management Science, 31,* 117–120.

Bender, L., & Schilder, P. (1937). Suicidal preoccupations and attempts in children. *American Journal of Orthopsychiatry, 7,* 224–234.

Benthin, A., Slovic, P., & Severson, H. (1993). A psychometric study of adolescent risk perception. *Journal of Adolescence, 16,* 153–168.

Beyth-Marom, R., Austin, L., Fischhoff, B., Palmgren, C., & Jacobs-Quadrel, M. (1993). Perceived consequences of risky behaviors: Adults and adolescents. *Developmental Psychology, 29,* 549–563.

Blackburn, I.M., & Davidson, K. (1995). *Cognitive Therapy for Depression and Anxiety.* London: Blackwell Science Ltd.

Bontempo, D.E., & D'Augelli, A.R. (2002). Effects of at-school victimization and sexual orientation on lesbian, gay or bisexual youths' health risk behaviour. *Journal of Adolescent Health, 30,* 364–374.

Borst, S.R., & Noam, G.G. (1993). Developmental psychopathology in suicidal and nonsuicidal adolescent girls. *Journal of the American Academy of Child and Adolescent Psychiatry, 32,* 501–508.

Bowlby, J. (1988). Defensive processes in response to stressful separation in early life. In Anthony, E. James (Ed.); Chiland, Colette (Ed.), The child in his family, Vol. 8: Perilous development: Child raising and identity formation under stress. Yearbook of the International Association for Child Adolescent Psychiatry and Allied Professions (pp. 23–30). Oxford, England: John Wiley & Sons.

Brent, D.A. (1995). Risk factors for adolescent suicide and suicidal behavior: Mental and substance abuse disorders, family environmental factors, and life stress. *Suicide and Life Threatening Behavior, 25,* 52–63.

Brent, D.A. (2001). Assessment and Treatment of the Youthful Suicidal Patient. In H. Hendin and J.J. Mann (Eds.), *The Clinical Science of Suicide Prevention* (pp. 106–131). Annals of The New York Academy of Science, 932. New York.

REFERENCES

Brent, D.A., Bridge, J., Johnson, B.A., & Connolly, J. (1996). Suicidal behavior runs in families: A controlled family study of adolescent suicide victims. *Archives of General Psychiatry, 53*, 1145–1152.

Brent, D.A., Johnson, B., Bartle, S., Bridge, J., Rather, C., Matta, J., Connolly, J., & Constantine, D. (1993a). Personality disorder, tendency to impulsive violence, and suicidal behavior in adolescents. *Journal of the American Academy of Child and Adolescent Psychiatry, 32*, 69–75.

Brent, D.A., Kolko, D.J., Allan, M.J., & Brown, R.V. (1990). Suicidality in affectively disordered adolescent inpatients. *Journal of the American Academy of Child and Adolescent Psychiatry, 29*, 586–593.

Brent, D.A., Perper, J., Moritz, G., Baugher, M., & Allman, C. (1993b). Suicide in adolescents with no apparent psychopathology. *Journal of the American Academy of Child and Adolescent Psychiatry, 32*, 494–500.

Brightman, B.K. (1990). Adolescent depression and the susceptibility to helplessness. *Journal of Youth and Adolescence, 19*, 441–449.

Brook, J.S., Whiteman, M., Finch, S.J., & Cohen, P. (1996). Young adult drug use and delinquency: Childhood antecedents and adolescent mediators. *Journal of the American Academy of Child and Adolescent Psychiatry, 35*, 1584–1592.

Burnett, P.C., & Fanshawe, J.P. (1996). Measuring adolescent coping strategies: A revalidation of the adolescent coping orientation for problem experiences. *The Australian Educational and Developmental Psychologist, 13*, 40–53.

Cantor, C.H., & Slater, P.J. (1997). A regional profile of suicide in Queensland. *Australian and New Zealand Journal of Public Health, 21*, 181–186.

Cantwell, D.P., & Baker, L. (1991). Manifestations of depressive affect in adolescence. *Journal of Youth and Adolescence, 20*, 121–133.

Carlton, P.A., & Deane, F.P. (2000). Impact of attitudes and suicidal ideation on adolescents' intentions to seek professional psychological help. *Journal of Adolescence, 23*, 35–45.

Carter, J. (ed.). (1999*). Partnerships for Learning. National Mental Health Strategy.* Canberra, ACT: Commonwealth Department of Health and Aged Care.

Centers for Disease Control. (1992). *Youth Suicide Prevention Programs: A Resource Guide*. Atlanta: Author.

Chou, C.P., & Bentler, P. (1995). Estimates and tests in structural equation modelling. In R.H. Hoyle (ed), *Structural equation modelling*, pp. 37–55. Thousand Oaks, CA: Sage.

Clark, D.C., Sommerfeldt, L., Schwarz, M., Hedeker, D., & Watel, L. (1990). Physical recklessness in adolescence. Trait or byproduct of depressive/suicidal states? *The Journal of Nervous and Mental Disease, 178*, 423–433.

REFERENCES

Cole, D.A. (1989). Psychopathology of adolescent suicide: Hopelessness, coping beliefs, and depression. *Journal of Abnormal Psychology, 98*, 248–255.

Commonwealth Department of Health and Aged Care. (1999). *National Youth Suicide Prevention Strategy – Setting the Evidence-Based Research Agenda for Australia* (A Literature Review), Commonwealth of Australia: Author. Retrieved from http://www.nhmrc.health.gov.au/publicat/synopses/mh12syn/htm

Connell, D.K., & Meyer, R.G. (1991). The reasons for living inventory and a college population: Adolescent suicidal behaviors, beliefs, and coping skills. *Journal of Clinical Psychology, 47*, 485–489.

Connell, H.M. (1972). Attempted suicide in school children. *The Medical Journal of Australia, 1*, 686–690.

Connolly, J., Geller, S., Marton, P., & Kutcher, S. (1992). Peer responses to social interaction with depressed adolescents. Journal of Clinical Child Psychology, 21(4), 365–370.

Connolly, J.A. (1988). Interpersonal skill deficits of emotionally disturbed adolescents: social problem-solving, self-reports of social behavior and self-esteem. Paper presented at NATO-ASI. Social Conference in Developmental Perspective. Les Arcs, France.

Conway, M., & Giannopoulos, C. (1993). Dysphoria and decision making: Limited information use for evaluations of multiattribute targets. *Journal of Personality and Social Psychology, 64*, 613–623.

Cornelius, J., Kirisci, L., & Tarter, R.E. (2001). Suicidality in offspring of men with substance use disorder: Is there a common liability? *Journal of Child & Adolescent Substance Abuse. Special Issue: Etiology of substance use disorder in children and adolescents: Emerging findings from the Center for Education and Drug Abuse Research. 10*(4), 101–109.

Craighead, W.E. (1991). Cognitive factors and classification issues in adolescent depression. *Journal of Youth and Adolescence, 20*, 311–326.

D'Augelli, A.R., Hershberger, S.L., & Pilkington, N.W. (2001). Suicidality patterns and sexual orientation-related factors among lesbian, gay and bisexual youths. *Suicide and Life Threatening Behaviour, 31*, 250–264.

Dalgleish, L.I. (1990). *Assessment of perceived risk in child protection: A model, some data and implications for practice.* Paper presented at the First International Conference on Risk Assessment, Leicester, England.

Davis A.T., & Kosky R.J. (1991). Attempted suicide in Adelaide and Perth: changing rates for males and females, 1971–1987. *Medical Journal of Australia, 154*, 666–70.

Davis, C., Martin, G., Kosky, R., & O'Hanlon, A. (1999). *National Stock Take of Early Intervention Programs.* Adelaide: The Australian Early Intervention

REFERENCES

Network for the Mental Health of Young People. Retrieved from http//auseinet.flinders.edu.au

Davis, C., Martin, G., Kosky, R., & O'Hanlon, A. (2000). *Early intervention in the mental health of young people: A literature review*. Adelaide, South Australia: Foundation Studios.

de Wilde, E.J., Kienhorst, C.W.M., Diekstra, R.F.W., & Wolters, W.H.G. (1992). The relationship between adolescent suicidal behavior and life events in childhood and adolescence. *American Journal of Psychiatry, 149*, 45–51.

DiFilippo, J.M., & Overholser, J.C. (2000). Suicidal Ideation in Adolescent Psychiatric Inpatients as Associated With Depression and Attachment Relationships. *Journal of Clinical Child Psychology, 29*, 155–166.

Dixon, W.A., Heppner, P.P., & Anderson, W. (1991). Problem-solving appraisal, stress, hopelessness, and suicide ideation in a college population. *Journal of Counselling Psychology, 38*, 51–56.

Dixon, W.A., Heppner, P.P., & Rudd, M.D. (1994). Problem-solving appraisal, hopelessness, and suicide ideation: Evidence for a mediational model. *Journal of Counseling Psychology, 41*, 91–98.

Dodge, K.A. (1993). Social-cognitive mechanisms in the development of conduct disorder and depression. *Annual Review of Psychology, 44*, 559–584.

Dodge, K.A., & Newman, J.P. (1981). Biased decision making processes in aggressive boys. *Journal of Abnormal Psychology, 90*, 375–379.

Dodge, K.A., Price, J.M., Bachorowski, J., & Newman, J.P. (1990). Hostile attributional biases in severely aggressive adolescents. *Journal of Abnormal Psychology, 99*, 385–392.

Donovan, J.E., & Jessor, R. (1985). Structure of problem behavior in adolescence and young adulthood. *Journal of Consulting and Clinical Psychology, 53*, 890–904.

Donovan, J.E., Jessor, R., & Jessor, L. (1983). Problem drinking in adolescence and young adulthood. *Journal of Studies on Alcoholism, 44*, 109–137.

Downey, V.W., & Landry, R.G. (1997). Self-reported sexual behaviors of high school juniors and seniors in North Dakota. *Psychological Reports, 80*, 1357–1358.

Durkheim, E. (1897). *Suicide*. Glencoe, IL: The Free Press, 1951.

D'Zurilla, T.J., & Sheedy, C.F. (1991). Relation between social problem-solving ability and subsequent level of psychological stress in college students. *Journal of Personality and Social Psychology, 61*, 841–846.

D'Zurilla, T.J., & Nezu, A.M. (1990). Developmental and preliminary evaluation of the social problem-solving inventory. *Psychological Assessment: A Journal of Consulting and Clinical Psychology, 2*, 156–163.

REFERENCES

Edwards, J., & McGorry, P.D. (2002). Implementing early intervention in psychosis: A guide to establishing early psychosis services. London: Dunitz Martin Ltd.

Eisenberg, L. (1995). Social policy and the reality of prevention. In B. Raphael & G. Burrows, *Handbook of Preventive Psychiatry* (pp. 31–50). Amsterdam: Elsevier.

Elkind, D. (1967). Egocentrism in adolescence. *Child Development, 38*, 1025–1034.

Elkind, D. (1985). Egocentrism redux. *Developmental Review, 5*, 218–226.

Ellickson, P.L., Bell, R.M., & McGuigan, K. (1993). Preventing Adolescent Drug Use: Long Term Results of a Junior High Program. *American Journal of Public Health, 83*, 856–861

Elliott, T.R., Sherwin, E., Harkins, S.W., & Marmarosch, C. (1995). Self-appraised problem-solving ability, affective states, and psychological distress. *Journal of Counselling Psychology, 42*, 105–115.

Evans, J. (1998). *Active analytic group therapy for adolescents.* London: Jessica Kingsley Publishers.

Faulkner, A. H., & Cranston, K. (1998). Correlates of same-sex sexual behavior in a random sample of Massachusetts high school students. *American Journal of Public Health, 88*(2), 262–266.

Ferrante, P., & Loh, N. (1994). *Crime and justice statistics for Western Australia:* 1994. Perth: The University Of Western Australia Crime Research Centre.

Fischhoff, B., Bostrom, A., & Quadrel, M. J. (2000). Risk perception and communication. In T. Connolly (Ed.), H.R Arkes, (Ed.), et al. Cambridge series on judgment and decision making: Judgment and decision making: An interdisciplinary reader (2nd ed.) (pp. 479–499). New York: Cambridge University Press.

Fisher, L., & Feldman, S.S. (1998). Familial antecedents of young adult health risk behavior: A longitudinal study. *Journal of Family Psychology, 12*, 66–80.

Fonagy, P., Steele, M., Steele, H., & Heggitt, A. (1994). The theory and practice of resilience. *Journal of Child Psychology and Psychiatry, 35*, 231–258.

Frick, P.J., & Jackson, Y.K. (1993). Family functioning and childhood antisocial behavior: Yet another reinterpretation. *Journal of Clinical Child Psychology, 22*, 410–419.

Furby, L., & Beyth-Marom, R. (1992). Risk taking in adolescence: A decision-making perspective. *Developmental Review, 12*, 1–44.

Garnefski, N., & Diekstra, R.F.W. (1997). Child sexual abuse and emotional and behavioral problems in adolescence: Gender differences.

Journal of the American Academy of Child and Adolescent Psychiatry, 36, 323–329.

Garofalo, R., Wolf, R.C., Kessel, S., Palfrey, J., & DuRat, R.H. (1998). The association between health risk behaviors and sexual orientation among a school-based sample of adolescents. *Pediatrics, 101*, 895–902.

Garofalo, R., Wolf, R.C., Wissow, L.S, Woods, E.R., & Goodman, E. (1999). Sexual orientation and risk of suicide attempts among a representative sample of youth. *Archives of Pediatric and Adolescent Medicine, 153*, 487–493.

Garrison, C.Z., Addy, C.L., Jackson, K.L., McKeown, R.E., & Waller, J.L. (1991). A longitudinal study of suicidal ideation in young adolescents. *Journal of the American Academy of Child and Adolescent Psychiatry, 30*, 597–603.

Garrison, C.Z., Jackson, K.L., Marsteller, F., McKeown, R., & Addy, C. (1990). A longitudinal study of depressive symptomatology in young adolescents. *Journal of the American Academy of Child and Adolescent Psychiatry, 29*, 581–585.

Gibbons, F.X., & Gerrard, M. (1994). Social-psychological factors in the initiation of adolescent health risk behaviors: A longitudinal study. Manuscript in preparation, Iowa State University.

Gibbons, F.X., Helweg-Larsen, M., & Gerrard, M. (1995). Prevalence estimates and adolescent risk behavior: Cross-cultural differences in social influence. *Journal of Applied Psychology, 80*, 107–121.

Goldston, D.B., Daniel, S.S., Reboussin, B.A., Reboussin, D.M., Frazier, P.H., & Harris, A.E. (2001). Cognitive risk factors and suicide attempts among formerly hospitalized adolescents: A prospective naturalistic study. *Journal of the American Academy of Child & Adolescent Psychiatry, 40*, 91–99.

Gonzalez, J., Field, T., Yando, R., Gonzalez, K., Lasko, D., & Bendell, D. (1994). Adolescents' perceptions of their risk-taking behavior. *Adolescence, 29*, 701–709.

Goodman, P., & Stoehr, T. (Ed.). (1978). The *Break–Up of Our Camp: Stories 1932–35*. Santa Barbara: Black Sparrow Press.

Gordon, D.E. (1990). Formal operational thinking: The role of cognitive-developmental processes in adolescent decision-making about pregnancy and contraception. *American Journal of Orthopsychiatry, 60*, 346–356.

Gould, M.S., Fisher, P., Parides, M., Flory, M., & Shaffer, D. (1996). Psychosocial risk factors of child and adolescent completed suicide. *Archives of General Psychiatry, 53*, 1155–1162.

Gould, M.S., Shaffer, D., Fisher, P., & Garfinkel, R. (1998). Separation/divorce and the child and adolescent completed suicide. *Journal of the American Academy of Child and Adolescent Psychiatry, 37*, 155–162.

REFERENCES

Green, V., Johnson, S., & Kaplan, D. (1992). Predictors of adolescent female decision making regarding contraceptive usage. *Adolescence, 27,* 613–632.

Groholt, B., Ekeberg, O., Wichstrom, L., & Haldorsen, T. (1997). Youth suicide in Norway, 1990–1992: A comparison between children and adolescents completing suicide and age- and gender-matched controls. *Suicide and Life Threatening Behavior, 27,* 250–263.

Gutierrez, P.M., Osman, A., Kopper, B.A., & Barrios, F.X. (2000). Why young people do not kill themselves: The Reasons For Living Inventory for Adolescents. *Journal of Clinical Child Psychology, 29,* 177–187.

Hartlage, S., Alloy, L.B., Vazquez, C., & Dykman, B. (1993). Automatic and effortful processing in depression. *Psychological Bulletin, 113,* 247–278.

Hasher, L., & Zacks, R.T. (1979). Automatic and effortful processes in memory. *Journal of Experimental Psychology: General, 109,* 356–388.

Hasher, L., Rose, K.C., Zacks, R.T., Sanft, H., & Doren, B. (1985). Mood, recall, and selectivity effects in normal college students. *Journal of Experimental Psychology: General, 114,* 104–118.

Hertel, P.T., & Rude, S.S. (1991). Depressive deficits in memory: Focusing attention improves subsequent recall. *Journal of Experimental Psychology: General, 120,* 301–309.

Hinshelwood, R.D. (1991). *A Dictionary of Kleinian Thought.* London: Free Association Books.

Hoberman, H.M., & Garfinkel, B.D. (1988). Completed suicide in children and adolescents. *Journal of the American Academy of Child and Adolescent Psychiatry, 27,* 689–695.

Hollis, C. (1996). Depression, family environment, and adolescent suicidal behavior. *Journal of the American Academy of Child and Adolescent Psychiatry, 35,* 622–630.

Hunter, E. (1993). Aboriginal health and history: Power and prejudice in remote Australia. Cambridge: Cambridge University Press.

Information Victoria. (1997). *Victorian Task Force Report: Suicide Prevention.* Victoria, Australia: Government of Victoria. Retrieved from http://hna.ffh. vic.gov.au/info/sptf/

Ingram, R.E. (1984a). Information processing and feedback: Effects of mood and information favorability on the cognitive processing of personally relevant information. *Cognitive Therapy and Research, 8,* 371–386.

Ingram, R.E. (1984b). Toward an information-processing analysis of depression. *Cognitive Therapy and Research, 8,* 443–478.

Ingram, R.E. (1990). Self-focused attention in clinical disorders: Review and a conceptual model. *Psychological Bulletin, 107,* 156–176.

189

Irwin, C.E., & Millstein, S.G. (1992). Risk-taking behaviors and biopsychosocial development during adolescence. In E.J. Susman, L.V. Feagans & W.J. Ray (Eds.), *Emotion, Cognition, Health, and Development in Children and Adolescents* (pp. 75–102). Hillsdale, NJ: Lawrence Erlbaum Associates, Inc.

Isen, A.M., & Geva, N. (1987). The influence of positive affect on acceptable level of risk and thoughts about losing: The person with a large canoe has a large worry. *Organizational Behavior and Human Decision Processes, 39*, 145–154.

Isen, A.M., & Means, B. (1983). The influence of positive affect on decision-making strategy. *Social Cognition, 2*, 18–31.

Jarey, M.L., & Stewart, M.A. (1985). Psychiatric disorder in the parents of adopted children with aggressive conduct disorder. *Neuropsychobiology, 13*, 7–11.

Jaycox, L.H., Reivich, K.J., Gillham, J., & Seligman, M. (1994). Prevention of depressive symptoms in school children. *Behaviour Research and Therapy, 32*, 801–816.

Jessor, R. (1992). Risk behavior in adolescence: A psychosocial framework for understanding and action. *Developmental Review, 12*, 374–390.

Jessor, R., & Jessor, S.L. (1975). Adolescent development and the onset of drinking. *Journal of Studies on Alcohol, 36*, 27–51.

Jessor, R., Van Den Bos, J., Vanderryn, J., Costa, F.M., & Turbin, M.S. (1995). Protective factors in adolescent problem behavior: Moderator effects and developmental change. *Developmental Psychology, 31*, 923–933.

Jetter, A. (1993). *Mississippi Learning.* New York Times Magazine, February 21, 28–35.

Jobes, D.A., Berman, A.L., O'Carroll, P.W., Eastguard, S., & Knickmeyer, S. (1996). The Kurt Cobain suicide crisis: Perspectives from research, public health, and the news media. *Suicide and Life Threatening Behavior, 26*, 260–272.

Joffe, R.D., Dobson, K.S., Fine, S., Marriage, K., & Haley, G. (1990). Social problem-solving in depressed, conduct-disordered, and normal adolescents. *Journal of Abnormal Child Psychology, 18*, 565–575.

Jorm, A.F., Angermyer, M., & Katschinig, H. (2000). Public Knowledge of and attitudes to mental disorders: a limiting factor in the optimal use of treatment services. In G. Andrews and A.S. Henderson (Eds.), *Unmet needs in psychiatry* (pp. 399–413). Cambridge: Cambridge University Press.

Kahneman, D. (1973). *Attention and effort.* New York: Prentice-Hall. Englewood Cliffs, NJ: Prentice-Hall.

REFERENCES

Kandel, D.B., & Andrews, K. (1987). Process of adolescent socialization by parents and peers. *International Journal of the Addictions, 22*, 319–342.

Kann, L., Warren, C. W., Harris, W. A., Collins, J.L., Williams, B.I., Ross, J.G., & Kolbe, L.J. (1996). Youth Risk Behaviour Surveillance – United States, 1996. In CDC Surveillance Summaries, September 27, 1996. MMWR, 45 (SS-4).

Kashani, J.H., Suarez, L., Allan, W.D., & Reid, J.C. (1997). Hopelessness in inpatient youths: A closer look at behavior, emotional expression, and social support. *Journal of the Academy of Child and Adolescent Psychiatry, 36*, 1625–1631.

Kazdin A.E., Esveldt-Dawson, K., French, N.H., Unis, A.S. (1987). Effects of Parent Management Training and Problem-Solving Skills Training Combined in the Treatment of Antisocial Child Behavior. *Journal of the American Academy of Child and Adolescent Psychiatry, 26*, 416–424.

Kelly, T.M., Cornelius, J.R. and Lynch, K.G. (2002). Psychiatric and substance use disorders as risk factors for attempted suicide among adolescents: A case control study. *Suicide and Life-Threatening Behavior, 32*, 301–312.

Kelly, T.M., Lynch, K.G., Donovan, J.E., & Clark, D.B. (2001). Alcohol use disorders and risk factor interactions for adolescent suicidal ideation and attempts. *Suicide and Life-Threatening Behavior, 31*, 181–193.

Kempton, T., Van Hasselt, V.B., Bukstein, O.G., & Null, J.A. (1994). Cognitive distortions and psychiatric diagnosis in dually diagnosed adolescents. *Journal of the American Academy of Child and Adolescent Psychiatry, 33*, 217–222.

Kety, S. S. (1990). Genetic factors in suicide: Family, twin, and adoption studies. In S. J. Blumenthal (Ed.), D. J. Kupfer (Ed.), *Suicide over the life cycle: Risk factors, assessment, and treatment of suicidal patients* (pp. 127–133). Washington, DC, US: American Psychiatric Association.

Kienhorst, C.W.M., de Wilde, E.J., Diekstra, R.F.W., & Wolters, W.H.G. (1991). Construction of an index for predicting suicide attempts in depressed adolescents. *British Journal of Psychiatry, 159*, 676–682.

Kienhorst, C.W.M., de Wilde, E.J., Van Den Bout, J., Diekstra, R.F.W., & Wolters, W.H.G. (1990). Characteristics of suicide attempters in a population-based sample of Dutch adolescents. *British Journal of Psychiatry, 156*, 243–248.

King, C.A., Hill, E.M., Naylor, M., Evans, T., & Shain, B. (1993). Alcohol consumption in relation to other predictors of suicidality among adolescent inpatient girls. *Journal of the American Academy of Child and Adolescent Psychiatry, 32*, 82–88.

REFERENCES

King, C.A., Segal, H., Kaminski, K., Naylor, M.W., Ghaziuddin, N., & Radpour, L. (1995). A prospective study of adolescent suicidal behavior following hospitalization. *Suicide and Life Threatening Behavior, 25*, 327–338.

Kosky R. (1982). Suicide and attempted suicide among Australian children. *Medical Journal of Australia, 1*, 124–6.

Kosky, R. (1983). Childhood suicidal behaviour. Journal of Child Psychology and Psychiatry and Allied Disciplines, 24, 457–468.

Kosky, R., McAlpine, I., Silburn, S., & Richmond J. (1985). A Survey of Child Psychiatry Outpatients: 1. Clinical and Demographic Characteristics. *Australian and New Zealand Journal of Psychiatry, 19*, 158–166.

Kosky, R., Silburn, S., & Zubrick, S.R. (1986). Symptomatic depression and suicidal ideation: A comparative study with 628 children. *Journal of Nervous and Mental Disease, 174*, 523–528.

Kosky, R., Silburn, S., & Zubrick, S.R. (1990). Are children and adolescents who have suicidal thoughts different from those who attempt suicide? *The Journal of Nervous and Mental Disease, 178*, 327–338.

Kosky, R.J., Sawyer, M.G., & Gowland, J.C. (1990). Adolescents in custody: hidden psychological morbidity. *The Medical Journal of Australia, 153*, 24–27.

Kosky, R.J., Sawyer, M.G., & Gowland, J.C. (1990). Adolescents in custody: hidden psychological morbidity. *The Medical Journal of Australia, 153*, 24–27.

Kosky, R.J., Sawyer, M.G., Fotheringham, M. (1996). The mental health status of adolescents released from custody: a preliminary study. *Australian and New Zealand Journal of Psychiatry, 30*, 326–31.

Kovacs, M., Goldston, D., & Gatsonis, C. (1993). Suicidal behaviors and childhood-onset depressive disorders: A longitudinal investigation. *Journal of the American Academy of Child and Adolescent Psychiatry, 32*, 8–20.

Larrick, R.P. (1993). Motivational factors in decision theories: The role of self-protection. *Psychological Bulletin, 113*, 440–450.

Lavery, B., Siegel, A.W., Cousins, J.H., & Rubovits, D.S. (1993). Adolescent risk-taking: An analysis of problem behaviors in problem children. *Journal of Experimental Child Psychology, 55*, 277–294.

Lehnert, K., Overholser, J., & Spirito, A. (1994). Internalized and externalized anger in adolescent suicide attempters. *Journal of Adolescent Research, 9*, 105–119.

Leichtman, M.D., Ceci, S., & Morse, M.B. (1997). The Nature and Development of Children's Event Memory. In P.S. Appelbaum, L.A. Uyehara & M.R.

Elin (Eds.), *Trauma and Memory: clinical and legal controversies* (pp. 158–87). Oxford: Oxford University Press.

Leslie, M.B., Stein, J.A., & Rotheram-Borus, M.J. (2002). Sex-specific predicators of suicidality among runaway youth. *Journal of Clinical Child and Adolescent Psychology, 31,* 27–40.

Lester, D., & Yang, B. (1998). *Suicide and homicide in the twentieth century: Changes over time.* NY: Nova Science.

Levy, J.C., & Deykin, E.Y. (1989). Suicidality, depression, and substance abuse in adolescence. *American Journal of Psychiatry, 146,* 1462–1467.

Lewinsohn P.M., Klein D.N., & Seeley J.R. (1995). Bipolar disorders in a community sample of older adolescents: prevalence, phenomenology, comorbidity, and course. *Journal of the American Academy of Child and Adolescent Psychiatry, 34,* 454–63.

Lewinsohn, P.M., Rohde, P., & Seeley, J.R. (1993). Psychosocial characteristics of adolescents with a history of suicide attempt. *Journal of the American Academy of Child and Adolescent Psychiatry, 32,* 60–68.

Lewinsohn, P.M., Rohde, P., & Seeley, J.R. (1996). Adolescent suicidal ideation and attempts: Prevalence, risk factors, and clinical implications. *Clinical Psychology: Science and Practice, 3,* 25–46.

Lewinsohn, S., & Mano, H. (1991). Multiattribute choice and effect: The influence of naturally-occurring and manipulated moods on choice processes. *Journal of Behavioral Decision Making, 6,* 33–51.

Lewis, D.O., Yeager, C.A., Lovely, R., Stein, A., & Cobham-Portorreal, C.S. (1994). A clinical follow-up of delinquent males: ignored variables, unmet needs, and the perpetuation of violence. *Journal of the American Academy of Child and Adolescent Psychiatry, 33,* 518–528.

Lewis, M. (1988). *Managing Madness: psychiatry and society in Australia, 1788 – 1980* (pp. 123–43). Canberra, Australia: Australian Government Publishing Service.

Linehan, M.M. (1993). Cognitive-behavioral treatment of borderline personality disorder. New York: The Guilford Press.

Linehan, M.M., Goodstein, J.L., Nielsen, S.L., & Chiles, J.A. (1983). Reasons for staying alive when you are thinking of killing yourself: The reasons for living inventory. *Journal of Consulting and Clinical Psychology, 51,* 276–286.

Litman, R.E. (1996). Suicidology: A look backward and ahead. *Suicide and Life Threatening Behavior, 26,* 276–286.

Litman, R.E., & Farberow, N.L. (1986). *Youth suicide in California.* Sacramento: California Department of Mental Health.

REFERENCES

Lochman, J.E., & Lampron, L.B. (1986). Situational social problem-solving skills and self-esteem of aggressive and nonaggressive boys. *Journal of Abnormal Child Psychology, 14*, 605–617.

Lochman, J.E., Wayland, K.K., & White K.J. (1993). Social goals: Relationship to adolescent adjustment and to social problem solving. *Journal of Abnormal Child Psychology, 21*, 135–157.

Lockman, J.E., Coie, J.D., Underwood, M.K., & Terry, R. (1993). Effectiveness of a social relations intervention program for aggressive and non-aggressive, rejected children. *Journal of Consulting and Clinical Psychology, 60*, 420–32.

Mano, H. (1992). Judgments under distress: Assessing the role of unpleasantness and arousal in judgment formation. *Organizational Behavior and Human Decision Processes, 52*, 216–245.

Marshall, J., & Watt, P. (1999). *Child Behaviour Problems: A Literature Review of its Size and Nature and Prevention Interventions.* Perth, Western Australia: The Interagency Committee on Children's Futures.

Marton, P., Connolly, J., Kutcher, S., & Korenblum, M. (1993). Cognitive social skills and social self-appraisal in depressed adolescents. *Journal of the American Academy of Child and Adolescent Psychiatry, 32*, 739–744.

Marttunen, M.J., Aro, H.M., & Lonnqvist, J.K. (1992). Adolescent suicide: Endpoint of long-term difficulties. *Journal of the American Academy of Child and Adolescent Psychiatry, 31*, 649–654.

Marttunen, M.J., Aro, H.M., Henriksson, M.M., & Lonnqvist, J.K. (1994). Psychosocial stressors more common in adolescent suicides with alcohol abuse compared with depressive adolescent suicides. *Journal of the American Academy of Child and Adolescent Psychiatry, 33*, 649–654.

Marttunen, M.J., Henriksson, M.M., Aro, H.M., Heikkinen, M.E., Isometsa, E.T., & Lonnqvist, J.K. (1995). Suicide among female adolescents: Characteristics and comparison with males in the age group 13 to 22 years. *Journal of the Academy of Child and Adolescent Psychiatry, 34*, 1297–1307.

Mazza, J.J., & Reynolds, W.M. (2001). An investigation of psychopathology in nonreferred suicidal and nonsuicidal adolescents. *Suicide and Life-Threatening Behavior, 31*, 282–302.

McDaniel J.S., Purcell D., & D'Augelli A.R. (2001). The relationship between sexual orientation and risk for suicide: research findings and future directions for research and prevention. *Suicide Life Threatening Behavior, 31*, (Suppl.), 84–105.

McKay, A.P., Fingerhut, L.A., Duran, C.R. (2000). *Health United States, 2000 with adolescent chartbook.* Hyattsville, MD: NCHS.

REFERENCES

McKay, J.R., Murphy, R.T., Maisto, S.A., & Rivinus, T.R. (1992). Characteristics of adolescent psychiatric patients who engage in problematic behavior while intoxicated. *Journal of the American Academy of Child and Adolescent Psychiatry, 31*, 1031–1035.

McLaren, K. (1992). *Reducing Offending: What Works Now?* (pp. 70–71). Wellington, New Zealand: Penal Division, Department Of Justice.

McLaughlin, J., Miller, P., & Warwick, H. (1996). Deliberate self-harm in adolescents: hopelessness, depression, problems and problem-solving. *Journal of Adolescence, 19*, 523–532.

Meadows, S. (1993). The Child as Thinker: The Development and Acquisition of Cognition in Childhood (pp. 8–94). London: Routledge.

Mitchell, M.G., & Rosenthal, D.M. (1992). Suicidal adolescents: Family dynamics and the effect of lethality and hopelessness. Journal of Youth and Adolescence, 21, 23–33.

Mitterauer, B. (1990). A contribution to the discussion of the role of the genetic factor in suicide, based on five studies in an epidemiologically defined area (Province of Salzburg, Austria). *Comprehensive Psychiatry, 31*, 557–565.

Moon, L., Meyer, P., & Grau, J. (1999). *Australia's young people: their health and well-being.* PHE19. Canberra: Australian Institute of Health and Welfare.

Moore, S., & Gullone, E. (1996). Predicting adolescent risk behavior using a personalized cost-benefit analysis. *Journal of Youth and Adolescence, 25*, 343–359.

Mukherje, S., & Graycar, A. (1997). *Crime and Justice in Australia* (2nd ed.). Leichhardt, New South Wales: Australian Institute of Criminology, Hawkins Press.

Mukherjee S.K. (1985). Juvenile Delinquency: Dimensions of the Problem. In A. Borowski and J.M. Murray (Eds.), *Juvenile Delinquency in Australia* (pp.19–42). Melbourne: Methuen Australia.

Murphy, C. (2003). The world's greatest kisser. Dark Love: The life and death of Rudolph Valentino (Book Review). *New Statesmen, 132, i4662*, 54.

Myers, K., McCauley, E., Calderon, R., Mitchell, J., Burke, P., & Schloredt, K. (1991). Risks for suicidality in major depressive disorder. *Journal of the American Academy of Child and Adolescent Psychiatry, 30*, 86–94.

Namerow, P.B., Lawton, A.I., & Philliber, S.G. (1987). Teenagers' perceived and actual probabilities of pregnancy. *Adolescence, 22*, 475–485.

National Health and Medical Research Council, Department of Health and Family Services, Commonwealth of Australia. (1997). *Depression in Young People: Clinical Practice Guidelines*. Canberra, Australia: Author.

Norton, G.R., Rockman, G.E., Luy, B., & Marion, T. (1993). Suicide, chemical abuse, and panic attacks: A preliminary report. *Behaviour Research and Therapy, 31*, 37–40.

O'Hanlon, A., Kosky, R., Martin, G. Davis, C., Dundas, P. (2000). *Model Projects for Early Intervention in the Mental Health of Young People: Reorienting the Services*. Adelaide: The Australian Early Intervention Network for the Mental Health of Young People. Retrieved from http://auseinet.flinders.edu.au.

Oeser, O. (1960). Society in Miniature: The Social Roles of Pupil and Teacher and Their Relevance to the Acquisition of Knowledge. In O. Oeser (Ed.), *Teacher, pupil and task* (2nd ed.). London: Tavistock Publishers.

Offer, D., Schonert-Reichl, K.A., & Boxer, A.M. (1996). Normal adolescent development: Empirical research findings. In M. Lewis (ed.). *Child and adolescent psychiatry: A comprehensive textbook* (2nd ed.). Baltimore, MD: Williams and Wilkins Publishers.

Offord, D.A., Adler, R.J., Boyle, M.H. (1986). Prevalence and sociodemographic correlates of conduct disorder. *American Journal of Social Psychiatry, 6*, 272–278.

Ohberg, A., Lonnqvist, J., Sarna, S., & Vuori, E. (1996). Violent methods associated with high suicide mortality among the young. *Journal of the American Academy of Child & Adolescent Psychiatry, 35*(2), 144–153.

Orbach, I., Rosenheim, E., & Hary, E. (1987). Some aspects of cognitive functioning in suicidal children. *Journal of the American Academy of Child and Adolescent Psychiatry, 26*, 181–185.

Pandey, G.N., Pandey, S.C., Dwivedi, Y., Sharma, R.P., Janicak, P.G., & Davis, J.M. (1995). Platelet serotonin-2A receptors: A potential biological marker for suicidal behaviour. *American Journal of Psychiatry, 152*, 850–855.

Patterson, G.R., & Bank, L. (1989). Some amplifying mechanisms for pathological processes in families. In M.R. Gunnar & E. Thelen (Eds.), *Systems and development: The Minnesota Symposia on Child Psychology* (Vol. 23, pp. 167–209). Hillsdale, NJ: Erlbaum.

Patterson, G.R., & Dishion, T.J. (1985). Contributions of families and peers to delinquency. *Criminology, 23*, 63–79.

Patterson, G.R., Reid, J.B., & Dishion, T.J. (1992). Antisocial boys. Eugene. OR: Castelia.

Patton, G.C., & Moon, L.J. (2000). The health of young Australians. *Medical Journal of Australia, 172*, 150–151.

Pepler, D.J., King, G., & Byrd, W. (1991). A Social-cognitively based social skills training program for aggressive children. In D. Pepler & K. Robb (Eds.), *The*

Development and treatment of childhood aggression (pp. 360–86). Hillside, New Jersey: Erlbaum Assoc Inc.

Pfeffer, C.R., Klerman, G.L., Hurt, S.W., Kakuma, T., Peskin, J., & Siefker, C.A. (1993). Suicidal children grow up: Rates and psychosocial risk factors for suicide attempts during follow-up. *Journal of the American Academy of Child and Adolescent Psychiatry, 32*, 106–113.

Pfeffer, C.R., Klerman, G.L., Hurt, S.W., Lesser, M., Peskin, J.R., & Siefker, C.A. (1991). Suicidal children grow up: demographic and clinical risk factors for adolescent suicide attempts. *Journal of the American Academy of Child and Adolescent Psychiatry, 30*, 609–616.

Phillips, D. P., & Cartensen, L.L. (1986). Clustering of teenage suicides after television news stories about suicide. *The New England Journal of Medicine, 315*, 685–689.

Piacentini, J., Rotheram-Borus, M.J., Gillis, J.R., Graae, F., Trautman, P., Cantwell, C., Garcia-Leeds, C., & Shaffer, D. (1995). Demographic predictors of treatment attendance among adolescent suicide attempters. *Journal of Consulting and Clinical Psychology, 63*, 469–473.

Piaget, J. (1968). *Six psychological cases.* London: University of London Press.

Pillay, A.L., & Shoubben-Hesk, S. (2001). Depression, Anxiety, and hopelessness in sexually abused adolescent girls. *Psychological Reports, 88*, 727–733.

Pinto, A., & Whisman, M.A. (1996). Negative affect and cognitive biases in suicidal and nonsuuicidal hospitalized adolescents. *Journal of the American Academy of Child and Adolescent Psychiatry, 35*, 158–165.

Platt, J.J., & Spivack, G. (1975). Unidimensionality of the Means-Ends Problem Solving (MEPS) procedure. *Journal of Clinical Psychology, 31*, 15–16.

Platt, J.J., Spivack, G., & Bloom, W. (1975). *Manual for the Means-Ends Problem-Solving Procedure (MEPS): A measure of interpersonal problem-solving skill.* Philadelphia: Hahnemann Medical College and Hospital, Department of Mental Health Sciences, Hahnemann Community MH/MR Center.

Pont, H.B. (1995). Maladjustment and socio-cognitive problem solving: The validity of quantitative and qualitative assessment. *British Journal of Clinical Psychology, 34*, 53–65.

Potas, I., Vining, A., & Wilson, P. (1989). *Young People and Crime: costs and prevention.* Canberra: Australian Institute of Criminology.

Power, P.J.R., Bell, R.J., Mills, R., Herrman-Doig, T., Davern, M., Henry, L., Yuen, H.P., Khademy-Deljo, A., & McGorry, P.D. (2003). Suicide prevention in first episode psychosis: the development of a randomised controlled trial of cognitive therapy for acutely suicidal patients with early psychosis. *Australian & New Zealand Journal of Psychiatry, 37*(4), 414–420.

REFERENCES

Priester, M.J., & Clum, G.A. (1993). The problem-solving diathesis in depression, hopelessness, and suicide ideation: A longitudinal analysis. *Journal of Psychopathology and Behavioral Assessment, 15,* 239–254.

Quadrel, M.J., Fischhoff, B., & Davis, W. (1993). Adolescent (in)vulnerability. *American Psychologist, 48,* 102–116.

Quinnett, P.G. (1987). *Suicide: The forever decision.* New York: Continuum.

Rao, U., Weissman, M.M., Martin, J.A., & Hammond, R.W. (1993). Childhood depression and risk of suicide: A preliminary report of a longitudinal study. *Journal of the American Academy of Child and Adolescent Psychiatry, 32,* 21–27.

Raphael, B. (2000). *Promoting the Mental Health and Well-Being of Children and Young People.* Canberra, Australian Capital Territory: National Mental Health Working Group, Commonwealth Department of Health and Aged Care.

Remafedi, G., French, S., Story, M., Resnick, M.D., & Blum, R. (1998). The relationship between suicide risk and sexual orientation: Results of a population-based study. *American Journal of Public Health, 88,* 57–60.

Rey, J. (1992). The epidemiological catchment area (ECA) study: implications for Australia. *Medical Journal of Australia, 156,* 200–3.

Rohde, P., Mace, D.E., & Seeley, J.R. (1997). The association of psychiatric disorders with suicide attempts in a juvenile delinquent population. *Criminal Behaviour and Mental Health, 7,* 187–200.

Rosario, M. Hunter, J., & Gwadz, M. (1997). Exploration of substance use among lesbian, gay, and bisexual youth: Prevalence and correlates. *Journal of Adolescent Research, 12,* 454–476.

Rotheram, M. (1982). Social skills and training with underachievers, disruptive and exceptional children. *Psychology in Schools, 19,* 532–9.

Rotheram-Borus, M.J., Trautman, P.D., Dopkins, S.C., & Shrout, P.E. (1990). Cognitive style and pleasant activities among female adolescent suicide attempters. *Journal of Consulting and Clinical Psychology, 58,* 554–561.

Rotherham-Borus, M.J., & Trautman, P.D. (1988). Hopelessness, depression, and suicidal intent among adolescent suicide attempters. *Journal of the American Academy of Child and Adolescent Psychiatry, 27,* 700–704.

Roy-Byrne, P.P., Weingartner, H., Bierer, L.M., Thompson, K., & Post, R.M. (1986). Effortful and automatic cognitive processes in depression. *Archives of General Psychiatry, 43,* 265–267.

Rudd, M.D. (2000). Integrating science into the practice of clinical suicidology: A review of the psychotherapy literature and a research agenda for the future. In R.W. Maris (Ed.), S.S. Canetto (Ed.); et al. *Review of suicidology* (pp. 47–83). New York: The Guilford Press.

Rudd, M.D., Rajab, M.H., & Dahm, F. (1994). Problem-solving appraisal in suicide ideators and attempters. *American Journal of Orthopsychiatry, 64*, 136–149.

Rutter, M. (1976). Isle of Wight studies, 1964–1974. *Psychological Medicine, 6*, 313–332.

Rutter, M. (1983). School effects on pupil's progress: Research findings and policy implications. *Child Development, 54*, 1 29.

Rutter, M. (1989). Isle of Wight revisited: Twenty-five years of child psychiatric epidemiology. *Journal of the American Academy of Child and Adolescent Psychiatry, 28*, 633–653.

Rutter, M., Cox, A., Tupling, C., Berger, M., & Yule, W. (1975). Attachment and adjustment in two geographic areas: the prevalence of psychiatric disorder. *British Journal of Psychiatry, 126*, 526–533.

Sadowski, C., & Kelley, M.L. (1993). Social problem solving in suicidal adolescents. *Journal of Consulting and Clinical Psychology, 61*, 121–127.

Sardonoff, C. (1989). *Latency* (pp. 85–146). Northvale, New Jersey: Jason Aronson Inc.

Sawyer, M.G., MacMullin, C., Graetz, B., Said, J.A., Clarke, J., & Baghurst, P. (1997). Social skills training for primary school children: A one-year follow-up study. *Journal of Child Health and Paediatrics, 33*, 378–83.

Sawyer, M.G., Arney, F.M., & Baghurst, P.A. (2000). *The mental health of young people in Australia*. Canberra, Australia: Commonwealth Department of Health and Aged Care.

Sawyer, M.G., Kosky, R., & Graetz, B. (2000). The National Survey of Health and Wellbeing: The child and adolescent component. *Australian and New Zealand Journal of Psychiatry, 34*, 214–221.

Schotte, D.E. & Clum, G.A. (1987). Problem-solving skills in psychiatric patients. *Journal of Clinical and Consulting Psychology, 55*, 49–54.

Shaffer, D. (1974). Suicide in childhood and early adolescence. Journal of Child Psychology & Psychiatry & Allied Disciplines, *15*(4), 275–291.

Shaffer, D., & Piacentini, J. (1994). Suicide and suicide attempts. In M. Rutter, L. Hersov, & E. Taylor (Eds.), *Child and adolescent psychiatry* (3rd ed., pp. 407–424). London: Blackwell Scientific Publications.

Shaffer, D., Fisher, P., Lucas, C.P., Dulcan, M.K., & Schwab-Stone, M.E. (2000). NIMH Diagnostic Interview Schedule for Children Version IV (NIMH DISC-IV): description, differences from previous versions, and reliability of some common diagnoses. *Journal of the American Academy of Child and Adolescent Psychiatry, 39*, 28–38.

Shaffer, D., Gould, M.S., Fisher, P., Trautmen, P., Moreau, D., Kleinman, M., & Flory, M. (1996). Psychiatric diagnosis in child and adolescent suicide. *Archives of General Psychiatry, 53*, 339–348.

Shapiro, R., Siegel, A.W., Scovill, L.C., & Hays, J. (1998). Risk-taking patterns of female adolescents: What they do and why. *Journal of Adolescence, 21*, 143–159.

Shedler, J., & Block, J. (1990). Adolescent drug use and psychological health: A longitudinal inquiry. *American Psychologist, 45*, 612–630.

Shneidman, E.S. (1985). *Definition of suicide*. New York: Wiley.

Shure, M.B. (1996). I can solve problems (ICSP): An interpersonal cognitive problem-solving program for children. In M.C. Roberts (Ed.), *Model Programs in Child and Family Mental Health* (pp. 34–46). Mahwah, New Jersey: Lawrence Erlbaum Assoc.

Silverman, A.B., Reinherz, H.Z., & Giacona, R.M. (1996). The long-term sequelae of child and adolescent abuse: A longitudinal community study. *Child Abuse and Neglect, 20*, 709–723.

Slaby, R.G., & Guerra, N.G. (1988). Cognitive mediators of aggression in adolescent offenders: 1. Assessment. *Developmental Psychology, 24*, 580–588.

Sofronoff, K. (1999). *Adolescent suicide and risk-taking behaviour*. Unpublished doctoral dissertation. University of Queensland.

Sofronoff, K., & Dalgliesh, L.I. (2001). The effect of alcohol and stress on adolescent problem-solving and decision making. Unpublished manuscript. University of Queensland, Australia.

Spence, S. H., & Sheffield, J. (2000). *The problem solving for life program: Preventing depression in Australian youth*. National Educational Service, Reaching Today's Youth, Summer.

Spirito, A., Francis, G., Overholser, J., & Frank, N. (1996). Coping, depression, and adolescent suicide attempts. *Journal of Clinical Child Psychology, 25*, 147–155.

Spirito, A., Overholser, J., & Hart, K. (1991). Cognitive characteristics of adolescent suicide attempters. *Journal of the American Academy of Child and Adolescent Psychiatry, 30*, 604–608.

Stacy, A.W., Newcomb, M.D. (1995). Long-term social psychological influences on deviant attitudes and criminal behaviour. In H.B. Kaplan (Ed.), *Drugs, crime and other deviant adaptations: Longitudinal studies* (pp. 99–127). Longitudinal research in the social and behavioral sciences: An interdisciplinary series. New York: Plenum Press.

REFERENCES

Stewart, S.E., Manion, I.G., Davidson, S., & Cloutier, P. (2001). Suicidal children and adolescents with first emergency room presentations: Predictors of six-month outcome. *Journal of the American Academy of Child & Adolescent Psychiatry, 40, 580–587.*

Stoney, G. (1998). Suicide prevention and the Internet. In R. Kosky, H. Eshkevari, R. Goldney & R. Hassan (Eds.), *Suicide Prevention: The Global Context*. New York: Plenum Press.

Strosahl, K., Chiles, J.A., & Linehan, M. (1992). Prediction of suicide intent in hospitalized parasuicides: Reasons for living, hopelessness, and depression. *Comprehensive Psychiatry, 33,* 366–373.

Tabachnik, B.G., & Fidell, L.S. (1989). *Using multivariate statistics* (2nd Edition). New York: Harper & Row.

Tarrant, B., & Woon, A. (1995). Adolescent suicide: An overview. *Australian Journal of Emergency Care, 2,* 26–30.

Trautman, P., Rotheram-Borus, M.J., Dopkins, S., & Lewin, N. (1991). Psychiatric diagnoses in minority female adolescent suicide attempters. *Journal of the American Academy of Child and Adolescent Psychiatry, 30,* 617–622.

Tremblay, R.E., Masse, L.C., Vitaro, F., & Dobkin, P.L. (1995). The impact of friends' deviant behavior on early onset of delinquency: Longitudinal data from 6 to 13 years of age. *Development and Psychopathology, 7,* 649–667.

UNICEF (1993). *Progress of nations*. New York: UNICEF.

Wagner, B.M. (1997). Family risk factors for child and adolescent suicidal behaviour. *Psychological Bulletin, 121,* 246–298.

Walsh, A. (1991). Intellectual Imbalance, Love Deprivation and Violent Delinquency: a biosocial perspective. Springfield, Illinois: Charles C. Thomas Publishers.

Watt, T.T., & Sharp, S.F. (2001). Gender Differences in Strains Associated with Suicidal Behavior Among Adolescents. Journal of Youth and Adolescence, 30, 333–348.

Weiner, D.A., Abraham, M.E., & Lyons, J. (2001). Clinical Characteristics of Youths with Substance Use Problems and Implications for Residential Treatment. *Psychiatric Services, 52,* 793–799.

Westefeld, J.S., Cardin, D., & Deaton, W.L. (1992). Development of the college reasons for living inventory. *Suicide and Life Threatening Behavior, 22,* 442–452.

Wichstrom, L., & Rossow, I. (2002). Explaining the gender difference in self-reported suicide attempts: A nationally representative study of Norwegian adolescents. Suicide and Life-Threatening Behavior, *32,* 101–116.

Winokur, G. (1991). Epidemiology and genetics of depression and mania. In M. T. Tsuang (Ed.), K.S. Kendler (Ed.); et al. *Series in psychosocial epidemiology volume 8: Genetic issues in psychosocial epidemiology* (pp. 153–174). New Brunswick: Rutgers University Press.

Woods, E.R., Lin, Y.G., Middleman, A., Beckford, P., Chase, L., & DuRant, R.H. (1997). The associations of suicide attempts in adolescents. *Pediatrics, 99,* 791–796.

Wright, W.F., & Bower, G.H. (1992). Mood effects on subjective probability assessment. *Organizational Behavior and Human Decision Processes, 52,* 276–291.

Wunderlich, U., Bronisch, T., Wittchen, H.-U., & Carter, R. (2001). Gender differences in adolescents and young adults with suicidal behaviour. *Acta Psychiatrica Scandinavica, 104,* 332–339.

Yang, B., & Clum, G.A. (1996). Effects of early negative life experiences on cognitive functioning and risk for suicide: A review. *Clinical Psychology Review, 16,* 177–195.

Yerkes, R.M., & Dodson, J.D. (1908). The relation of strength of stimulus to rapidity of habit-formation. Journal of Comparative Neurology and Psychology, *18,* 459–482.

Zlotnick, C., Donaldson, D., Spirito, A., & Pearlstein, T. (1997). Affect regulation and suicide attempts in adolescent inpatients. *Journal of the American Academy of Child and Adolescent Psychiatry, 36,* 793–798.

Zubrick, S.R., Kosky, R., & Silburn, S. (1987). Is suicidal ideation associated with puberty? *Australian and New Zealand Journal of Psychiatry, 21,* 54–58.

Index

203

like 'alien Jews' had to be excluded from the British nation, while 'primitive blacks' had to be ruled by it. Indeed 'aliens' and 'blacks' provided the foil against which the British nation was defined.

A slightly different picture started to emerge with the decline of the British Empire. After the Second World War in particular, more and more territories fought for and won their independence, although most continued to be part of the Commonwealth and as such their citizens were still subjects of the Crown.

The all-inclusive legal definition of British nationality as created by the 1914 British Nationality Act (and reinforced by the twilight-of-Empire 1948 Act)[2] became less and less compatible with this new reality. For a while this contradiction was not particularly problematic for the British state. Postwar Britain, like most other industrialised countries, urgently needed cheap migrant labour for its expanding economy. Immigrants from the colonies and Commonwealth countries provided a major and convenient source for this labour power.

However, when it became clear that not only was Britain's economy starting to contract, but also that black Commonwealth immigrants were increasingly claiming their rights as British subjects to settle permanently in Britain, the shared legal status of black and white British subjects was rapidly removed. This was achieved through immigration legislation, whilst the increasingly tenuous myth of a common citizenship for black and white Britons was maintained by, for the time being, leaving British nationality legislation intact.

Successive governments in the 1960s passed a series of immigration Acts which progressively reduced the status of black British subjects to one which approximated that of 'aliens'. Under the explicitly racist principle of patriality, introduced by the 1971 Immigration Act, broadly speaking only those British subjects who were born in the British Isles and their descendants (that is basically white people) were entitled to settle in Britain.[3] The gap between British immigration and nationality legislation was finally closed by the 1981 Nationality Act which essentially linked the patriality principle to British nationality. Those British subjects not eligible, on grounds of birth or descent, for full British citizenship literally became second-class citizens. As British Dependent Territories Citizens or British Overseas Citizens they have no right whatsoever to live in Britain.[4]

Running in parallel with these developments has been the rise of a different kind of anti-black racism – that has come to be known as the 'new racism' (Barker 1981). This relies not so much on the view that black people are inferior but instead on the premise that different cultural groups simply do not mix. If the old variant, with its emphasis on the intellectual superiority of white people, acted as a suitable legitimation of imperial rule, the new brand provides the ideological justification for separation in the form of strict immigration controls (although there are still many fanatically racist and nationalist groups which peddle with crude notions of 'inferior stock').

In recent years this new brand of racism has appeared regularly – almost casually and in passing – as if it is just common sense. The *Daily Star*'s commentator Robert McNeill argued on 17 April 1984 that 'any fool knows . . . that the process which Darwin called natural selection means that, on the whole, people prefer their "ain folk" – their own ethnic stock', while feature writer Jill Tweedie wrote in the *Guardian* that 'so much is a kind of racism built into humanity that it could well be considered a primeval, possibly genetic, inheritance from our most distant ancestors, of whatever race or colour' (24 January 1984). Of course it was this kind of theme which Prime Minister Margaret Thatcher was developing when she said in a television interview in 1978 that 'People are really rather afraid that this country might be rather swamped by people with a different culture and . . . if there is any fear that it might be swamped people are going to react and be rather hostile to those coming in.'

In practical terms the 'new racism' has both fuelled and legitimised the most stringent immigration controls to date. At the last two general elections the government boasted that immigration was lower than at any time since controls for Commonwealth citizens were introduced in 1962; Tamil and Iranian refugees are regularly refused asylum; and, most recently, there is the new Immigration Bill which will remove the automatic right of women and children to join their husbands and fathers who immigrated to Britain before the 1971 Immigration Act was passed.

But for some advocates of the 'new racism' this is still not enough. However tight, immigration controls cannot stop black people already living here from having children. The only 'solution', from this point of view, is to make black people 'go home'. It is not only fascists who promote this view. Enoch Powell MP has done so for decades. Others on the far right of the Conservative Party, such as members of the Monday Club's Immigration and Race Relations Committee, have increasingly pushed for a policy of so-called 'voluntary repatriation' particularly in the context of inner city strife (Gordon & Klug 1986).

EUGENICS AND THE PATRIARCHAL NATION

Racist ideologies and in particular those based on pseudo-scientific notions of innate superiority, have been linked to the construction of gender relations. This link was particularly strong in Britain's imperial days and focused around the eugenicist notions of selective breeding and genetic inheritance. These were based on the supposed need, as leading eugenicist Prof. Karl Pearson put it, to create a 'reserve of brain and physique' (Fryer 1984: 181). Such ideas became increasingly influential around the turn of the century as the relatively poor British military performance in the Boer Wars brought fears of 'national inefficiency' and 'unhealthy stock'. Through this, public attention became focused on the destitute state in which the working class lived. Concern grew over the supposedly 'lowering effect' on 'British stock' of uncontrolled breeding by the working class. As middle and upper class families were more likely to have access to information on birth control, the eugenicists were concerned that they would be 'swamped' by the working class. The consequence, as they saw it, would be that Britain would eventually be unable to compete with other industrial powers and, worse still, would lose its eminence among nations.

To safeguard the health of the nation eugenicists gave women, or rather middle class women, a pivotal role. The elevation of motherhood was emphasised at the expense of women developing other skills. In a lecture on 'The Woman's Question' in 1885, for example, Pearson stated that 'Those nations which have been the most reproductive have, on the whole, been the ruling nations . . . if child-bearing women must be intellectually handicapped then the penalty to be paid for race-predominance is the subjection of women' (Semmel 1960: ch.2).

Given the central role allocated to women as physical reproducers of the nation by the prevailing ideology of the time, it is not surprising that nineteenth- and twentieth-century British nationality law was explicitly patriarchal. Firstly, women were only allowed to reproduce the British nation on behalf of their husbands. They could not pass on their nationality to their children in their own right. So if an unmarried British woman gave birth to a child outside the British Empire he or she would be born stateless. (But, for reasons already explained, any child born within the British Empire regardless of parentage, would automatically be a British subject.) Secondly, a woman's own nationality was determined by that of her husband. If she married an 'alien', that is a man without British subject status, she was defined 'out' of the British nation and was expected to take on the nationality of her spouse (in practice she could only do so if she married a man whose country's citizenship laws provided this facility). At the same time, a 'foreign' woman who married a British man automatically entered the fold – she did not have to go through a naturalisation process to become British.

The patriarchal nature of British nationality law was actually strengthened in the late nineteenth century. It was the 1870 Naturalisation Act which was the first to explicitly state that a British woman was deemed an 'alien' if her husband was not British (although generally speaking under Common Law such women tended to be treated as 'foreigners' anyway). Although suffragettes and feminists campaigned for this to be amended by the 1914 Nationality Act, the all-male parliament stood firm. In the words of Lewis Hardcourt, Secretary of State for the Colonies, to allow a woman to retain her own nationality 'when she deliberately marries an alien' would be 'departing from the practice of the whole civilized world . . . with the exception of Venezuela and Spain' (WING 1985: 14).

It was not until 1948 that women won the right to retain their nationality on marriage – three decades after women over 30 got the vote. And it was not until 1981 that they won the right to transfer their citizenship to their own children born abroad. In addition to eugenistic notions on the role of women, ideological factors similar to those which led to immigration control being introduced in Britain for the first time at the turn of the century helped to shape the patriarchal nature of British nationality law. As already noted, the common status conferred on all subjects of the Empire by the 1914 Act was to mark their incorporation into British rule. If there had to be coherence in the Empire all the more so in the family! Opponents of equality in nationality law argued that as men were the head of the family they must define its national identity. If a woman married 'out' then she automatically put herself outside the nation. Otherwise, so the argument ran, there could be anarchy with women claiming dual citizenship. If this were the case no clear demarcation would exist between those who did and those who did not owe loyalty to the British state and the Empire.

SOCIAL POLICY AND THE RISE AND FALL OF THE BRITISH BIRTH RATE

The question of the reproduction of the nation also had a profound effect on the development of social policy with regard to women and reproduction in this period. There was a school of eugenics, many fabian–socialists included, which argued that for the sake of the British nation the population *as a whole* needed boosting both in terms of quality and of quantity – and that programmes to encourage population growth should not be restricted to the middle and upper classes. Once again the role of women was crucial in this scheme. In the fabian tract of 1907, for example, fabian leader Sidney Webb argued for the 'endowment of motherhood' – that is, financial recognition by the state that child-bearing was for the national good.

This era saw the dawning of what came to be known as the welfare state. The 1906 Liberal government introduced a series of new social reforms (Fraser 1975). In addition to a genuinely held Liberal commitment to boosting the living standards of the poor, the state was concerned to improve the physical well-being of the population as a whole to make the British people fit defenders of the Empire. At the same time 'aliens' were to be denied access to these new benefits. Under major pieces of legislation introduced around the turn of the century eligibility for welfare depended upon immigration status (Cohen 1985). Among the new reforms were policies aimed at encouraging women to breed and at improving the health of their offspring, such as the introduction of maternity insurance, health visitors and child welfare.

At the same time what amounted to a national panic set in over the declining British birth rate, particularly after the First World War. It began to fall from the late 1870s onwards and by 1933 it was at its lowest point yet. Demographic experts were predicting that the time was approaching when the British population would be down to 16 million. The extent of the anxiety around this related to Britain's continued imperial role. In 1935 Prime Minister Neville Chamberlain warned that the time would come when 'the British Empire will be crying out for more citizens of the right breed and when we in this country shall not be able to supply the demand' (Rowbotham 1973: p. 144).

Books like *The Twilight of Parenthood* and *The Menace of British Depopulation* predicted national decline. In 1944, in an essay entitled 'The English People', George Orwell lamented the fact that 'Britain today has a million and a half fewer children than in 1914' and advocated a more graduated system of taxation 'to encourage child bearing and to save young children from being obliged to work outside the home' (Riley 1981: 89). Such views were typical of those to be found in a range of periodicals, books and speeches of the time.

In 1943 the issue of how to reverse the decline in the national birth rate was discussed in both Houses of Parliament. Methods proposed ranged from elevating the status of motherhood in a generalised way to providing financial and social inducement to make child-rearing less onerous. Finally in 1944 a Royal Commission on Population was set up.

It took five years for the Commission to report. By this time there had in fact been a reverse in the trend and the birth rate increased substantially from 1941 onwards. This was noted by the Commission but it nevertheless warned that if this was not maintained the population would seriously decline. This in turn threatened Britain's imperial rule, its wealth and the future development of the world.

> The growth of population in Great Britain was in fact an essential condition not only of the development of Britain itself, but also of the growth of the new overseas countries inhabited mainly or largely by people of British descent, and of the spread of British culture and influence all over the world through emigrants, commerce and capital investment. (Royal Commission on Population 1949: ch.2)

The solution advocated by the Commission to avoid the impending doom of a declining British population was the creation of social conditions which would allow the instinctive desire for a family to be sufficiently met. These ranged from income tax relief to more nursery provision, from improved house design to increased access to labour-saving devices.

Similar proposals and more were contained in the 1942 Beveridge Report which heralded the introduction of the modern welfare state. Again eugenicist notions provided the context for some of the policies advocated. Children's Allowances (now Child Benefit) were recommended not only to guarantee a minimum income and to ensure that unemployment benefit did not exceed the earnings of those in work, but to encourage population growth:

> With its present rate of reproduction, the British race cannot continue: means of reversing the recent course of the birthrate must be found . . . children's allowances can help to restore the birthrate, both by making it possible for parents who desire more children to bring them into the world without damaging the chances of those already born, and as a signal of the national

interest in children, setting the tone of public opinion. (Beveridge 1942: 154)

The Family Allowances Act was passed by the 1945 coalition government. Benefit was paid directly to the mother on the birth of her second child. A survey of hospital patients in 1946 found that nearly all the women interviewed believed that family allowances had been introduced to boost the birth rate rather than to alleviate their hardships (Riley 1981: 94).

One possible 'solution' to the so-called 'population problem' that was firmly ruled out by the British state was encouraging immigration to Britain by the non-Anglo-Saxon inhabitants of the British colonies. This was in spite of the fact that official concern about population *growth* in some of the colonies was being expressed at this time. A 1945 Royal Commission on social conditions in the West Indies recommended the establishment of birth control clinics and there was growing support among British administrators in India for measures to curb the birth rate (Smith 1973).

The crudest of eugenicist reasons were used to rule out immigration to Britain to boost the British population. The 1949 Royal Commission on Population declared that such immigration would:

Involve serious problems of assimilation beyond those of training and housing. Immigration on a large scale into a fully established society like ours could only be welcomed without reserve if the immigrants were of good human stock and were not prevented by their religion or race from intermarrying with the host population and becoming merged in it . . . there is little or no prospect that we should be able to apply these conditions to large scale immigration in the future. (Royal Commission on Population 1949: ch.2)

THE BABY BOOM AND RACIST POPULATION CONTROLS

After the decline in the birth rate had reached its peak in 1933, there was a rapid rise from 1941 onwards culminating in the 'baby boom' of the mid-1950s to the mid-1960s. In 1976 it was projected by the government's actuary department that the UK population would increase by a further 15 million by the year 2000, to reach over 70 million. This led to a flurry of activity in official quarters. The Labour government under Harold Wilson set up an unpublicised committee of senior civil servants to advise the government on how to control

Britain's population growth. There were plans afoot to establish a central population unit in the Cabinet Ofice, but Labour lost power to the Tories before this could be implemented. Then in response to a resolution signed by more than 300 MPs, the new Select Committee on Science and Technology initiated an enquiry into population growth, which reported in 1971.

While the prime focus of the national attention on population growth may well have been the future *size* of British population, it is clear that concerns about the *composition* of that population were also pronounced. The cruder aspects of eugenics were completely discredited by the social democratic consensus which dominated the British state in the 1960s and 1970s. But, although largely unacknowledged, such ideas clearly lay behind the development of immigration controls to curb the entry of black British subjects to the UK in those decades.

The justification given by successive governments for this legislation was population growth. The problem, so the argument ran, was not one of inferior stock or even of cultural incompatibility but of too many people competing for too few resources in an overcrowded island. This was frequently the kind of position adopted by Labour Party leaders in the 1960s and 1970s. It was not that they themselves were racist, they would protest. They were opposed to racial discrimination and passed laws against it. They were simply responding to the will and anxieties of the people! In 1967 Prime Minister Harold Wilson approached former Tory minister David Renton about studies that the Labour government had initiated into the policy implications of an increased population. He wrote in a letter: 'if any of these implications appeared to be intolerable we could then consider what needed to be done' (Select Committee on Science and Technology 1971). The following year the Labour government introduced the 1968 Commonwealth Immigrants Act to stop British Asians living in East Africa from being automatically entitled to come to Britain. The Act was passed amidst fears that large numbers of British Asians were on the point of taking up their right to live in the UK, due to expulsions and persecution in some East African countries. It did not prevent *all* immigration – only immigration by those without British *ancestry*.

Again the 1971 Immigration Act was introduced by Edward Heath's Conservative government in the same year that the Select Committee on Population Policy produced its first report. Among other things it noted that 'the fertility rate of the immigrants in this country is . . . slightly higher than the British characteristic average'. It urged the government to 'act to prevent the consequences of population growth becoming intolerable for the every day conditions of life', and proposed that a special government office be set up to study and advise on population policy. Among its remit would be 'internal and external migration and consequences' (Select Committee on Science and Technology 1971). The all-party committee was very disappointed when the government refused to act on its recommendation to set up a permanent office. But the new Immigration Act showed that the government was indeed concerned to curb population growth, not by the population as a whole, but by 'non-patrials', i.e. black UK citizens. The year after the new Act was passed the same government took Britain into the EEC, opening the door to whoever wished to seek work in the UK – provided they were European![5]

The drift of post-1971 immigration policy has been almost entirely devoted to separating black families so as to keep the size of the black British population tightly controlled. This has chiefly been achieved by constructing women as wives and mothers or 'dependants', much as in pre-1981 nationality legislation. Whilst, until recently, theoretically entitled to follow their husbands wherever they may live (a right much more easily exercised if their husbands happen to be white), women – including those born in the UK – have not even been given a paper right to bring over foreign-born husbands to live with them.[6] Legally defined as 'dependants', they of course cannot be married and bring over 'dependants' of their own. As former Home Secretary William Whitelaw put it in a speech to the Central Council of the Conservative Party in 1978: 'it surely cannot be unreasonable to argue that in accordance with the customs of Europe and the Indian subcontinent, the abode of the husband in a marriage should normally be viewed as the natural place of residence of the family' (speech distributed by the Conservative central office).

In practice this policy has been used almost exclusively to prevent *black* women from bringing over husbands from abroad and, in particular, to prevent Asian women from engaging in 'arranged marriages' with men from the Indian sub-continent. Even where the Home Office acknowledges a marriage is 'genuine', the couple have to have met before the marriage and 'prove' that the 'primary purpose' of their marriage was not immigration, before they are allowed to settle in Britain.

When the European Court ruled in 1985 that British immigration law discriminated against women, the government responded to this binding judgement by reducing the rights of men to those of women. Had they not done this, of course, more black families would have been united with the concomitant growth in the black population of Britain.

The 1970s was also the period in which the government started to collect statistics to gauge the size of the black, rather than just the immigrant, population. A question on the birthplace of respondents has been asked since the 1841 census. But in 1971 a question was introduced to the census on birthplace of parents to estimate the number of people from the 'New Commonwealth' (that is, all Commonwealth countries *excluding* Australia, Canada and New Zealand) living in Britain, including those who were themselves born in the UK.[7] Two years previously the birthplace of parents started to be recorded on birth certificates for the first time and the birthplace of the deceased was marked on death certificates. By combining all this information, together with figures on net immigration, the government is able to produce annual published estimates of the 'New Commonwealth' population as well as figures of the 'New Commonwealth' birth rate. Successive governments have justified counting the black population of Britain on the grounds that it is necessary for devising social policies to deal with the discrimination and 'disadvantage' they face. But it is difficult not to share the scepticism of black groups who ask how many times they need to be counted before such policies are forthcoming. However sincere those in the 'liberal lobby' may be in insisting that such statistics are put to beneficial use, their significance is not lost on sections of the media or some Tory MPs. For them these statistics are a way of gauging the British stock – a means of assessing what proportion of the British population is black and what proportion is 'truly British'. Articles in the press reflect this preoccupation. And not just the 'popular' press: 'immigrant mothers lead baby league' was the headline of an article in *The Times* (14 September 1985) following publication of the latest statistics on births to parents from the 'New Commonwealth'. 'More than half the births in four London boroughs last year were to mothers born outside the UK', the story read. Likewise Tory MPs such as Tony Marlow (and the now deposed Harvey Proctor) have used the opportunity of the annual head-count of the black population to publicise dire warnings about the future awaiting Britain. 'This country is being progressively colonised', Marlow stated on one such occasion. 'It is a peaceful invasion but one which threatens to destroy our heritage and our traditions' (*Daily Mail*, 9 April 1982).

The preoccupation with *who* comes in has also affected eligibility for benefits under the modern welfare state, much as in the early part of this century. As discussed earlier, one of the main factors involved in shaping British social policy has been the production of a physically fit nation capable of carrying out its responsibilities in the world. The belief that the health of the nation equals the wealth of the nation is now so widely accepted as to be unquestioned. And hand in hand with this assumption has been the conviction that the benefits of the welfare state are for the British only – foreigners keep out!

In fact when the postwar welfare state was first created mere presence in the UK was sufficient for entitlement to national assistance and to health treatment. But this soon changed. Following parliamentary pressure the 1949 National Health Service Act empowered the Minister of Health to make regulations to exclude from free treatment people who were not 'ordinarily resident' in the UK. Numerous government circulars were issued over the years underlining who was ineligible for free care until regulations tying hospital treatment under the NHS to residency tests were enacted in 1982.

Under the 1971 Immigration Act, all non-patrial 'dependants' seeking admission had to prove that they would not have 'recourse to public funds'.[8] Now 'dependants' who are not British citizens are placed in the same situation. Under the 1980 Social Security Act 'sponsors' can be charged with a criminal offence if they refuse to maintain a 'dependant' relative whom they have brought over. There is no time limit, in theory at least, on this liability. Whether they come for a short period or are permanent residents, non-naturalised 'dependants' are deemed second-class citizens, ineligible for the benefits they pay for in taxes. Under the new Tory Immigration Bill these restrictions will be extended to apply to the 'dependants' of those who settled in the UK *before* the 1971 Immigration Act was introduced in 1973. Families who have been divided for years, often because of delays and obstacles in immigration procedures, will now remain divided because the original settler, who will have been paying taxes for 15 years or more, will be forced to maintain and accommodate the entire family without access to public funds or state housing.

It must be said, however, that although successive British governments have engineered a wide range of social and immigration policies in an attempt to get the 'population mix' right, they have never interfered *directly* in the national birth rate. In a Council of Europe paper published in 1981, Britain was one of 12 countries which was described as having no policy of direct intervention in the national fertility rate.[9] While there were prosecutions of birth control advocates in the late nineteenth and early twentieth centuries, birth control itself has never been strictly illegal in Britain. Similarly, although family allowances, along with other social policies, were partly introduced to render child-bearing less burdensome and thereby increase the birth rate, modern child benefits were *not* withdrawn in the period when fears of a population explosion were at their greatest.

It could be argued that the introduction in 1967 of widely available contraceptive advice and of abortion on 'social' as well as medical grounds did come about when concern over population growth was at its peak. The official rationale for introducing such measures was to increase the choice of the individual. Given the extent of popular support for contraception and abortion, this probably was the major factor involved. The attention paid to the birth rate at the time was arguably no more than an additional conducive factor.

Testimonies from black women, however, have provided disturbing evidence that they receive greater encouragement from some sections of the National Service to have abortions or sterilisation in the face of unplanned pregnancies than white women do. This issue became sufficiently significant to split the National Abortion Campaign in 1983. The Reproductive Rights Campaign was formed to reflect the fact that for all women to have 'the right to choose' how to control their own fertility there needed to be a movement which catered for the conflicting pressures faced by black and white women. If white women argued that they were denied the freedom of choice *not* to breed, too often black women complained that they were prevented from deciding *to have* children when they wished to (Bryan *et al.* 1985: 100–10).

Similarly, it has been alleged that Asian women, in particular, have been more liable to receive the injectable contraceptive, Depo Provera, than white women. This is a particularly reliable form of birth control but one whose attendant health risks are said by some contraceptive specialists to be very high.[10] This is not to imply that there is a eugenicist-inspired state conspiracy to prevent black women from having children. It is to suggest that the official attention paid to the black birth rate, even though it is alleged to be for purely benign reasons, has permeated into the general consciousness. As a result it seems that some medical workers act out of their own initiative to encourage black women to terminate unplanned pregnancies and to use any method available to avoid them in the future. In some cases, no doubt, there are health workers who do not even require the state to encourage them to take preemptive action to control the black birth rate.

CONCLUSIONS

In the construction of the modern British nation the role of women has been crucial. As it is assumed that nationality is something transmitted by birth, it is women, of course, who physically reproduce the nation, as any strategy for limiting the boundaries of a nation to a particular people has recognised. However, in spite of periodic panics over projections of a declining or exploding British population – for example, in the 1930s or 1960s – there has been no concerted state plan to directly control the birth rate (although there has been evidence of independent coercion by health workers on black women to control their fertility). Neither has a policy of repatriation been introduced in modern Britian, although there have been cases of this in the past,[11] and the threat that the government will be pushed down this path by pressure from the far right, in and outside the Tory party, has never disappeared.

At the same time – drawing on the persisting myth of a continuous lineage of white Anglo-Saxons with exclusive rights to the benefits of Britain – the British Isles *have* been largely reserved for the white British, with black Britons and those defined as 'aliens' kept out. This has mainly been achieved through a deliberate immigration policy pursued by successive British governments.[12] Policies implemented for a variety of purposes, such as the introduction of family allowances, have also contributed by helping to boost the quality and quantity of white Britons. Whilst it is always possible to invent conspiracy theories, there are historical developments which occur through deliberate state planning. Keeping Britain for the white British has been one of them!

And what of the future? If the majority grouping within the state continues to see Britain's best interests as lying within the EEC – and the current trend of British capitalism suggests they will – then the British national identity, which the right in particular tenaciously hangs on to, may gradually be superceded by a European one. The freedom of movement granted to European workers in the early 1970s, compared with the barriers put in the way of non-patrial British workers, marked the possible beginning of this process. The introduction of a European passport, bitterly resented by the far right, may prove to be the next. From an internationalist perspective the move from narrow Englander to pan-Europeanism may well act to offset the most inward-looking aspects of traditional British nationalism. But there is no guarantee that some of the crudest racist and eugenicist notions will be relinquished in this development, nor that policies to encourage women to reproduce will fade into history. In April 1984 the European Parliament called for 'concerted action' to reverse the 'drastic decline' of the Community's birth rate. The parliament was told that the population of the member states would drop from 8.8 per cent of the world's total in 1950 to 4.5 per cent by the year 2000, and a presidency paper on the subject warned: 'a nation without enough children would be a sad nation. The same applies to Europe as a whole' (*Guardian*, 13 April 1984). With some European countries, notably France and Germany, expelling their 'guest workers' as unemployment sets in, there is little reason to hope that any European nation of the future will be less racist than the British nation of the past.

NOTES

1. Legally speaking the category of British citizen was not created until the 1981 British Nationality Act came into force in 1983. Until then the term 'British subject' was used to denote roughly what we now understand by British citizen.
2. Under this Act, passed by the postwar Labour government, all citizens of Commonwealth countries, whether independent or not, continued to be 'British subjects'. As such they, along with Irish citizens, were not subject to British immigration control (until 1962) and were granted full civic rights if resident in Britain. Broadly speaking, those born in independent ex-colonies also became citizens of their new countries, whilst those born in Britain and any of the remaining colonies became citizens of the UK and colonies.
3. Patrials were *either* UK citizens who were born or adopted or registered or naturalised or resident for five years or more in the UK *or else* they were Commonwealth citizens with a British-born parent *or* a Commonwealth wife of a patrial man. Under the Immigration Rules for administering the Act, Commonwealth citizens with a British-born grandparent

were, and are, also entitled to live in the UK indefinitely. Clearly unless a black UK citizen was actually born in Britain or had lived there for more than five years, they were unlikely to be patrial whereas few white Commonwealth citizens, whether or not born or living in Britain and whether or not UK citizens, were unlikely to be 'caught out' by the patriality clause because of their ancestry.

4. BDTCs are only entitled to live in the colony they already inhabit. BOCs, mainly Asians living in East Africa, are not *entitled* to live anywhere, as a result of this status, and have to queue for discretionary vouchers to live in the UK.

5. Under EEC law nationals of other EEC member states are granted a residence permit provided they find work in the UK within six months.

6. Although wives of men settled here have had an entitlement to join them which has been denied to husbands and women settled here, in practice thousands of wives and children have been refused entry each year since 1973. A paper given by Home Office civil servants in 1983, leaked to the *Guardian* in April 1985, revealed that long queues for entry to Britain by families in the Indian sub-continent are maintained as the 'primary regulator' of immigration from that part of the world.

7. In the 1981 census this question was altered to 'birthplace of head of household'. Using statistical formulae the black population as a whole is calculated on this basis.

8. Unless they were the wives or minor children of Commonwealth men settled in the UK before the 1971 Act came into force, in which case they had an absolute right of entry.

9. The member states which were reported to have interventionist fertility policies were France, Greece, Liechtenstein and Luxembourg. Out of 20 states, nine expressed concern over their country's birth rate because they considered it to be too low.

10. A report by obstetrician Wendy Savage, 'The Use of Dep Provera in East London' in *Fertility and Contraception*, vol. 12, no. 3 (July 1978), showed that this contraceptive is administered in hospitals with a large proportion of Asian women patients. It did not conclusively demonstrate, therefore, that Asian women are generally more likely to be given Depo Provera and, to my knowledge, no such study has yet been conducted.

11. *Examples* include the expulsion of all Jews from England in 1290; the removal of some 'Black Moors' from Elizabethan England; legislation permitting the deportation of destitute Indian seamen in the 1890s, despite their British subject status; and the repatriation of hundreds of black people following the 1919 anti-black riots in Liverpool and Cardiff.

12. This is despite the fact that the demographic estimates of the late 1960s have proved to be grossly exaggerated. The UK population is expected to rise by less than a million by the end of the century. There was almost no population growth between 1971 and 1981 with the birth rate reaching a new low in 1977. Moreover, it is predicted that the annual net outflow of people from the UK will be 31 000 on average until the

end of the century (Hubbak 1983). This is in keeping with the past. Other than in the late 1950s and early 1960s emigration has exceeded immigration to Britain virtually every year since British settlers started migrating to the colonies from the 1820s onwards.

BIBLIOGRAPHY

Barker, Martin (1981) *The New Racism: Conservatives and the Ideology of the Tribe* (London: Junction Books).
Beveridge, William (1942) *Social Insurance and Allied Services*, CMND 4606 (London: HMSO).
Bryan, B., S. Dudzi & S. Scafe (1985) *The Heart of the Race: Black Women's Lives in Britain* (London: Virago).
Cohen, Steve (1985) 'Anti-semitism, Immigration Controls and the Welfare State', *Critical Social Policy* (Summer).
Council of Europe (1981) *Population Policies in the Member States of the Council of Europe*, CDDE (81) 6.
Dale, Jenny & Peggy Foster (1986) *Feminists and State Welfare* (London: Routledge & Kegan Paul), 73–92.
Davin, Anna (1978) 'Immigration and Motherhood', *History Workshop*, 9–52.
Fraser, D. (1975) *The Evolution of the British Welfare State* (London: Macmillan).
Fryer, Peter (1984) *Staying Power: the History of Black People in Britain* (London: Pluto).
Gordon, Paul & Francesca Klug (1986) *New Right, New Racism* (London: Searchlight).
Gordon, Paul & Anne Newnham (1985) *Passport to Benefits: Racism in Social Security* (London: Runnymede Trust/CPAG).
Hubbak, David (1983) *Population Trends in Great Britain* (London: Simon Population Trust/Policy Studies Institute).
Nairn, Tom (1977) *The Break up of Britain* (London: Verso).
Riley, Denise (1981) 'The Free Mothers: Pronatalism and Working Mothers in Industry at the End of the Last War in Britain', *History Workshop*, 11 (Spring).
Rowbotham, Sheila (1973) *Hidden from History* (London: Pluto).
Royal Commission on Population (1949) *Report*, CMND 7695 (London: HMSO).
Select Committee on Science and Technology (1971) *Population of the UK*, H.C. 379 (London: HMSO).
Semmel, Bernard (1960) *Immigration and Social Reform: English Social Imperial Thought 1895–1914* (London: George Allen & Unwin).
Smith, T.D. (1973) *The Politics of Family Planning in the Third World* (London: Allen & Unwin).

West Indian Royal Commission (1945) *Report*, CMND 6607 (London: HMSO).

Whitelaw, W. (1988) *Speech to the Central Council of the Conservative Party* (Conservative Central Office).

WING – Women, Immigration and Nationality Group (1985) *Worlds Apart: Women under Immigration and Nationality Law* (London: Pluto).

3 Women, Nation and the State in Australia
Marie de Lepervanche

INTRODUCTION

In Australia's multi-cultural society of the 1980s both state and federal legislation outlaws race and gender discrimination. Even so, Australia's major political, legal and educational institutions, as well as many social customs, are derived from British liberal democratic models which privilege British over non-British and male over female. Women also remain affected by the class structure and ethnic/racial mix present-day Australia and by the legacy of social practices that had their origin in the formation of a 'white' Australian nation. In the move towards federation of the colonies, accomplished in 1901, racist practices against Aboriginals, Asian and Melanesian immigrants, legitimated by 'scientific' notions of biological differences, helped weld the 'white' nation. Only in the 1970s was the 'white' Australia policy finally abandoned, together with the abandonment of a policy which had enjoined immigrants and Aboriginals to assimilate to Anglo conformity. Since 1973 public policy has emphasised the celebration of ethnicity, yet despite the multi-cultural rhetoric some nationalisms are more acceptable than others.

The chapter is going to look at the history of ethnic/racial divisions in Australia as have been constructed by the Australian state, and at the specific roles women played in these processes. In particular it is going to look at women as the 'breeders of the white race'.

EARLY ETHNIC/RACIAL DIVISIONS

From the days of first white settlement until the end of the Second World War the ethnic composition of the white population was always heavily Anglo-Celtic. Even so, colonial settlers were often troubled by race differences which set whites apart from the indigenous Aboriginals in the first place and later from Indian indentured labourers, Chinese gold diggers, Afghan cameleers and Melanesian

36

cane workers. By the end of the last century Australians had clearly distinguished themselves and the acceptable white Europeans from undesirable (predominantly Mediterranean) Europeans and non-Europeans. Yet, even among the British, class, ethnic and gender divisions affected people's lives differently. From colonial times until comparatively recently a distinct cultural division between Protestant British and (Irish) Roman Catholic coloured Australian social life. In the nineteenth century the Catholic Irish working class component of the population contributed substantially to the development of the Australian Labour movement, while the colonial establishments remained attached to all things British and Protestant. But, despite their 'ethnic' disadvantages, Irish Catholics were never excluded from Australian society as much as Aboriginals and Asian immigrants were. White settlement deprived the Aboriginal people of their land, and colonial, state and federal legislation restricted their residence, their right to vote, their employment, freedom of movement, their marriages and the custody, care and education of their children. While white British settlers were encouraged to establish their families and populate the land, Aboriginal family life was disrupted or destroyed. Legislation concerning 'half castes' even determined who was and was not Aboriginal and who did and did not receive pensions. Only during the 1960s were Aboriginals enfranchised and counted in the federal census. Although modified land rights and anti-discrimination legislation exists today, the extent of white racism can be gauged by the continuing high rates of Aboriginal infant and child mortality, in their shorter life expectancy, their high unemployment figures, poor health and educational disadvantages and in their over-representation in prison statistics. The contact experience for Aboriginal women also included sexual as well as other forms of exploitation by whites (Grimshaw 1981).

Asians and Melanesians were introduced to the colonies in the last century as indentured labour for pastoral and plantation properties. After gold was discovered in the 1850s, free Chinese also arrived and competition for gold brought hostile reactions from Europeans. These Asian and Island immigrations were predominantly male. Not only were whites frightened that the 'lower races' might breed if coloured women entered but, as Saunders comments, those Pacific Island women who did enter, and whose menfolk provided the Kanaka (indentured Melanesian) labour in Queensland's sugar fields, were not themselves acceptable initially as indentured servants 'because their reproductive capacities could endanger the whole structure of an easily replaceable, fluid, servile labour force' (1982: 32). Colonial and later state legislation inhibited Asian settlement and activity, and with federation in 1901 the Immigration Restriction Act (otherwise known as the 'white' Australian policy) was passed, which impeded Asian immigration until the 1960s.

Before the Second World War a number of northern and Mediterranean Europeans had established the nucleus of later 'ethnic' settlements. Even so, their entry was restricted during the 1920s and some southern Europeans were even categorised as non-white (Evans *et al.* 1975: 6). During the 1930s, refugees from Hitler were also regarded with suspicion, especially by trade unionists. Many pre-war immigrant men started small businesses and their wives and daughters, if present, usually contributed to the family enterprise, although their labour was frequently unpaid (Martin 1984).

IMMIGRANT ETHNIC AND GENDER VARIETY

Immediately after the Second World War immigrant programmes were explicitly linked with measures to exclude the 'yellow hordes' to the north and to maintain the white British character of the 'race' within. The Pacific war had increased anxieties about defence and, together with a need for labour power, this prompted the massive postwar immigration programme. Compared with the pre-war predominantly male immigrations, the postwar programme favoured a more balanced sex ratio, and the newcomers were expected to enter the urban industrial labour force rather than agricultural work.

By the 1960s the British emphasis had become diluted as the demand for labourers forced Australia to seek immigrants from non-British and eventually non-European sources. The 'white' Australia policy was liberalised to permit the entry of professionally or technically qualified Asians and their dependants. But unlike New Commonwealth immigrants in the UK who have entered the industrial working class, the postwar Asian settlers have tended to occupy petit bourgeois or middle class positions and do not constitute 'problems', although in recent years some racist hostility has erupted againt Vietnamese refugees, many of whom hold working class jobs.

By the 1980s Australia had received more than 3 million immigrants from more than 60 nations. Only in Israel has immigration had a greater relative impact on the composition of the population, workforce and social life in general (Collins 1984: 8). In 1947 most

Australians in the workforce were Anglo-Celtic and male: only one-fifth of the total workforce was female. By 1981, 37 per cent of employed persons were female and the workforce in general was more immigrant in origin and less Anglophone (Collins 1984: 11).

Among OECD (Organisation for Economic Co-operation and Development) nations Australia has one of the most sex-segregated labour markets by occupation and superimposed on these divisions are differences of ethnic origin: ideologies of sexism and racism sustain these distinctions (Power 1975). In 1971 where 55.9 per cent of Greek-born and 54.7 per cent of Yugoslavian-born women were employed as process workers and labourers, only 9.3 per cent of Australian-born women were. In 1984 63 per cent of female employees were concentrated in clerical, sales and service occupations: others (and particularly Mediterraneans) were in manufacturing jobs (Collins 1984). This kind of ethnic and sex segmentation disadvantages immigrant women particularly: their conditions are poor, their health suffers and they are liable to stereotyping as 'naturally' stupid and suited to boring, repetitive work.

Postwar immigration to Australia was initially accompanied by the publicly sanctioned policy of assimilation to Anglo conformity, in force until the early 1970s even after Australia had begun to recruit labour from the Middle East and Asia. As late as 1968 the Minister for Immigration was quoted as saying 'We must have a single culture.'

For a while the non-British were referred to as 'national groups' but during the 1970s they became transformed into 'ethnic groups' after Labour came to power in 1973 and multi-culturalism became government policy. Behind this acceptance of cultural variety there was, first, the settlement of more non-British than ever before in Australian history. Second, many of these newcomers had begun to demand a voice in social affairs, had the vote and were critical of assimilation policy. Third, a number of Australians shared these sentiments and were increasingly critical of some problems immigrant assimilation entailed; and a poverty survey of Melbourne had shown that 16.2 per cent of Greeks and 15.3 per cent of Italians were below the poverty line compared with 7.7 per cent of the total population who were below this income level. By the mid-1970s public response had apparently undergone a complete metamorphosis: the new emphasis was on cultural diversity. Newcomers were invited to celebrate their ethnicity and the rhetoric of assimilation was formally abandoned (cf. de Lepervanche 1980).

CITIZENS, PERMANENT RESIDENTS AND FAMILY REUNIONS

Australia does not sanction the introduction of guest workers. Immigrants are expected to apply for permanent residence and eventually become citizens. In 1948 the Nationality and Citizenship Act first defined Australian citizenship; before then Australians were British subjects, like others in the Commonwealth. Amendments to the Citizenship Act in 1973 removed some of the anomalies with respect to citizenship which had previously discriminated against non-European British subjects, and in that year non-European immigrants first became eligible for assisted passages which had previously been available only to white British and some selected European settlers.

To produce citizens, the family reunion provisions have constituted important planks of immigration policy. Initally defined in 1947 to include extended family members, the term 'family reunion' has since contracted and expanded in meaning. When assimilation ideology gave way to multi-culturalism in the 1970s, for example, the ideal family was the nuclear mode, and working immigrant women often 'failed' to conform. After ethnic pressure for liberalising family reunion provisions, concessions were made in 1982 with respect to adult brothers and sisters and adult children, although new guidelines in July 1985 stressed the *immediate* family (spouses, dependent children and aged parents) rather than the extended unit. Special provisions are available for introducing fiancé(e)s.

The stress on women as producers of families goes back a long way, despite a number of nineteenth-century male immigrations. The first assisted immigrants to this country were 50 women from Cork who arrived in 1831. They were expected to:

> exert a sobering influence over the moral debauchery held to be rampant in the colony as a result of the excess of single men; they were to become the wives of labouring men and the mothers of their children and they were to provide menial domestic (later factory) labour in the homes and industries of the colonial elite . . . [Later] preference in assistance was given to young married couples, their children and to single women between eighteen and thirty years who came to the colony under the protection of a married couple. Thus, the ideal female immigrant had . . . to . . .

be *dependent* on the patronage of some form of male-headed household. (Martin 1984: 109)

Some women have migrated independently, but since 1945 most women and especially non-English-speaking female settlers have been dependants of men. In official eyes they have been expected to establish and/or maintain family units and relations in the interests of anchoring their male compatriots emotionally, and to provide consumption units for Australia's expanding capitalism. But their experiences in this country do not conform neatly to the planners' tidy sexual division of labour. Among new female arrivals, workforce participation high, between 50 per cent and 85 per cent in the decade 1970–80 (Martin 1984: 112). Without the customary support of kin and neighbours available in their homelands, many of these women see their lives torn between jobs and children. Together with Australian-born women, they are also the victims of grossly inadequate childcare.

Some of the (male) experts on the family in the 1960s saw immigrants, and especially women, as 'problems' because their supposed seclusion within family life impeded their assimilation. Others feared that children of working mothers were disadvantaged, although one expert considered a more liberal resolution to the contradictions women experienced: 'We must beware of drawing false conclusions about the results of . . . employment on the home life and upbringing of immigrant children . . . many wives assist . . . in running a cafe or small store . . . they are therefore "at home" when the children return from school' (Price 1966: 18–19).

As Martin has noted, most analyses of immigration tend to see production as male enterprise and consumption and population growth within the family as female responsibilities. Thus the 'ideological division of our world into masculine and feminine spheres, corresponding to a production/consumption split, is reproduced in migration policy and has governed female migration to Australia' (1984: 111). This ideological divide has indeed been a fundamental tenet of white Anglo male hegemony in Australia, and the social construction of women as dependent breeders has been oppressive for all women. But for those immigrant women who have endured extreme exploitation in their paid work, as well as subordination in the domestic sphere, the oppression has been particularly acute. Yet these kinds of variation in women's experience are not always recognised. In more ways than one, women tend to be severely stereotyped in male discourse or absent from it altogether as the following material illustrates.

BREEDERS OF THE WHITE RACE

The traditional sexual division of labour in the domestic sphere and workplace has been continually sanctioned in portrayals of the Australian way of life and national character, which have invariably been by white men. Until well into the 1950s the 'typical Australian' was a white man with British forbears; he came from the bush and practised mateship. A second type of Australian identity emerged in the 1960s: although still male, Anglo-Celtic and white, he was no longer from the bush but thoroughly middle class and suburban. By the 1970s when we were urged by the state to celebrate the different ethnic backgrounds of postwar immigrants, the Australian national character transformed into a number of versions. One was multicultural and supposedly sophisticated, while another remained distinctly 'ocker' and male (cf. Oxley 1979: 193). Throughout this literature, if women did appear they were white, English speakers associated with domestic life where they remained rather dumb, even dangerous, greedy or distracting the men from carrying out their important tasks (cf. Horne 1972: 193; Conway 1978: 25).

Without the vote until 1902, women were conspicuously absent from parliamentary decision-making at federation; they were in 'the home' as objects of 'protection', particularly from those not eligible for inclusion in the new nation, namely the male non-white immigrants from Asia and the Pacific who were permitted domicile or eventually excluded by the 'white' Australia policy. According to clergymen, politicians and journalists, the black and yellow men had posed a threat to virtuous white women. As the *Queensland Evangelical Standard* put it in 1876:

> The Asiatics were not children but savages, with irrepressible savage natures of a kind most dangerous to the safety of unprotected females . . . What happiness can any poor foolish country woman of ours expect from uniting in marriage with soft, pulpy, childish but passionate kanaka or the lithe, yellow-skinned mummy of the Celestial Empire? (quoted in Evans *et al*. 1975: 262)

The Asiatic 'threat' was not the only one: the Australian birth-rate fell from 38 per 1000 to 27 per 1000 in 1900, which caused alarm in government circles as policy was geared to increasing the country's (white) population. Explanations for the falling birth-rate included the use of contraceptives which were allegedly contributing to 'race suicide'. In New South Wales a report by the Commonwealth Statistician noted that the limitation of family size was a selfish and decadent phenomenon. The advertising of contraceptives was made illegal (McQueen 1978: 60). One of the Birth Rate Commissioners in 1903 labelled the women's rights movements a 'formidable adversary to fecundity' (quoted in Bacchi 1980: 148), and a lecturer in physiology at Melbourne University, attacking the emancipation of women for the decline in the birth rate concluded, in his presidential address to the Australasian Association for the Advancement of Science in 1901:

> The propagation of the Anglo-Saxon race has been placed largely under voluntary control, owing to the education of women. The extent to which this control is resorted to may determine the fate of the Empire . . . it is not possible to cheat God Almighty without paying a very heavy penalty both personally and racially. (Quoted in Bacchi 1980: 149)

Although by 1910, one-fifth of the workforce was female and many others worked (and still do) in material production on farms and in small businesses for which they are not paid and for which they get no public recognition as workers, it was widely accepted that a woman's job was to care for her husband and children. Justice Higgins 'Harvester' Judgement of 1907 had even instituted a policy which sanctioned by law the existing practices of sex segregation in social life: he introduced the notion of a 'living' wage sufficient to keep a man, his wife and three children (Baldock 1983: 34). All unskilled male workers were to receive this basic wage, despite the fact that 45 per cent of the male workforce was single at the time of the judgement. There was no basic wage established for women, and in 1912 Justice Higgins instituted separate pay rates for women's work without any regard for productivity: women were to get a male rate if they did 'men's work' and competed with men, but if they did 'women's work' they were paid a woman's (lower) wage. The judgement deemed that the 'normal needs' of men were greater than

women's, as men had to support the family whereas women supported only themselves. Curiously, a survey in 1928 showed that 30 per
cent of women were partially or wholly supporting other family
members (Cass 1983: 62).

Simultaneously as white women were encouraged to be home-
makers, the rapid urban expansion of the late nineteenth century
generated concern for health and sanitation as much as for families,
and advice through health agencies and public lectures was continually directed at women. In Melbourne working class suburbs,
'Meetings for Wives and Daughters' were held to 'secure the
co-operation of the home-ruler, be she mother, wife or daughter, by
interesting her personally in the work of sanitary reform' (Reiger
1982: 75). There were very few non-European women in Australia at
this time, except for Aboriginals and they tended to be herded into
reserves or left to their own devices in the bush or on the edges of
country towns. Older Aboriginal women, particularly, struggled to
keep their families together while they endured severe ill-health, low
life expectancy, high infant and child mortality rates and harassment
by white (usually male) officials, which often led to 'the institutionali-
sation of the young and the sexual exploitation of girls resulting in
illegitimate births' (Grimshaw 1981: 91). High rates of male unemployment, the absence of their menfolk as itinerant labour and their
heavy drinking did not make the women's lives any easier (Grimshaw
1981).

The domestic labour and much of the breeding that engaged white
women during the last years of the nineteenth century provided the
grim fodder for the slaughter at Gallipoli and in France between 1914
and 1918. Over 330 770 men went overseas and 63 163, or nearly one
in five, died on active service. Only one in three escaped wounds,
capture or death (Gammage 1975: 283).

Women are conspicuously absent from the war histories except in
so far as they served as nurses, did war work or 'gave in sacrifice' their
sons, husbands and lovers for the 'noble' cause. Moreover, the
constructive enterprise of giving birth during these war years was
accorded solely to the men: the disaster at Gallipoli even became the
'birthplace' of Australian nationhood (Bean 1981).

Women had not entered the workforce in vast numbers during the
First World War. Where they were in paid employment before and
after the war their jobs were concentrated in 'female' industries, such
as domestic service and clothing factories (Power 1975: 229). Until
1942 their minimum wage was 54 per cent that for male workers

(Baldock 1983: 26). These circumstances weakened their potential for general political or industrial activity. The feminist agitation that did occur centred on matters of citizenship and suffrage and on women's ability to bear children. Before and after getting the vote in 1902, women had 'campaigned for legal reforms on the issues which *they* perceived as significant: the social injustices and exploitations of women and children' (Allen 1979: 107). In stressing their differences from men as the basis of their demands for citizen rights, women even attracted some converts from the patriarchal establishment to support them in the years 1891–1901. Most of these politically active women were middle class and in the years preceding the First World War the issues that received parliamentary sponsorship were those supporting middle class concepts of childhood and family life. But even these activities were not always successful. In debates in the New South Wales parliament over the Bill to raise the age of consent from 14 to 16, members denounced the measures as an 'intolerable interference with the liberty of men and as a contravention of nature: in a sub-tropical climate, it was said, girls ripened into women earlier than in England' (Allen 1979: 111).

Before the First World War the only Commonwealth provision to recognise women independently as citizens with sex-specific claims was the universalist maternity allowance of 1912 from which Aboriginal and Asian women were excluded (Roe 1983: 7). The accent on white children populating the nation emerged again in debates on child endowment in the 1920s. Associated with wage fixation legislation, child endowment (paid to wives) was introduced by New South Wales, for example, in 1927. In arguing for the benefit, women maintained that there was no guarantee that husbands would share their 'living' wage equitably with their wives and children, and emphasised the contribution of women's domestic labour, the recognition of their rights and their children's to a separate income, as well as the necessity of supplementing the 'living' wage itself. They also saw endowment as a precondition for equal pay (Cass 1983a: 56–64). Men's arguments revolved around a clash of class interests that saw Labour stress the 'living' wage and its need for supplementation, while Conservatives, worried about profits and the possibility of the provision to mothers threatening the conjugal relationship and male authority, stressed the notion of the 'capacity of industry to pay' (Cass 1983: 55). Male concerns with 'race suicide' if women did not perform their 'natural' duty also surfaced. The New South Wales Minister for Public Health and Motherhood, in his support for welfare, complained:

the black races are breeding ten to one of the white races. The
civilised races are being over educated. Women try to avoid the
hardship of bearing and breeding children. They want to enjoy life
and the bearing of children is looked upon as an encumbrance and
a hindrance . . . The only way to alter the balance in favour of the
white races is to ensure that the women who are prepared to do
their duty should not be penalised, as is the case today. (New South
Wales Parliamentary Debates 1920: 4087, quoted in Cass 1983a:
68–9)

It is sobering to remember that the maternal mortality rate in
Australia actually rose between 1910 and 1930. In the 1920s it
accounted for one-sixth of deaths of married women in early and
mid-adult life (Roe 1983: 10).

State intervention in the form of social security benefits has
traditionally focused on nuclear families and children: widows
received benefits long before single mothers – to help them care for
their children in the 'national interest'. And men could claim tax
relief for supporting a daughter/housekeeper even in the 1940s. Not
until 1973, when the Whitlam Labour government introduced the
supporting mother's benefit, were single women granted a status of
child rearer independent of men. In 1977 the benefit was extended to
lone fathers (Roe 1983: 12–13).

The national preoccupation with women as dependent mothers and
wives has taken many forms. One authority in 1919 even argued that
all the paraphernalia of police and punishment could be scrapped 'if
only mothers would understand their duty and learn how to do it'
(quoted in Reiger 1982: 81). During the next decade before the 1930s
depression set in, the Empire Settlement Act (1922) was passed.
With associated legislation, this enabled Britain and Australia to
encourage oppressed white Britons to settle in the open spaces of
Australia where, together with the local population and with the help
of The Racial Hygiene Movement (forerunner of the Family Planning
Association), they were urged to reproduce and improve the race. At
the Movement's conference in 1929 the Commonwealth Film Censor
even spoke on sex and the soul. Though part of our animal nature, he
argued, sex can provide an 'uplifting experience' linking man to his
maker and 'the name of this stair by which men climb to god is
woman' (Reiger 1982: 82). A few years later in 1938 when Australia
observed the 150th anniversary of Phillip's landing, women as

breeders were again celebrated in pageant and verse. An example from a poetry competition included:

> Ye girls of British race
> Famous for your beauty
> Breed fast in all your grace
> For this is your duty.
> As Anzac gave in war
> So daughters at your call
> Will quick respond the more
> To replace those that fall.
> (quoted in McQueen 1978:158)

During and after the 1930s the birth rate declined and immigration intakes dropped. The Commonwealth Arbitration Court abandoned the 'living' wage in 1931 for the principle of fixing wages according to the 'capacity of industry to pay'. Wage reductions of 10 per cent ensued in all industries and some jobs previously classified as men's work were redefined as women's work, and were consequently less well paid. The differential pay rates meant that working women provided particularly cheap labour, but unlike the introduced cheap labour from Asia and Melanesia in the last century, women could not be excluded from the country and the threat they posed to male workers continued to concern the male-dominated unions.

Those women who did stay at home and breed often faced considerable hardship and struggle, as their letters submitted as evidence in the National Health and Medical Research Council's *Inquiry into the Decline in the Birth-Rate* (1944) testify. As one woman wrote: 'The falling birth-rate is due to . . . the ancient order of master and chattel . . . Let the state pay the mother a living wage for herself and for each child and so leave her independent of her husband's pay envelope and she will have her family' (quoted in Cass 1983b: 172). The then Director General of Health, who compiled the women's written testimonies, did not question the sexual division of labour, although he noted that the social condition of the women 'must be profoundly altered if this nation is to survive' (quoted in Cass 1983b: 172).

The implementation of federal social welfare policies to promote and support fertility ensued from this Inquiry. The 1944 report denounced abortion and defined the family as the site for redistribution policies. It was assumed that women's unpaid domestic labour and childcare were the foundation of welfare, full employment and population policies. The state intervened, therefore, not to introduce increased individual wages, but to provide a 'social wage' in the form of child endowment and maternity allowances and to subsidise housing and health care (Cass 1983b: 174).

The effects of immigration on Australia's population and its costs to the state were the concern of the National Population Inquiry (NPI) in 1970. When Labour assumed power in 1972, the terms of the Inquiry were extended to consider, among other things, the abandoning of immigration control based on colour, creed and race. Australia continued to need people. In the NPI *Supplementary Report* (1978) there is a clear focus on fertility decline as a social issue, but as Cass argues, despite government's well intentioned view of the 'national interest', 'it has not been recognised that the political and economic conditions of advanced industrial capitalism have militated *against* fertility, especially the fertility of working-class women and of working-class migrant women' (1983b: 177). Like its predecessor in 1944, the 1978 *Report* assumed the traditional sexual division of labour in the family to be 'natural', and that women will leave the workforce to rear children (Cass 1983b: 181). No class analysis or feminist insight is evident in these reports. Class and gender inequalities were implicitly accepted as public expenditure in the social welfare sphere contracted. Official government compaigns to establish 'national family policies' continue to adhere to ideological notions that the family is the 'natural' unit and provider of services to the state. Cuts in the value of the social wage to women (expenditure on childcare) help sustain the dependency of women and push them into providing an 'invisible welfare system' based on their unpaid domestic labour (Cass 1983b; 185). With the depressed economic climate in the 1980s, high unemployment rates and increasing single-parent families, there has also been a transfer of female dependency from male breadwinners to the state (Roe 1983: 18). However liberating in one respect, welfare provisions have perpetuated this dependency and women remain conspicuous among the 'permanent poor'.

As the birth rate fell in the 1970s Australian women were again urged to breed. Their failure to do so was even cited as a cause for the recession, and in 1977 the Anglican Archbishop of Sydney was reported as criticising both state and federal governments for funding Women's Health and Rape Crisis Centres because they allegedly advocated easy access to abortion, promiscuity and lesbianism. According to the Archbishop, the centres 'disturb and destroy the inherited moral standards and values of our nation' and actively promote 'drastic change in normal human relationships (*SMH*, 5 October 1977). During the 1979 abortion debate in federal parliament the Minister for Health was reported as deploring the prevalence of abortion and the increased use of contraception. Both, he said, had upset planning projections and it would require a massive immigration programme to effect a population increase. Another MP concluded that Australia was on the path to self-genocide (*SMH*, 23 March 1979).

The general injunction to breed has been extended to immigrant women arriving in Australia since the Second World War, but their experiences have varied depending on their location in their culture of origin, their class position in Australia and their ability to speak English. Although women in the family occupy a central position in popular belief, in state population and welfare planning programmes, in political propaganda and in various ideologies, women do not form a homogeneous category in social life.

As government policy on family reunion prefers immediate dependants (usually the wives and daughters of men), the state exercises a stricter control over immigrant families than over local ones, ensuring that wherever possible the nuclear rather than the extended family is reproduced (Martin 1984: 117). For women from the UK, northern Europe and north America or those from middle class backgrounds with professional or managerial breadwinners from any country, or who are independent, this limitation may not prove so much of a hurdle. But women from Mediterranean and some Asian countries

are caught squarely in the contradiction between consumption/ social reproduction and production, and are socially punished for being there. For economic reasons, for cultural reasons, from isolation and boredom, they are driven into paid work at a stage in their life cycle when they are 'supposed' to be at home caring for and rearing their families, setting up the family unit and furnishing it accordingly. (Martin 1984: 115)

For some Mediterranean and Middle Eastern women the social punishment goes further. Those from societies where women's roles are justified by strong ideologies of machismo or honour have sometimes found it difficult to sustain social relations outside their ethnic communities or even outside their families. As an Italian woman explained, after marriage 'the life of slavery then began (*vita di schiavitu*)' (Huber 1977: 23). The woman's work experience is often fraught with tension too because, although the family needs the money, the woman is not accustomed to factory work or mixing with outsiders. In some cases husbands forbid their wives to mix with Australians who are perceived to be too permissive. Where these women have been victims of sexual harassment at work they have even been afraid to tell their husbands lest they accuse them of having encouraged the advances (Bottomley 1984: 4).

Among Lebanese Muslim women, for instance, their participation rate in the workforce is even less than that for Australian women because of cultural pressures which define

> the primary role of women . . . as that of homemaker and child-bearer. This role is reinforced by various patriarchal ideologies, the most common of which is the ideology of honour. Men invest their honour in the virtue of their women and thereby idealise and control them. One consequence is that women's mobility is often very restricted since their independence is always seen as potentially threatening to the reputation of males and their families. (Humphrey 1984: 40)

Yet for those whose class position entails economic insecurity and hardship, the religious community does give support even though this in turn encourages traditional family relations and early marriage for women. For young women brought up in Australia this can lead to conflicts over gender roles, cultural identity and social continuity (Humphrey 1984: 41). Orthodox Jews have similar problems with respect to conflicts arising from Jewish law concerning religious marriage and divorce.

Among some Italian, Greek, other Mediterranean settlers, some Asians and Muslim Lebanese arranged marriages are still customary. Greeks in Australia, for example, 'are more married than Greeks in Greece' and proportionally more Greek Australian women have had their marriages arranged by parents and relatives (73 per cent) compared with women in Greece (25 per cent) (Bottomley 1984: 5,8). Arranged marriages among Punjabi Sikh farmers in Australia are also customary (de Lepervanche 1984: 154–8).

In cities where more welfare services are available, some immigrant women have rejected customary gender subordination, particularly after ˋbashings and rapes by husbands and fathers: they have sought refuge in Women's Health Centres, Refuges and Rape Crisis Centres in the face of opposition from their men (*SMH*, 22 November 1980; Bottomley 1984: 6). These problems highlight the need for strong feminist representation from ethnic groups as the present policy of multi-culturalism, however liberating in some respects, can preserve traditions that can have unfortunate consequences for women. But some women have been on the move: in 1981 a woman of Italian immigrant origin was elected to the New South Wales Legislative Council; the Italian Federation of Workers and their Families (FILEF) has an active women's group and other groups include the Australian Arab Women's Association, the Turkish Women's Association and the Hellenic Women's Association (Bottomley 1984). Even so, ethnic politics are male-dominated and decidedly petit bourgeois in complexion; some ethnic leaders try to maintain conservative and sexist customs that have already been lost or diluted in the homeland (Bottomley 1984), and gains made for women's autonomy have been resented by these ethnic spokesmen as well as by Australian men. Multi-culturalism in Australia is still a very male ideology which does not resonate with the specificities of class and gender differences.

In any discussion of family reunion and the maintenance of communal boundaries, it is important to remember that white sexist domination has many ramifications. In the use of Depo Provera, for example, certain categories of women, including Aboriginal school-girls and some immigrant women, are more disadvantaged than others (Bottomley 1984: 4). The Australian Drug Evaluation Committee ruled in 1977 that this drug cannot be promoted as a contraceptive, but its use as a contraceptive may occur on a trial or 'investigational' basis if administered to a patient on the basis of her 'informed consent' (Fraser & Weisberg 1981). Yet Aboriginal school-girls in Oodnadatta have been given injections of Depo against their will as they have been 'living in danger' from itinerant railway workers. A local resident of the town explained that the drug had been provided by a special Aboriginal health unit within the South Australian Health Commission (*SHM*, 7 December 1984).

A curious twist to Australian racist and sexist practices has been the 'recent spectacular growth in the Filipino marriage market' (Watkins 1982: 73). Statistics from the Australian Department of Immigration show that 384 Filipino brides entered Australia in 1978–79 and 607 were introduced in 1979–80 when an additional 111 financées also migrated. More brides were expected in future years (I have heard from an unofficial estimate that there are 3000 in the country) as Australian men 'are now looking for Asian brides to fulfil what they see as the traditional role of a wife' (Watkins 1982: 82).

They describe the Asian women as 'very faithful, not forceful, and co-operative – traits they have found lacking in Australian women' (Watkins 1982: 73).

Yet the status of other Asian immigrants, mostly in working class or petit bourgeois jobs if they are not unemployed, has been recently under attack, particularly from white middle class spokesmen claiming to speak for those 'ordinary Australians' who see their jobs and way of life threatened by the 'Asianisation' of Australia. Since 1980 racist criticism of Asian settlers, especially Vietnam refugees, many of whom have entered under the family reunion provisions, has increased. Simultaneously with attacks on Aboriginal claims to land rights (particularly by mining interests), the anti-Asian racism has appeared in numerous graffiti and in the press, accompanied by calls to preserve Australia's British (or at least European) heritage. The question of who has the right to people the nation and to own its land is very definitely contested terrain, despite the state's official policy of multi-culturalism. Curiously, while some increases in Asian immigration have been met with outpourings of ethnocentrism and, it would appear, some government response, there is very little public protest about movements of foreign capital that gives rise to newspaper headlines such as 'Australia a haven for Asian investors' (*SMH*, 12 November 1984) or 'Businessmen defend the "unethical" Japanese' (*SMH*, 27 October 1984).

The most articulate critic of present immigration policy, Geoffrey Blainey, a Melbourne University professor of history, has argued that 'a family-reunion scheme is overwhelmingly a racial-reunion scheme' (1984: 98) whereas the 'typical nation practises discrimination against migrants, for the sake of national unity' (1984: 52). If Australia continued to treat all peoples of the world as equally eligible as immigrants, he writes, and the Asian percentage became the dominant stream, the 'Asian and Third World domination of the migrant lists would be self generating, and Australia would eventually become an Asian nation' (1984: 119). In the last few years, he argues, successive Australian governments have cut 'the crimson threads' of kinship with Britain and thereby disowned our past (1984: 159), and now the 'desire to turn Australia into a new nation, a nation of all nations . . . contradicts the increasing sense of national pride that has become so vivid since the Whitlam era' (1984: 153). Blainey's nationalism, like other nationalisms of the New Right, draws on the notion of a universal human nature which 'naturally' distinguishes other cultures from its own, which it prefers. By invoking 'nature' and 'natural' differences between cultural (ethnic) groups, such people can deny their racism.

CONCLUSION

In comparison with men's, women's status generally remains disadvantaged with respect to ownership of wealth, job opportunities and the sharing of power. Women have no real control over material production, the production of knowledge in general or of scientific/ technological knowledge in particular. They are poorly represented in top positions in the commercial and professional worlds, in trades unions, in universities and in parliament. When they are in paid employment they are concentrated in 'female' industries or in the lower ranks of the occupational hierarchies (Power 1975). Their average weekly wage in the 1980s has been only 67 per cent that of men's, and childcare facilities are grossly inadequate for working women (Power *et al.* 1984). Single mothers particularly feature prominently in poverty figures (Cass 1983a) and both Aboriginal and immigrant women are subject to racist as well as sexist practices. All women are currently the objects of a considerable amount of right wing rhetoric about their place in the family, even though their 'nurturing' propensities and their 'matrist' values have even been considered dangerous to the state and to civic consciousness on the grounds that they allegedly emphasise 'sensate comfort, unconditional communal support and satisfaction' all of which, according to Ronald Conway, contributed to 'Australia's steep rise in unemployment' in the 1970s (1978: 27).

Australian women have not remained passive or submissive in the face of these male constructions. Immigrant women have mobilised among themselves, Aboriginal women have been prominent in lobbying for land rights and in setting up welfare centres for their own people (Grimshaw 1981: 86). Women in general have also joined in political action in bringing about changes in the divorce and rape laws, to institute maternity leave and to introduce the anti-discrimination legislation of the 1970s and 1980s. Even so, Australian civil society and the state remain constructed in opposition to female nature, domestic life and the production of children, all of which raises the question: what kind of patriarchy are we confronting? An answer to this question can be found in the work of Carole Pateman.

As Pateman argues, one of the foundations of today's opposition between the sexes is the modern form of partriarchy inherent in the *fraternal* social contract which must be distinguished from the (European) patriarchalism of three centuries ago. Both forms accept that 'women (wives), unlike sons, were born and remained naturally subject to men (husbands)', but the economic dependence of wives increased with the development of capitalism and 'reinforced the appearance of a natural subordination' (Pateman 1983: 6). Thus, although liberal theory has argued for liberty, equality and fraternity for individuals, the individuals have been men as 'brothers'. The social contract constitutes then a patriarchy of men as a fraternity who exercise power over women and who benefit from women's subordination: 'The crucial distinction between the partriarchy of the fathers and the modern, liberal patriarchy of the brothers is that the latter is created separately from and in opposition to the family' (Pateman 1983: 9).

This distinction informs the difference between man, constructed as the breadwinner, protector and defender of women and woman the breeder, a difference perhaps most vividly expressed in the state's requirement that men in wars have had to surrender their bodies in defence of the state in 'the truly, exemplary act of citizenship' (Pateman 1983: 18). Not surprisingly, then, in Australia until the 1960s 'war widows headed the hierarchy of women welfare recipients' and 'an ambivalent attitude towards women without men' prevailed (Roe 1983: 11–12).

The 'intimate connection between masculinity, citizenship and . . . bearing . . . arms' is opposed to the women's proper role of creating and preserving life under male protection (Pateman 1983: 20), and the general form of social contract is therefore 'an (apparent) exchange of (spurious) protection for obedience. Contract gives the appearance of voluntarism and freedom to domination and subjection that is, in many aspects, still ascriptive in character' (Pateman 1983: 21). The rights women have won as citizens have therefore only served to 'highlight the opposition between a formal civil equality made after a male image and the real social position of women *as women*' (Pateman 1983: 23). As Pateman concludes:

> Despite the important divisions between men of different races and classes . . . feminists are showing how men, as men, have a common interest; or, it is to their rational advantage to uphold the contract, since *as men* they gain material and psychological benefits throughout the whole of socio-political life, in the family, production and the state. (1983: 23)

Bearing Pateman's argument in mind, it is clear that, like the white race and nation of the early twentieth century, the ethnic groups and multi-cultural Australian state of today are cultural constructions created by men. Admittedly, women's traditional role has been crucial in producing and maintaining these imagined communities, yet too little is known about the specific gender, class and ethnic contexts in which women have been contributing to the 'national interest', accomplishing the state's purpose or have been excluded from it (cf. Anthias and Yuval-Davis this volume).

The rhetoric around the Bicentenary of 1988 in which multi-cultural Australia celebrated white settlement has sharpened awareness of state control of, and surveillance over, the nation, national identity and the national interest. The various ethnic groups within the state and their diverse cultures provide a focus for concern in the construction of state policies on immigration, citizenship, education and the family. Women need to be particularly vigilant in monitoring the state's version of this national interest: their own interests and the state's may well be in contradiction.

BIBLIOGRAPHY

Abbreviations:
ABS Australian Bureau of Statistics, Yearbook of Australia 1985 (Canberra, 1985)
SMH Sydney Morning Herald

Allen, J. (1979) 'Breaking into the Public Sphere', in J. Mackinolty & H. Radi (eds), *In Pursuit of Justice* (Sydney: Hale & Iremonger) 107–17.
Bacchi, C. (1980) 'Evolution, Eugenics and Women', in E. Windschuttle (ed.), *Women, Class and History* (Melbourne: Fontana/Collins) 132–56.
Baldock, C.V. (1983) 'Public Policies and the Paid Work of Women', in C.V. Baldock and B. Cass (eds), *Women, Social Welfare and the State* (Sydney: Allen & Unwin) 20–53.
Bean, C.E.W. (1981) *The Story of Anzac: The Official History of Australia in the War of 1914–18*, 2 volumes (Brisbane: University of Queensland Press).
Blainey, G. (1984) *All For Australia* (Sydney: Methuen Haynes).
Bottomley, G. (1984) 'Mediterranean Women in Australia: An Overview', paper presented at a Symposium of Mediterranean Women's Organisations, Delphi, Greece, 5–8 April.

Cass, B. (1983a) 'Redistribution to Children and to Mothers: a History of Child Endowment and Family Allowances', in C.V. Baldock & B. Cass (eds), *Women, Social Welfare and the State* (Sydney: Allen & Unwin) 54–84.

Cass, B. (1983b) 'Population Policies and Family Policies: State Construction of Domestic Life', in C.V. Baldock & B. Cass (eds), *Women, Social Welfare and the State* (Sydney: Allen & Unwin) 164–85.

Collins, J. (1984) 'Immigration and Class: the Australian Experience', in G. Bottomley and M. de Lepervanche (eds), *Ethnicity, Class and Gender in Australia* (Sydney: Allen & Unwin) 1–27.

Conway, R. (1978) *Land of the Long Weekend* (Melbourne: Sun Books).

de Lepervanche, M. (1980) 'From Race to Ethnicity', *Australian and New Zealand Journal of Sociology*, vol. 16, no. 1, 24–37.

de Lepervanche, M. *Indians in a White Australia* (Sydney: Allen & Unwin).

Evans, R., K. Saunders and K. Cronin (1975) *Exclusion, Exploitation and Extermination* (Sydney: ANZ Book Company).

Fraser, I.S., & E. Weisberg (1981) 'A Comprehensive Review of Injectable Contraception with Special Emphasis on Depo Medroxyprogesterone Acetate', *Medical Journal of Australia*, vol. 1, no. 1, special supplement.

Gammage, B. (1975) *The Broken Years: Australian Soldiers in the Great War* (Harmondsworth: Penguin).

Gordon, L. (1975) 'Race, Suicide and the Feminist Response', *Hecate: A Women's Interdisciplinary Journal*, vol. 1, no. 2, 40–53.

Grimshaw, P. (1981) 'Aboriginal Women: a Study of Culture Contact', in N. Greive & P. Grimshaw (eds), *Australian Women: Feminist Perspectives* (Melbourne: Oxford University Press) 86–94.

Horne, D. (1972) *The Australian People* (Sydney: Angus & Robertson).

Huber, R. (1977) *From Pasta to Pavlova* (Brisbane: University of Queensland Press).

Humphrey, M. (1984) 'Islamic Law in Australia', in *Islam in Australia*, Proceedings of a Seminar held at Macarthur Institute of Higher Education, Sydney, May, 36–47.

McQueen, H. (1978) *Social Sketches of Australia 1888–1975* (Harmondsworth: Penguin).

Martin, J. (1984) 'Non-English Speaking Women: Production and Social Reproduction', in G. Bottomley & M. de Lepervanche (eds), *Ethnicity, Class and Gender in Australia* (Sydney: Allen & Unwin) 109–22.

Oxley, H. (1979) 'Ockerism: the Cultural Rabbit', in P. Spearritt & D. Walker (eds), *Australian Popular Culture* (Sydney: Allen & Unwin) 190–209.

Pateman, C. (1983) 'The Fraternal Social Contract: Some Observations on Patriarchal Civil Society', paper presented to the Australian Women's Philosophy Conference, Adelaide.

Power, M. (1975) 'Women's Work is Never Done – By Men: a Socio-Economic Model of Sex-Typing in Occupations', *Journal of Industrial Relations*, vol. 17, no. 3, 225–39.

Power, M., S. Outhwaite, S. Rosewarne, J. Templeman and C. Wallace (1984) 'Writing Women Out of the Economy', paper presented to From

Margin to Mainstream: a National Conference About Women and Employment, Melbourne, 16 October.

Price, C.A. (1966) 'Post-War Migration: Demographic Background', in A. Stoller (ed.), *New Faces: Immigration and Family Life in Australia* (Melbourne: Cheshire) 11–29.

Reiger, K. (1982) 'Women's Labour Redefined: Childbearing and Rearing Advice in Australia 1880–1930s', in M. Bevedge, M. James and C. Shute (eds), *Worth Her Salt: Women at Work in Australia* (Sydney: Hale & Iremonger) 72–83.

Roe, J. (1983) 'The End is Where We Start From: Women and Welfare Since 1901', in C.V. Baldock & B. Cass (eds), *Women, Social Welfare and the State* (Sydney: Allen & Unwin) 1–19.

Saunders, K. 'Pacific Islander Women in Queensland: 1863–1907', in M. Bevedge, M. James and C. Shute (eds), *Worth Her Salt: Women at Work in Australia* (Sydney: Hale & Iremonger) 16–32.

Watkins, D. (1982) 'Filipino Brides: Slaves or Marriage Partners?' *Australian Journal of Social Issues*, vol. 17, no. 1, 73–84.

4 Mothers of the Nation: a Comparative Analysis of Nation, Race and Motherhood in Afrikaner Nationalism and the African National Congress

Deborah Gaitskell and
Elaine Unterhalter

The concept of nation has a different content according to the way in which the social forces are aligned at any particular moment and the nature of the prevailing ideologies. Far from being an incontrovertible given, 'nation' is one of the most elastic of concepts. This is particularly clear in the case in South Africa. Very different notions of nation have been developed by the dominant classes on the one hand and the dominated on the other.

Race has permeated the perceptions of nation of virtually all the dominant classes but its centrality has been most unambiguously expressed within Afrikaner nationalism. At certain points important proponents of Afrikaner nationalism have totally fused the concept of nation with that of the white race. Thus in 1972 a National Party cabinet minister, Connie Mulder, declared 'Soon there will be no black South Africans' (quoted in Lacey 1982: 3). He anticipated apartheid refined to such a point where 85 per cent of the population of his country had lost their nationality on account of their race and the South African nation had become the people identified as of white race.

Some 60 per cent of the white population of South Africa are Afrikaans-speaking. Most, but not all, Afrikaners can be deemed 'nationalists', although, as discussed below, important divisions have appeared in nationalist ranks throughout the twentieth century.

Although there has been a strand in African nationalism that has identified the nation only with the black race, this strand has never been dominant in South Africa (Lodge 1983: 80–4). The movement that has led the opposition to the political subordination of the black population, their segregation and exploitation, and which today, 75 years after its foundation, commands mass popular support is the African National Congress (ANC). The Freedom Charter, compiled in 1955 after a country-wide campaign by the ANC to collect popular views on an alternative society to that which existed under apartheid, expresses in its preamble: 'We, the people of South Africa, declare for all our country and the world to know: that South Africa belongs to all who live in it, black and white, and that no government can justly claim authority unless it is based on the will of the people' (Suttner & Cronin 1986: 262). The Freedom Charter remains the guiding manifesto of the ANC. Although the ANC is outlawed in South Africa and can only operate underground, the Freedom Charter is not banned and has been adopted in the 1980s by a number of key organisations of the mass democratic movement, most notably the student and youth congresses with more than a million members and two of the largest trade unions. While Afrikaner nationalism is dominated by a formulation of the nation that identifies special privileges for those deemed of white race, the African nationalism of the ANC is explicitly non-racial and lays great emphasis on a vision of the nation in which race is not a determinant, but democracy is.

Although there are two very different concepts of the nation ideologically and physically at war in South Africa, some observers remark there are similarities in the content of Afrikaner nationalism and African nationalism (Marks & Trapido 1987: 2, 23; Matisonn 1987: 5). This chapter looks at one such superficial similarity, the way both political organisations have constructed an ideology of 'the mother of the nation', and discusses how different the content of those ideologies are, partly because of the different concepts of the nation, partly because of the different circumstances of black and white women, and partly because the state, shaped by a complex of social forces, has itself given a different content to motherhood according to race and class. We focus particularly in each case on periods of nationalist mobilisation. This entails looking closely at Afrikaner nationalism in the post-Boer War period and the 1920s and 1930s on the one hand, and at the ANC in the 1950s, and 1970s and 1980s on the other.

MOEDERS VAN ONS VOLK: MOTHERHOOD IN AFRIKANER NATIONALISM

Throughout this century, to the extent that Afrikaner women have appeared at all in the rhetoric and imagery used for the 'ethnic mobilisation' (Adam & Giliomee 1979) of the Afrikaner *volk* ('people'), they have figured overwhelmingly as mothers.

Three different representations of Afrikaner motherhood since the turn of the century can be identified and each relates to a changing conception of race and nation. Despite some overlapping, a rough periodisation is possible, corresponding to the periods after the three watershed dates in 1902 (the Afrikaner defeat by the British in the South African War, entailing imperial rule over their formerly independent Boer republics); 1914 (the formation of the first Afrikaner National Party – NP); and 1948 (the accession to power of the first wholly Afrikaner nationalist government, which has remained the ruling party ever since). In each case, the nation is perceived differently. First, the Afrinaker nation mourns as a suffering victim; then on the basis of racial and cultural distinctiveness, the nation mobilises to redress political and economic disadvantage; finally, the Afrikaner nation attains state power completely independently but is eventually compelled because of challenges to its authority to expand its appeal to all members of the white race and then attempt to enlarge the boundaries of the nation to encompass black groups. Notions of motherhood shift accordingly.

In the first phase, after 1902, Afrikaner motherhood is exalted as saintly in suffering, admired for stoicism in victimisation, its strength an inspiration to the rest of the defeated nation. The emphasis is on nobility, passivity, virtuous nurturing and protection of children. This appears to be an image shaped by male cultural entrepreneurs, the women themselves as silent as in their stereotypical portrayal. In the aftermath of the Boer War, the former Boer generals, Botha and Smuts, were working to build conciliation between English- and Afrikaans-speaking white South Africans – and were duly rewarded with the leadership of the first government of a united South Africa, in 1910. The less prosperous, more politically threatened segment in the Afrikaner community – petit bourgeois journalists, teachers, clerics and writers – however, began building a more exclusive nationalist movement in which their occupational group could be assured of a stake (Hofmeyr 1987). The Second Language Movement of those years produced Afrikaans literature which twinned the recent cycle of suffering and death in the war with the earlier suffering of the *Voortrekkers* (Afrikaner emigrants from the British Cape Colony in the 1830s), not only at the hands of the British but especially from the Zulu and other African peoples encountered in that 'Great Trek'. The sufferings of Afrikaner mothers were central to the emotive portrayal of the nation's agony since both were seen as blameless victims. Thus in Gustav Preller's historical writings about the Trek, 'the noble blood of women, girls and tiny babes' matted the grass after a Zulu attack, 'women's breasts were severed, their bodies mutilated and ravished', nursing infants pierced with Zulu spears (Preller, quoted Moodie 1975: 6). Likewise, in the early accounts of Boer suffering during the war, the 26 000 women and children who died in the British concentration camps loom large, the outrage and pathos of their fate a staple of the nationalist litany on into the 1950s (le Roux 1986: 196). Those days in the camps were 'days of lamentation and bitterness . . . The moaning and weeping of sick mothers, the crying and pleading of little children dying of hunger in cold tents mounted up to heaven. But in vain' (Smith, quoted Moodie 1975: 9–10).

One of the few poems of lament of this time to give great prominence to Afrikaner women, C.L. Leipoldt's *Vrede-Aand* ('Peace Night'), has a powerful evocation of this maternal loss and tribulation. But it also pays tribute to the women as 'the strongest of us all' for, helped by God, the 'heroine and wife' bore 'the heaviest burden'. The inspiration of women's spirituality is stressed, for women's soul is the 'leading light'. As a final apostrophe, he exclaims, 'Woman! Our nation's treasure' (Grove & Harvey 1962). Again, it was the agony of the camps, woman as suffering mother of the nation, which the Women's Monument, opened at Bloemfontein in 1913, commemorated. Within a circular enclosure stands a bare-headed woman, holding a dying child, another woman in Voortrekker dress staring out across the veld. In panels on either side, again mothers and children feature, first entering the concentration camp (under the caption 'For freedom, volk and fatherland') and then an emaciated child dying in a camp tent, his mother by his side, a panel headed 'If you do not despair, I shall not forsake you' (Moodie 1975: 19). Maternal desolation and isolation were to embody the deep sense of devastation which the people felt in defeat.

In the second phase of Afrikaner nationalism, motherhood within the volk is perceived as far more active and mobilising. This coincides with the attempt of the disinherited Afrikaners to rebuild their cultural distinctiveness for parity with or even domination of the English. The home is focused on as women's appropriate arena for fostering Afrikaner national identity through their child-rearing and domestic responsibilities. These were the years after the two former Boer republics and the two British colonies had come together in the Union of South Africa, ruled by coalition Afrikaner–English governments which consciously strove from 1910–24 and again from 1933–48 to minimise division between the two white 'races' (to use the terminology of the time). Only from 1924–33, and even then in coalition with white Labour Party politicians for the first five years of that 'Pact', did the more vehement Afrikaner nationalists hold power. But it was in those years that Afrikaans (instead of Dutch) achieved equal official status with English (in 1925). Hertzog had perceived the Afrikaner nation as needing to mobilise to overcome its inequality *vis-à-vis* the English; for the second wave of nationalism beginning later in this period, parity was not enough and Afrikanerdom had further economic and cultural nationalist mobilising to do.

Popular literature like the magazine *Brandwag*, launched in 1910, aimed very specifically to capture the home for the Afrikaner language, culture and people. It chose to concentrate 'on a point where the land lies unprotected', for it was 'determined to steal a place in the Afrikaans family which is at present empty or is filled with foreign nonsense like Home Notes, Home Chat and Home Journal' (quoted in Hofmeyr 1987: 114). There was, Isabel Hofmeyr suggests, a community of interest between the Afrikaner women seeking to enhance their importance and status within both the domestic sphere and the limited public arena open to them in the women's welfare and political movements starting up after the Boer War, and the men of the Afrikaner Language Movement. For the male writers and ideologies there was 'an over-riding interest in making the Afrikaans family a solid reality' because the home was at that stage almost the only place where some form of Afrikaans was consistently spoken. Anglicisation was proceeding apace in the workplace, for the urban economy was at this stage largely in the hands of English-speaking capitalist concerns and the Labour Party espousing the white workers' cause had English roots. In church until 1918–19 ordinary Afrikaners heard Dutch sermons and sang Dutch hymns, while it was hard for parents to ignore the lure of English education when language could prove a vital asset for employment. It was 'not for nothing that Afrikaans was so frequently called "the mother tongue"'; if anyone was going to socialise children as Afrikaners in this situation where the male-dominated worlds of church and work used Dutch or English, it was the women, hence it was essential for Afrikaners to capture the home for the new nationalist outlook (Hofmeyr 1987: 113).

From the mid-1920s it was *Huisgenoot* ('Family/Home Companion') which, with its less literary and more pictorial appeal, became perhaps the most widely read magazine in South Africa. Through articles, advertisements, pictures and stories, such journals were engaged in redefining and repackaging Afrikaner everyday life to portray what was 'authentically' Afrikaans in 'Food, architecture, interior decoration, dress, etiquette, health, humour, landscape, monuments, the plastic arts, music . . . and so on'. Thus a woman who adopted this all-embracing ethnic identity and nationalist loyalty could increase her status at home, but also within women's organisations, 'by appearing publicly as an Afrikaner woman, who also taught others how to be Afrikaner women' (Hofmeyr 1987: 114). This was a devotion to be poured out not just towards families but also the volk. By contrast, in the nationalist appeals of African community, the home could not feature as a starting point of strength in quite the same way. The shattering effect of conquest and apartheid on the African family meant the school, the workplace and the community replaced the importance of the home as a centre of nationalist mobilisation. Afrikaners in the 1920s and 1930s, however, hoped their homes would be a maternal powerhouse of domestic ethnic mobilisation.

There was much more ambivalence in the Afrikaner community about women's contribution in the public political arena as opposed to the domestic sphere, precisely because of woman's supposedly divinely ordained role as wife and mother. By the 1920s the Women's Enfranchisement Association of the Union (WEAU) had been campaigning for a decade for the female franchise but its small, exclusively white membership was almost entirely English-speaking, educated, privileged urban women (Walker 1982: 21). Afrikaner women's hostility to the suffrage movement because of its image of 'foreignness' and imperialist sympathies was bolstered by, for instance, the opposition of the Dutch Reformed Church (DRC – to which the vast majority of Afrikaners belong) to women's suffrage. A 1920 DRC synod condemned it on biblical grounds: the vote belonged 'to the man as the head of the family' – three biblical texts were quoted at this point – 'and not to the women who, in accordance with the story of creation, was given to man as a helpmate (Genesis 2.18)' (Walker 1979: 22). So women's auxiliary role in the family precluded the vote.

And yet, no doubt in their 'helpmate' role, the Women's National Party was founded in July 1915 to work in conjunction with Hertzog's party. It was the growing support for female suffrage from these Afrikaner nationalist women as the 1920s progressed, and in the context of increased Afrikaner urbanisation and female employment, that led the NP to re-evaluate its stance. Race intertwined with nation and gender in a complex way because of South Africa's constitutional specificities: the nationalist premier Hertzog espoused votes for white women because that would dilute the black vote in the Cape. (In the African and 'coloured' franchise there was a legacy of its nineteenth-century status as a British colony.)

Thus in 1930, under Hertzog, white women were enfranchised in a racially exclusive Bill: 'In this Act . . . "woman" means a woman who is wholly of European parentage, extraction or descent' (Walker 1979: 23–4). It could be argued, then, that the female 'political nation' in South Africa was constituted in racially exclusive terms by state policy for the country as a whole some years before this was the case for men. (Cape Africans lost the vote for the Union parliament in 1936 and Cape Coloureds in 1956.) But in a sense this was only possible for white women precisely because of the nature and basis of their political mobilisation – around an exclusive ideology of motherhood and the isolation within the home which it implied.

In a sense, the major political watershed of 1948 does not really herald the third phase of Afrikaner nationalist conceptions of motherhood and the state. The creation and defence of the Afrikaner home continued to be the Afrikaner woman's prime service to the volk into the 1960s. Only in that decade was there a marked shift to a more inclusive conception of the white nation, which in turn, particularly by the late 1970s, led to a broader appeal to black and white mothers which has become in the 1980s an attempt to usurp the fully national call to women of the ANC.

The changing conception of the white nation was rooted in the fact that an Afrikaner capitalist class came into being. Afrikaners in the cities had made remarkable progress in their attempts to catch up with the long-entrenched wealth of the urban English speaker. The home was therefore no longer in the forefront of ethnic struggle.

Instead of being a key base from which to reconstruct the Afrikaner nation, it became a focus for the display of the new-found prosperity which ethnic mobilisation had made possible. Afrikaner wives and mothers moved into a less defensive phase, proud of the affluent lifestyle which they now shared, many of them, with their fellow whites. Instead of anglicisation absorbing Afrikanerdom, both language groups had a materialistic consumer culture in common.

Afrikaner women occupied a less important role in nation building in these years. In a notorious incident, they were urged to 'have a baby for Republic Day', to celebrate five years since leaving the Commonwealth (1961–6), but their ideological and political contribution as opposed to their biologically reproductive role was much marginalised. Their invisibility in the public political arena persisted.

The broadening of nationalist support among the white population at large from the mid-1960s (Stultz 1974: 165) was attended by a new sharp division within Afrikanerdom from the late 1960s, the first serious fracturing of their ethnic unity in two decades and a split which intensified further in the early 1980s. Much of this bitter in-fighting has implicitly been about the blurring of the boundaries of the nation: first to accommodate English speakers within the wider white nation and now latterly even appearing to expand the white nation to accommodate or effect the alignment of the other two minority races, the coloureds and Indians. Thus, just as Hertzog split with Botha and Smuts in 1914 over relations with Britain and English-speaking whites, and Malan did in turn with Hertzog in 1934, so the HNP ('Re-established' Nationalist Party) in 1969 and the Conservative Party in 1982 have broken nationalist ranks.

Afrikaner mothers have been mobilised in this in-fighting in at least two ways: firstly to help defend the nation against 'total onslaught' portrayed as coming both from beyond its borders and from within the local black population; and secondly to try to establish contact with co-optable members of other racial groups. The image of motherhood is therefore contradictory. It is both that of the mother–defender of the nation and that of the mother identifying with other mothers in the nation to help preserve a disappearing status quo.

The mobilisation of Nationalist Party women was being pursued in the late 1970s within the militaristic framework which was becoming pervasive in South Africa society. An NP pamphlet of 1978, *Women our Silent Soldiers*, compiled by wives of cabinet ministers and edited by the party's Chief Information Officer, called for party loyalty and solidarity within 'the total onslaught on us as a nation' (Goodwin

1984: 222 ff. for pamphlet quotes). Official propaganda was anxious to assure Afrikaner women that they were just as important as 'the boys on the border': 'women are the indispensable "soldiers" within our country's borders and their spiritual power is South Africa's secret weapon'. Women were also 'doing service' every day, 'without call-up instructions, without military pay, but in the service of the things which are dear to us – our families, our countries, our nation'.

Ostensibly the focus for Afrikaner women's nationalist activity has not changed from the pre-1948 period: it was still within the home that their service to country and nation were primarily to be performed. But the home's insertion into a wider context in which whites are warding off threats to their survival is emphasised throughout. Women are not now being urged to make Afrikaner homes but to defend them from hostile forces and, by their competent coping with family finances, for instance, help free the male members of their households to play their part in the inevitable military struggle. But the maternal education of the soldier is vital: as the 1978 pamphlet emphasises 'A woman's most important task is the educational task. A child develops pride in his cultural assets, his language, his nation and his country largely through his mother's guidance.'

In this third phase of heightened popular mobilisation against apartheid and increased international pressure on the South African state Afrikaner women are also lending themselves to inter-racial ventures with an emphasis on the common experience of motherhood across race divides, apparently attempting to pre-empt the ANC's efforts in this direction. Frede van Rooyen founded Kontak in 1976 after the Soweto revolt had begun. By 1983, appointed by the Minister of Internal Affairs, she chaired a committee trying to bring coloured and other groups closer, her warm personality and enthusiasm an asset to the state in the run-up to the launch of the new constitution. When the boundaries of the political nation were about to be extended, Afrikaner women were enlisted to promote reconciliation.

The further extension of this strategy comes in the national 'bridge-building' campaign started in October 1986, led by NP woman MP, Rina Venter, and consciously evoking common motherhood which Afrikaner women share with black: 'They are starting discussion groups and social groups and are inviting them to tea, where they discuss their problems . . . They want to understand how they feel about their political aspiration, their children's situation – things like that' (*Star*, 3 October 1986). A social worker and former president of the South African *Vrouefederasie* ('Women's Federation'), Dr Venter saw her foremost role as a mother. Her work, however, 'has left her aware of women's strength in unity, and she believes in their ability to triumph over violence, self-interest and political wrangling to join in their common interests as mothers and creators of life' (*Star*, 1 November 1986). The version of motherhood here is crucial: mothers are still seen in a very limited domestic role, united in a concern for their children. Unlike the ANC case, a focus on motherhood does not open up broader issues of women's situation and need for emancipation. Furthermore, when the situation of mothers in different race groups is in fact so manifestly different, and in a context where radical transformation of South African society is not on the agenda, 'bridge building' on the basis that the home is what mothers have in common becomes farcical.

Thus the notion of Afrikaner motherhood, its relation to the state and its contribution to national struggles, has gone through major shifts over time, as Afrikaner power in South Africa has suffered serious setbacks, then gradually reasserted itself, then faced new crises of legitimation. In the first phase, the nation's defeat in the Boer War was most feelingly focused on and remembered in the fact of the suffering of Afrikaner mothers. In the second phase, the national call for mobilisation of political support for separate Afrikaner identity as well as the mobilisation of Afrikaner wealth had its counterpart in domestic cultural mobilisation which was seen as pre-eminently the work of women as mothers. In the third phase, after some years when Afrikaner mothers rejoiced in being able to display the successful achievement of financially secure and culturally distinct homes, the power of motherhood has been invoked to assist in the survival of white domination. From the point of view of the regime mothers have a crucial role in personally supporting and validating military solutions to the opposition to apartheid, on the one hand, while on the other the cultural distinctiveness of their maternal role is now being downplayed in favour of the potential support of the white government which it may be possible to augment via inter-racial contact among mothers based on their common biological role. These changing conceptions of motherhood have clearly had their roots in material reality, in the social and economic circumstances of Afrikaner women. The suffering mothers and children of the early iconography reflected not only the grim reality of the 26 000 deaths in British concentration camps, but also the hardships of re-establishing family life after the war. Physically, motherhood for whites involved suffering, not least because white infant mortality rates in the first decades of the twentieth century were high by the standards of the day. The links are particularly striking in the second phase, at the height of concern about the problem of newly urbanised Afrikaner-speaking 'poor whites' struggling to survive in town.

The sharp contrast between the white working class suburbs of Johannesburg and the more affluent parts of the city, for instance, in respect of infant mortality rates intensified in the depression years of 1929–30 (Unterhalter 1982: 631). Social investigators also set much store by the contribution mothers could make to combating poverty and racial 'degeneracy' and this provides further explanation for the emphasis of popular Afrikaner literature of the interwar period on woman's home-making role.

In the third phase of Afrikaner motherhood, solidarity with English-speaking mothers was indeed rooted in the major shift in economic fortunes which had occurred by the 1970s. In 1978, 60 per cent of the white labour force in public and semi-public jobs were Afrikaans, while the Afrikaner share of the private sector had grown from 9.6 per cent in 1938–9 to 20.8 per cent in 1975. Income distribution between the two white groups had also evened up: in 1946, whites earned 74 per cent of the income in South Africa, the English getting 44.5 and the Afrikaners 29.5 per cent; by 1976, each got exactly half (31.5 per cent) of the whites' 63 per cent share of national income (Adam & Giliomee 1979: 165, 172).

MOTHERS OF THE NATION: MOTHERHOOD AND THE AFRICAN NATIONAL CONGRESS

In posters, pamphlets, songs and speeches in the postwar period, and particularly in the phases of mass popular mobilisation in the 1950s and again in the 1970s and 1980s the ANC, and the mass democratic organisations that share its aspirations, have laid much stress on the image of the mother; indeed the general appeal to all women has been in terms of their common potential experience of motherhood, although there have been important qualitative differences in the portrayal of the mother in different periods.

In the 1950s the major anti-apartheid women's organisation in South Africa was the Federation of South African Women (FSAW), whose largest affiliate was the ANC Women's League. The FSAW campaigned vigorously against the introduction of passes for African women, which would regulate where African women could live and work. In their campaign they stressed the identity of African women as mothers. For example, a statement presented by the FSAW to local government officials throughout the country in 1957 stressed: 'As wives and mothers we condemn the pass laws and all they imply' (quoted in Kimble & Unterhalter 1983: 26). Frances Baard, a trade union organiser and member of the ANC Women's League and FSAW in the 1950s recalled the discussions among women in the anti-pass campaign:

> We knew that you would be carrying a child, or have your child on your back, and the police will be coming behind you wanting your pass and you won't be able to run away and jump over that fence there and that will be the time the police will get you, or else your child will fall and get hurt because you are trying to run away from the police. And then who is going to look after the children when they take you to jail because you haven't got your pass, or your pass is not right? We explained to the women what would happen if we accepted these passes and no one wanted them. (Baard 1986: 47–8)

Motherhood is stressed partly because this is seen as a common experience of women, in towns and rural areas, in wage employment or working in the informal sector. It also seems that the outrage at the introduction of passes for women focuses on women's status as mothers. The implicit reasoning runs that as mothers African women deserve better treatment than the brutality routinely handed out to their men.

In its campaign to win the support of white women for African women's opposition to passes, the FSAW also stressed motherhood, but here the importance of this appears to be because motherhood was an experience black and white women shared. A pamphlet distributed by the FSAW in 1958 in white residential areas appealed to white women on the issue of passes for African women: 'In the name of humanity, can you as a woman, as a mother, tolerate this?' (quoted in Kimble & Unterhalter 1983: 26). The 1960s was a decade of severe repression in South Africa; the ANC was forced underground, and mass democratic organisations ceased to function. However, in the 1970s, initially locally and then regionally, organised opposition re-emerged as black workers went on strikes and began to build up trade unions and school and university students initiated

protests at their inferior education which escalated, in the face of
vicious police shootings of unarmed children in Soweto in 1976, into a
year-long uprising in which official buildings were burned, local
communities galvanised into rejection of the regime and thousands of
young people left the country to join the ANC and its armed struggle
against the apartheid regime.

   In the anger and the commitment to national liberation that were
generated in this period there is frequent reference to the totemic
symbol of the mother. In a collection of poems by ANC women
published in 1983 there is a section on the Soweto events and their
aftermath. Out of eight poems in this section five are about
motherhood. There are two distinct images of mothers: first, there is
that of the suffering careworn mother, whose pain goads her daughter to join the liberation struggle. For example Rebecca Matlou, in
her poem entitled 'Mother Patriot' describes a woman shot dead in
the streets of Soweto in June 1976, and ends 'She must be avenged.'
The second image is of the mother, in her suffering, nurturing the
revolution. In Baleka Kgositsile's poem the mother inspires the
children with commitment to revolution:

> your sweat and tears
> let our future burn in them
> that they create
> years of the child
> let their hunger
> bear their anger
> let our children live
> and live
> (Matlou 1983: 44)

In a similar vein Ilva Mackay in her poem 'Mayibuye' fuses the image
of the mother with the revolution, so that on liberation 'our mothers
shall be returned to us' (Mackay 1983a: 46).

   Young people were prominent in the uprising of 1976, which partly
might account for the stress on images of motherhood; there was also
a sense, in this period, that after the long period in which resistance
had lain dormant, repressed, it was now being reborn, and this sense
too might have inspired so many poems around the theme of
motherhood. The images of motherhood suggest strength and suffering and sadness. The mother is an inspiration to the daughter, but it is
the daughter who is the protector of the mother and in that guise and

in her decision to join the struggle and build a new society becomes the mother to future unborn generations. This appears an interesting contrast with Afrikaner nationalist literature, where it is the self-sacrificing mother, whose sacrifice rather than whose strength is the inspiration, generally to the *son* who is the poet.

From the late 1970s to the present the actions of the armed wing of the ANC Umkhontho we Sizwe, operating underground in South Africa, began to increase in number and mass democratic organisations were recreated. Many women's organisations were established and began to build regional and national structure and campaign on many issues. As in the 1950s there is once again an appeal to women of all races in terms of their common motherhood. So Albertina Sisulu, president of the United Democratic Front (UDF), the umbrella body representing some 400 local and regional anti-apartheid organisations, in an address to one thousand people at the University of Cape Town in June 1986 said: 'No selfrespecting woman can stand aside and say she is not involved while police are hunting other mothers' children like wild dogs in the townships . . . A mother is a mother, black or white. Stand up and be counted with other women' (*Argus*, 3 June 1986). The National Executive Committee of the ANC, in its address to the South African people in January 1987 issued this call:

Black mothers have to live with the agony of having to bury their children every day. Too often they have to search for their sons and daughters who have perhaps been arrested or perhaps disappeared forever without trace. Across the barricades, the white mothers see their children transformed and perverted into mindless killers who will not stop at murdering the unarmed, and will surely turn their guns on the very mothers who today surrender their sons willingly or unwillingly to the South African death force. These black and white mothers must reach across the divide created by the common enemy of our people and form a human chain to stop, now and forever, the murderous rampage of the apartheid system. (African National Congress 1987: 8)

The same speech also affirmed:

The mothers of the nation, the womenfolk as a whole are the titans of our struggle . . . Our revolutionary movement has long recognised the fact that an oppressive social order such as ours could not but enslave women in a particularly brutal way. One of the greatest

prizes of the democratic movement must therefore be the unshack-
ling of the women. (African National Congress 1987: 8)

In all these calls there is a fusion of women and mothers. This must
partly be read in the context of the vernacular African languages
where the word for adult woman and the word for mother are the
same and in the context of African societies, where the upbringing
of children is much more widely shared between households than is
the case in white areas. But these calls are also predicated on an
appeal to qualities of motherhood, like care and concern, which
straddle racial boundaries and which are seen to be powerful forces
that can be harnessed to destroy apartheid and create national
unity. In contrast to the appeal to women as mothers in the 1950s,
the first period of mass mobilisation, the focus now is not so much
on outrage at the treatment of mothers, but at the power mothers
exercise in society, which itself places on the agenda questions of
women's emancipation.

In many ways the changing perception of motherhood, particularly the contrast between the first phase and the third, arises out of
the changing circumstances of women. In the 1950s still a relatively
small percentage of women were wage earners: only 23 per cent of
women of all races aged 15–59 in 1950, compared with 33 per cent in
1980 (Jaffee & Caine 1986: 11). A sizeable number of women who
were mothers, both black and white, were dependent on the wages
of male workers. Within the cities where the ANC drew its major
support many of the women members worked in the informal sector
and lived in households with a number of male relatives (Kimble &
Unterhalter 1983: 22–9). In these circumstances it is hardly surprising that motherhood was perceived as a status that needed protection. In the 1980s, as well as a very marked increase in the number
of women employed in wage labour, there is also a significant
increase in the number of female-headed households. A study based
on the 1980 census found that 30 per cent of African households in
metropolitan areas, 47 per cent of households in bantustan towns
and 59 per cent of households in bantustan rural areas were headed
by women (Simkins 1986: 33–8).

There appears a marked correlation between women's political
activism and women bringing up families on their own (Cole 1986:
Unterhalter 1988). These material circumstances of black women –
their increasing wage employment, their increasing hardship
because of living without the support of male relatives and their

increasing mobilisation into women's organisations, trade unions, street committees and civic associations – seem to go a considerable way to explaining the new vision of motherhood in the ANC as something dynamic and activist, rather than passively in need of protection. In the 1980s it appears that it is largely highly educated, upper middle class, white women who have identified with black women, partly as an extension of their professional work as lawyers, teachers or social workers. The image of motherhood expressed in the speeches might well touch that embodied in their work. By contrast, in the 1950s the white women activists were mainly working in the progressive organisations as secretaries or journalists, often part-time, as they had young children, and thus probably shared protective ideas of motherhood.

Political pressures from within the dominant classes: combined in the first phase to force the regime to legislate for a particular form of nation and particular conditions of motherhood for the black population. The nation was conceived as segregated on racial lines and the state was prepared to suppress political organisations like the ANC and the black trade union movement in order to achieve this. It was against this background that the politics of protecting the non-racial democratic nation was created. Within its concept of the nation the regime dictated under what circumstances a black woman could be a mother, where she had to live and work, who she could marry and have sexual relations with.

In the second phase the regime, still supported by the same social forces from within the dominant classes, sought not only to segregate the nation according to race, but to create separate nations for Africans according to ethnic classifications and to decree South Africa as a nation of only those deemed white. Even more stringent controls were placed on where black women might live with their children, as African women with children were perceived by the regime as a threat to the strategy of returning all Africans to the bantustans. Act 42 of 1964 removed the right of African women to settle in urban areas, even though their fathers and husbands might be legally resident and working in those areas. From 1967 it became impossible for women from the bantustans even to take work legally in the urban areas as they were not allowed to register with the labour bureaus from which the contract workers were chosen. In the view of the ruling National Party, as expressed by a member of parliament for a white middle class area: 'We do not want the Bantu woman here simply as an adjunct to the procreative capacity of the Bantu population' (quoted in Simons 1968: 282). The severe hardships these policies imposed on African women, condemned to poverty in the bantustans and constantly harassed in pass raids, incensed the children of 1976, who joined the uprising (Strachan 1984). Within schools, universities and churches, relatively untouched by the repression of the political organisations the ideology of the suffering black nation rising against its oppressor was created, strongly influenced initially by notions of black consciousness but politically oriented to the aspirations of the ANC for a non-racial democratic state (Lodge 1983: 321–62). The actual experience of the suffering of mothers shaped the articulation of the ideology of motherhood and influenced the notion of nation in this period.

In the third phase cracks began to appear amidst the social forces supporting the regime. Important sectors of monopoly capitalism and some members of the white petit bourgeoisie began to mount a critique of the regime, largely because of its failure to secure lasting economic growth or political stability. Some representatives of these classes saw a non-racial democratic state as the only form of state able to secure the conditions for the reproduction of capitalist accumulation. Sectors of the white working class and petit bourgeoisie, at the other end of the political spectrum, opposed the regime because of its limited exercise in constitutional change, giving segregated parliamentary representation to coloureds and Indians, allowing the formation of black trade unions and reformulating the pass laws. These disputes in the ruling bloc partly arise from the growing mobilisation of the population and their success in articulating their grievances and insisting the ANC must be unbanned and the democratic rights of all South Africans must be recognised; equally the divisions within the ruling bloc provide a wedge which allows the mass democratic movement and the ANC to try to detach important allies from the regime. Within this context the regime has developed an ideology of the nation facing a 'total onslaught'. The nation is no longer identified only with those deemed white, but is expanded to encompass all those, white and black, who oppose the national liberation movement. In its search for black allies the regime has made important concessions with regard to conditions of motherhood. The pass laws were formally abolished in 1986, although important restrictions remain on the movement of African women – many thousands have flocked into urban areas outside the bantustans; the citizenship rights of certain Africans, who were deemed aliens as citizens of bantustans that had been decreed independent, were restored; the legislation outlawing inter-racial marriages was repealed. While these concessions in no way amount to support for black mothers they were conceived as an attempt to divide the African population. In the event, the reforms have proved too little too late and have only further spurred the organisations and militancy of black women, transforming their perception of motherhood from a protective status to a dynamic force for change.

CONCLUSION

Superficially, one can trace similarities in the way both Afrikaner and African nationalists have viewed and used motherhood in their periods of mobilisation for power. The suffering Boer War mothers are exalted and provide a stimulus to national mobilisation just as the suffering pass-carrying mothers or the mothers of Soweto did. But a different concept of the nation operates, an exclusive Afrikaner nation as opposed to the ANC belief in the non-racial democratic South African nation. Furthermore, the suffering of motherhood has led in the ANC to a call for women's emancipation; this has never been part of the trajectory of Afrikaner nationalism, where women have consciously been kept in the home and out of public life.

Other important contrasts exist also. When the power of the state was imposing passes, African women saw the need for allies and addressed a cross-racial appeal to other mothers. For Afrikaner women, their current resort to cross-racial appeals comes when their tenure of state power is perceived to be threatened by the growth of the opposition movement. Their response early in the century to the threat of anglicisation was not to seek allies but, with ethnic logic, to build up group strength partly through an exclusive, distinctive Afrikaner motherhood. Political rights for women became a priority only when their use to race and nation was clear, and they have not displaced the centrality of women in the home from Afrikaner ideology.

We began by describing the nation as the most elastic of concepts. Motherhood, this discussion of Afrikaner and African nationalist views has made clear, is likewise a very fluid and manipulable notion, especially in the context of a divided society where class and race divisions overlap. There have been very strong parallels between the form in which the nation is perceived and the form in which motherhood is viewed. Appeals to motherhood have been couched in ethnically very exclusive terms as well as in racially inclusive ways. The different circumstances of black and white mothers have shaped the relation between ideas of nation, state and motherhood. Legislation has made motherhood materially much easier and potentially more fulfilling for some groups than others, highlighting the contradiction between white assertions of the nobility of mothers and their destructions and denigration of motherhood and family life for black people. In the present, motherhood is explicitly part of the terminology and strategy of struggle of both Afrikaner nationalism and the ANC, but the implications of motherhood remain very different on both sides, just as both sides envisage a very different future for women and the nation as a whole.

BIBLIOGRAPHY

Adam, H. & H. Giliomee (1979) *Ethnic Power Mobilized: Can South Africa Change?* (New York and London: Yale University Press).

African National Congress (1987) *8 January 1987 ANC Calls for Advance to People's Power* (Lusaka/London: ANC).

Baard, F. (1986) *My Spirit is not Banned* (Harare: Zimbabwe Publishing House).

Brink, E. (1987) '"Maar 'n Klomp 'Factory' Meide"': Afrikaner Family and Community on the Witwatersrands during the 1920s', in B. Bozzoli (ed.), *Class, Community and Conflict: South African Perspectives* (Johannesburg: Raven Press).

Carter, G. (1958) *The Politics of Inequality: South Africa since 1948* (New York: Prager).

Cole, J. (1986) 'When Your Life is Bitter You do Something: Women and Squatting in the Western Cape Tracing the Origins of Crossroads and the Role of Women in its Struggle', in D. Kaplan (ed.), *South African Research Papers* (Department of Economic History, University of Cape Town).

de Klerk, W.A. (1976) *The Puritans in Africa: a Story of Afrikanerdom* (Harmondsworth: Penguin Books; first published 1975).

Goodwin, J. (1984) *Cry Amandla! South African Women and the Question of Power* (New York and London: Africana Publishing Company).

Grove, A.P. & C.J.D. Harvey (1962) *Afrikaans Poems with English Translations* (Cape Town: Oxford University Press).

Hofmeyr, I. (1987) 'Building a Nation from Words: Afrikaans Language, Literature and Ethnic Identity, 1902–1924', in S. Marks & S. Trapido (eds), *The Politics of Race, Class and Nationalism in Twentieth Century South Africa* (Harlow: Longman).

Jaff, F. (1975) *Women South Africa Remembers* (Cape Town: Howard Timmins).

Jaffee, G. and C. Caine (1986) 'The Incorporation of African Women into the Industrial Workforce: its Implications for the Women's Question in South Africa', unpublished paper presented at the conference on The South African Economy after Apartheid, Centre for African Studies, University of York.

Kimble, J. and E. Unterhalter (1983) '"We Opened the Road for You, You Must Go Forward". ANC Women's Struggles, 1912–1982', *Feminist Review*, vol. 12, 11–36.

Lacey, M. (1982) 'Resettlement Policy in its Historical Context', in E. Walt (ed.), *South Africa: a Land Divided* (Johannesburg: Black Sash).

le Roux, P. (1986) 'Growing up an Afrikaner', in S. Burman & P. Reynolds (eds), *Growing up in a Divided Society: The Contexts of Childhood in South Africa* (Johannesburg: Raven Press).

Lodge, T. (1983) *Black Politics in South Africa since 1945* (London: Longman).

Mackay, I. (1983) 'Mayibuye', in S. Molefe (ed.), *Malibongwe. ANC Women: Poetry is also their Weapon* (Stockholm: African National Congress).

Marks, S. & S. Trapido (1987) 'The Politics of Race, Class and Nationalism', in S. Marks & S. Trapido (eds), *The Politics of Race, Class and Nationalism in Twentieth Century South Africa* (London: Longman).

Matisonn, J. (1987) 'Meeting the ANC in West Africa: from Dakar to Burkina Faso', *Work in Progress*, vol. 49, 3–5.

Matlou, R. (1983) 'Mother Patriot', in S. Molefe (ed.), *Malibongwe. ANC Women: Poetry is also their Weapon* (Stockholm: African National Congress).

Moodie, T.D. (1975) *The Rise of Afrikanerdom: Power, Apartheid and Afrikaner Civil Religion* (Berkeley and London: University of California Press).

O'Meara, D. (1983) *Volkskapitalisme: Class, Capital and Ideology in the Development of Afrikaner Nationalism, 1934–48* (Cambridge: Cambridge University Press).

Simkins, C. (1986) 'Household Composition and Structure in South Africa', in S. Burman & P. Reynolds (eds), *Growing up in a Divided Society: The Contexts of Childhood in South Africa* (Johannesburg: Raven Press).

Simons, H.J. (1968) *African Women: their Legal Status in South Africa* (London: C. Hurst).

Strachan, B. (1983) *Never on our Knees: Youth in Apartheid South Africa* (London: United Nations Association of Youth).

Suttner, R. & J. Cronin (1986) *Thirty Years of the Freedom Charter* (Johannesburg: Raven Press).

Stultz, N.M. (1974) *Afrikaner Politics in South Africa, 1934–1948* (Berkeley and Los Angeles: University of California Press).

Unterhalter, B. (1982) 'Inequalities in Health and Disease: the Case of Mortality Rates for the City of Johannesburg, South Africa, 1910–1979', *International Journal of Health Services*, vol. 12, no. 4, 154–71.

Unterhalter, E. (1988) 'Class, Race and Gender: the Social and Economic Origins of Women's Resistance to Apartheid', in J. Lonsdale (ed.), *South Africa in Question* (London: James Currey).

Walker, C. (1979) *The Women's Suffrage Movement in South Africa* (Cape Town: Centre for African Studies, UCT).

Walker, C. (1982) *Women and Resistance in South Africa* (London: Onyx Press).

Newspapers

Argus, Cape Town
Star, Johannesburg

5 Sexuality and Economic Domination in Uganda
Christine Obbo

INTRODUCTION

In East Africa there co-exist two main views concerning women as biological and social reproducers and their membership within particular communities. On the one hand it is regarded as unimportant if one's mother, for example, is a foreigner as long as one has been successfully socialised according to the descent group ideology. It is held that the community gains through women marrying from one ethnic community into another. However, there is another view which perceives all women married to 'foreigners' as lost to the community. And by the same token women who marry into the community are perceived as being outsiders to the communities into which they marry. These contradictory views co-exist and are held by individuals often of the same group; they are more generally voiced by men who come from societies with a patrilineal descent system, as is the case usually in Uganda, although they exist as aspects of the dominant ideology which women hold also.

This chapter is concerned with the place of women's reproductive role in traditional ideologies defining 'the proper woman'.

Attitudes towards childless women, family planning and women's dress are indicators of the ways in which women's sexuality is defined and controlled. Arguments about scarce resources or foreign economic monopoly are often couched in terms of discussions about women and sexuality. The 'sexual protection' of women has a long history the world over and has a central place in patriotic discourses linked to nationalism and the defence of ethnic boundaries.

Both officially and privately ethnic chauvinism is regarded as mistaken and as a hindrance to Ugandan nationalism. However, sexism is treated as a given and therefore as unproblematic and natural: as specifying the commonsense existence of men and women. Differences between men and women are systematically and consistently emphasised to the detriment of women and as postulating subordination. This is evident in both public and private discussion and

arguments represented in conversations that men have as well as
those reported systematically in the media.

ISSUES AFFECTING WOMEN

In all Ugandan social or ethnic groups[1] women are defined primarily
as reproducers of new group members; and as reproducers of social
relations through their nurturing and socialisation roles. However,
these important roles, which are regarded as paramount for social
well-being, are used also as arguments to deny women a full and
equal share in employment and access to social resources generally.
Women's day to day lives are controlled and governed by a number
of factors. First, internal societal or ethnic ideologies determine, on
the one hand, the relationships between men and women through the
systems of kinship and marriage; and on the other, the distribution of
resources and access to resources and opportunities. Second, national
policies regarding remuneration in employment (such as equal pay
for equal work, or maternity and sick leave as well as other fringe
benefits like car loans, housing, travel and vacations) benefit a
minority of professional and educated women but leave the majority
of employed women vulnerable to the whims of male employers and
supervisors. There is no national policy or legislation protecting or
offering a way to redress sexism at work. Third, government policies
effectively benefit urban dwellers (mainly an elite minority) over and
above the majority of workers in subsistence agriculture and the
unskilled, unschooled urban migrants, most of whom are women.
Fourth, Western influence has served to reinforce many of the
internal social ideologies and has created new problems for women.
For example, values concerning the 'good Christian wife' are reinforced at high status levels by the importation of Victorian Christian
teachings. Female emancipation and equality is preached but at the
same time woman's place is seen as in the home and it is claimed that
she should be pure, domestic and virginal. There is no doubt that the
ideas about chastity found in both traditional and Christian ideologies
serve to control women's sexuality. Again cash-crop farming and
rural–urban migration were the direct result of foreign domination,
foreign trade and generally the recent infiltration of a capitalist
economy. Women have become the major agricultural producers of
cash crops and food, and serve to sustain the national economy and
subsidise the low urban wages paid to men. Needless to say, all this is

rationalised in terms of 'mothers feeding their families'. Consequently when women migrate to towns they are often criticised and labelled as a 'wasted resource' because they are regarded as most needed in the rural areas.

The decree in 1973 regulating female attire asserted that Ugandan women should look dignified like 'our mothers', and was premised on the often voiced belief that women who wear tight or short dresses are morally loose. Urban women were coerced to obey the decree by mobs of men or by soldiers who were empowered to arrest and even enjoy sexual licence over such women. During the 1950s, 1960s and 1970s assumptions of moral looseness were definitely behind behaviour towards them, such as economic harassment, physical coercion, arrests and deportation to the rural areas. Often there was the added financial drain of having to pay court fines.

The ideological coercion is clear: women in the urban areas are forced to subsist on prostitution, thus devaluing their worth as 'mothers' in the public eye; women in the rural areas are 'good mothers' because they produce for subsistence through the labours of their hands. However, no woman wishes to be considered a bad woman, because this devalues her as a 'mother' in the eyes of her family and community. However, at issue is women's access to work in the urban areas, which migrants perceive as providing greater opportunities to improve their situation and enabling them to surmount the mere subsistence levels of the rural economy.

DOMINANT SOCIETAL IDEOLOGIES OF GENDER

All social groups in Uganda are organised according to patrilineal principles which give men dominance in marriage and property relations. Women's biological role as child-bearers is regarded as their primary social role and defines their social worth. Consequently most women want an unlimited number of children, but in practice may only have a few due to their fertility levels or the antenatal and postnatal survival chances of their children. However, some women want only a few children either because they suffer unduly during pregnancies and deliveries, or because they do not want to be aged by the constant bearing of children. Highly educated mothers generally want fewer children, whom they can support and educate well. Again, from all available evidence, a woman with one or two children is regarded as a 'one-eyed person' deserving pity, and a woman with no children is pitied for her misfortune in 'being barren', and is despised. These attitudes are strong even in areas like Buganda where the fertility levels are low and infertility not uncommon, due to dietary deficiencies and the impact of venereal disease.

Ugandan men from all societal groups and socio-economic levels want proof of a woman's fertility[2] (Molnos 1973). Pre-marital pregnancies occur among both uneducated girls who give in to male pressure and educated girls and women who may be living with their boyfriend, often in the hope of speeding up matrimony. Thus women's strategies as they negotiate their roles as women, and as full members of their societies, find them by and large conforming to dominant values about women's roles. Women find themselves in a double bind, concurrently trying to prove that their chastity is beyond reproach and that they will prove faithful to their husbands; and at the same time having to show their desirability as marriage partners through demonstrating their reproductive potential. Men of course continue to practise the double standard according to which they not only enjoy sexual relations before marriage but as married men have access to other men's wives and daughters.

Women's handling of the double bind in their lives and the double standards practised by men often reflects their social and economic position. Status-conscious women or those with high economic status will behave in different ways from women with low 'status', and will tend to turn a blind eye to their husbands' infidelities, although they will often develop a passionate dislike for the 'other woman' whom they regard as 'home wreckers' and 'bad women' generally. In this way, high status women become trapped by the ideology of the 'good woman' as a faithful wife and mother. The high status women contrast their moral uprightness with the improbity of the other 'bad women'. They fail to take account of the uneven distribution of resources and power between men and women; and between the privileged educated few and the unprivileged masses who are constantly striving to transcend this condition. Of course, it is not uncommon (although ideologically upholding the ideas of chastity) for elite women to have affairs with elite men.

RESOURCES AND PRODUCTION

Land ownership is the most important asset for all Ugandans, irrespective of cultural and socio-economic position. Even in pastoral societies where livestock ownership is the most visibly important economic resource, it goes without saying that one needs access to land in order to feed the animals. The issue of land ownership is particularly important to women because they see it as the passport to other societal resources. In nearly all Ugandan societies women had, and still have, access to land by virtue of being wives and mothers. Women as wives are expected to assist, or as some see it, to work for, their husbands. This is repeatedly revealed when women identify men as managers and controllers of the household labour force and women as the controlled labourers who have to budget their time in order to fulfil their duties as mothers, wives and producers as well as responsible citizens whose duty is to attend the sick and bereaved. Women who fulfil their roles as mothers, i.e. reproducers of the community, fare better than those women who do not. But the numbers of women who reject marriage have increased as women have gained greater access to land and other sources of incomes. However, all things being equal, women would rather have both economic security and marriage; but only elite women seem relatively successful in maintaining the balance. Women are generally critical of other women who are taken in by the male declaration that they have joint property ownership. The difficulties that divorced or widowed women face in overcoming the social and economic disadvantages and even dispossession that often beset them are well known. It is commonly agreed by both men and women that the poorest man in Uganda is one who has no female relative or wife to work for him. In relation to this, a hotly debated issue is the effect to the household economy if women were allowed ownership of land (or among pastoralists, cattle). It is generally believed that women would be more likely to abandon their husbands, 'what then would be the purpose of marriage if women controlled their own land or property?'[3] This brings out clearly that women are dependent upon marriage for economic survival given their lack of land ownership and access to other valuable economic resources. In the Buganda province of southern Uganda since 1900 it has been possible for the female relatives of powerful men to acquire individual freehold ownership rights through receiving gifts or purchasing land. Needless to say, rich women can gain access to more land than poor women. In a number of districts a few forceful women have gained access to land by applying to district boards. However, by and large rural women have increased their share in societal resources by using their contribution to subsistence production as the bargaining point.

The incorporation of Uganda into the international capitalist system had the effect of increasing female employment through the addition of cash crops to subsistence production. This is crucial to understanding the low ability of employers in the towns to pay wages to men, particularly those from labour-exporting regions. Most of these men had wives who acted as unpaid agricultural workers, and the state has quietly incorporated them into the economy as unpaid workers who have functioned to subsidise low urban male wages. The colonial government regarded African men as urban 'visitors' whose rightful place was in the rural areas. Social scientists have tended to label the migrants as 'target' workers – e.g. spending a few months or a year working to buy a bicycle, a cow or a sewing machine or to build a tin roofed house, and then returning to the rural areas. In reality the migrants alternated their urban employment with home leaves which allowed them to continue existing social and property relationships in the village and to conceive children. By the mid-1950s, social scientists regarded them as 'circulating' migrants; and by the mid-1960s as the heads of two-household families who shuttled between town and country.

During the 1960s the five-year plan of the independent government of Uganda advocated employment opportunities that would improve the lives of rural dwellers and thus bridge the gap between rural and urban real incomes. In other words the government was aware of the need to alleviate rural poverty, unemployment and underemployment if people were to stay in the rural areas. Yet in their rhetoric, government ministers treated the urban migrants as lazy rustics who had inadvertently drifted to the towns and who therefore should be returned to the land for gainful employment.

However, in all these attempts to define and understand the urban migrants, the discussion centred on men who were assumed to be the major 'breadwinners'. Women, who remained in the rural areas, generating a second income through cash-crop production, and ensuring that the migrants and the children were well fed and in good health, were rarely mentioned. The women found themselves in a double bind, on the one hand producing within a capitalist system for which they received no remuneration; and on the other hand subjected to an ideology that regarded land as a resource that belonged to men. Furthermore, urban policies and public stereotypes clearly spelled out the view that migration to towns was not appropriate for women.

SEX AND NATIONALISM

Women's 'security' is often the last frontier men have to defend when all the other battles against colonialism and imperialism are lost. Human societies always portray their women as more virtuous than women of other groups and therefore in need of protection. Never mind that each society also coerces women to be 'good women' through imposing a number of sanctions against 'bad women'. Sexual involvement with foreign men, for example, makes a woman 'bad'. In Africa generally and Uganda in particular such involvement is seen as a perpetuation of colonialism and imperialism: that is both as a form of cultural–political and economic domination. On the other hand women are expected to submit to the sexual advances of indigenous men who dominate political and economic life. Thus men in the modern African state reserve the right to specify and control women's sexuality in much the same way as found in the more traditional relations of Ugandan society. The following section will treat in detail the following: first, Idi Amin's attempt to reconstitute the 'authentic Ugandan woman' during the 1970s; and second, an episode from the 1940s nationalistic struggles against Asian commercial monopoly which indicates the links between nationalism and gender.

In 1972 when Idi Amin was consolidating his control over various sections of Uganda, he legislated as a popular measure that women had to wear long dresses, i.e. well below the knees and preferably ankle-length. Women who normally wore the long traditional garbs (Kikoyi, Ssuka or buluti) joined men in criticising those wearing Western-style dress, mainly women who were in gainful employment in the towns, usually educated women of professional status. This controversy revealed many areas of clash in Ugandan society. Thus women stood opposed to women – an essential element of the criticism here related to the abandonment of traditional folk ways and culture. In addition, highly educated women and wives of elite men in general also condemned those women who dressed 'indecently' in order to trap men. This was an obvious reference to those women in the supporting or service jobs such as secretaries, bank tellers, shop assistants and barmaids whose wages were inadequate and who were always at the receiving end of sexual advances from their bosses. Some women in this group may have found it necessary to supplement their wages by acquiring a lover to pay their rent: and still many others found it imperative to entertain their male superiors in order to keep their jobs or earn promotions. Thus professional or elite women who themselves faced sexual harassment at work, but were more able to deal with it, were critical of the less educated professional women who were seen as 'loose' and out to seduce, 'snatch the purses' of or 'steal' their husbands. In other words, when it came to competing for men, elite women found it convenient to ignore the first-hand knowledge of sexual harassment which sometimes operates to deny promotions.

The whole matter of dress was an indicator of how much control not only Amin but Ugandan men in general had over women. During a meeting convened by Amin to talk with women leaders, elite women initially wholly supported his legislation dictating women's dress and condemning 'bad women' who dressed 'indecently'. But as the meeting progressed they found themselves on the defensive. This happened when Amin claimed that some Uganda women were doing 'terrible things', i.e. practising prostitution with the Europeans at the Kenyan port of Mombasa and thus ruining the name of Uganda. While no one could emphatically deny that there were Ugandan prostitutes at Mombasa, the leaders of the women's group found it necessary to inform Amin that some of those women were in fact married to Europeans. Subsequently, their spokesperson and later minister and ambassador was accused of misusing government funds to buy jewellery, and then of engaging in sexual activity with an unknown European at Orly Airport in France. Amin's ultimate act of cutting her down to size was achieved by publishing alleged nude pictures of the minister when she was a top Vogue magazine model living abroad. In the logic of the moment, it did not matter that she was wearing body stockings. What was at issue was that she had exposed her body to a white photographer and who knows what else! The connection was being made in the public perception that a woman who undresses for foreign men – for whatever purpose – is a prostitute. The identification of non-conformist women in the area of dress and behaviour with prostitutes reached a head. The minister was put under house arrest and according to reliable sources, her waist-long hair was chopped off with broken bottles. According to those who were familiar with the circumstances it was her refusal to submit to Amin's sexual demands that led to this brutal treatment. Thus women must not only be willing to admit to the sexual advances of powerful men but they must not get involved with foreign men who represent colonialism and economic exploitation.

This point is best illustrated by a letter written in 1956 as part of the early nationalistic struggle against British colonialism and Asian commercial dominance. The letter is significant because it appeared in a vernacular newspaper intended for African not Asian or European readers. It expressed grievances against economic exploitation in general and the sexual exploitation of women in particular:

(a) . . . 'parasites' which suckle Uganda . . . rob us and make us poor . . . the Indian traders . . . are a millstone weighing many pounds around the neck of Africans . . . They trick us and rob us saying that they are selling goods to us reasonably at proper prices whereas in fact they are profiteering. (b) They employ our young children, boys and girls, at very low wages in fact the shs 2/ which is given to them does not suffice to obtain a shirt or frock to help them out of difficulties which have induced them to work. As a result the boys learn pick-pocketing and the girls become prostitutes. Also the Indians are responsible for these young girls taking up the profession. For instance, look at the number of mulattos or people with mixed color and the majority of them belong to the Indians of Uganda. What causes this mixture is their desire to enrich themselves. The result is nothing but misery because these mulatto children have nothing to help them, neither do they leave them anything when they go back to India, even though when they go back they have amassed a great deal of money from this country. (c) The personal servants and the people who work for the Indians are people who are always found to be exceedingly dirty and untrustworthy. It is amongst them that we find ignorant people who speak in an obscene manner and who have not the manners of polite people. This therefore shows that they are not fellows and they copy this from their masters, the Indians. The personal servants and also employees of some Europeans are found however, to be paid good wages and are also clever, and clean at the same time. (G.R. Kizza, April 1946; quoted in Low 1971: 131–2)

This letter raises many pertinent issues regarding nationalism, racism and women's sexuality. Whereas earlier letter writers had deplored Asian economic exploitation and their patronising attitudes (Z.K. Sentongo, July 1941; quoted in Low 1971: 54). This letter also condemns Asians as uncouth and irresponsible. It is not clear whether little girls were initiated into sex to supplement their poor wages or whether once initiated they were employed specifically for sexual services. Amongst other things the point of the letter seems to be that the Asians were not only encroaching upon the economic rights of African men but upon their sexual rights as well. What seems clear is that the penetration of capitalism had pushed people to seek labour in an Asian-controlled place. It was part of Pax Britannica to use buffer zones. The African chiefs served as the political buffer of indirect rule while the Asian traders were the economic buffer between the colonialists and the 'natives'. The letter is very positive about Europeans as employers and as people whose cleanliness and manners were presumably faultless and imparted to their employees.[4] However, the Indians are seen as the opposite, presumably because they are in close contact with the 'natives' whom they despise and feel free to abuse verbally or sexually. Elkan found in the industrial town of Jinja that men objected to women's employment in factories because they would be at risk of bearing half-caste children through sexual relations with Asian employers (Elkan 1956: 1–6).

It is important at this point to backtrack and outline the economic and political context of the letter. In East Africa (Kenya Colony, Uganda Protectoratate and Tanganyika Territory), colonial society was organised like a three-tiered pyramid. At the top were the Europeans who controlled the political economy; in the middle were their protégés, the Asian civil servants and traders and at the bottom were the Africans, referred to as 'natives'. There was another group mentioned in the letter, the mulattos or 'half-castes'. Such children were reared in all three colonial social tiers depending on how the Asian or European fathers felt about their offspring. It would seem that those raised in African homes found total acceptance. Those raised by European fathers with the help of all-white boarding schools in England or Kenya, and African *ayahs* ('nursemaids') exhibited the most confusion. This was due to the conflict between their experiences of racism against people of colour (i.e. not quite white) and the fact that their holidays were spent with African domestics (among whom may have been their mothers) whom they had learned to despise. In the colonial social ranking system, the half-castes were ranked below the Asians. But in the zone where the Arabs seemed to float half-castes were ranked in descending order, after Europeans, Asians and Arab. (At least that was the ranking in colonial boarding schools.) The Europeans felt most guilty about their half-castes, although they would not fully accept them in their community. When Uganda attained political independence in 1962 colonial and neo-colonial cultural imperialism was blatantly promoted by the 'friends of Uganda', as the ex-colonials and new arrivals called themselves. The Ugandan Asian continued business as usual and still controlled the theatre and newspapers which were important vehicles for the dissemination of so-called 'cultural information' in the urban areas. One incident stands out clearly. When in 1962 Uganda, for the first time ever, entered a Miss World beauty contest, a half-caste with a European father was selected as Miss Uganda. Her confusion surfaced in London during press conferences when she claimed that her father was a rich coalminer. No coal has yet been discovered in Uganda and the girl's father was a civil servant.

CONCLUDING REMARKS: SEX AND POWER

In the final analysis, the racial tiering reflects the political economy and the relationships it generated. Property generally divides people into exploiters and exploited. Capitalist ideology stresses the freedom of individuals to sell their labour, but obscures the limited choices people have, which makes such freedom difficult, and the facts of exploitation. The colonial economic structure is the basic agent of change in relation to other social institutions. The employment of young children and particularly the sexual exploitation of girls is a case in point.

The issues of controlling or exploiting women's sexuality is a recurrent theme in relation to women's employment. As late as the 1960s, the employment of girls and women, though regarded as necessary in some cases, was seen as problematic. Salaried men often stopped the employment of qualified wives because 'their bosses will seduce them'. Uneducated men, whose wives worked for wages, bitterly resented the elite who controlled access to opportunities and employment, appropriating the sexual services of their wives. Ambitious, unmarried and salaried men all insist that they wish to marry women who will work and earn. However, these same men, as well as those with non-working wives or those who resent their wives' working, claim that women obtain and maintain jobs through being sexually accessible or that women take away jobs from men who are more deserving of work.

The argument presented in this chapter is that women's biological reproductive role has been used in debates about nationalism and those concerned with the need to control women. McKinnon has argued that 'Marxism and feminism are theories of power and its unequal distribution. They provide accounts of how social arrangements of patterned disparity can be internally rational yet unjust.

They argue, respectively, that the relations in which many women work and a few gain, in which some fuck and others get fucked are the prime moments of politics' (MacKinnon 1982: 156, 517). However, in all political moments the available options determine people's strategies. Women's conscious or unwitting choices often serve to reproduce and reinforce attitudes and practices in which their sexuality and its control are used by men to abuse them, to deny them certain privileges and to symbolically pursue struggles. In summary, this chapter has indicated that Uganda is predominantly a man's world in which sexuality – 'that social process which creates, organizes, expresses and directs desire, creating social beings we know as women and men, as their relations create society' (MacKinnon 1982: 516) – like other domains of society is controlled by men who reserve the right to dictate what women's sexuality should be. Patriotic arguments in defence of nationalism or ethnic boundaries incorporate in a central way notions of women's sexuality both in terms of sex and biological reproduction.

NOTES

1. The information presented in this paper was gathered between 1971 and 1974, and has been updated through subsequent letters and short-period research in 1977.
2. Ideas surrounding female sexuality and fertility in select East African societies have been adequately covered in Molnos (1973). The Ugandan groups covered in the volumes include the Baganda (Mere N. Kisekka; Martin Southwold); the Nyoro (John Beattie); the Lugbara (John F. Middleton); the Lango (Richard R. Curley); the So (Charles S. Laughlin and E.R. Laughlin); the Jie (John E. Lamphear); the Kiga (Rachel Van der Meeren-Yeld); and the Nkole (Musa T. Mushanga).
3. Co-operative officer during a discussion following a lecture given by the author on 19 May 1983 to 20 co-operative officers from Uganda at the University of Winsconsin-Madison.
4. The writer of the letter was a Mugandan. The Gandan maintained ethnic boundaries by claiming that everyone who was like Europeans was dirty and not like them. For example, this argument was used when they demanded separate hospital wards at Mulago. The argument also came up constantly during my fieldwork as an explanation of why Nyoro or Ruandan women were unacceptable as marriage partners. But since there were Gandan men married to Nyoro and Ruandan women, the explanation for this was: 'She is practically like us! She has

learned to be clean.' It is therefore alright having a Nyoro mother as long as she bears you in the clan (*Nyoko aberanga Munyolo nakuzaala Mukikka*). With regard to the Asians, most Ugandans groups considered them dirty because they spat in public, blew their noses using their bare hands and loudly cleared their mucus in their noses and swallowed it.

BIBLIOGRAPHY

Elkan, Walter (1956) 'The Employment of Women in Uganda', mimeo 1–6. Also published in *Bulletin de l'Insitut inter African du Travail, Brazzaville*, vol. 4 (1957) no. 4, 8–23.

Low, D.A. (1971) *The Mind of Buganda: Documents of the Modern History of an African Kingdom* (London: Heinemann).

MacKinnon, Catherine A. (1982) 'Feminism, Marxism, Method and the State: an Agenda for Theory', *Signs* vol. 7 (Spring) 516–17.

Molnos, Angela (1973) 'Cultural Source Materials for Population Planning', in Angela Molnos (ed.), *East Africa: vol. 3, Beliefs and Practices* (Nairobi: East Africa).

6   National Reproduction and 'the Demographic Race' in Israel

Nira Yuval-Davis

The issue of national reproduction in Israel, both in terms of its ideological boundaries and in terms of the reproduction of its membership, has always been at the centre of zionist discourse. During the 1980s, however, it has gradually come to overshadow even the issue of security as a precondition for Israel's survival. However, Golda Meir, the prime minister of Israel at the time, already confided in the early 1970s that she was afraid of a situation in which 'she would have to wake up every morning wondering how many Arab babies have been born during the night'! (quoted in Kahane 1983: 52).

A 'demographic race' between Jews and Arabs in Israel is seen as crucial to the survival of Israel, not only as the state apparatus of the population living in it, but as the state for Jews everywhere. Revealingly, the official aim of the Israeli demographic centre which was established as a unit attached to the Israeli prime minister's office in April 1967, is 'to act systematically to realize a demographic policy directed at creating an atmosphere and conditions for encouraging a higher birth rate, which is so vital to the future of the *Jewish people*' (my emphasis – NY-D; Demographic Centre 1979: 1).

This statement has to be read whilst bearing in mind that more than 75 per cent of world Jewry, according to statistics produced by that same demographic centre, live outside Israel. On the other hand, 17 per cent of Israeli citizens and about a third of the people under the direct control of the Israeli government (including those living in the territories occupied by Israel since 1967) are not Jews.

Israel was established for a specific purpose, and as the achievement of a specific political movement – zionism. While, as most of the chapters in this volume reveal, the definition of boundaries of national collectivities and their relationship to the state is very often problematic, in Israel it is especially so.[1] This can be understood partly in terms of the specific historical construction of the Jewish people as a territoryless people/caste with a religious civilisation in which Palestine was regarded as the 'land of the Fathers' and 'the Promised Land'. Like many other ethnic collectivities in Europe and particularly in the Third World, the dichotomy of nation/religion has not suited the historical construction of the Jewish people. Zionism has been only one response, and for a very long time a minority one, of the Jews in the 'modern' world to this history; in particular to their displacement and persecution with the rise of capitalism and nationalism in Europe in which their traditional mode of existence could not survive any longer (Leon 1970; Halevi 1986). The zionist movement aspired to the 'normalisation' of the Jewish people, through the establishment of a Jewish state in an independent territory in which, ideally, all Jews would eventually settle. The problems of defining the boundaries of the Israeli national collectivity stem, therefore, not only from the specific character of the Jewish people, but are also a result of the history of zionist settlement in Palestine and the establishment of a settler colonial society there. This relates to contradictions in Israeli social structures and social forces, in relation to Jews outside Israel and non-Jews within Israel, as well as ethnic, religious and class divisions amongst Israeli Jews themselves. All of these contradictions are expressd in debates in Israel around demographic issues.

Demographic policies often seem to be determined by worries over sufficient labour power for the national economy. Indeed the literature on reproduction often assumes it to be the complementary facet to economic production, or rather a precondition to it (e.g. Edholme *et al*; 1976 McIntosh 1981). A closer examination of national demographic policies (as well as state welfare policies), however, will often reveal that national political rather than economic interests lie behind the desire to have more children, or rather, more children of a specific origin.[2] In Israel, where economistic calculations have never seriously determined major political decisions (even in the heart of an extremely economic crisis (Yuval-Davis 1984), this is certainly the case. This chapter will therefore concentrate on examining the nationalist angle in the ideological debates and policies which have surrounded the question of the birth rate in Israel. It will then consider the ways in which the political and ideological pressures to define and reproduce the national collectivity in Israel have constituted Israeli Jewish women as its national reproducers.

DEMOGRAPHIC POLICIES AND THE 'NEED' FOR A JEWISH MAJORITY

Israeli demographic policies have had two hegemonic goals:

(a) the first has been to maintain and, if possible, increase Jewish domination in Israel, both in terms of a numerical majority and also in terms of military and technological superiority over the Arabs;

(b) the second one, which gradually plays a more and more central role in the preoccupation of the Israeli policy makers, has been to reproduce and enlarge 'the Jewish people' all over the world and for Israeli Jewish mothers to have enough children to 'compensate' for the children lost in the Nazi Holocaust and to what is called in Israel the 'Demographic Holocaust' and assimilation.

Traditionally, as a settler society, immigration (*Aliya*) was considered to be both the quickest as well as the cheapest and most efficient method of increasing the Jewish zionist presence in Palestine. The 'need' for a Jewish majority has always been the cornerstone in zionist thinking. Ben-Gurion, debating in the *Knesset* (the Israeli parliament) in 1949 (during the war which expanded Israel's territory far beyond the territory allocated to it by the UN), explained:

A Jewish state . . . even if only in the west of Palestine is impossible, if it is to be a democratic state, because the number of Arabs in the western part of Palestine is higher than that of the Jews . . . we want a Jewish state, even if not all over the country. (Protocols of the Knesset, 4 April 1949)

The priority of a Jewish majority in Israel in zionist strategy has been one of the issues debated all along between the 'left' and 'right' of the zionist movement, especially before the establishment of the state and after 1967. A Jewish majority has always been more important to the zionist 'left'. However, even the zionist 'left' was prepared to accept a majority of only 55 per cent in the first instance, as was planned in the UN partition plan of 1947 which was to divide Palestine into a Jewish and Palestinian state (this never actually materialised as a result of the 1948 war). The zionist 'left', however, planned various ways to expand that majority (Bailin 1985).

During the 1948 war, Israel enlarged by more than 50 per cent its allocated territory, having divided the planned Palestinian state with

Jordan. This could have meant a Jewish state with an overwhelming Palestinian majority. However, most of the Palestinians under Israeli rule either escaped during the battles and were never allowed to return, or were expelled by force. This, plus the major Jewish immigration, in its first few years of existence, to Israel from postwar Europe and from the Arab countries, reduced the Palestinian minority in Israel in the early 1950s to no more than 11 per cent. Still, in the hope of reinforcing this ration, Ben-Gurion initiated in the early 1950s rewards (of IL100 – even then more of symbolic than substantial value) for 'herione mothers', defined as those who have had ten children or more. Israeli Jewish mothers continued to be urged to have more children.

The birth rate within the Jewish and Palestinian population in Israel was not, however, even. In the early 1960s the situation arose whereby, on the one hand mass Jewish immigration to Israel stopped, and on the other hand the rate of birth also started to drop amongst the more traditionally oriented Israeli Jews. At the same time, the Palestinian birth rate in Israel did not decrease significantly, while Palestinians' life expectancy increased (by 1967 the Arab minority in Israel constituted 15 per cent in comparison with the 11 per cent of the early 1950s).

The 'ultimate threat' of the gradual growth of the Palestinian community in Israel and the 'erosion of the Jewish majority' kept on growing as a political issue, especially after the 1967 war and the public debate about annexation of the occupied territories with its massive Palestinian population. But the concern has been growing also in relation to the Palestinians who live within the 1949 borders, who are Israeli citizens, and who, for the first time in the 1980s started to be counted, for sheer numbers, as an important electorate lobby.[3]

In the mid-1960s (before the 1967 war and around the time of the establishment of the demographic centre), major confiscations of Arab lands were carried out in the Galillee. The official name of this policy, initiated by Levy Eshkol, the prime minister at the time, was to 'Judaise Galillee'. When this goal failed a public debate developed, triggered by a secret document leaked to the press which was written in 1967 by a civil officer called Konig. Various means were suggested to fight this tendency, which included, among others, encouraging Arab emigration from the country by limiting Arab prospects of employment and studies, cutting Arab child national insurance benefits and more. Since then, the 'demographic race' and the annual Jewish and Arab birth rate continue to be discussed prominently in the Israeli national press, accompanied by gloomy demographic predictions and/or attempts to refute them.

The Israeli Palestinians have not been reluctant participants in the 'demographic race'. Large numbers of children, especially boys, has always been important in Arab rural society, which was organised around the extended family. Modernisation has had contradictory short term effects on the rate of growth of the population. The rate of life expectancy has grown; the rate of mortality has fallen, and both these facts have overwhelmed the beginning of the trend of falling birth rates (Ronen 1982).

Since the 1970s the number of children has become also a conscious political weapon among Palestinian nationalists. This has been true about the whole of the Palestinian movement. In the 'post-Konig report' period, slogans like 'The Israelis beat us at the borders but we beat them at the bedrooms' started to be heard, and poems, a traditional mobilising means in Arab societies, were written in this spirit.[4] The Israeli authorities more or less admitted that no active policies of population control which are used in other Third World countries have any chance of finding co-operation from either the 'traditional' or the 'modern' elements in the Arab sector. Nevertheless, social welfare clinics were established, and Palestinian women are the only ones in Israel who can obtain free contraceptives.[5]

Since the Israeli government is unable effectively to control the number of Palestinian children being born, quite a lot of Israeli government policies have concentrated on bringing more Jews from abroad and gradually, when that happened less and less, promoting and encouraging the growth of the Jewish birth rate in Israel itself. This was done both through propaganda work and with material incentives. For example, 'The Fund of Encouraging Birth' was established in 1968 by the Housing Ministry to subsidise housing loans for families with more than three children. These benefits, like larger child allowances, were given basically only to Jews, under the euphemistic definition of 'families who have relatives who have served in the Israeli army'.

Clearly all these policies have been of greater symbolic than of practical value when we take into consideration what is actually involved in bringing up a child. But even on this symbolic and auxiliary–practical level, these policies were not universally approved of in Israel.

One line of objection was raised by militant liberals and leftists.

They joined the Israeli Palestinians in pointing out the racist character of using the state apparatus to discriminate against Palestinians and to block their access to a whole line of state benefits. Right wing nationalists, however, also objected to using the state apparatus for that purpose – they would have preferred the Jewish Agency, which caters only for Jews and not for all Israeli citizens.

Another line of opposition to these policies was on the grounds that, while promoting national goals, these policies were not taking into account class (and therefore also intra-Jewish ethnic) divisions in the Israeli society – as the number of children rather than the income of the family was used as the qualifying criterion for child and housing benefits.

This line of opposition reflected a growing concern in the early 1970s with issues of poverty and ethnic antagonism within the Jewish collectivity. Class differentiations between Ashkenazi (of Occidental origin) and Oriental (mostly of Arab countries origin) Jews in Israel grew rather than shrunk in the 1960s (Smooha 1978; Bernstein and Svirsky). This situation changed somewhat in the 1970s through the influx of a large number of Palestinians from the occupied territories into the Israeli labour market and the consequent economic upward mobility of sections of the Oriental Jews. Nevertheless, the Jewish poor in Israel today are still overwhelmingly of Oriental Jewish origin (E. Farjun; A. Ehlich 1983). Growing popular protest movements within what is often called 'The Second Israel' (the best known one but by no means the only one being the Israeli Black Panthers) have brought this reality to the political arena as well, especially as the Oriental Jews have become the majority of the Israeli electorate.

The government committee which examined these issues found that 75 per cent of the children who grew up in Israel in economic deprivation have come from large families of four-plus children, mostly from Oriental Jewish families, and they constitute about 40 per cent of all Israeli children (Prime Minister's Committee 1974).

It is important to note in this context that, although a Jewish majority in Israel was very important to the zionist movement, it was also always very aware that in the Arab east it will always be a very small minority. The petit bourgeois socio-economic background of most of the zionist settlers before the establishment of the state, their technological and organisational superiority over the underdeveloped Arab world, imperialist support as the most consistent local allies and the nationalist myth of 'there is no alternative', all enabled the continuous success of Israel in its wars against the Arabs (at least until the Lebanon War). Quality, then, rather than quantity was the crucial factor. (In the late 1970s and 1980s the situation has been changing and Israeli newspapers reported with anxiety that there is a much higher number of university graduates in the Arab world than in Israel as well as a growing deterioration in the quality of the Israeli army human power (e.g. Sharit 1985).

It was therefore, again, primarily a national concern, as well as an attempt to appease the growing protests of 'Second Israel' (as the Oriental Jews are frequently known), which affected a significant development in the direction of welfare policies in Israel in the 1970s, measures such as the introduction of social security, 'slum rehabilitation' programmes etc. For a while the (Jewish) family's economic situation rather than the number of children became the official criterion for housing support.

This political trend, resulting from the fear of too many children growing up in poverty-stricken households in Israel, can also be said to be one of the major factors which, combined with ideological pressures, have brought about abortion legislation in Israel. This occurred after years when there were no official policies on abortion, which had resulted from the fear of running into political trouble whatever decisions would be taken (Yishai 1978). In fact, abortion legislation has become one of the major mobilisation factors of the growing right wing nationalist and religious camp. For them, not only abortions but family planning in general for families smaller than four children is objectionable.[6]

For large sections in the pro-natal lobby in Israel, having many children is not just an inevitable outcome of keeping religious codes concerning procreation, an expression of Jewish traditional values or even a means of making Israel stronger by enlarging the number of potential soldiers. It is not even a question of simply keeping a Jewish majority in Israel. It is also a way of reproducing and enlarging the Jewish people which has dwindled, first through the Nazi Holocaust (caused by anti-semitism) and then through the 'Demographic Holocaust' (caused by assimilation and intermarriage when there is not enough anti-semitism).[7]

If, at the beginning of the zionist endeavour, it was the Jewish mothers in the Diaspora who produced human power for the Yishuv settlement in Palestine, it was now the 'duty' of the Israeli Jewish mothers to produce even more children for the sake of the Jewish people as a whole. In 1983 the 'Law on Families Blessed with

Children' was passed, giving a whole range of subsidies to families with more than three children.

The lobby which organised the pro-natal politics in the early 1980s revived the 'Efrat committee for the encouragement of a higher Jewish birth rate' which had been dormant for most of the 1970s. In the early 1980s it became powerful enough to establish centres and branches all over the country. It was able to incorporate within its ranks major elite figures from all professional fields, both religious and secular, and to gain an official place as a governmental consultative body on natal and demographic policies committees (together with the official women's organisations). Efrat gained much of its public power through linking the debate on the Jewish birth rate with the public campaign around the abortion issue.

As part of its coalition agreement with the religious parties, the Begin government, when it came to power in the late 1970s, abolished the one category in the abortion law which enabled legal abortions to be carried out on the grounds of 'social hardships' (the other categories are: the age of the woman; the pregnancy being a result of 'forbidden relations'; health of the fetus; and health of the woman). This angered the feminist lobby, but was not enough to appease the anti-abortion lobby, especially as liberal social workers on the abortion committees have tended to apply the woman's health category instead.[8] Along with the usual reasoning of anti-abortion lobbies who treat abortions as murders came the emotive call to the Jewish mothers to do their national duty and replace the Jewish children killed by the Nazis. An extreme example of this ideology was a suggestion, narrowly defeated, of the Advisor of the Minister of Health of the time, Haim Sdan, to force every woman considering abortion to watch a slide show which would include, in addition to horrors of dead fetuses in rubbish bins, the pictures of dead children in Nazi concentration camps. After a large public campaign this specific proposal was defeated and Sdan eventually resigned. Nevertheless, 'the war on the demographic war' continues.

It is worth remarking, however, that at the time of writing this chapter, in the mid-1980s, the effects of the overall economic, political and ideological crisis in Israel were making their marks on the various policies which have been used in the 'demographic race'. Within an overall context of drastic cuts in real wages and the threat of rising unemployment, the effectively reduced state incentives have lost, to a great extent, any practical effects that they might have had a few years previously. This, plus a growing negative balance of immigration and emigration movements to and from the country, have gradually turned attention more and more to the transfer of Palestinians from the country, as the only possible valid long-term solution for keeping the zionist character of the Israeli state.[9]

Nevertheless, on January 1986 Avidov-Hacohen MP, of the Likud Party, suggested making 1987 an official year for 'the encouragement of Jewish birth rate in Israel'. Hooting and laughter followed his speech in the Knesset from its more liberal and leftist members and wonderful satires followed in the press. But his suggestion has had enough support not to be defeated. One of the Knesset committees received the task of promoting this proposal as part of its agenda.

JEWISH WOMEN AND 'THE NATION'

We have seen how Israeli Jewish women have been 'recruited' in the 'demographic war' to bear more children as their national duty to the Jewish people in general and in the Israeli Jewish people in particular. It is debatable to what extent the ideological pressures, child benefits or other formal and material collective measures are the crucial factors for having a child, or when an unplanned pregnancy occurs, for keeping it. The emotional needs of people in a permanent war society (when husbands and sons might get killed at any moment) and cultural familial traditions probably play a much more central role than anything else. Whatever the main reason, the fact is that Israeli Jewish women, especially professional middle class women, do bear more children than their counterparts in other advanced capitalist societies.[10] And their role as suppliers of children to 'the nation' directly affects the availability of contraceptives and abortions. As mentioned before, there are no free contraceptives in Israel (except for Palestinians) and abortion legislation is a focus of major public political debates – not unique to Israel, but with a very explicit nationalistic emphasis in comparison with campaigns in other countries where the 'moral right' has been fighting against abortion legislation.

Historically – until the 1960s, and since the beginning of the zionist movement – it has been mainly Jewish mothers in the Diaspora who 'supplied' the human power for the zionist settlement to be possible. The zionist endeavour can be described as involving an organisation with clear international division of labour – in the Diaspora the members and supporters of the movement supplied financial and political support and human power, and in Palestine, at the 'front', these resources were used to promote the zionist project of establishing an exclusively Jewish society over Palestine (Hecht and Yuval-Davis 1978; A. Ehrlich 1980). This division of labour continues to date, as without the financial and political support of the Jewish Diaspora, Israel could not have continued to exist. In the supply of human material, however, the balance has gradually shifted and the discussion today focuses, as we have seen, on the role of Israeli Jewish mothers in replacing the overall shrinking Jewish national collectivity all over the world rather than, or in addition to, the other way around.

Within the zionist Yishuv itself, pressures were out on Israeli Jewish women to bear more children since the beginning of the limitation on the number of Jewish immigrants to Palestine under the British mandate.[11]

However, initially the main emphasis of Jewish motherhood in Israel had more to do with its qualitative aspect – of producing the 'New Jew', 'the Sabre', the antithesis of the 'Diaspora Jew' whose negative image the zionist movement shared with European anti-semitism – rather than necessarily with the quantity of children. The latter was envisaged as coming mainly from Jewish Aliya from abroad. The role of the Israeli woman was to participate in the national struggle, mainly in supportive roles (Yuval-Davis 1982; 1985), and in addition, to produce proud, rooted and 'normal' children.

The development of the specific ideological construction of women as national reproducers in Israel has had much to do with the specificity of the historical development of Israeli society as a permanent war society. The ideological placement of women in this respect was best summed up by M.P. Geula Cohen:

> The Israeli woman is an organic part of the family of the Jewish people and the female constitutes a practical symbol of that. But she is a wife and a mother in Israel, and therefore it is of her nature to be a soldier, a wife of a soldier, a sister of a soldier, a grandmother of a soldier. This is her reserve service. She is continually in military service. (Hazelton 1978: 113)

There have been many myths concerning the role of Israeli women as soldiers (Yuval-Davis 1985). Basically, however, and to a great extent as in the civil labour market, women in the army serve in subordinate and supportive roles to that of men, unless in roles which directly correspond to the ideological tradition of women in looking after the welfare of their menfolk. The few women who are engaged in combative occupation do so in order to release men for front duties from which women soldiers are officially banned. Also, as Geula Cohen says, women, unlike men, are released mostly from reserve service which is the mass popular base of the Israeli army where men serve at least one month a year until they are 50 years old, as their most important national role. The women's national role then becomes to produce babies who would become soldiers in future wars.

This ideological construction can explain why groups like 'Women against the War' and 'Parents against Silence' have been so effective in their protest against the Lebanon War. They have touched the heart of the ideological assumption that the Israel Jewish society is fighting only because 'there is no other alternative' for continuous collective survival, and therefore the individual's sacrifices (constructed specifically according to gender and age and to a certain extent class and ethnic origin) are willingly made. When we look at the effects of the national reproductive role of Israeli Jewish women, however, it is important to remember that we are dealing here not only, and even not mainly, with effects which relate to the actual number of children they produce and for what. We are also concerned with the ideological and legal constraints in which this role of theirs is being constructed.

Jewish women in Israel, and for that matter in the Diaspora as well, are being incorporated actively in the zionist endeavour, not only in supplying humanpower to the national collectivity, but also legally and symbolically, as markers of its boundaries. A Jew, according to the Law of Return, which entitles any Jew from anywhere in the world to automatic citizenship in Israel, and following the Jewish orthodox religious law, is somebody who was born to a Jewish mother (unless s/he is a religious convert). Motherhood, therefore, rather than fatherhood determines membership in the collectivity.

However, this matrilineal tradition does not mean that Jewish society is a matriarchal one. It is not even fully matrilineal – as the family name of the child is that of her/his father, and not the mother. The collective matrilinearity in determining who is a Jew was suitable to the existence of the Jewish community as a persecuted minority, in which pogroms and rapes were historically a recurring phenomenon.

As such, motherhood was a safer way of determining inclusive boundaries, and tight measures were taken in the religious code to secure the legitimate reproduction of the boundaries of the Jewish collectivity marked by its women.

Jewish women in the Diaspora in principle can choose whether or not to remain subjugated to the religious code. Not so Israeli women. The Israeli state apparatus has added its coercive power to the traditional voluntary Jewish communal power in several crucial instances, and given it monopolistic rights. This requires explanation, as the zionist movement generally presented itself as a 'modern alternative' way of being Jewish to the traditional religious one. However, in spite of the fact that the majority of the zionists were, at least originally, vehement secularists the zionist movement never completely broke away from Jewish orthodoxy. The zionist movement needed the religious tradition for justifying its claim over Palestine as its homeland, rather than the land of its indigenous population; it also needed the recognition of at least major sections of the orthodox Jewish communities, as the zionist movement claimed to represent all the Jews all over the world.

This is why (in addition to more *ad hoc* government coalition calculations) there has always been a partial incorporation of the Jewish religious legislation into the Israeli state legislation and hence its usage for determination of 'who is a Jew'.

To be born Jewish is more than being a child of a Jewish mother. One has to be born to a Jewish mother in the 'proper' way – otherwise one is considered a *mamzer* ('bastard'), would not be considered a Jew, is not able even to become a Jew by conversion, and one's descendants cannot marry other Jews 'for ten generations'. Bastardy in Judaism is not a question of being born outside wedlock as sexual intercourse, according to Jewish religious law, is one of the ways marriage can be contracted (as long as it is another Jew – rapes during pogrom did not receive such a 'sanctification'). Bastardy is a question of being born to a woman who is having a forbidden relationship of adultery or incest – and that includes even women who are divorced by civil (rather than religious) court, which unlike civil marriages are not recognised by the religious court, and who are having children from their second husband.

The major ideological justification which has been given for the incorporation of orthodox religious personal law into Israeli legislation and accepting its definition of 'who is a Jew' has been that doing otherwise will 'split the people'. It was claimed that accepting the authority or other Jewish religious denominations, such as the Conservative and Reform Judaism, let alone secular legislation, would make it impossible for orthodox Jews to marry anyone but other orthodox Jews, for fear of incorporating unintentionally the forbidden mamzers into their family. The paradox is, of course, that in reality no orthodox Jew marries a non-orthodox one (or even newly 'born again' orthodox Jews who come from secular families – exactly because of this fear). Moreover, outside Israel the majority of Jews do marry and divorce in a non-orthodox fashion, even if they marry before a Rabbi, and in Israel itself private contracts in lawyers' offices have become more and more popular as an established alternative to official marriages. The attempt to control the Israeli collectivity boundaries and its patterns of reproduction in an homogeneous way by incorporating the severe orthodox religious law into the Israeli state legislation has, therefore, not really succeeded. On the other hand, it has had a fundamental influence on the position of women in Israel.

Several attempts have been made since the establishment of the state of Israel to guarantee equal rights for women in terms of employment and payments, as well as to protect their rights as workers when becoming mothers. This legislation suffers from limitations similar to other legislations found in this area in Western states, in which women are constituted in the law primarily as wives and mothers. Also as in other countries, this legislation does not manage to alter the basic segregation and inequality between women and men in the labour market (Land 1978; Wilson 1977). What is more specific to Israel, however, is the fact that all the attempts to guarantee women's overall equal constitutional rights in principle have failed. This was not so much the result of direct intervention by the religious parties, as that of preventative actions of the other zionist parties who were afraid of the withdrawal of the support of the religious parties from their coalition governments which would damage the zionist claim to be 'the representative of the Jewish people'. This is why Rabin, the Labour government prime minister in 1975, declared that a Fundamental (i.e. quasi-constitutional) Law of Women's Equality will never be passed in Israel. However, as early as the 1930s, at the height of its ideological zeal, the Labour zionist movement (which defined itself as secular) was ready to give up women's right to vote. This was in order to prevent withdrawal of the extreme religious communities from the Yishuv institutions (the zionist settler community). What 'saved' the women then was the fact that the extremist religious parties withdrew anyway (Azaryahu 1977).

Women do have the right to vote in Israel, although in the last few years they have been prevented from doing so in local elections in some extreme religious settlements, especially among the settlers in the occupied territories (like Immanuel). But in the 1950s, Golda Meir was prevented from becoming a candidate for the mayorship of Tel-Aviv as, according to the Halakha, it was claimed, 'women are not allowed to govern men' – and this position never changed. Golda herself was eventually 'allowed' to become prime minister because, it was argued, formally her role there was that of 'first among equals'.

The most serious effects of the incorporation of religious laws into state legislation on women's status relate to their position in family law, where control of their constitution as bearers of the national collectivity is most carefully guarded. They are not allowed to become judges in the orthodox Rabbinical state courts which have the monolopy to decide in issues of marriage and divorce, and their evidence as a rule is not accepted, especially if there are male witnesses. In relation to the guardianship of children and to maintenance, there are two parallel court authorities, secular and religious. In the latter, especially, constructions of what should be the proper duties of a wife are exclusively decided by a small reactionary patriarchal group of Rabbinical judges. If these 'duties' are to be unfulfilled they result in a woman losing all her maintenance rights and being declared 'a rebel'. The inequality between the sexes affects also the women whose husbands disappear – in peacetime and even more so in Israel's continuous wars. Unlike men, they are not allowed to remarry until some proof can be brought that their husbands are certainly dead, and if they move to live with another man and have children by him, the latter are declared as *mamzerim*, outsiders to the Jewish national collectivity for ever.

A CONCLUDING REMARK

This chapter has examined some of the factors determining the relationship between women's position and their roles in Israeli society and the central concern of zionism for the reproduction of the Israeli national collectivity as 'Jewish'. To this purpose it has focused on the series of debates accompanying various demographic policies which have attempted to reinforce it. It shows that issues of marriage and divorce, birth control and child benefits are intimately linked with claims over territories and citizenship rights, class divisions and plans of mass transfer.

The first proposal for a private Member of Parliament's Bill that was raised by Rabbi Kahana, the leader of the neo-nazi Kach Party was, therefore, no mere coincidence. Rabbi Kahana's party has been the fastest growing political power in Israel in the last few years. He preaches for the mass expulsion of Palestinians from all over Israel as well as the occupied territories and a few years ago established in Jerusalem the museum of 'the Future Holocaust', predicting an end of American Jewry similar to that in Nazi Germany. His proposed Bill (which was invalidated on legal grounds so as to avoid formal voting on the issue in the Israeli parliament) suggested the legal prohibition of sexual relations between Jewish women and Arab men. Women and their sexuality are seen as the gate-keeping elements for the boundaries of the national collectivity.

This leads directly to the question, to what extent feminist struggle is possible within zionist discourse (Hecht and Yuval-Davis 1978; Lehzman 1987). It is a sobering revelation in that respect to read an editorial not by Kahana, but by the liberal zionist Uri Avner, one of the most consistent fighters in Israel for democracy, civil rights and women's equality. Avnery, who in the mid-1960s used to mock the demographic-race mentality as 'rabbit psychology', states as an acceptable fact in the mid-1980s that 'The new Jewish community in this country, from the beginning of the Zionist Aliya until today, simply cannot absorb anybody who is not Jewish' (*Haolam Hazeh*, 24 April 1985).

Are Kahana's supporters right when they claim that he is the most consistent zionist?

NOTES

1.   See part I of my paper 'The Jewish Collectivity and National Reproduction in Israel' in *Khamsin 13, Women in the Middle East* (London: Zed Books, 1987). The present chapter is based on parts II and III of that paper.
2.   See, for example, Beveridge Report (1942: 154): 'With its present rate of reproduction, the British race cannot continue; means of reversing the recent course of birth rate must be found.' And in the Soviet

Union, like in Israel, they rewarded 'herione mothers' for those with ten children and more (*Guardian*, March 1979).

3. During the last election campaign, for the first time the election campaign by the major zionist parties in the Arab sector in Israel did not take place mainly via traditional Hamula heads. This was especially true for the party headed by General Ezer Weizman.

4. In May 1976, the poet Owani Sawit was arrested after reading some of his poems in the 'Day of the Land' memorial, including a poem in which he promised: 'Hey murderer/ Do you really believe that you can murder my people?/ This is an impossible mission/ If you murder six, we shall bring to the world sixty on that same day' (Arabic).

5. I was told by a social worker, that as long as these clinics were headed by Palestinian women, they tended to co-operate with the Israeli authorities on policies of family planning, although from a very different motivation – of care for individual women rather than control of overall numbers. During the 1980s, Palestinian men have become heads of some of these clinics and it is rumoured that attitudes towards family planning have changed considerably.

6. The secretary of the Efrat committee explained to me that, as so many Jewish women get married and start bearing children only after their military service (at the age of 20), any family planning aimed at limiting child-bearing to once every few years would necessarily limit severely the number of children such women could have before menopause.

7. Professors Baki and Dela Pergulas of the Hebrew University are continually quoted in the press, predicting the shrinking of world Jewry from the present 11.5 million to 8 million by the year 2000 and to 5 million by the 2200, and pointing out that by now 43 per cent of world Jewry births are taking place in Israel (although less than 25 per cent of world Jewry actually live there).

8. The table in the Efrat bulletin (no. 15–16) shows that in 1979 there were 15 925 legal abortions in Israel, of which 1665 were granted under the category of the age of the women; 4465, forbidden relations; 2165, danger to the embryo; 1299, danger to the woman; and 6331, the social situation of the woman. The last category was abolished in 1980 and in 1980 the number of abortions came down to 14 703. However, in 1982, the number of legal abortions was 16 839, 1775 for age; 6632 for forbidden relations; 2626, danger to the embryo; and 5796, danger to the woman. Clearly the last category has been used by the abortion committees as a substitute for the category which was abolished.

9. During July–August 1987 the debate on the desirability of the transfer of the Palestinians out of Israel and the occupied territories held major newspapers' headlines in Israel. This happened when central figures in the Israeli establishment (to differentiate from supposedly marginal rightists like Rabbi Kahana), like ex-General Rekhavam Zeevi and the Undersecretary of the Ministry of Security, Michael Dekel, spoke publicly in defence of the idea, and moreover presented themselves as mere followers in that respect of the major pre-1948 labour zionist leaders, like Berl Kazenelson and David Ben-Gurion.

10. The average number of children of Jewish women in Israel in 1984 was

2.7, while it was less than two, if not one, in most Western countries. For systematic comparison of the situation of women and the family in Israel and in other countries, see Y. Peres and R. Katz, *Megamot*, 26.1, 30–43 (Hebrew).

11.   I myself am an 'historical product' of Ben-Gurion's call for 'Internal Aliya' (immigration) in the early 1940s when the news of the Nazi Holocaust started to arrive. . .

BIBLIOGRAPHY

Azaryahu, S. (1977) *The Organization of Hebrew Women for Equal Rights in the Land of Israel* (Hebrew) (Keren Leezrat Haisha).

Bailin, Y. (1985) *The Price of Unification: the Israeli Labour Party until the Yom-Kipur War* (Hebrew) (Revivim).

Beveridge, W. (1942) *Report on Social Insurance and Allied Services* (London: HMSO).

Davis, U. (1987) *Israel: Apartheid State* (London: Zed Books).

Demographic Centre (1979) *Goals and Means of Demographic Policy* (Hebrew) (Labour and Welfare Ministry).

Edholm, F. O. Harris & K. Young (1977) 'Conceptualizing Women', *Critique of Anthropology*, vol. 3, no. 9, 101–30.

Ehrlich, A. (1980) 'Zionism, Demography and Women's Work', *Khamsin* no. 7, 87–106.

Ehrlich, A. (1983) 'The Oriental Support for Begin – a Critique of Farjun', *Khamsin*, no. 10, 40–6.

Farjun, E. (1983) 'Pax Hebraica', *Khamsin*, no. 10, 29–39.

Ghilan, Maxim (1974) *How Israel Lost its Soul* (Harmondsworth: Penguin).

Halevi, I. (1986) *History of the Jews* (London: Zed Books).

Harris, O. & M. Strivens (1981?) 'Women and Social Reproduction', unpublished paper.

Hazleton, L. (1978) *Israeli Women – the Reality behind the Myth* (Hebrew) (Idanim).

Hecht, D. & N. Yuval-Davis (1978) 'Ideology without Revolution: Jewish Women in Israel', *Khamsin*, no. 6, 97–117.

Kahane, M. (1983) *Thorns in Your Eyes* (Hebrew) (Jerusalem, Institute of Jewish Ideas).

Land, H. (1978) 'Sex Role Stereotyping in the Social Security and Income Tax System'. in J. Chetwynd & O. Hartnett, *Sex Role Systems* (London: Routledge & Kegan Paul).

Leon, A. (1970) *The Jewish Question, a Marxist Interpretation* (Pathfinder Press).

Lehrman, D. (1987) 'Feminism in Israel – a Common Struggle?', *Khamsin* 13, 94–8.

McIntosh, M. (1981) 'Gender and Economics', in K. Young, C. Wolkowitz & R. McCullugh (eds) *Of Marriage and the Market* (London: CSE Books).

Orr, A. (1983) *The Unjewish Staff* (Ithaca Press).

Peres, Y. & R. Katz, 'Family and Familiality in Israel' (Hebrew) *Megamot*, vol. 26, no. 1.

Prime Minister's Committee (1974) *Report on Children and Youth in Distress* (Hebrew).

Ronen, H. (1982) 'Israeli Arabs Multiply Faster than the Chinese', *Bamakhane* (army weekly; Hebrew), 17 November.

Shahak, I. (1981) 'The Jewish Religion and its Attitude to Non-Jews', *Khamsin* nos. 8 & 9, 27–61 & 3–49.

Shamgar, L. (1979) 'War Widows in Israeli Society, (Hebrew), Ph.D thesis, Hebrew University.

Sharit, A. (1985) 'Is Israel Withdrawing from the Army?' (Hebrew), *Koteret Rashit*, 15 May.

Smooha, S. (1978) *Israel – Pluralism and Conflict* (London: Routledge & Kegan Paul).

Svirsky, S. & D. Bernstein (1980) 'Who Worked in What, for Whom and for What' (Hebrew), *Booklets for Research and Critique*, no. 4, 5–66.

Wilson, E. (1977) *Women and the Welfare State* (London: Tavistock).

Yishai, Y. (1978) 'Abortion in Israel – Social Demand and Political Responses', *Policy Studies Journal*, vol. 7., no. 2 (Winter)

Yuval-Davis, N. (1982) *Israel Women and Men: Divisions Behind the Unity* (Change Publications).

Yuval-Davis, N. (1984) 'The Current Crisis in Israel', *Capital and Class*, no. 22 (Spring) 5–14.

Yuval-Davis, N. (1985) 'Front and Rear: the Sexual Division of Labour in the Israeli Army', *Feminist Studies*, vol. 11, no. 3 (Autumn) 649–76.

Yuval-Davis, N. (1987) 'Marxism and the Jewish Question', *History Workshop Journal*, no. 24 (October) 82–110.

7 Women and Reproduction in Iran
Haleh Afshar

INTRODUCTION – IRAN: STATE AND NATION

With the rise of fundamentalism and the imposition of its values on the daily lives of Iranians, women are firmly directed towards domesticity and selected as the bastions of honour and familial respectability. The family is seen as the centre and motherhood as the nexus of nationhood. The imposition of motherhood as the sole national obligation of Iranian women has been exacerbated by the long-running war against Iraq. The reproduction of future martyrs has become the patriotic duty as well as the function of womanhood. This chapter examines the political context within which this has occurred alongside an examination of women's position in contemporary Iran.

Iran is a land of diverse tribal and regional people with one religion; 99 per cent of Iranians are Muslims and of these almost 90 per cent are Shi'ias. But though united in religion, Iranians are widely divided in their ethnic origins, cultural backgrounds and social practices. Persian, which is now recognised as the national language, is merely the language of the largest minority which has, through state control of the educational system and the media, been imposed as the *lingua franca*. The process of unification of the nation through explicit state policies dates from the modernisation policies of Reza Shah Pahlavi in the 1920s.

The secularisation process was part and parcel of Reza Shah's attempt to modernise Iran within a very short period of time. He saw two major obstacles to this process: the religious establishment, which remained the bastion of traditional and 'backward' ideology; and tribes who presented a major threat to the emerging centralised national government. All the major tribal groups were defeated within the first decade of the Pahlavi's rule (1921–78). To ensure their continuing subjugation, Reza Shah placed all the major tribal chieftans, *Kavanin*, under house arrest in the capital Tehran. Subsequently, both Reza Shah and his son Mohamad Reza Shah married

110

daughters of tribal chieftans to forge a political alliance with these groups and secure their allegiance. The *Kavanin* made the best of the situation by acting as intermediaries between the regime and their people, and seeking to represent the interest of the minorities in the capital. In the long run, the children of many of these chieftains grew up in the city and went abroad to be educated. They returned home as town dwellers, and found it difficult, if not impossible, to return to the rigours of nomadic life. At the same time, Reza Shah sought to force tribal people to abandon their migratory lifestyle and settle in selected villages, although this policy was only partially successful and at times exacerbated tribal feuds.

There are deep divisions among tribal groups and regions. Tribal groups, who are ethnically of different origins, stretch across national boundaries. The Kurds live in Turkey, Iran and Iraq, and the Baluch in Pakistan as well as Baluchestan. Similarly, the Arab Khamsin tribes in the south are closely related to their Arab relatives across the river Shat'al Arab. But tribal allegiances did not and do not imply unity; the Kurds are divided among themselves and, as the Iraquis observed, the Khamsins in Khuzestan were not willing to support their Arab brethren in their invasion of Iran.

The central policy authority in Iran has traditionally relied on inter- and intra-tribal differences to maintain its control. The policy continued during the Pahlavi era and the divisions between ethnicity, tribalism and nationhood played an important role in permitting the establishment of a relatively secure and secular centralised government. Nevertheless, tribalism continues to provide both a strong sense of identity and a basis for struggle against the encroachment of state policies in the country.

THE STATE AND THE RELIGIOUS ESTABLISHMENT

The religious establishment has traditionally provided an alternative arena for the struggles against the state. Shi'ias do not recognise a secular head of state empowered to exercise political control over the nation. The only legitimate ruler, according to the Shi'ia, is the Imam, the direct male descendent of the prophet. The Iranian constitution of 1906 asserted that the nation's religion is the Isthna Asahri Shi'ia Islam, and endorsed much of the Islamic dictum, particularly where the domestic sphere was concerned. Accordingly men were recognised as the legal head of the household and enabled to exercise considerable power over their wives and children including the unequivocal rights of divorce and custody of children.

Although the religious establishment retained a critical view of the state, it shared the bureaucracy's distrust of minorities and denied the validity of the many regional and local varieties of interpretations that Islam has had in Iran. Religious beliefs can become diluted in different regions and have frequently been influenced by local superstitions, saints and sufis. These local cults can easily be accommodated by the flexibility of Islamic ideology. But the religious establishment has always resisted such fragmentation of its central authority and the *ulama* have usually supported policies that imposed and maintained a sense of national unity. This is surprising since, in essence, nationhood is a relatively unimportant concept in Islam. The whole Muslim community, *Ummat*, is seen as one people guided by total submission to the rule of Islam which, by its nature, transcends national and international boundaries.

Despite its conservative nature, the Iranian religious establishment has spearheaded many revolutions and uprisings in Iran's recent history. In the first instance, these were to protect traditional interests as a whole and the merchant classes in particular against the penetration of foreign interests in the country. There is a close alliance between the bazaar, the commercial and financial centre of the merchant economy, and the *ulama*. The Shah's decision to welcome foreign capital immediately alienated both the church and the merchants. Nevertheless, by the turn of the century the Shah continued to hand out commercial monopolies to foreign capital. Iranian banking, customs and excise, oil and even the gendarmerie were handed over to foreign control at a rapid pace. The bazaar and the *ulama* reacted by staging a revolution and calling for a constitional monarchy. The ensuing constitution in 1906 appointed a group of *ulama* to supervise all future legislations with the right to veto over those that contravened Islamic dictum.

The constitution did not recognise any of the national minorities and Farsi was declared as the *lingua franca*. The *ulama*, who aspired to *umma* and its concepts of universality, saw the emergence of a centralised Muslim state as a useful step towards a utopia of Muslim unity. Tribal and ethnic divisions, as well as differences in languages and religious interpretations were, in turn, viewed as potential threats to such an ideal state.

With the arrival of the Pahlavis, the *ulama* began losing much of their control over the social and political life of the country. They had been the main source of education, carried out exclusively for boys, and main source of legal decisions, running the *shariat* ('religious') courts and controlled all registries, public endowments and private trusts (Keddie 1961–2). Reza Shah instituted secular education and judiciary systems. He imposed secular taxes, which undermined *khoms*, and set up an extensive and secular bureaucracy, gradually eroding much of the power of the clergy, and curtailing their lucrative source of income.

The secularisation process was to prove of great benefit to women, who began to gain access to education and the formal labour market.

WOMEN AND SECULARISATION

The Iranian constitution of 1906 barely recognised women as legally independent individuals. Despite their important contribution to the revolution, they were not given the vote and were legally defined as dependent wives and daughters within male-headed households. It took Iranian women nearly 30 years to gain equal access to education and another 30 to get the vote. Men's arbitrary rights of polygamy and divorce took yet another decade.

Reza Shah's modernisation policies, however, proved invaluable to the liberation of women. In 1937, Reza Shah issued a decree for compulsory unveiling. Iranian women were officially barred from wearing the all-enveloping *chador* and required to appear in public dressed in Western-style clothes. Iranian men were also encouraged to wear Western-style clothes, as were civil servants. The ban on the veil was preceded in 1936 by the simultaneous admission of male and female students to the newly inaugurated University of Tehran. Women, in their capacity as mothers, were viewed as crucial links in the modernisation process, and an effective means of transmitting the secular ideology to the new generations.

Nevertheless, the civil code, enacted in 1932, did not radically change the social and legal position of women. The law closely followed the Islamic Sharia laws, the only deviation was the raising of the age of marriage to 15 for girls and 18 for boys.

By contrast the criminal code, enacted in 1940, was modelled on the *code Napoléon* and its formulation closely followed the Belgian model. It was a final blow to the *ulama*'s legal authority and abandoned much of the Islamic practices, such as equating the word of one male witness with that of two females, or banning women from practising the law. Nevertheless, the code accorded men the right to murder their adulterous wives, mothers or sisters without giving similar rights to women.

WOMEN, MARRIAGE AND THE WOMEN'S MOVEMENT

The Shah's liberating measures provided an opening for the women's movement to continue its struggle for emancipation and equal rights particularly in the domestic sphere. Within the family women in general and wives in particular were accepted as socially subordinate and unequal, and had little legal recourse against husbands. Polygamy was legal: four permanent and numerous temporary marriages, *siqeh*, which could be for as short or as long a period as the husband wished. Men had the legal and unilateral right to divorce and custody of children (boys at four and girls at seven years), without any right of access for mothers. It was the man who decided where the family should live, and whether the wife was permitted to work or travel abroad; in both cases women had to obtain formal permission granted in the presence of a public notary. Ironically, although a wife's identity was clearly defined in terms of her husband, women were not legally permitted to change their surname to that of their spouse on marriage.

Marriage was a formal means of granting control over women, their sexuality, their fecundity and their daily lives to the husband. Women retained their Islamic right to their personal wealth and property and the inalienable right of inheritance. But their husband could so circumscribe their lives as to make these material rights irrelevant.

All Iranian women were unavoidably subject to the marriage laws, since it was illegal for them to marry foreigners without the formal permission of the Ministry of the Interior. Foreigners who married Iranian women were required either to become Muslims or to suffer imprisonment for infringing the law. Curiously enough, it was the foreign husband and not the woman who was so punished. Iranian men, however, were not subject to such restrictions; they could marry anyone they wished at any time and any place. But, since civil marriages were not recognised by the state, all those who married Muslim men had to convert to Islam. The father bestowed his name, nationality and religion on the children and thus it was legally impossible for Muslims to have legitimate non-Muslim children.

The women's movement gained some impetus from the secularisation policies and spent the period 1940 to 1962 in formulating and fighting for its demands. The major issues were the vote, direct and equal access to the labour market and curbs on the extensive domestic control by husbands. The early 1960s were years of political turbulence which included massive street demonstrations and strikes, organised by middle class and professional women. Finally in 1963 women got the vote. Once enfranchised middle class women made rapid strides in the public sphere, by 1978 there were 38 women judges, one woman minister, five deputy ministers, one ambassadress and 400 university lecturers.

By the 1970s the arena of the women's struggles had shifted to the domestic sphere. Already in the mid-1960s the institution of marriage was showing signs of weakness in Iran. The country had the fourth-highest rate of divorce in the world and one in every four marriages resulted in separation. In all these cases women lost the custody of their children and had little other than their *mahre*, a sum negotiated and recorded in the marriage contract which is payable to the bride for the consummation of the marriage. Normally this is received by wives on divorce rather than at the time of marriage. Given that husbands could prevent their wives from working and stipulated where and how they lived, divorced women often found themselves unemployed, in a strange city, with few friends or relatives and no visible means of livelihood.

The 1967 and 1975 Family Protection Laws finally curbed polygamy and men's unilateral right of divorce. The Family Law Courts were interposed between men and their Islamic rights of marriage and divorce. The first wife's consent was required before a second marriage was permitted and custody was made subject to the court's decision, and women who gained custody were entitled to claim alimony. The husband's right to decide on a wife's occupation was tempered by a similar right on the part of wives; for the first time ever Iranian women seemed poised on the brink of legal equality.

The Shah, whose personal opinions of women were quite unacceptable, chose to support their case for a number of reasons. In the context of the rapidly modernising economy women provided a plentiful and cheap source of labour and could be used to displace the more troublesome men in many of the processes of production. To do so women had to be relatively free to choose their employment. As to the middle class women, they were an obvious and vociferous support base for the Shah who, particularly in the early 1960s, had little popularity.

The land reforms which began in 1962 alienated the wealthy landed gentry and the religious institution who controlled much endowed and shrine lands. Similarly, the merchants who used land holdings as secure investment were vehemently opposed to these measures. At the same time, the Shah's decision to close the *Majlis* ('Parliament') and rule by decree alienated many of the middle classes and severely undermined his legitimacy as a ruler. Without the support of the army, the monarchy would not have survived the decade. As it was, rebellions, strikes and demonstrations were the order of the day. In this context the support of women was seen as a valuable political asset. Furthermore, the central role that women played in the socialisation of future generations was seen as an obvious means of gaining the backing of future generations for the rule of the Shah. His influential twin sister, Ashraf Pahlavi, was appointed as head of the Women's Organisations and the way was paved for radical legal reforms.

Not all women, however, supported the feminists. In particular the insistence on sexual freedom and the rejection of marriage, family and the traditional notions of shame, modesty and dignity alienated the majority of Iranian women. For the impoverished working class women the provisions of the Family Protection Laws were largely irrelevant. They did not know about them and had no means of securing those rights. Access to the formal labour market was, however, a welcome opportunity with their domestic duties. Furthermore, it was frequently the husband and father of employed women who negotiated and obtained their wages. Thus the economic boom of the 1960s did not necessarily benefit the working class women.

Some middle class women were also weary of feminism. The more traditional mothers feared the disregard for family honour exhibited by their daughters. Often mothers of feminists resorted to marrying off their younger daughters straight from school to prevent them from embarking on the immoral venues of liberation. As to the majority of Iranian men, they saw the liberalisation process both as a direct threat to their position of social and economic superiority and as a rapid erosion of their familial status. Not surprisingly the Islamic backlash found extensive support.

Once more the clergy spearheaded a revolution in 1978. The anti-American and anti-imperialist rhetorics were backed by constant references to the national loss of honour and dignity. This usually meant the loss of control over sexuality and reproductive activities of women, and a resulting loss of face and national identity. Women as well as men supported the claims that the country as a whole was losing its moral standards. The religious backlash offered among other things the reinstatement of the natural social order and the affirmation of family as the core and motherhood as the nexus of nationhood.

It would be all too easy to dismiss these views as anti-feminist and retrograde, but since the mass of Iranian women did and still do share these views it is essential to analyse why they emerged, why they found such a wide acceptance and why they continue to attract an inordinately large number of women.

It is crucial in this context to understand the emotive and cultural importance of concepts such as honour and dignity. Muslim women in general and Iranians in particular did and still do accept the burden of respectability. In Iran as in many other Third World countries, family honour is defined in terms of the sexuality of women and the ability of men to control and exchange women and their reproductive powers. Women themselves share these views which attribute disgrace to those who choose to deviate from the norm. It is those women who have deeply imbibed the male ideologies who are now instrumental in both maintaining and transmitting these traditional standards.

Marriage is central to the transfer of control over reproduction and the marriage market, which is largely organised and run by women. Mothers are instrumental in choosing prospective marriage partners and assessing their wealth, health and suitability. Thus, although men negotiate the actual marriage contract, women control the future of their children. Not surprisingly mothers see the process as desirable and empowering and a means of becoming something of a matriarch within the domestic sphere. So long as the traditional values are maintained all mothers have the prospect of power and prestige. Once the married couple produce children, then grandmothers are accorded the prestige of the custodians of family health, welfare and morality. Traditional ceremonies run by women and for women initiate and protect each and every stage of child-rearing and enhance the authority of older women over the family as a whole. Even working class women whose wages support the husband and numerous children see motherhood as an essential part of their life and cherish the prospect of retiring into grandmotherhood. For them children are the only available source of financial security at old age and grandchildren a means of gaining familial control and authority.

To deny the aspirations of the majority of women towards self-fulfilment through motherhood would in practice mean the denial of an active support base for any 'feminist' movement in Iran today.

To see marriage and motherhood as oppressive institutions imposed by men to control women is correct in terms of the theoretical analysis. But it is irrelevant in terms of tactics and strategy in a country where the majority of women lamented the liberation of their daughters because it resulted in the denial of marriage and blocked the natural progress towards maternal control of the domestic sphere. This resistance was not confined to the lower and lower middle class women; it was as much an intra-class division as an inter-class one.

Women in Iran, as women elsewhere, were faced with a widely segregated labour market, where few had any hope of gaining a secure livelihood through their waged employment and where all continued to carry out their domestic obligations. It is therefore hard to see any firm grounds for them to support what they saw as degrading materialistic policies which denied their importance as mothers, yet gave them little power and opportunity to succeed outside the marital framework. Repressive as they are, the current Iranian policies of domestication of women create a clear and important role that many women appreciate and value; motherhood is now a national duty and publicly revered.

MOTHERHOOD AS A NATIONAL DUTY

In adopting motherhood as a national duty, the current regime is endorsing the views of the more traditionalist women, as well as appealing to those who did not find life under the Pahlavis particularly liberating. Most women were all too aware of their marginality to the oil boom and the ensuing bonanza. But now they have been given a central role to play, a role which they have always had but have never been applauded for by the entire state propaganda machine. The new regime is cleverly equating domesticity and motherhood with being 'pivotal in securing the continuation of Islam and its values'.[1] Women are told they are crucial because they 'raise brave men in their laps' (Khomeini, *Kayhan*, 17 May 1980). This 'natural' function ensures the very survival of the system. Khomeini, the 'great leader of the revolution' categorically confirms this view: 'so long as you ladies play your part and raise our youths, this Islam will go forward' (*Kayhan*, 14 March 1985).

The expansionist aims of this 'forward' movement are for the moment absorbed at the Iraqi borders. The Iranian government, however, has no intention of ending this war which has taken the lives of thousands of youths. What is required of women now is to play their 'decisive part' in this encounter and 'raise good children for the battle fronts' (*Kayhan*, 30 November 1986), to protect Islam and 'achieve all the ambitions of humanity' (Khomeini, *Kayhan*, 17 May 1980). Motherhood has become a public duty as well as an heroic one. 'You heroic women of Iran, you carry hope and wisdom on your back and the future generations in your hands. It is you who must bring the cargo of revolution to a safe harbour'.[2]

It is by returning to the heart of the family that Iranian women have become 'central', 'pivotal', 'invaluable' etc, attributes that were not commonly given to the 'weaker sex' in the pre-revolutionary days. The family is offering salvation to all woman-kind and saving them from the horrors of feminism and society from total destruction:

> Women in some western countries have strayed from the natural limits of their unborn selves and gone beyond the social and natural requirement. This has brought suffering and destruction to the women themselves and to society as a whole.
>
> As a result of such inappropriate behaviour in the west, in the name of women's liberation, whole generations of children are left uncared for and unprotected. They have become like soulless, mechanical beings devoid of human sensitivities.[3]

It must be noted that in the context of the current public discourse in Iran, 'the family' is meant to be interpreted as motherhood: 'In truth only a wise, caring and religious mother can raise an ideal child, no man has the capability of fulfilling such a role. This is a characteristic ability that nature has bestowed on women.'[4] The synonymous use of *family* and *motherhood* is so prevalent that male orators never think of mentioning fatherhood as a necessary part of 'the family'. Men, Iranian women are told, 'have to carry the heavy burden of heading the household and it falls upon them to manage its complicated financial transactions'.[5] It is not easy for those middle class women who fought for equality throughout the century to accept defeat. Yet many women have come to see motherhood as an achievement as well as a national duty.

MOTHERS AND MARTYRDOM

The question of feminism and inequalities may have had a very
different impact had there been no war. But the Iranian revolution
has for but one of its eight years of existence been at war. This war
has used men as gun fodder. The entire nation is mobilised and males
of all ages, as young as 12 or as old as 65 are encouraged to come
forward and give their lives for the cause. An atmosphere of hysteria
is nurtured by the media, the religious establishment and the
government, and all are promised a gateway to heaven through the
saintly road of martyrdom. Martyrdom, however, is the sole domain
of men. It is one of the 'separate and special rights reserved for men
in Islam'.[6] Women are merely the mothers, wives or sisters of
martyrs. In this atmosphere of heightened hysteria, women have
become the guardians of cradles and coffins (Afshar 1982). Mothers
of martyrs attend Friday prayers, address the gathered multitudes
and talk of the 'blood-stained shrouds' of heroes. Some announce
that they have given as many as five sons to the revolution and will
have more on offer (*Kayhan*, 5 October 1985).

Newspapers report the sweet sorrows of mothering martyrs:

> The messengers of hope and pride, they were at the graveside of
> the martyrs. The place which enshrines our hopes and sorrows and
> those of thousands, no tens of thousands of scarlet oaths of love;
> the place which is the centre of hope for smitten mothers and which
> exerts a calming influence on all.
>
> Mothers of martyrs, their wives, sisters, children and their
> relatives all visit the graves on pilgrimage to celebrate the new
> year. Under their salt tears they smile in the knowledge of the
> eternal happiness, seeing the soldiers fulfilling their engagement to
> shed their blood and march triumphantly towards eternal spring.
> (*Kayhan*, 29 March 1987)

It is as mothers that women have created both the youths and their
bravery:

> This love and commitment which has sprung among our youth is
> rooted in the sacred tears that fall from the eyes of the mothers of
> martyrs at the feet of our martyred imam Hosein. The tears
> entwined with the milk that the suckling babies drink at the
> fountain of their mother's breast. What a unique mana and reward.
> This mixture of tears and milk imbibed while hearing about the

heroic deeds of the martyrs of Islam, this is the spiritual food that raises our devout martyrs. (*Kayhan*, 17 March 1985)

Mothers are encouraged to follow the examples set by those who gave their sons to the cause of Shi'ism, a sect born of blood and martyrdom. Mohamad's son in law Ali sought to follow the prophet and become the caliph of Muslims. In the event he failed to do so and finally took up arms against the sunni caliph. It was an unequal struggle and Ali and many of his male descendants died in some of the bloodiest of battles. Iranians have revered all these imams, and their heroic deaths are the themes of stories repeated regularly; particularly during the month of Muharam when these battles occurred. Men and women have traditionally gathered to hear of these heroic deeds, and cry for their saints. The imagery of tear-stained suckling babies does reflect the reality of the experience of many of the less wealthy classes. It has always been assumed that crying for the imams paved the way to heaven for the believing shi'ias.

Since the revolution this oral tradition has been taken on board by the newspapers who frequently print similar tales. One that is obviously addressed to women was published in the popular daily newspaper, *Kayhan*:

> Vahab ibn Abdolah ibn Habab Kali was one of the followers of martyred imam Hosein. His mother said unto him 'rise my son and help the descendant of the Prophet.' He responded 'Rest assured that I would not fail in this duty.' He went forth and killed many a foe and returned. 'Oh mother, are you pleased with the deeds of your son?' His mother responded 'I will be totally satisfied only when I see that while leading the men of imam Hosein, May God Hail his Soul, you are killed in battle.' (17 March 1985)

An anonymous young woman writing to *Kayhan* exhalts the ability of women to cope with suffering and reminds her sisters of Omeh Leila:

> Be like the wife of Imam Hosein Omeh Leila who watched while the enemy cut the throat of her husband, then her son and all her children before her very eyes. The heartless enemy killed them in that desert of Kerbala without even giving them a drop of water to quench their saintly thirst. (15 May 1985)

Such obviously bloodthirsty language is not viewed as obscene by the readers. In fact, it is thought to reflect the powerful poetry and the graphic experience of suffering for a just cause.

The language of death and joy are intertwined. Martyrs announce in their last letters home: 'I chose to espouse the gun and share my life with the holy war *jehad*, May God bless this union.'[7]

But, whereas martyrs may marry death, women and particularly war widows are expected to remarry fast and continue to reproduce: 'Widows of martyrs must not be hidebound by archaic traditions of sorrow and mourning, they must gather their offspring and move on to a new husband.'[8] Since women have been squeezed out of the public sector, those who lose their breadwinners become an instant problem. Despite many statements of intent, the government has nothing, other than glory, to bestow on wives of martyrs. They have been officially classified as 'the unprotected', and in 1983 the Majlis passed a bill instructing the government to 'submit, within a three months period, the necessary legislation and appropriate budget for protection of the unprotected women and children'.[9] But although by 1987 the government was spending an annual average of 15 billion rials on the children of the martyrs and war casualties (*Kayhan*, 19 April 1987), their wives remain 'unprotected' and continue to be viewed as a social 'problem'.

Even worse is the 'problem' of single girls. The speaker of Majlis Hojaloleslam Hahsemi Rafsanjani has publicly denounced the terrible phenomenon of 'unmarried women' as 'Western-style urban depravity'. At a Friday prayer meeting he lamented the fact that:

> almost one in every seven women has no husband . . . What can we do with them? The society must think about this problem. We have 4 to 5 per cent more men than women and the number of unmarried men is also greater than that of women . . . Obviously the Islamic solution is to encourage these women to get married. The Majlis must try and introduce measures to secure this process. We must think about this one-seventh of our female population and think how we would feel if we were so deprived. (*Kayhan*, 2 November 1985)

Naturally, the unmarried men are not seen as a 'deprived' and 'problematic' lot, they are destined to 'espouse' martyrdom. Now the pressure is on women to marry disabled war returnees or embark on temporary or polygamous marriages. 'Honour', 'grace' and 'pivotal' roles are all the preserve of mothers, all other women, particularly the unmarried ones, are merely 'problems' that can only be solved by marriage and reproduction.

The new regime embodies the ideological backlash against feminism. All the legal ground gained in the past 70 years was repealed within the first seven months of the Islamic rule. Men have regained their right to polygamy, though in the case of permanent marriages this is made subject to the approval of Family Courts. Permission is granted to all men who are deemed able to support more than one wife and to all who wish to marry war widows regardless of their economic means. Temporary marriages are not subject to any control nor to any maximum numbers. Men are entitled to have an unlimited number of concubines who, like permanent wives, must 'obey' their husbands and never deny them their sexual demands. Men can also divorce at will. Temporary wives have no recourse to the law, permanent wives may go to court to claim their *mahre*. Fathers and paternal ancestors have legal custody of all children and their consent is needed by a spinster who wishes to marry.

Not only have men gained total control of the domestic sphere, but also women are now required to become socially invisible by adopting the Iranian *chador*, a garment that covers them from top to toe, or a similar Islamic *hejab* ('veil'). Those who refuse to do so are subject to 79 lashes, which are administered immediately. Nurseries have been closed down as 'dens of subversion' and mothers of young children are not permitted to work full-time. Although officially women are not barred from seeking employment, with the exception of teaching and nursing, they are finding it ever more difficult to obtain jobs.

CONCLUSION

The problems of living in an Islamic society, aggravated by the soaring prices of food and accommodation and the cuts in civil service salaries have made it impossible for many women to espouse the idealistic views of Islamic domestication. The struggles of daily life, the ever-longer queues, the ration cards that cannot be exchanged for food, the empty shelves in government shops, shortages of everything for those who have little money and abundance for the wealthy who can pay the exorbitant black market prices, are all contributing to the increasing disillusion among many of the poorest women. But the loss of hope is in many cases tempered by the massive war hysteria and the emphasis placed by the state in its expressed admiration for and endorsement of motherhood. Mothers of past and future martyrs are called upon at every turn to save the nation, its honour and its war against the oppressor. Mothers of martyrs are not only honoured by speeches but also entitled to extra rations, to better resources and to favourable treatment across the board. The combination of expressed honour and actual economic rewards makes it easier for mothers of martyrs to live in the hope of seeing the Islamic utopia which has a special place for such mothers. Motherhood has become a personal aspiration for unmarried women who are forever encouraged to embark on the 'sacred duty of motherhood' as soon as it is physically possible. The family is hailed as the saviour of the future of the nation and the women are the instruments chosen by God and the country to secure this future. Women have become part and parcel of the mechanisms for producing and educating 'martyrs'. As educators of martyrs they are deemed to be in full-time employment and in need of neither formal education nor paid employment outside the home. Girls' schools are increasingly concentrating on a segregated curriculum training women to become good mothers of martyrs and the few university places that are available are strictly segregated. Women are not admitted to scientific and engineering subjects and even agriculture and rural development has been defined as unsuitable for women. This, in a country where women are the sole cultivators of the staple food, rice.

The clergy and the media continue to exalt the 'natural' sensitivity of women and their 'natural' reluctance to embark on any intellectual pursuit quite unsuited to their tender psyche. They have become designated as unequal before the law, they are unable to give evidence unsupported by a male witness and are in many cases entitled to half as much justice as their male counterpart (Afshar 1985). All this because of the assumption that women have no place in the public and formal sector and require no protection in the private domestic one.

The inherent contradictions of this world view of domesticity and the real need of most mothers to work in order to pay the exorbitant rents, the ever-rising prices is proving a more effective means of raising women's consciousness than the polemics of feminists' arguments presented by middle class women. The situation is exacerbated now that the bombs are falling on cities and attacking homes in the capital city, for there is nowhere to go and little protection. The government is of the view that self-reliance is needed if the country is to survive. Self-reliance is proving more and more to be reliance on women to secure the survival of the family. But for most women, although the expectations are emphatic, there are few legal means of achieving this end. The contradictions between the ideology of domestic bliss and the reality of survival through the war is becoming too extreme. The war hysteria is increasingly tempered by demands for a peaceful settlement and many women find themselves supporting the call for peace since they are less and less able to fulfil their heroic role of warmongers.

NOTES

1. Hojatoleslam Hosein Mirkhani, Director of the Political Ideology Unit of the Tobacco Co., *Kayhan*, 22 June 1986.
2. Maryam Behrouzi, MP for Tehran, speaking in the Majlis (parliament).
3. Hojatoleslam Hashemi Rafsanjani, Majlis Speaker, *Kayhan*, 26 July 1984.
4. Ibid.
5. Ibid.
6. Hojatoleslam Movahedi Kermani, MP and member of Islamic Propaganda Unit, *Kayhan*, 2 March 1986.
7. Martyr Naser Farrajalahi, *Kayhan*, 8 October 1981.
8. Ayatolah Mohamadi Guilani, member of the Council of Guardians.
9. Law for the Protection of Unprotected Women and Children.

BIBLIOGRAPHY

Keddie, N. (1961–2) 'Religion and Irreligion in the Early Iranian Nationalism', *Comparative Studies in Society and History*, vol IV, 289.

Afshar, H. (1982) 'Khomeini's Teachings and their Implications for Iranian Women', in *In the Shadow of Islam* (London: Zed Press) 27–75; and *Feminist Review*, no. 12 (October) 59–72.

Afshar, H. (1985) 'The Legal, Social and Political Position of Women in Iran', *International Journal of the Sociology of Law*, no. 13, 47–60.

8 Women and the Turkish State: Political Actors or Symbolic Pawns?

Deniz Kandiyoti

In 1987 Turkey was a country offering the perplexing spectacle of a sit-in and hunger strike by ultra-religious women students demanding the right to don the veil to go to classes (a right officially denied), and a small group of feminists marching through the streets to demonstrate against violence against women, virtually in the same week. While to an outside observer this may seem merely a healthy manifestation of political pluralism, the roots of the contemporary situation have to be sought in the specificities of the woman question in Turkey and of its evolution through time.

The role played by the Turkish state after the establishment by Mustafa Kemal Ataturk of a secular republic in 1923 on the remnants of the Ottoman Empire, has represented nothing short of an all-out onslaught on existing social institutions and mores surrounding the status of women. It is little wonder therefore to find that most discussions of the woman question in Turkey tend to centre around the republican legal reforms, their meaning and possible strategic importance for the state. These reforms were extensive. The Turkish Civil Code adopted in 1926, inspired by the Swiss Civil Code, outlawed polygamy, gave equal rights of divorce to both partners, and granted child custody rights to both parents. Women's enfranchisement followed in two steps: women were first granted the vote at local elections in 1930 and at the national level in 1934. These rights were not obtained through the sustained activities of women's movements, as in the case of Western suffragist movements, but were granted by an enlightened governing elite committed to the goals of modernisation and 'Westernisation'. It is a fact that the reforms remained merely formal for a long time especially in the rural areas most weakly integrated into the national company, and class-biased in that they primarily benefited the women of the urban bourgeoisie. Nonetheless, their very existence signalled a new positioning of the state *vis-à-vis* the woman question which deserved to be explained.

First-generation republican women writers tended to stress the intrinsic necessity of these reforms in the development of a democratic, civic society (Taskiran 1973; A. Inan 1964). More recently, Tekeli has suggested that women's rights have played a strategic role both against the political and ideological basis of the Ottoman state and with respect to establishing proofs of 'democratisation' *vis-à-vis* the West. She argues that singling out women as the group most visibly oppressed by religion, through practices such as veiling, seclusion and polygamy, was central to Ataturk's onslaught on the theological Ottoman state which culminated in the abolition of the caliphate in 1924. The timing of the legislation on women's suffrage in the 1930s, on the other hand, is interpreted as an important attempt on the part of Ataturk to dissociate himself from the European dictatorships of the time (nazi Germany and fascist Italy) and claim Turkey's rightful place among Western democratic nations (S. Tekely 1981).

While this intepretation concurs well with analyses of the strategic role of women's rights in other revolutionary situations (Massell 1974; Molyneux 1981: 167–202), an exclusive emphasis on the finalities of the republican reforms may unwittingly obscure the historical developments which led up to them. The aim of this chapter is to demonstrate that the 'woman question' has been central to the different ideological and political reactions to the dissolution of the Ottoman empire in the latter half of the nineteenth century and the beginning of this century. Since the eighteenth century the Ottoman Empire was increasingly unable to hold its own either against Western economic/military supremacy or against the rise of nationalist, secessionist movements in its provinces. This weakening of imperial power ushered in a period of political search and redefinition which lasted until the First World War and culminated in the Kemalist republic in 1923 (Berkes 1964; Shaw & Shaw 1977; Lewis 1961; Timur 1968). It is particularly over this period that the 'crisis' of Ottoman culture and of the Ottoman family system appeared on the political agenda. As a result, women made an irreversible entry into political discourse and the question of their rights became a privileged site for debates concerning questions of modernisation vs. cultural conservatism and integrity. In what follows, I will attempt to trace the development and transformations of the woman question during the period leading up to the Republic in order to highlight how the treatment of this question closely paralleled successive shifts within the Ottoman/Turkish policy and reflected its changing political priorities.

The drive for Ottoman 'modernisation' is officially traced to the Tanzimat period (1839–76), despite earlier attempts at technical innovation in the military sphere. By the time of the Second Constitutional Period in 1908, the relative merits of the Islamist, Ottomanist and Turkish solutions to the impasse of the Ottoman state had become a matter of public debate. It is important to emphasise that the various, overwhelmingly male, protagonists of the woman question also represented distinct ideological positions on a way out of the floundering empire. The dilemma posed by Westernisation and the need for progress on the one hand and the maintenance of Ottoman culture and integrity on the other strongly coloured the debate on the status of women and infused the general polemic with high levels of emotionality.

The Islamists saw the reasons for decay in the corruption and abandonment of Islamic law and institutions and advocated a return to the unadulterated application of the Sharia. Their political solution revolved around a pan-Islamic empire consolidated around the institution of the caliphate. Although the adoption of Western technology was deemed acceptable in the military and economic spheres, Western culture must on no account be allowed to contaminate the values of Islam. Not surprisingly, the position of women came to represent the touchstone of such contamination and any attempts to discuss issues such as polygamy, veiling and unilateral male repudiation in divorce could be denounced as morally corrupt or irreligious.[1] This contrasted sharply with the views of the Westernists, who maintained that the superiority of the West resided not only in its technology but in its rationalistic, positivistic outlook, freed from the shackles of obscurantism and stifling superstition. To varying degrees, they held Islam responsible both for obscurantism and for what they saw as the debased position of women (which some went as far as pinpointing as the major symptom of Ottoman backwardness (Mardin 1962). The Ottomanists ever since the Tanzimat reforms had been trying to formulate a balance between Westernism and traditionalism by achieving an 'Ottoman' synthesis (Mardin 1962).

Loyalty neither to Islam (actively mobilised during the reign of Abdulhamit II, 1876–1909) nor to the Ottoman cause would prove effective. By the turn of the century an Anatolian-based, predominantly Turkish nation was becoming an established fact. The current of Turkism which lay the foundations of Kemalist nationalism played a key ideological role in ensuring the transition from an empire based on the multi-ethnic *millet* system to a nation–state. It is within this current that we see the principal stirrings of feminism in Turkey which have left their mark on all subsequent treatments of the woman question. The specific form and content of the discussion on women's emancipation under Ataturk's republic is thus directly traceable to the birth and development of Turkish nationalism. This point will be illustrated with particular reference to Ziya Gokalp who is considered as the main ideologue of Turkism and who has put forward a clear and detailed position on the woman question. This chapter will explore the key moments in the transformation of the woman question in the Ottoman Empire leading to the birth of Turkish nationalism, culminating in the era of Kemalist reforms. The implications of this analysis for an understanding of the contemporary situation will be spelt out in the conclusion.

THE TANZIMAT REFORMS AND THEIR AFTERMATH

The decline of the Ottomans signalled by two centuries of military defeat and territorial retreat called for more radical reforms than earlier attempts at modernisation which had been confined to the adoption of Western military technology, training and organisation. The Tanzimat period set the scene for extensive reforms in the fields of administration, legislation and education. They were instrumental in the rise of a new class of Ottoman bureaucrats, relatively secure in their position within a secularised bureaucratic hierarchy, and weakened the overall political influence of the clergy (*ulema* as well as their monopoly over the educational system. These reforms have been the subject of conflicting intepretations, denounced by some as total capitulation to the West and assessed by others as the foundation of all later developments in the creation of a secular state. It seems beyond doubt that the Ottoman Empire suffered serious peripheralisation *vis-à-vis* European powers since the sixteenth century, so that the Tanzimat reforms can be seen as being primarily aimed at creating a central bureaucracy which could become an instrument of the smooth integration of the Ottoman state into the world economy (H. Inan 1983: 9–39). Already the trend of capitalising on Ottoman military misadventures to wrest trade concessions and force the lifting of tariff barriers was well established.[2] Indeed, the official document that ushered in the Tanzimat, the *Gulhane Hatt-i Humayunu* ('Imperial Rescript of Gulhane') had as its net effect the extension of legal assurances to non-Muslim and non-Turkish mercantile groups affiliated to European commercial interests. The new role that the Tanzimat bureaucracy had to adopt meant that it had to articulate itself to the needs of what they saw as 'modernisation' and to the expectations of Western powers in a manner that alienated the groups and classes which were excluded from the new 'modernised' structures (such as craftsmen, artisans, the urban lower middle class, petty civil servants and not least the ulema) and in fact stood to lose from them. These classes were to become the focus of a resistance which often took Islamic forms. Thus the Tanzimat reforms were to create deep cleavages in Ottoman society which were reflected both at the institutional level and that of culture more generally.

An interesting case in point is the dual legal system which emerged in a series of attempts at both renovation and compromise. Despite the importation of numerous European laws in the Tanzimat period as well as Abdulhamit II's autocratic rule, the personal status code affecting women directly had been untouched by new legislation. The preparation of the Ottoman Civic Code by a commission headed by Cevdet Pasha represented a compromise, by attempting a modern Ottoman code based on the Sharia. However, a religious opposition headed by the Sheyh-ul-Islam subsequently persuaded Abdulhamit to disband the commission which had only completed the legislation concerning debts and contracts, thereby blocking any further changes in the fields of family and inheritance laws. This created a dual juridical system whereby secular courts (*mahkeme-i nizamiye*) functioned under the aegis of the Ministry of Justice, while religious courts (*mahkeme-i ser'iyye*) remained under the jurisdiction of the Sheyh-ul-Islam. Nonetheless, the Tanzimat introduced some modest legislative advances concerning women with the promulgation of the 1856 Land Law (*arazi Kanunu*) granting equal rights of inheritance to daughters and the ratification of a treaty abolishing slavery and concubinage. Similarly there were some innovations in the field of women's education. However, Taskiran (1973), in her review of these advances, comments on the pressures resulting from the strict segregation of the sexes. For instance, she mentions the fact that due to the scarcity of trained female teachers all courses except needlework had to be taught by elderly male teachers.

The Tanzimat period did not necessarily stand out as a period of substantial change in matters regarding women but rather as a period of intellectual ferment when ideas about Ottoman society, the family and the position of women started to be debated in a variety of fora and media, from the newspaper column to the novel. The cultural cleavages between a Western-looking bureaucratic elite and popular classes committed to and protected by Ottoman communitarian conservatism were reflected in key literary productions of the time in which the Westernisation of upper class males and the position of women in society represented privileged and recurrent themes. Mardin's (1974) analysis of the post-Tanzimat novel suggests that whereas such as Ahmed Mithat Efendi echoed the popular unease with Westernisation through satirical treatment of the superficial, Western-struck male, there was a discernible consensus among the elite with regard to women's emancipation which was discussed in universalistic 'civilisational' terms. This, however, was an issue which apparently had the potential to create important cleavages among men of different social extraction. To the lower classes, any change in the position of women had been and remained anathema and a sign of moral decay. Nor was the elite necessarily consistent: retrenchment into conservatism *vis-à-vis* women always remained just below the surface. For instance, as late as 1917, and at a juncture when the Empire was in grave peril, the Committee for Union and Progress halted all progressive leanings and constituted a committee to discuss the suitable length for women's skirts. Enver Pasa removed one of his commanders in the Dardanelles whose daughters he had seen sunning themselves on the Bosphorus (Rifki Atay 1974: 433–4). This and similar observations lead Seni to conclude that the divisions between the traditionalists and modernists may have been more apparent than real:

> If the modernists distinguish themselves from the conservative current in terms of the real measures adopted for the emancipation of women, they do not escape the moralism and puritanism of their opponents. It would seem that the control of women also cristallizes a part of their Ottoman identity since when they feel that identity, the Ottoman Empire, to be under threat they backtrack in their position and regress to more conservative attitudes. (Seni 1984: 89)

There is thus a clear continuity, in her view, between the imperial edicts of the sixteenth century making women's attire and movements the object of direct legislation and later more modernist interventions on women's behalf, including Kemalist reforms: they all emanate from an Ottoman state tradition that recognises no sources of legitimacy outside itself.

While it is easy to concur that women's bodies have been and are still today used as vehicles for the symbolic representation of political intent, it is more difficult to overlook or dismiss the very real transformations that Ottoman society underwent in the transition to the republic and their independent impact on the position of women. Nor do these transformations stand in any mechanical or easily understandable relationship to the woman question. On the contrary, the attempts to absorb new positions into existing views of the world or ideologies often created complex, convoluted bodies of discourse.

There is little doubt that the Tanzimat elite was deeply influenced by the ideals of the French Enlightenment and that some of this influence was reflected in writings on the position of women. Not surprisingly, however, that most strenuous efforts of early feminists were directed towards making their demands compatible with the dictates of Islam. Even Fatma Aliye Hanim, the most noteworthy woman writer of her time who distinguished herself through a lively polemic on polygamy with the conservative Mahmut Esat Efendi, clearly inscribed herself within such a perspective. Nor was it an accident that the longest-lived woman's weekly of the time, *The Ladies' Gazette*, declared itself to be serving three principles: being a good mother, a good wife and a good Muslim.

In contrast to the nationalist stance of later periods, Islam was the only available body of discourse in which the woman question could be debated. Ozankaya's discussion of the work of Semseddin Sami, one of the most enlightened Tanzimat thinkers, illustrates the limitations of even the best-meaning attempts at tackling the woman question (Ozankaya 1985). Sami is ultimately unable to openly criticise Islamic rules regarding divorce, polygamy and wife-beating even though one can quite easily sense his unease with them throughout his text, titled *Women*. Universal human rights, rationalism and positivism notwithstanding, even the most progressive proposals regarding women had a strong instrumentalist flavour about them. Traditional marriages and repudiation were denounced as the source of 'social ills' weakening and corroding the social fabric, the ignorance of women meant that they were lacking as educators and mothers and finally the gulf between the sexes created by the traditional family system was a source of alienation and unhappiness for both. Yet I disagree with contention that these concerns represented an emulation of Western, particularly Victorian ideals of

monogamy and female domesticity by a rising bourgeois ruling class
(S. Tekeli 1982: 179). I think there are specific and very significant
reasons for the fact that men were the most outspoken critics of the
Ottoman family system and, on occasion, the most fervent advocates
of romantic love or at least marriages based on mutual compatabili-
ty.[3] The traditional Ottoman family, based on deference to the *pater
familias* and seniority, arranged marriages and spatial and social
segregation of the sexes was not conducive to rapport and closeness
between spouses, much less to romantic love. It should not suprise us
that it was 'modern' men who could openly reflect upon the oppres-
siveness of traditional family structure although women were more
visibly the victims of it. Women, on the other hand, may have been
more timid or at least cautious in this respect. It is revealing that the
author Omer Seyfettin accuses women themselves of standing in the
way of more companionate relations between the sexes (Seyfettin
1926, 1963). This is hardly surprising in a society which offered
women no shelter outside the traditional family and a tenuous one
inside it; where the options, however undesirable, of spinsterhood,
'genteel' female occupations and female religious orders were totally
unavailable. Duben (1985: 117) also notes the high rate of remarriage
among widows in contrast to the Mediterranean and Russian patterns
of the time, so that at no stage were women visible as the managers of
their own property. At least initially, women may have had a great
deal to lose and very little tangible gain in following the steps of their
more emancipated brothers. The 'passive' attitude of women on this
issue was to last well into the republic and continue to draw fire from
progressive men.

THE SECOND CONSTITUTIONAL PERIOD: THE SEARCH
FOR A NATIONAL BOURGEOISIE

Beneath Tanzimat liberalism were powerful undercurrents which had
a strong material basis. The Tanzimat reforms had failed to stem the
tide of nationalism in the Christian Balkan provinces and had
essentially strengthened the hand of local Christian merchants who
were the preferred trading partners of European powers in Ottoman
lands. In Berkes' terms, the more Westernisation proceeded, the
more Turks felt excluded from it (Berkes 1965). After an abortive
attempt at constitutional monarchy (1876–8), followed by an Islamist
backlash under the rule of Abdulhamit II, the Second Constitutional

Period was ushered in by the Young Turk's Revolution. The Committee for Union and Progress, who were the architects of the 1908 revolution, did not delay in seeing that the Ottoman nationalism which united Muslim and non-Muslim subjects in the overthrow of Abdulhamit's despotic rule in a bid for 'freedom' could not stem the secessionist movements in the ethnically heterogeneous provinces. Toprak suggests that Turkish nationalism, which was born from the liberal currents of the 1908 revolution, also represented a reaction against liberalism, especially against economic liberalism which had cost the Muslim artisan so dear.

> The nationalism which the Second Constitutional Period put on the agenda, aided by the extraordinary circumstances of World War I, produced a yearning for the creation of a Muslim–Turkish 'middle class', which after the loss of the war was to constitute the cadres of the National Struggle in Anatolia. (Z. Toprak 1982: 21)

The search for alternatives to liberalism produced a major shift in thinking about society and economy in the direction of corporatism which in the case of the Second Constitutional Period represented a blend of solidarism emanating from French corporatist thought and Ottoman guild traditions (Z. Toprak 1980: 41–49). Throughout the war years the Committee for Union and Progress (CUP) consistently struggled to create a middle class consisting of Turkish–Muslim entrepreneurs, stressing the ethnic dimension of the problem persistently and favouring Muslim over non-Muslim. The effects of this national mobilisation on women have not received the attention they deserve except in connection to the war effort, a point to which we shall return later. It seems probable, however, that women were not totally unaffected by the new societal priorities. A suggestive though inconclusive example may be found in the effects of a law imposing Turkish as the language of correspondence to foreign firms operating in the Ottoman Empire in 1916. These firms had previously employed foreigners and now had the choice of either folding up or recruiting local employees. Meanwhile, vocational evening classes especially in the fields of commerce and banking were instituted by CUP clubs, in an obvious attempt to create skilled cadres that were competent in these fields. Special business classes for women were also started. Especially at a juncture where male labour was getting scarcer because of the war, the Advanced School for Commerce had opened a section for women in the Women's University (*Inas Darulfununu*) which was so popular that a second section had to be opened

(Z. Toprak 1980: 83). Undoubtedly this type of vocational training must have been instrumental in creating new employment opportunities for women. However, the real social upheaval that propelled women into the workforce in greater numbers was the First World War itself.

THE EFFECT OF THE WARS

The overthrow of Abdulhamit's absolutist rule and the greater freedom promised by the 1908 revolution raised hopes among women that they would also benefit from the new principles of liberty and equality. However, these hopes soon turned to disillusionment and bitterness. A woman's periodical, on the occasion of the fifth anniversary of the Constitution proclaimed that it was 'men's National Celebration Day' (Taskiran 1973: 38). Nonetheless, the Second Constitutional Period saw an increase in the numbers of women availing themelves of education opportunities, increases in the number of women's associations and periodicals and especially a tendency for women themselves to participate more actively in the women's struggle. Many writers on this question put these developments down to the effect of the wars on women's greater involvement in public life (S. Tekeli 1982: 198; Abadan-Unat 1981: 8).

Already during the Balkan War middle class women were involved in social welfare activities. The women's branch of the Red Crescent had started training Turkish nurses. However, it is during the First World War that the massive loss of male labour to the front created a demand for female labour, not unlike the case of the other warring nations. The growth of female employment did not remain confined to white collar jobs but involved attempts at wider mobilisation throughout the Anatolian provinces. A law passed in 1915 by the Ottoman Ministry of Trade instituted a form of mandatory employment which rapidly swelled the number of women workers. Women volunteers were organised into workers' platoons to help the army with support services. In the agrarian sector, the Fourth Army formed Women Workers' Brigades. The Islamic Association for the Employment of Ottoman Women, founded in 1916, was instrumental in employing women workers under conditions insuring them an 'honest' living. But if the war effort created interest in women as workers there was no less interest in an intensification of their role as mothers and reproducers of the nation. It is interesting and significant that the Empire's first pro-natalist policies also had the employees of the Islamic Association for the Employment of Ottoman Women as their target, for whom mandatory marriage by the age of 21 for women and 25 for men was introduced. The Association used newspaper columns for matchmaking, provided girls with a trousseau and staged well appointed wedding ceremonies. Those who passed the marriage age limit or did not accept the matrimonial candidates proposed by the Association had 15 per cent of their salary withheld and were excluded from membership. Conversely, marriage was rewarded by a 20 per cent salary increase and similar increases for the birth of each child (Z. Toprak 1982: 317–18, 412). Thus women's service to the nation as workers and breeders was made explicitly co-extensive. Nonetheless, concession had to be made to the necessities of female employment: in 1915, for instance, an imperial decree allowed the discarding of the veil during office hours. It is clear, however, that this increased female presence in the labour force was viewed with considerable ambivalence. The conditions of women's work tended to scrupulously respect the segregation of the sexes. They were apparently often forced by the police to return home if their skirts were shorter than the officially prescribed length (Yener 1955: 8). There is little doubt that this period must have been full of confusion and contradictions, leading to mildly comical incidents. In September 1917 the following announcement was posted on Istanbul walls by the police:

> In the last few months shameful fashions are being seen in the streets of the Capital. All Muslim women are called upon to lengthen their skirts, refrain from wearing corsets and wear a thick *charshaf*. A maximum of two days is allowed to abide by the orders of this proclamation.

This announcement was the subject of such indignation and furore that higher level administrators were forced to rebuke their overzealous subordinates and retract the order. The new announcement read as follows:

> The General Directorate regrets that old and retrograde women were able to induce a subaltern employee to publicize an announcement ordering Muslim women to go back to old fashions. We announce that the previous orders are null and void. (J. Melia 1929: 147–8)

Clearly, despite women's entry into the workforce in unprecedented numbers and strenuous advocacy for their rights, changes in mores were slow to come. Meanwhile the intelligentsia continued to bemoan enforced segregation and the impossibility of civilised communication between the sexes. The rights demanded by feminists of the time (voiced in publications such as *Mahasin*, which started appearing in 1908; *Women*, again published in 1908 in Salonica; and *Women's World* from 1913) were relatively modest by later standards. They were the right to education, to go out in the streets and to places of entertainment and a limited right to work with freedom from police harassment. Greater equality within the conjugal union was a largely taboo subject despite the ongoing polemic on the evils of polygamy. Women themselves felt compelled to defend monogamous and more companionate marriages in the name of 'social hygiene' rather than on grounds of greater equality and basic human rights.[4]

The compromises apparent in the 1917 Family Code are quite indicative of the different pressures at work in Ottoman society. This law aimed at completing the task left unfinished by the *Mecelle* (the Ottoman Civic Code referred to previously) by legislating aspects of personal status which had been totally abandoned to the rulings of religious authorities. It was the first written family code in the Muslim world. The contractual aspect of the marriage was to apply to all religious groups in the Empire, it being understood that this could be followed by the appropriate religious ceremonies. Marriages without consent were decreed illegal and divorce was made more difficult by the introduction of a conciliation procedure. However, not only was polygamy not abolished but it was actually legalised even though its practice was made more difficult by stipulating the consent of the first wife. Interestingly, the commission headed by the Minister of Justice, Seyyit Bey, wavered on the question of polygamy and finally accepted it not only in view of the clear Koranic licence in this respect but also on demographic grounds, since numerous wars had created an imbalance in the sex ratio. Needless to say, such a law failed to satisfy either those who wanted to see fundamental changes in the family system considered to be 'in crisis' or those who saw the changes as clear-cut infractions of Koranic law. Minorities were also discontented with what they saw as a curtailment of the authority of their own religious authorities and in 1919 complained to the forces then occupying Istanbul and obtained a repeal of the clauses regarding Christian marriages. This law nonetheless remained in force until 1926 in Turkey and much later in the Ottoman periphery (until 1953 in Syria and Jordan, for instance). It represents an interesting exercise illustrative of the muddled attempts of Ottoman legislators to introduce progressive change. These attempts were to encounter great opposition and resistance throughout this period and extend to Kemal Ataturk's own National Assemblies regardless of women's often praised contributions to the War of National Liberation.

WOMEN AND THE STRUGGLE FOR NATIONAL INDEPENDENCE

The end of the First World War brought about the dismemberment of the defeated Empire and the control of Anatolian provinces by occupying Western powers. The landing of Greek forces in Izmir in May 1919 and the occupation of Istanbul by the British unleashed a wave of popular protest in which women were not merely participants but public speakers in open-air meetings, where they made impassioned calls for the defence of the motherland (Taskiran 1973: 68–73). Many women joined Mustafa Kemal's forces of resistance in Anatolia. Associations for Patriotic Defence started springing up in the Anatolian provinces. Women did not join these directly but set up their own parallel organisations. The Anatolian Women's Association for Patriotic Defence was founded in Sivas in November 1919. The active members were the wives, daughters and sisters of local provincial notables and higher level state employees as well as some teachers and educational administrators. In other words, these were the women of the nascent local middle class which the Second Constitutional Period did so much to nurture. During the War of National Liberation there was a large-scale mobilisation of the whole nation in which Anatolian peasant women played a key and visible role glorified in public monuments as well as patriotic literature. Yet the coalition of nationalist forces which united behind Mustafa Kemal included men of religion who were going to remain inflexible on the woman question to the last and constitute a focus of active and vocal resistance throughout the first and second National Assemblies. In fact in 1924, soon after the declaration of the republic there were some regressive steps in legislation in the field of civil law (Berkes 1973: 68–73). Some of the advantages gained through the 1917 code by endorsing polygyny were endangered by a draft law eliminating the need for consent by the first wife and lowering the legal marriage

age for girls to nine years old. This proposal, which was subsequently rejected, was part of the playing out of the opposition between religious and Kemalist forces in the National Assemblies, an opposition which was finally resolved by the abolition of the caliphate and the abrogation of the Sharia. There is no doubt that the woman question became one of the pawns in the Kemalist struggle to dismantle the theocratic remnants of the Ottoman state (Taskiran 1973: 106–9). Some progressive men were using newspaper columns to take women to task over their acquiescent posture in this debate. Necmettin Sadak wrote thus in the daily newspaper *Aksam*:

> Finally an important issue concerning Turkish womanhood has arisen. The National Assembly has started debating the Family Law proposal. This proposal . . . has passed through the Sharia and Justice commissions without a murmur from women. Almost all newspapers have cried out against this law. However, our women who engage in demonstration with or without justification and at every possible occasion, did not act. We have witnessed this silence with surprise as well as some despair. Where were our young ladies filling sections of university classes, where those founding political parties in the pursuit of chimera? The Turkish Republic is insulting you with its own laws, why are you not crying out? (21 January 1924).

The process of mobilisation and co-operation of women into the ideological struggles of the republic can thus be seen to be significantly different from early feminist movements in the West. In this latter, the women's struggles took place against a background where legislation was lagging considerably behind the socioeconomic realities of advancing industrialism and a growing labour movement. In Turkey, it was an ideological lever operating on a substantially unchanged economic base, at least as far as women's economic and familial options were concerned. Yet the specific forms that feminist discourse took continued to be indicative of the search for a new legitimacy in the transition to the republic. From this perspective, the transformations of the woman question can be better understood with reference to republican state ideology than to any other single factor. The main legitimising discourse for the woman question in Turkey has been that of Turkish nationalism, which has its roots in the Turkism of the Second Constitutional Period.

TURKISH NATIONALISM: A NEW FRAMEWORK FOR THE WOMAN QUESTION?

The woman question remained for a long time caught in the dilemma between Westernism and Islam without a third term to moderate the debate. The Turkish movement represented an attempt at recuperation of a national identity which could be grounded in a national 'culture' rather than solely in Islam. This was in many ways a most difficult enterprise.

As Berkes (Berkes 1965: 52–3) points out, the Turks were the last to achieve a sense of nationality in the whole Ottoman formation. In the Ottoman context, Turkish nationalism could even be perceived as divisive in a situation where other ethnic minorities were restive, and it certainly found no favour among the Islamists for whom the notion of a Turkish nation constituted a threat to the Islamic *umma* (collectivity of believers). Turkish nationalism initially took the form of a populist reaction to Westernism not unlike, and certainly heavily influenced by, the Narodnik movement in Russia and the Turkish Russian emigrés. The leading ideologue in this transition has undoubtedly been Ziya Gokalp (1876–1924), the author of *The Principles of Turkism*. Parla suggests that 'Gokalp's system fixed the parameters within which mainstream political discourse and action has been conducted in Turkey' (Parla 1985: 7). This is also true of his influence on the treatment of the woman question throughout the period of republican reforms. Gokalp, who was greatly influenced by Durkheim's sociology, substituted his notion of society with that of 'nation', emphasising the national–cultural rather than Islamic sources of morality. His work represents strenuous attempts at defining the nature of the collectivity called 'nation'. He settles on the idea of a collectivity based on common language and culture and representing the highest form of social solidarity. Gokalp took great pains to distinguish the concepts of culture and civilisation from one another. In his view Islamic and Western civilisation influences need not be incompatible with Turkish national culture, although admittedly his brand of Islam, ethical Sufism, is highly secular, and his preferred Western sources are drawn from European corporatism. Gokalp's search for authentic national–cultural patterns led him to an eclectic examination of myth, legend, archeological and anthropological evidence on pre-islamic Turkic patterns. In his *Principles of Turkism* he spells out the programmatic implications of Turkism and its application to the fields of language, aesthetics, morality, law, religion, economy and philosophy. His views on 'moral Turkism' especially on family and sexual morality represent a significant departure from earlier approaches to the woman question. He suggested that family morality based on old Turkish cultural values included norms such as communal property in land, democracy in the 'parental' family as opposed to the autocracy of the patriarchal family, the equality of men and women and monogamy in marriage. He traces some of the origins of what he labels as 'Turkish feminism' (using these exact words) to the fact that Shamanistic religion and rituals were based on the sacred power vested in women. This made men and women ritualistically equal, an equality which was seen to permeate every sphere of life including the political. The patrilineal and matrilineal principles were equally important, children belonged to both parents, women could control their own independent property and, interestingly, were excellent warriors ('amazons', to use Gokalp's own terminology). This amounted to a pre-Islamic 'golden age' for women which was made much of by subsequent feminist women writers. As far as Gokalp was concerned the Turks had lost their old morality: 'The reason why Turkists are both populist and feminist is not simply because these ideals are valued in this century; the fact that democracy and feminism were the two main principles of ancient Turkish life is a major factor in this respect' (Gokalp 1978: 148).

This position was not greeted with a total lack of scepticism. Mehmet Izzet, for instance, suggested that Gokalp's ideas might have been greatly influenced by pragmatic considerations: 'At a time when Islamic law was being abolished, when improvements in women's position were sought and changes in family life along the Western model were being introduced, interpreting this movement as a return to ancient Turkish law and national identity would ensure greater goodwill and sympathy' (Eroz 1977: 13). Berkes (1982: 114) also comments rather wryly on the fact that by some happy coincidence the elements of Turkish culture which Gokalp took such pains to distinguish from Western civilisations matched this latter with uncanny ease. Indeed, in terms of the position of women what might have been rather unpalatable in the form of Western influence gained a new legitimacy when it was recuperated by national discourse.

For Ataturk, who was to distance himself from Islam much further than Gokalp himself ever envisaged, the latter's definition of the nation was to provide a very valuable tool. In assessing Kemalist nationalism it is important to remember some of the special circumstances under which Mustafa Kemal's struggle for independence took place. The Istanbul government headed by the sultan-caliph had reached an agreement with the occupying powers to stamp out Kemalist resistance. In April 1920 the Sheyh-ul-Islam issued a *fetva* (canonical proclamation) declaring holy war against the 'Ankara rebels'. A military court condemned Ataturk and a group of his supporters to death and the defection of his forces to the Army of the Caliphate was only reversed after the outrage created by the humiliating treaty of Sevres. Henceforth religious reaction (*irtica*) was to be identified as one of the main enemies of Kemalist nationalism.

Yet unlike Islam, which had very deep roots in the Ottoman–Turkish polity, Turkish nationalism was an ideal which had yet to search for its symbols and discourse. This search, already inaugurated in the work of Turkists and Ziya Gokalp in particular, was to culminate in a major onslaught on Turkish history and an extensive rewriting of it. This task was given to the Association for the Study of Turkish History which was set up by Ataturk himself and which reported its findings to the First Turkish History congress which was held in Istanbul in 1932. This history traced back its origins to Central Asiatic beginnings when the Turkish peoples and the Chinese were the main actors on the scene of civilisation. All the subsequent civilisations of Asia Minor and Mesopotamia were considered as so many links in the chain of Turkish civilisations. Compared to the relatively recent conversion of the Turks to Islam in the tenth century, this history could be traced much further back, to 5000 BC. This was the new framework in which the woman question in Turkey started being discussed by the first generation of Kemalist feminists. The most prominent among these, Afet Inan, who was also Ataturk's adoptive daughter, devotes a long section to a consideration of Turkish women before Islam in her classic book, *The Emancipation of the Turkish Woman* (A. Inan 1962) where she echoes Gokalp's convictions about women's high status and greater equality in pre-Islamic times.

This type of discourse is prevalent among many Third World feminists, but the actual content of it changes according to what it is that is being recuperated by the discourse that claims to be feminists.[5] In the Turkish case, it was nothing less than national identity itself which was deemed to have a practically built-in sexual egalitarianist component. Even though the actual realities of entrenched Ottoman–Turkish patriarchy[6] and the influence of Islam made such pronouncements seem rather remote and endowed them with a mythical quality, they continued to be part of the official discourse on women in Turkey. This meant, furthermore, that an alternative model for Turkish womanhood could be proposed and discussed.

I have suggested elsewhere (Kandiyoti 1988) that the writer Halide Edip Adivar, herself a fighter for the nationalistic cause, played a major role in creating images of the new Turkish woman. Her nationalist heroine is cast as a self-sacrificing 'comrade-woman' who shares in the struggles of her male peers. She is depicted as an asexual sister-in-arms whose public activities never cast any doubt on her virtue and chastity. This echoes the position of Ziya Gokalp who, in his attempt to establish a new nationalist morality in which the equality of women could be justified as an integral part of Turkish cultural mores, nonetheless took great pains to emphasise in his section of 'sexual mores' that the principal characteristic of the Turkish woman was her *iffet*, i.e. chastity and honour. Thus, there appears to be one persistent concern which finally unites nationalist and Islamist discourses on women in Turkey: the necessity to establish that the behaviour and position of women, however defined, are congruent with the 'true' identity of the collectivity and constitute no threat to it. It is perhaps not surprising that the prime area of potential threat centres around women's appropriate sexual conduct and its control, so that the dread of loss of control and anxieties about degeneracy and corruption easily get displaced onto a third term, 'Westernism', which becomes a highly charged, polyvalent symbol.

CONCLUSION

In this chapter, I have attempted to show how the woman question in Turkey became part of an ideological terrain upon which concerns about the changing nature of the Ottoman order and the question of Ottoman and later Turkish national identity were articulated and debated. I have argued that the mobilisation of Turkish women and their co-optation into the political struggles around the dissolution of the Empire and the birth of the republic served as an ideological lever and that the single most important factor accounting for the transformations of the woman question could be found in nationalist state ideology.[7] I have not addressed the material conditions of different classes of women in Turkey, nor their transformations under the impact of socio-economic changes (see Kandiyoti 1977, 1982, 1983, 1984), but instead focused on the crucial role of state ideology. I have alluded quite consistently throughout the text to the possible connection between the demands of the national economy (as in the need for female labour during the First World War), processes of class formation (as in attempting to understand the alliance of forces behind the Kemalist movement) and social practices and ideologies relating to women. However, I have left the link between socio-economic transformations and ideologies relative to women as totally indeterminate and problematic, allowing for the possibility that ideology may be used to both reflect and negate, promote and compensate for such transformations. I would like to conclude by drawing out both the continuing relevance of my analysis to an understanding of more contemporary developments, and the ways in which it needs to be expanded and modified.

At a superficial level, current debates on women continue to express the tensions between Westernisation, Islam and Turkism, and one cannot help but note the persistence of both the concerns expressed and the imagery used to express them. The issues of women's dress and conduct are still used by the state to signify political intent,[8] although women nowadays increasingly appear as active participants and militants in causes concerning them. Yet it would be quite misleading to interpret this semblance of continuity as an extension of past ideological debates playing themselves out within an essentially unmodified state tradition. Although the terms and symbols of the debate may seem thoroughly familiar, it must be acknowledged that they operate in a totally transformed national and international context. Thus any further analysis of the woman question in contemporary Turkey would have to take fuller and more explicit account of changing economic realities and class alignments, the struggles between rival ideologies within the Turkish political spectrum, and their degree of representation at the level of the Turkish state.

Since the First Republic, Turkey has undergone several drastic reorientations in its domestic economic policies and in its mode of insertion into the world economy, with important consequences for the country's class structure, as well as the nature of the Turkish state apparatus (I. Tekeli *et al.* 1984). The fact that Kemalist republicanism (and its cultural Westernism) is no longer the sole ideology emanating from the centre, and that a new political elite with a strong religious orientation, its own cadres and political organisation now exists has been the subject of much recent commentary (B. Toprak 1978, 1981; Saribay 1985). The implications of these transformations for different classes of women in Turkey are as yet hard to ascertain beyond being able to assert that the issue of their roles and place will remain an actively contested domain. The 1970s witnessed a resurgence of polemical writing on women which was more diversified than ever before, since it involved the 'Marxist' left and growing Islamist currents alongside a previously dominant Kemalist position and a proliferation of women's organisations operating as extensions to political parties and movements (Yorgun 1985: 78–83). This has meant that the new protagonists of the woman question became more self-consciously politicised and better organised. It has also meant, however, that just as in the past women have only been able to operate in co-opted political structures, defining their own demands as marginal or secondary to what each tendency saw as their 'main' struggle, i.e. the fight against 'backwardness', imperialism or class struggle, as the case may be. Interestingly, only Islamist currents accord a central place to the position of women, at least at the level of discourse, since they see keeping women in their religiously sanc-tioned traditional roles as absolutely crucial to the maintenance of the Islamic social order. At a time when the tensions between political authoritarianism and democratic pluralism are openly on the Turkish political agenda, it will be interesting to see whether women's movements and feminist currents are able to finally emerge as an added voice in the search for democratisation, or whether women's concerns will continue to be played out in a manner that reduces them to being symbolic pawns. While my incursions into the woman question between the Tanzimat period and the republic do not provide any answers to these contemporary questions, they hopefully suggest a method to begin tackling them.

NOTES

1.   In this connection Caporal draw attention to the fact, unlike the Arab Middle East and Muslim Russia where vigorous modernist Islamic currents could be seen, Ottoman Islam has remained more consistently conservative. B. Caporal, *Kemalizmde ve Kemalizm Sonrasinda Turk Kadini* (Ankara: Turkiye Is Bankasi Kultur Yayinlari, 1982) 736.

2. For instance, Mahmut II's attempts to consolidate Ottoman central authority over the provinces brought him into conflict with Mehmet Ali the powerful governor of Egypt, who he was finally able to subjugate with Britain's naval and military support. The price for such support was the commercial treaty of 1838 which opened the vast Ottoman market to British manufacturers by lifting trade restrictions and tariff barriers.

3. There is a vast literature by male writers of the time on the evils of traditional marriages and the unhappiness and alienation resulting from them. For an impassioned defence of romantic love, see Omer Seyfettin *Ask Kalgasi* (Istanbul: Bilgi Yayinevi, 1964). Seyfettin writes: 'Here in our surroundings, the surroundings of the Turks, love is strictly forbidden. It is as forbidden as an infernal machine, a bomb, a box of dynamite.' (p. 52).

4. This in itself is not surprising and the arguments are frequently reminiscent of the earlier Western feminists such as Mary Wollstonecraft in her *Vindication of the Rights of Women* (1792).

5. Witness the attempts of Muslim feminists to recuperate Islam itself by invoking an Islamic 'golden age' for women which possesses many of the positive characteristics attributed to the pre-Islamic Turkish pattern, including women's equality as warriors (for the faith, in this latter case). As examples, see El Saadawi's 'Women and Islam', and Al-Hibri's 'A Study of Islamic Herstory', both in A. Al-Hibri (ed.), *Women and Islam* (Oxford: Pergamon Press, 1982).

6. Anthropological studies show that despite some regional variations in marriage practices, the patrivirilocal household was normative in Turkey. For a review of the evidence, see Duben (1985).

7. The primarily symbolic function of the rights granted to women may be evidenced in their steadily declining representation in parliament since the First Republic, and especially after the transition to a multi-party system. In the three chambers elected between 1935 and 1946 the number of women representatives was 18, 15 and 16 (rising up to 4.5 per cent with 18 deputies), whereas after 1946 women's representation dropped below 1 per cent and there were never more that 11 representatives at any time. This is readily understandable if we think of it as a shift from a single-party system where the appointment of women by an 'enlightened' vanguard, in line with state ideology, is actually possible to a multi-party democracy where patron–client relationships in the male world play a key role in political competition. For an interesting discussion of male patronage and sponsorship of women politicians in Turkey, see Y. Arat 'From the Private to the Political Realm: Women Parliamentarians in Turkey', in F. Ozbay (ed.), *The Study of Women in Turkey: An Anthology* (UNESCO, forthcoming).

8. As recently as 1982, a Minister of Youth and Sports decreed that schoolgirls would not be allowed to wear short-sleeved blouses and shorts as in the past, but tracksuits covering their limbs completely instead. This announcement was followed by outcries in the more progressive newspapers and satirical cartoons depicting fully veiled

women exercising. Conversely, the growing Islamist current among
university youth has been using the official ban on veiling in the
classroom as a vehicle for militant protest.

BIBLIOGRAPHY

Abadan-Unat, N. (1981) 'Social Change and Turkish Women', in N.
Abadan-Unat (ed.), *Women in Turkish Society* (Leiden: E.J. Brill).
Arat, Y. (forthcoming) 'From the Private to the Political Realm: Women
Parliamentarians in Turkey', in F. Ozbay (ed.), *The Study of Women in
Turkey: an Anthology* (Paris: UNESCO).
Berkes, N. (1964) *The Development of Secularism in Turkey* (Toronto:
McGill University Press).
Berkes, N. (1965) *Baticilik, Ulusculuk ve Toplumsal Devrimler* (Istanbul:
Yon Yayinlari).
Berkes, N. (1973) *Turkiyede Caqdaslasma* (Ankara: Bilgi Yayinevi).
Duben, A. (1985) 'Nineteenth and Twentieth Century Ottoman–Turkish
Family and Household Structure', in T. Erder (ed.), *Family in Turkish
Society* (Ankara: Turkish Social Science Association).
Eroz, M. (1977) *Turk Ailesi* (Istanbul: Milli Egitim Basimevi).
Gokalp, Z. (1978) *Turkculuqun Esaslari* (Istanbul: Inkilap ve Aka Kitabev-
leri Koll. Sti).
Inan, A. (1962) *The Emancipation of the Turkish Woman* (Paris: UNESCO).
Inan, A. (1964) *Ataturk ve Turk Kadin Haklarinin Kazanilmasi* (Istanbul:
Milli Egitim Basimevi).
Inan, A. (1983) 'Osmanli Tarihi ve Dunya Sistemi: Bir Degerlendirme'
Toplum ve Bilim, vol. 23, 9–38.
Kandiyoti, D. (1977) 'Sex Roles and Social Change: a Comparative Apprai-
sal of Turkey's Women', *Signs*, vol. 3, 57–73.
Kandiyoti, D. (1982) 'Urban Change and Women's Roles: an Overview and
Evaluation', in C. Kagitcibasi (ed.), *Sex Roles, Family and Community in
Turkey* (Bloomington: Indiana University Turkish Studies), 101–20.
Kandiyoti, D. (1982) 'Economie monétaire et roles des sexes: le cas de la
Turquie', *Current Sociology*, vol. 31, 213–28.
Kandiyoti, D. (1984) 'Rural Transformation in Turkey and its Implications
for Women's Status', in *Women on the Move: Contemporary Changes in
Family and Society* (Paris: UNESCO).
Kandiyoti, D. (1988) 'Women as Metaphor: the Turkish Novel from the
Tanzimat to the Repubic', in K. Brown *et al* (eds), *The State, Urban Crisis
and Social Movements in the Middle East and North Africa* (Paris:
L'Harmattan).
Lewis, B. (1961) *The Emergence of Modern Turkey* (London: Oxford
University Press).
Mardin, S. (1962) *The Genesis of Young Ottoman Thought* (Princeton:
Princeton University Press).

Mardin, S. (1974) 'Superwesternization in Urban Life in the Ottoman Empire in the Last Quarter of the Nineteenth Century', in P. Benedict and E. Tumertekin (eds), *Turkey: Geographical and Social Perspectives* (Leiden: E.J. Brill).

Massell, G. (1974) *The Surrogate Proletariat: Muslim Women and Revolutionary Strategies in Soviet Central Asia, 1919–1929* (Princeton: Princeton University Press).

Melia, J. (1929) *Mustafa Kemal ou la renovation de la Turquie* (Paris), quoted in B. Caporal, *Kemalizmde ve Kemalizm Sonrasinda Turk Kadini* (Türkiye Iş Bankasi Kultur yayin lani).

Molyneux, M. (1981) 'Women in Socialist Societies: Theory and Practice', in K. Young, C. Wolkowitz & R. McCullagh (eds), *Of Marriage and the Market: Women's Subordination in International Perspective* (London: CSE Books).

Ortayli, I (1983) *Imparatorlugun En Uzun Yuzyili* (Istanbul: Hi Yayin).

Ozankaya, O. (1985) 'Reflections of Semseddin Sami on Women in the Period before the Advent of Secularism', in T. Erder (ed.), *Family in Turkish Society* (Ankara: Turkish Social Science Association).

Parla, T. (1985) *The Social and Political Thought of Ziya Gokalp 1876–1924* (Leiden: E.J. Brill).

Rifki Atay, Falih *Baris Yillari* quoted in Mardin 1974.

Sadak, Necmettin (1924) 'Hanimlarimiz ve Aile Hukuku Kararnamesi' *Aksam* (21 January), quoted in Taskiran 1973.

Saribay, A.Y. (1985) 'Turkiyede Siyasal Modernlesme ve Islam', *Toplum ve Bilim*, vol. 29/30, 45–64.

Seni, N. (1984) 'Ville ottomane et réprésentation du corps féminin', *Les Temps Modernes*, no. 456–7 (July–August), 66–95.

Seyfettin, Omer (1926) *Gizli Mabet*, in *En Güzel Hikayeler* (vol. II) (Istanbul: Sander Yayinlari, 1976), 220–8.

Seyfettin, Omer (1963) *Bahar ve Kelebekler*, in *En Güzel Hikayeler* (vol. II) (1976).

Shaw, S.J. & E.K. Shaw (1977) *History of the Ottoman Empire and Modern Turkey*, vol. 2 (Cambridge: Cambridge University Press).

Taskiran, T. (1973) *Comhuriyetin 50. Yilinda Turk Kadin Haklari* (Ankara: Basbakanlik Basimevi).

Tekeli, I. C. Keider, E. Turkcan, G. Yalman, N. Ekzen, O. Purel & K. Boratov (1984) *Turkiyede ve Dunyada Yasanan Ekonomik Bunalim* (Ankara: Yurt Yayinlari).

Tekeli, S. (1981) 'Women in Turkish Politics', in N. Abadan-Unat (ed.), *Women in Turkish Society* (Leiden: E.J. Brill).

Tekeli, S. (1982) *Kadinlar ve Siyasal Toplumsal Hayat* (Istanbul: Birikim Yayinlari).

Timur, T. (1968) *Turk Devrimi: Tarihi Anlami ve Felsefi Temeli* (Ankara: Sevinc Matbaasi).

Toprak, B. (Sayari) (1978) 'Turkiyede Dinin Denetim Islevi', *Siyasal Bilgiler Fakultesi Dergisi*, vol. 1/2.

Toprak, B. (Sayari) (1981) 'Religion and Turkish Women', in N. Abadan-Unat (ed.) *Women in Turkish Society* (London: E.J. Brill).

Toprak, Z. (1980) 'Turkiyede Korporatizmin Dogusu', *Toplum ve Bilim*, vol. 12, 41–9.

Toprak, Z. (1982) *Turkiyede Milli Iktisat (1908–1918)* (Ankara: Yurt Yayinlari).

Yener, E. (1955) 'Eski Ankara Kiyafetleri ve Eski Giyinis Tarzlari', *Dil Tarih ve Cografya Fak. Dergisi*, vol. 13, no. 3, quoted in Abadan-Unat (1981).

Yorgun, P. (1985) 'The Question and Difficulties of Feminism in Turkey', *Khamsin*, vol. 11, 70–85.

9   Women and Nationalism in Cyprus
Floya Anthias

INTRODUCTION

Given the centrality of nationalism in the political history of Cyprus within the last 50 years or so it is not surprising that the issue of nationality should be the one remaining bastion of formal male superiority in the present territorially divided state. The recent Sex Equality legislation (Chappa 1987: 11) has one proviso – the exclusion of regulations concerning nationality from its reform. It remains a male privilege to pass on automatic citizenship to one's children. A woman of Cypriot origin can only do so if she is unmarried and there is no legal father. On the other hand, if she is married to a foreigner she is denied this as an automatic right although as a permanent resident she may apply for her children to be granted nationality.

This chapter analyses some of the ways in which gender relations within the Greek-Cypriot population of Cyprus interlink with ethnic ideology and nationalist practice. As such it does not address the issue in relation to Cyprus as a whole. Cyprus also has a Turkish–Cypriot population which at the present does not accept the legitimacy of the state structure and has declared its own independent state – hence the island is territorially and ethnically divided. However, similarities and differences with the Turkish-Cypriot sector will be noted where possible.[1]

Cyprus is a small island in the eastern Mediterranean which is still defined in international law as one nation–state. It contains within it two ethnic and religious communities which are territorially separated, six armies, a no-man's land, a foreign invader and an illegal second state which purports to represent the Turkish-Cypriot community (Hitchens 1984). There is at the moment of writing a stalemate on the issue of what is to be the resolution to this latest phase of what is called the 'Cyprus problem'. The fate of the 200 000 Greek-Cypriot refugees in the south of the island is still in the balance. The movement of populations along ethnic lines, with the

Turkish invasion of Cyprus in 1974, has created territorial separation of the two main ethnic groups on the island for the first time in its long history of foreign invasion and domination. In addition about 60 000 settlers from the Turkish mainland have been imported as part of the demographic 'race' on the island – prior to 1974 only 18 per cent of the population were Turkish-Cypriot. The incorporation of the refugees within what is now effectively the Greek-Cypriot sector in the south of the island has led to a fundamental restructuring of Cypriot society on all fronts. Rapid social change has occurred in the traditional roles and expectations of women, particularly amongst refugee women and younger women in general. Class relations have been complicated by the growth, for the first time, of a landless proletariat, the dispossessed refugees and by the new social division of refugee/non-refugee.

In discourses and policies emanating from the Greek-Cypriot state (when now referring to the state in Cyprus we mean the legitimate state in the Greek-Cypriot sector) women and gender divisions find expression primarily on two levels. First, there is the symbolic level that uses those characteristics ascribed to women to foster the interests of the nation. Symbolism around women's reproductive role and sexual nature are important here. The links between the notions of 'mother' and 'nation' are found almost universally and in many societies special honour is due to the 'mother of the patriot' and Cyprus is no exception here, particularly since national issues and struggles are a central feature of political and social life. At the more practical or policy level many of the concerns of the nation–state have women as a central subject; all those, for example, that are aimed at structuring or restructuring the form of the family which may be instigated by a concern with controlling the mode of reproduction of state subjects in its fullest sense. We can single out as particularly significant all those policies that are aimed at women's reproduction, such as population policies, which in many ethnically divided societies would attempt to maintain or change existing demographic patterns. Rules relating to the conditions under which a legitimate national subject is reproduced are also significant here such as those which may prohibit or provide disincentives to marry outside one's ethnic group. Laws that specify the conditions under which a woman might or might not belong to the national collectivity and have the right to reproduce its subjects, such as nationality laws, are also important.

NATION AND STATE IN CYPRUS

In Cyprus the form of the Cypriot state was externally imposed (Attalides 1979), meeting the needs and desires of neither of the two main ethnic groups on the island – the Greek-Cypriot and the Turkish-Cypriot. Indeed what put insurmountable obstacles to the formation of a common national consciousness within the state structure was its construction via thoroughgoing bi-communalism and separate development for the two groups, with reference to political representation, education and family law, all those processes that can act, where they are common, to cement a nation–state.

Cypriots have never talked about a Cypriot *nation* as such although they have recognised and indeed desired the nation–state structure. The constitution, established in 1960 when Cyprus won its blighted and circumscribed independence, is still valid in international law. One unified nation–state was created, although bi-communalism was written into the constitution at all levels (Kyriakides 1968). Two separate communities were formally designated, the Greek-Cypriot and the Turkish-Cypriot, with their own specified political representation. The Greek-Cypriot community, according to the constitution, comprises all citizens who are of Cypriot origin, have Greek as their mother-tongue or who share the Greek cultural tradition and belong to the Greek Orthodox religion. The Turkish-Cypriot community, on the other hand, comprises all citizens who are of Cypriot origin and have Turkish as their mother-tongue or share the Turkish cultural tradition and are Muslims. The other communities on the island, the Armenians and Maronites, who comprise approximately 3 per cent of the population, can opt to belong to either, although most have opted to belong to the Greek-Cypriot community. However, the issue of who belongs to each community and who belongs to the state is more complicated than might appear from the above legal definitions. For example, non-residents of Cypriot origin – that is, migrants and their descendants – have a formal and automatic right to be included in these communities and the right to residence. They also have automatic right to Cypriot citizenship, which is a requisite for employment in the public sector. Only those who were not resident in Cyprus between 1955 and 1960 for any period cannot hold dual nationality and must forgo their other nationality (e.g. British) if they wish to become Cypriot citizens. In this way, the communities who comprise the state extend beyond the geographical and juridical spheres of the state of Cyprus and are defined by their ethnicity. It is worth noting here that more people of Cypriot origin live outside Cyprus than within its territorial boundaries.

In order to discuss the links between gender divisions and the nation state we need now to give a brief summary of the developments that have led up to the present day.

ETHNIC DIVISIONS

Cyprus has suffered from continuous colonisation because of its strategically favourable geographical position. In 1571 the Ottomans captured Cyprus from the Venetians and introduced what became a Turkish-Cypriot population. Under the Ottoman 'millet' system, which gave internal autonomy to separate religious communities, the Greek-Orthodox Church assumed a position of dominance and became the political and moral representative of the Greek-Cypriot population. Britain was leased the island in 1878 and formally annexed it at the Treaty of Lausanne in 1923. Cyprus finally won its independence in 1960.

The British colonial phase from 1878–1960 gave an impetus to the growth of polarised ethnicities and heralded the growth of ethnic conflict (Coufoudakis 1976). Conflict between Greek-Cypriots and Turkish-Cypriots, however, is a fairly recent phenomenon – the first outbursts dating to only about 30 years ago. Indeed, there is much evidence to show that the two groups lived under what has been termed 'traditional co-existence' (Kitromilides 1977), that solidarity bonds existed between them and that conversions to Islam were fairly common. A common 'Cypriot' dialect incorporated within it a mixture of Greek and Turkish as well as Italian and French.

Although both Muslims and Christians shared the common economic life of rural Cyprus they also had their own separate cultural practices (Attalides 1977). Although they attended each other's festivities, they rarely intermarried. Mixed marriages were not regarded as desirable by the Greek Orthodox Church. For Muslims, on the other hand, mixed marriages were possible between Muslim men and non-Muslim women but not the other way round. Under Ottoman rule there is some evidence that some Christian girls were forced to marry non-Christian men. For example, William Turner (Aimilianides 1938: 32) says: 'They [the Turks] frequently marry the Greek women of the island, as their religion permits a Turkish man to marry an infidel women though to guard against an abandonment of Mahometanism it forbids a Turkish woman to marry an infidel.'

Intermarriage also took place between Christians and the sect of Linobambakoi, who were crypto-Christians, that is were Muslims but spoke and dressed like the Greek-Cypriot population. These had either converted to Islam to avoid the tax that non-Muslims paid or were Latins who were forced to convert to avoid being pursued out of the country (Kitromilides 1977). Most had Christian names and celebrated Christian religious feasts. Until 1889 mixed marriages, like all marriages, were not the concern of civil law but religious law. After 1889, if one of the parties was a British subject this was a case for civil law (excluding Greek-Orthodox and Muslims). In the 1920s mixed marriages had to be by civil law (Aimilianides 1938).

It is not possible in this chapter to give an account of the processes by which the 'passive' ethnicity of the two groups was converted into an active nationalist consciousness and practice. Suffice it to say that the role of British colonial rule was of fundamental importance (Attalides 1979; Anthias & Ayres 1983), as was that of the Greek Orthodox Church. The failure of the socialist movement to harness some of the genuinely anti-colonialist and liberationist tendencies that existed may also be a relevant factor (Anthias & Ayres 1979). All these internal processes, however, have to be seen in the context of the intervention by Western political interests in Cyprus in the war for spheres of influence and the use of Cyprus as a military base for NATO (Hitchens 1984).

Ethnic conflict has its origins in the Greek-Cypriot *Enosis* (union with Greece) movement and the Turkish-Cypriot response, *Taksim* ('partition') (Attalides 1979). Although Cyprus was granted formal independence in 1960 the constitutional arrangements proved unworkable. In 1963 Turkish-Cypriots withdrew from the constitution and into their own enclaves – the physical separation of the two communities saw its beginnings here. In 1974, after a right wing coup staged by the extremist nationalist Greek-Cypriot group EOKA B, under the aegis of the fascist Junta in Greece, Turkey invaded the island, annexing 40 per cent of Cyprus territory in the north of the island. The enormous economic and social changes that have followed cannot be dealt with in this chapter, although those that are particularly relevant for the links between gender, ethnicity and the state will be explored in the following section.

WOMEN AND THE NATION IN CYPRUS

Immediately after 1974 posters appeared everywhere in the south of the island depicting an anguished black-clothed woman, her face tormented and her clothes ragged, and underneath the words 'Our martyred Cyprus'. This representation contained both the symbolism of Cyprus as a woman mourning for her loss and the reality that actual women faced, whose sons and other family had been killed and whose homes were abandoned in the war. This part of the chapter will consider a number of ways in which women relate to national concerns. Firstly, it considers the ways in which sexuality and marriage link to ethnic exclusivity. Secondly, it looks at the role of women within the national liberation struggle. Thirdly, it gives an account of discourses around refugees and the centrality of women within them. Finally, it turns to population policies which are concerned with ensuring the continuing demographic majority for Greek-Cypriots.

Sexuality and marriage

The control of women within the family ensures that women marry within the collective and according to the cultural, legal and religious rules that prescribe what constitutes a 'good Greek Orthodox' woman. The Greek-Cypriot family is nuclear in ideal form, but may include cohabitation by other members of the family, especially widowed parents. Traditionally, there existed an arranged marriage system. Marriages were usually locally based and co-villagers were generally preferred as marriage partners, since their family history was known and they could be trusted.

Great stress was always placed on female sexual purity and 'honour'. Marriage involved the transfer of property through the dowry contract (*proikosymphono*), which was required by the ecclesiastical courts on betrothal. Both parties needed to be Greek Orthodox in order to marry in church. Marriage and family law still remain under the jurisdiction of the ecclesiastical courts. Intermarriage with the other ethnic groups on the island was extremely rare and for women always entailed the rejection of their own culture and religion, since communal identity was established through the husband.

Marriage arrangements were generally conducted through intermediaries who were older married women who were 'in the know' concerning who was available for marriage. They were entrusted with the initial bargaining in relation to the dowry. More recently close relatives or the parents will make the initial approaches, with their children generally having the right of veto in what can be regarded as a collective decision on the part of the family group (St Cassia 1980). As a general rule men move into their wives' locality since it has been common for the woman to bring a dowry house on marriage for the last 50 years or so (Loizou 1976).

The sexual control of women functions to ensure that the males of the group produce their biological descendants and the 'purity' of their 'stock' is assured. In Cyprus until quite recently women were allowed no contacts with men outside the family unit and the family's honour was dependent on female sexual purity. Women could be divorced if they were discovered not to be virgins on their wedding night – a bloodied sheet was displayed as 'proof' of the wife's virginity during the marriage celebrations. Men, on the other hand, were encouraged to find sexual outlets and to prove their 'manhood' – usually through going regularly to prostitutes in the towns.

Women were important in a number of ways as keepers of the cultural rules that controlled women. Firstly, they were the guardians of the family's honour ensuring that daughters and other unmarried female members of the family were closely supervised to avoid tainting by male contacts and by gossip. Secondly, they tended to be the intermediaries in marriage transactions. Thirdly, they had the most active role within the community in keeping the religious rules and rituals and celebrating the seasonal festivities of Greek Ortho-doxy. They whitewashed houses, decorated the epitaphios, organised the performance of rites, baked sweetmeats for the *panegyria* and so on. It was they who organised the household space symbolically, decorating the house with religious pictures and family photographs, particularly of weddings and baptisms. It was women, generally, who kept contact with relatives who had migrated and it was they who possessed practical knowledge of families and made reputations or marred them in the village community.

The dowry contract (even after it was legally abolished in 1979) specified the terms under which marriage was to be enacted in relation to property. Since the 1940s this entailed an increasing expectation that brides should provide the home, whereas men brought into marriage long-term resources such as income. Apart from the clear advantages this gave women with property in the marriage market it facilitated the quick neo-local settlement of the young couple. Its implications for the development of capitalism are various: the maintenance of low wages on the assumption that no rent was paid; lopsided economic development through investment in property; and the impetus given to consumerism. These are all evident in contemporary Greek-Cypriot life.

The form of the marriage transaction, with its stress on locality, shared values and religion and the transference of property, encouraged intermarriage within social groupings, particularly religious and cultural ones, and contributed to the lack of intermarriage between Greek-Cypriots and Turkish-Cypriots.

There have been a number of changes that need to be noted, although in respect to marriage as an economic transaction and the dowry they have not been significant.[2] Women's position in general, however, has changed. In the few studies in which the position of women and their general attitudes have been the subject of investigation, it appears that girls especially in the towns and from the more educated levels expect and are given much more freedom of movement (Mylonas *et al.* 1982). The increasing participation of women in the labour market (House 1980) and in secondary and higher education are important indicators of social change as well as having consequences for women's position within the household although not necessarily of a 'liberating' kind. A visitor to one of the major towns will quickly notice the existence of a youth sub-culture in clothing and style which is modelled on western Europe and America and includes, for example, boys and girls frequenting hamburger bars and ice-cream parlours. However, these aspects of modern life have not penetrated the most rural areas. On the other hand, frequent visits from relatives living abroad, particularly the London Cypriots, as well as imported television programmes, like 'Dallas' and 'Dynasty', have inevitably left their mark on local traditional values and lifestyles. There has been less change, not surprisingly perhaps, as regards sexual behaviour. The stress on female sexual purity and the prohibition of extra-marital contact remains, although more contact and friendship cannot be prevented between the sexes with women's greater incorporation in the economy and education.[3] Marriage partners are more likely to be chosen by the young people themselves with an expectation of approval by the parents. However, the dowry house is not only retained as an ideal but has become more conspicuous and competitive as economic affluence has grown. It is recognised as a 'social reality' even though there is evidence that many young people disapprove of it (Mylonas *et al.* 1982). Indeed, the state reinforces the dowry rule by providing government housing for women refugees intending to marry but not for men, in order not to disadvantage refugee women in the marriage market. Whatever the intentions of this provision, it serves to give continuing formal recognition and assent to the dowry system.

Motherhood was the most central of the roles that women were expected to play traditionally. However, knowledge about contraception was often absent and its availability was limited. In any case the church prohibited the use of contraceptives and they were generally regarded as sinful. The ideological valuation of motherhood remains in contemporary Cyprus despite the greater use of contraceptives and the rapid decline in the birth rate (House 1981). In a study of the village Lysi immediately prior to 1974 (Markides *et al*. 1978), the majority of first births arrived a year after marriage, a 'proof' of male virility and an assertion of women's 'natural' mothering role.

Until 1974 abortion was legally prohibited, although, in practice, women were able to obtain abortions where they could afford them. The law was amended after 1974 when soldiers violated many women during the Turkish invasion. Abortion was legalised on grounds of rape or other circumstances which would cause a serious undermining of the status of the pregnant woman or her family, where two doctors testified that a pregnant woman was endangered by pregnancy or childbirth, or if the baby risked physical or mental abnormality. It is telling that this dramatic reform, undertaken under the auspices of the ecclesiastical courts, should be instigated not by the fact of rape itself but by rape by Turkish soldiers and fears about the possibility of bearing the children of the 'enemy'. This national 'enemy' was by now conceptualised as the Turkish Army and, by default, the population it was supposedly defending on the island, the Turkish-Cypriots.

The constitution of 1960, when Cyprus was granted independence, established formal political equality between men and women. Despite this, the constitution reinforced the dependence of women on men for communal identification. It established that a married woman belongs to the community to which her husband belongs, and that a male or female child under the age of 21 who is not married belongs to the community to which his or her father belongs. If the father is unknown the child belongs to the community to which his or her mother belongs. The father was designated as the legal guardian of children under the age of 18. Only in cases where there was no father was the mother the legal guardian (Cyprus Social Research Centre 1978).

Women and the national liberation struggle

The form that the national liberation struggle took in Cyprus was contextually related to the form of nationalism that arose within the Greek-Cypriot population and was articulated most forcefully by right wing and chauvinist elements. The EOKA fighters themselves, however, were in the main young Cypriot men and women from both rural and urban backgrounds who were fired by the Enosis ideology. This had become, by this time, the dominant form of ethnic consciousness for all sectors of the Greek-Cypriot population (Anthias & Ayres 1983).

Given the small population of the island and the military presence of the British as well as the co-optation of Turkish-Cypriots by the British as auxiliary policemen and in the militia, EOKA could only be effective as an urban guerilla movement.

Women's role in EOKA has rarely been given prominence. For example, none of the accolades given to ex-EOKA fighters during the post-independence period were received by women. Only as mothers of fallen heroes (like Afxendiou and Pallikarides) were women publicly acclaimed. The important 'rear' activities of women (Yuval-Davis 1985) greatly contributed to EOKA's success, however.

Women played a distinct role in the EOKA movement in relation to men. Firstly, they acted as foils for EOKA fighters and would often accompany men, for whom the British had put out warrants, into the mountains to secret hide-outs (as their wives, fiancées or sisters). In the context of Cypriot values this jeopardised their sexual honour since the company of strange men was frowned upon. There was always the risk that they would be seen or that their fathers or brothers would find out. As they were sworn to total secrecy by the organisation, it was difficult for them to account for their actions. In addition there was always the possibility of sexual harassment, although it appears that this rarely occurred, but some liaisons and romances did develop as one might have expected.

Secondly, women did not carry weapons as such, although they often transported them. For example, after an attack on British soldiers, which usually took place in a crowded street they would receive the weapons used by the men. As searches for weapons were usually only made on men, this minimised the risk of arrest.

Thirdly, women were responsible for carrying information and acted as messengers, often carrying notes and letters which were small enough to be concealed in their underclothes. They also acted as correspondence clerks gathering mail and sorting it out, and some had polygraphic machines hidden in their houses for printing pamphlets which they distributed. This was a task done primarily by schoolgirls.

Fourthly, there were a number of women's units who would actually go out after dark and throw bombs or carry bombs to pass to men.

All these were clearly vital activities and indicate that the risks that women took were often as great as men. Nonetheless, women on the whole were regarded with less suspicion by the British. There were, however, instances of women being arrested and charged. In addition it is important to note that women's involvement had implications for their personal emancipation – many prior to this had barely talked to a man let alone struck up common links.[4]

In the public consciousness, however, the image of women that predominated during this period was one of 'mother of our young martyrs', as tragic, black-clothed women, willing to offer their most precious possession, their sons, for the motherland. Concrete rewards were given neither to women fighters nor to the mothers of heroes after the struggle ended, however, and most of these women retreated into anonymity.

Discourses round refugees – the centrality of women

Women in Cyprus traditionally occupy the domestic sphere, and the loss of their homes and villages after the war was therefore regarded as particularly tragic (Evdokas *et al*. 1976; Phatoura *et al*. 1981; Anthias 1987). The loss of a supportive kinship network, of the community that they had lived their day to day lives in since birth (residence is usually matrilocal) and finally of their dowry-house came as a great and lasting shock to most women.

Homelessness on a vast scale was the most pressing problem the Cypriot state had to face in the immediate aftermath of the war. Initially, the refugees camped in the open ground wherever they could and very soon refugee camps were set up partly with aid from international refugee funds. The massive displacement of the population and the loss of 70 per cent (Public Information Office 1983) of the productive potential, along with major ports and airports, led to mass unemployment.

Since refugees lost their land and homes as well as whatever other property they possessed, they are unable to provide their daughters with a dowry house on marriage. We have already indicated that the state provides a house for intending brides but not refugee bride-grooms, on the assumption that women bring a house into the marriage transaction. In the case particularly of refugee men, it means if they marry a 'foreigner' they will not have a home and therefore will have to move into rented accommodation. Given that incomes have taken into account that most people don't pay rent (to the benefit of employers), they will be disadvantaged.

In order to be able to afford 'something better' than the housing financed by the state, many women have entered paid employment often for the first time. The loss of land and property have been one of the factors that have led to greater incorporation of women into the labour market, within the light manufacturing or service sectors of the economy that have themselves witnessed a rapid expansion (House 1980).

Whilst in the Turkish-Cypriot sector the authorities attempt to wipe out any signs of pre-1974 Cyprus by renaming roads and villages with Turkish names and eliminating any remnants of Greek-Cypriot habitation, the reverse is true in the Greek-Cypriot sector (King & Ladbury 1982). Impermanency is reinforced through the careful maintenance of Turkish-Cypriot names and signs and a rhetoric of 'return'. This is clearly seen as important in the political goal of re-establishing an independent unified state structure for which the return of refugees to their homes and villages is central. The pursuit of a 'comfortable impermanency', as ex-President Kyprianou has called it, has left its marks in a number of ways, however. One of the most significant is the creation and perpetuation of the 'refugee' category, with the continual retelling of the story of loss and uprooting and the reification in the public consciousness of 'our villages' and 'our homes'. Women particularly are central in this, since the villages and homes are experienced as 'lost' in a more fundamental way for them. The few studies that have been done (Evdokas *et al*, 1976; Phatoura *et al.* 1981; Anthias 1985) have indicated the greater cost to women and the greater reliance on 'return' for overcoming their continuing difficulties.

This construction of a refugee category locked in impermanency has also functioned to create an artificial unity to the refugee population where class differences are as evident as within the population as a whole. This supposed social homogeneity within the category and the reinforcement of the division between refugee and non-refugee militates against class discourse as well as drawing attention from those refugees from the commercial entrepreneurial class who have been given favourable financial terms by the Cypriot state in order to encourage the restructuration of Cypriot class division and society along the old lines.

Despite the ideology of return, it is widely recognised that not all refugees will be able to return to their homes and villages, given the interests of Turkey and the Turkish-Cypriots. This serves to construct a real division between refugees from those regions that are most likely to return in the event of a political settlement (such as those from Famagusta) and the rest, thus replacing the dominance of the real division of class differences within the refugee population to one of regional difference. Yet the rhetoric of return remains as a political weapon purveyed by the media, the schools and to a lesser extent the political parties. This leads to a highly contradictory situation – on the one hand a sense of impermanency and thus insecurity for a large proportion of the population, and on the other hand knowledge that the real alternatives to their present situation are very limited.

The case of a particular category of women created by the war, the wives of missing persons, those 2000 or so Greek-Cypriots whose whereabouts are unknown, illustrates most poignantly the impor-tance of women and the family ideologically. These, unlike refugee women (although many of them are refugee women also) have not been given special help by the state (Roussou 1986). Many are economically dependent on their relatives and have had to revert to the pre-adult status that single and divorced women are subjected to, expected to obey their fathers and to forgo male contacts. Local gossip often acts as an effective policing mechanism. The rights of widows of dead soldiers are denied them, as their husbands have not been formally declared dead. They have no rights over their hus-bands' property nor can they become legal guardians of their children. No provisions were introduced to ensure that these women had access to their husbands' property. The moral and social pressure not to institute divorce proceedings which would allow them to marry again is great. The church still objects to granting divorce in many cases and will do so only if the woman has already established another relationship and home with another man.

DEMOGRAPHIC POLICIES

Two of the declared demographic aims of the Cypriot state are to reverse the decline in the birth rate and to raise the labour force participation of women. It is recognised (House 1981) that the potential conflict between these two goals requires policy intervention. In addition there is a concern with emigration. As the third Emergency Action Plan, 1979–81, states: 'As regards population, the Plan aims at the formulation of a proper policy which will gradually lead to the reversal of the various adverse trends and developments in the past few years, particularly as regards emigration and the fall in the birth rate' (Statistics and Research Department, Cyprus 1979: 52). The crude birth rate has fallen from 30 per 1000 between 1946 and 1950 and 25 per 1000 between 1961 and 1965 to 18.5 per 1000 in 1976, representing a decline of 40 per cent over the whole period. By 1985 the rate had increased slightly to 19 per 1000 (Agathangelou 1987: 5). There is an inverse relationship between fertility and education as well as between the crude birth rate and labour-market participation and fertility and urban settlement (House 1981).

It appears unlikely, however, that there can be a reversal of trends towards greater educational attainment for women and urbanisation, both of which are negatively linked to fertility. The state in any case desires an increase in women's economic activity.

A number of measures have been taken to encourage larger families. First of all are those provisions which are exclusively for families with more than four or in some cases more than five, children. For example, there has been free medical treatment available to all members of families with more than four children since 1983. Fare subsidies on public transport are provided, government building-plots are offered at reduced prices and large families have priority in all government housing-schemes. In addition, the eldest son of a large family serves a truncated military service and income tax relief is given for children under 16 attending secondary school and to working mothers for each child looked after in an approved nursery or kindergarten. There has also been an increase in marriage and maternity allowances which have been gradually introduced with the revision of the social insurance law.

In addition to these measures to encourage fertility there have been attempts to improve nursery and day-care provision in order to

allow mothers to work. Sex equality measures are also being introduced to protect pregnant women from dismissal, and maternity
leave with pay is being improved.

Finally, the Technical Committee on Population in its final report
recommended the provision of a monthly family allowance per child
to be given to families with at least four children below 18 for the
third and older children (Chappa 1987).

As part of its demographic policy, the state makes substantial
attempts to prevent the loss of ethnic identity of the large number of
Cypriots who emigrated (Anthias 1981). The Cypriot state sends an
educational mission with teachers and other personnel to Britain, for
example, where the largest number of Cypriots abroad have settled.
Soon after the Turkish invasion (1977) a small government department was set up (Service of Overseas Cypriots), to strengthen the
unity between Cypriots abroad and Cyprus and maintain identity and
culture. In addition, in order to limit the exodus of Cypriots abroad,
temporary employment in other countries is arranged at times of high
unemployment for particular groups.

Various incentives for repatriation have been introduced (Chappa
1987), and there have been special attempts to persuade intellectuals
and professionals to return. But, given the absence of a university
and of a culture open to critical discourse, as well as problems of
graduate unemployment, such moves are doomed to failure.

CONCLUSION

Cyprus appears to be locked in a permanent state of impermanency.
The possibility of a solution on the basis of some form of a federal
state structure has repeatedly faltered (Anthias 1987). While this
stalemate exists, there is the danger of the resurfacing of nationalist
extremism. Until the indigenous political leaders and intellectuals on
both sides can provide a critique and an alternative to the received
wisdoms that often pass as the history of the last 30 years, little hope
exists of overcoming attitudes that stand as powerful obstacles to a
permanent peaceful solution. In the north, Denktash's position as
leader has not been seriously challenged and the presence of the
Turkish army discourages open debate on the Cyprus problem. There
is widespread discontent, however, in the north with the lack of
economic progress; the high level of unemployment; the uncertainty
that Turkish-Cypriot 'southerners' face; the conflict with settlers

brought in from Turkey to change the demographic balance of Cyprus; and the continued interference from Ankara. Only an internationally recognised negotiated solution can resolve these difficulties and this requires concessions on both sides.

Women have been affected by ethnic and national struggles and have been used in a number of ways in the 'national interest'. It is a challenge to both class organisations and to women to resist their co-optation in the nationalist cause and rework alliances with the equivalent forms on the Turkish Cypriot side in the interests of their whole of the *Cypriot* nation.

NOTES

1. There are difficulties in gaining access to information in respect of the Turkish-Cypriot sector, as little published work is available in English, the author does not speak Turkish and, as a Greek-Cypriot, faces difficulties in entering the Turkish-Cypriot sector.
2. As Cypriot society has become more differentiated so have practices relating to marriage and the dowry, with differences between urban and rural areas and in relation to class. In the main, however, the dowry remains significant in marriage choice and the expectations relating to property transference have grown with increasing affluence.
3. To a large extent it has always been the case that women from the higher economic classes have been more 'Westernised' in respect to sexual relations and this remains the case today with women from the towns and professional groupings more likely to accept sexual relations outside marriage than other women.
4. This account is based on information gathered through interviewing a number of women who had been active in EOKA and I am grateful for their willingness to share their experiences with me.

BIBLIOGRAPHY

Agathangelou, A. (1987) 'Patterns and Determinants of Fertility in Cyprus', paper presented to National Workshop on 'Population and Human Resources Development', Nicosia, 13–15 April.

Aimilianides, A. (1938) *The Law Relating to Mixed Marriages* (Greek) (Nicosia: Kypriakai Spoudai).

Anthias, F. (1981) 'Ethnicity and Class amongst Greek-Cypriot Migrants', Ph.D thesis, University of London.

Anthias, F. (1987) 'Cyprus', in C. Clarke and T. Payne (eds), *Politics, Security and Development in Small States* (London: Allen & Unwin).

Anthias, F. (1985) 'The Refugee Issue and Social Change in Cypriot Society', unpublished paper.

Anthias, F. & R. Ayres (1979) 'Nationalism and Socialism in Cyprus', CSE Conference Papers, Conference of Socialist Economics.

Anthias, F. & R. Ayres (1983) 'Ethnicity and Class in Cyprus', *Race and Class*, vol. 25, no. 1, 58–76.

Attalides, M. (ed.) (1977) *Cyprus Reviewed* (Nicosia: Social Research Centre). Edinburgh.

Attalides, M. (1979) *Cyprus: Nationalism and International Politics* (Edinburgh: Press).

St Cassia, P. (1980) 'A Study of Peyia', D Phil. thesis, University of Cambridge.

Chappa, I. (1987) 'Population Policy Issues in Cyprus – Past, Present and Future', paper presented to national workshop on 'Population and Human Resources Development', Nicosia, 13–15 April.

Coufoudakis, V. (ed.) (1976) *Essays on the Cyprus Conflict* (New York: Pella Publishing).

Cyprus Social Research Centre (1978) *Cypriot Women, Rise and Downfall* (Nicosia: Public Information Office).

Evdokas, T., L. Mylona, K. Paschalis, K. Olympios, S. Chimona, E. Kalava, N. Theodorou & E. Demetriadou (1976) *Cyprus Refugees* (Greek) (Nicosia: Social–Psychological Studies).

Hitchens, C. (1984) *Cyprus* (London: Quartet Books).

House, W.J. (1980) *Labour Market Segmentation and Sex Discrimination in Cyprus* (Nicosia: Statistics and Research Department).

House, W.J. (1981) *Socio-economic Determinants of Fertility* (Nicosia: Statistics and Research Department).

House, W.J. (1985) *Cypriot Women in the Labour Market* (Geneva: ILO).

King, R. & S. Ladbury (1982) 'The Cultural Reconstruction of Political Reality in Greek and Turkish Cyprus since 1974', *Anthropological Quarterly*, vol. 55, no. 1, 1–16.

Kitromilides, P. (1977) 'From Co-existence to Confrontation: The Dynamics of Ethnic Conflict in Cyprus', in M. Attalides (ed.) (1977).

Kyriakides, S. (1968) *Cyprus, Constitutionalism and Crisis Government* (University of Pennsylvania Press).

Loizou, P. (1976) 'Changes in Property Transfer among Greek-Cypriot Villagers', *Man* NS, vol. 10, 503–23.

Markides, K., E. Nikita & E.Rangou (1978) *LYSI: Social Change in a Cypriot Village* (Nicosia: Social Reseach Centre).

Mylonas, I., K. Paschalis, E. Kalava, N. Patsalidou & A. Erotokritou (1982) *The Cypriot Woman* (Greek) (Nicosia: Social–Psychological Studies Group).

Phatoura, M. *et al.* (1981) *Cypriot Refugees* (Greek) (Thessalonika University).

Public Information Office (1983) *Cyprus – The Refugee Problem*.

Roussou, M. (1986) 'Women and Political Conflict in Cyprus', in R. Ridd and H. Calloway (eds), *Caught up in Conflict* (London: Macmillan).

Statistics and Research Department, Cyprus (1979) Third Emergency Action Plan.

Yuval-Davis, N. (1985) 'Front and Rear: the Sexual Division of Labour in the Israeli Army', *Feminist Studies*, vol. 11, no. 3, 649–76.

10 Women as the Family: the Foundation of a New Italy?

Lesley Caldwell

INTRODUCTION

This chapter argues that it is through understanding the legacy of the past, particularly the immediately preceding 20 years, that we can more clearly see how the Italian liberal democratic state has attended to women. It stresses the attempts to establish women as a separate constituency fundamental to the construction of a new Italian nation, a nation distinctively different from that aspired to by fascism. It argues that all women were to be legislated for and attended to as part of the progressive stamp of the new republic; at the same time they were, in their traditional familial role, and above all as mothers, to be enlisted in the building of this new nation. By reference to statements from the 1943–8 period, it aims to show some of the problems involved in the new state, fundamentally adhering to traditional understandings of women's needs, obligations, rights and duties, while at the same time endorsing aspirations for progressive legislative reforms in their favour.

WOMEN AND THE STATE IN POST-SECOND WORLD WAR ITALY

The period following the arrest of Mussolini (July 1943) and the collapse of the fascist regime was one of massive political and social upheaval. Italy was devastated by the continuation of the world war raging in Europe generally and in the national territory in particular. In 1946 a referendum established the republic and dissolved the monarchy; women were given the vote in that year. Economic and social reconstruction involved the establishment of a new political machinery that would direct a different form of state. An interim

168

government, 1946–8, distinguished by two different coalitions, was made responsible for drawing up the constitution.

In the period 1943–8 there were inevitably whole areas of continuity with fascism. These included the form of personnel, of laws, of some state institutions and of the re-endorsement of the fascist state's agreements with the Vatican. This continuity is of particular interest in matters of women and the family. Moreover, it suggests that the importance of the ideological and cultural dimensions of the transformation were more porblematic than the dismantling of the more straightforwardly repressive aspects of fascism. The continuities, as Pavons (1974: 140) insists, built on the continuities of a particular class domination and socio-economic structure. They are also the result of the political choices followed through in the 1943–7 period and the continuities represented by the line of heads of government in which there was no rupture. These choices were not only the result of the estimation and strategies of the political parties involved but also of the pressures from the Allies for reconstruction in a particular way.

The historical role of Catholicism is also central in understanding developments in the Italian national state from 1946 onwards. The late unification of Italy (1861) was effected against the claims of organised Catholicism and one way the church attempted to counter the power of the centralised state was through the development of cultural, educational, financial and welfare networks.

The area of welfare assistance is especially relevant here, since much discussion of state support involves the provision of services that are seen as supplementing and extending the needs attended to families, especially by mothers. The state law of 1890 that grouped welfare institutions under state control in practice often left that control to the church. This is important because the way the church and certain apparatuses of the state have combined and divided areas of responsibility which in other countries have been more tightly brought under state control is an important aspect of the Italian situation after 1948, where, until the 1970s, church-supported institutions have supplemented and provided what the state does/did not in care and provision for children, the old, the sick and so on.

The 20 years of fascism relates both to the church (although this cannot be discussed here) and to the position of women. In Italy it is above all fascism that introduced legislation regarding social assistance and insisted on the obligation of the state to provide for the family (Saraceno 1981). This was linked to a concern with the forging of a strong and healthy Italian nation through an overt set of policies that aimed at population increase. These policies were especially, though not exclusively, directed at women as mothers; they included encouragement to get married and to produce large families.[1] The fascists also introduced advanced legislation relating to working mothers; they restructured but did not substantially alter the family law that had been in operation since 1865; they introduced penalties for abortion and forbade the spread of information on contraception. Perhaps of even greater importance for the discussion here, they operated an extended propaganda campaign on the importance of women's place in the family and the personal and national importance of motherhood. This represents a generalisable trend in the twentieth-century state towards responsibility for regulation of increasingly large areas of the apparently personal and private life. L'ONMI, *Opera Nazionale Maternita Infanzia*, was the first state organisation with national responsibility for the needs of mothers and children. Founded in 1925, it lasted till 1975. It is the institution of prime importance here.

There was continuity in laws regarding the protection of motherhood and infancy; the norms governing welfare for illegitimate and abandoned children or foundlings; the health law; the family law (revised 1975); the juvenile court and its organisation; the forms of regulation of 'criminal' minors; the penal code. The latter has still not received complete revision, although some of its Articles have been revoked. Of specific relevance here are the Articles referring to abortion, to the sale and advertisement of contraceptives and the differential criminal status of adultery. The modes by which women are separately attended to in these laws reproduce the emphases of fascism but they also further legitimise church positions. The heritage left by the fascist state, the powerful position of the Catholic Church and the growing state concern for families and for mothers reveals a powerful interlocking set of mechanisms in postwar Italy. Official state documents like the constitution, in existence alongside discriminatory laws, construct and legitimise particular accounts of women and of relations between mother and child. These make demands for freedom from traditional female roles for women more difficult to enact. Arguably it was only in the 1970s that a significant shift occurred in the legal position of women as bearers of reproductive capacities which do not automatically negate their other rights as Italian citizens.

In Italy the Catholic Church has reinforced the tendency to regard women as biological reproducers and nurturers and to regard them highly. There are clearly parallels between fascist rhetoric on motherhood and the church's stress on women as mothers first and foremost. When similar views about women are reproduced in official state accounts their importance is further extended by the association with church accounts. This highlights the difficulty of offering alternative accounts or positions when the preceding years had been dominated with a concern with women as reproducers and as builders of the nation only in so far as they *were* reproducers. The new Italian state, through official texts and other statements, insists that it is distancing itself from the fascist regime in that it sees women as equal partners in the construction of a new nation. However, in certain of its statements (say, Article 2 the constitution), it guarantees female equality, but in other of the Articles of the constitution it formally disavows this equality (Article 37). In its more general claims and appeals to all women it inveighs against the position offered to woman under fascism, but continues to endorse laws formulated under the fascist regime. The new state inevitably utilises and draws upon accounts of what it is to be a woman, and an Italian woman, that substantially reproduce those of fascism.

Examination of the debates surrounding the constitution reveals an inability and a refusal to go beyond cultural assumptions about women as biological reproducers. This works alongside the Catholic account of the family, women's primary position in it and the ordering of more general civil rights on that basis. And it is this that contributes to the long delays in reforming whole areas of the law that are seen to touch women in their familial obligations first and foremost. The legislators for the new nation, for all their insistence on the imperative need to take their distance from fascism, are caught in an extremely contradictory view of women and their proper and just place in a new and progressive democracy. For, as fascism demonstrated in a more clear cut way, the emphasis on reproduction entails other implications for the social position of women, implications that in hierarchically ordering their capacities and legislation either protectively or repressively about them may be used to justify other sets of sanctioned but potentially oppressive practices. The uncritical identification of Italian women as mothers, common to fascism and the Catholic Church, forms the basis of discussion in the establishment of the liberal democratic republic. The position offered to women is one that seeks to endorse their rights as citizens while insisting that motherhood is their major contribution to the building of a new collectivity, a nation united. A generalised rhetoric appeal to all women is the norm. Its basis is that of biological sex and the capacity to reproduce, and it is completely taken for granted. But the meanings associated with this are only established with reference to the structuring conditions of women's lives and there is a vast step from the attribution of a potential to the concrete conditions in which actual women may, can and do exercise three capacities. Here age, class situation, marital status and geographical location are important, and it is by reference to specific laws that ways of legislating for women as wives, as mothers, as older women and as workers may be distinguished.

But the discussions about the place women are offered or called upon to occupy in the new Italian nation make their appeal to a presumed unity whose basis is the cultural traditions that link the biological and the social. It is clear that there is a disjunction between the number of central structuring issues glossed over by the appeal to all women and the omnipresence of these other appeals. Public rhetorics of difference, the claims through which the demonstrable gap between the former shamed regime and the present–future one which the strengths of democracy are paramount, were an extremely important target. How 'women' feature in statements of the period gives important indicators on how they are discursively constituted in the new Italy and the kinds of roles assigned to them.

At the General Sitting of the Constituent Assembly on International Women's Day, 8 March 1947, it is one of the 22 women representatives who confirms the identification of women and the family. She uses it to draw out two important emphases: the first is the idea of the Italian nation as a family, that is attended to by women; and the second the union of national and Christian (i.e. Catholic) ideas in support of this:

> We do not forget, and we never shall forget, that our first task, and the highest and most social one, is the family; that motherhood is our privilege and because of that, we have claimed, are claiming, from the new constitution those new legal dispositions, like the family wage, like limits of women's work, that allow us to fully attend to our family function:
> Moreover, today, we feel that a much broader family demands our sacrifices and dedication; that all the Italian people are our family and that we must work to bring the spirit of the family into this social family. This is precisely the Christian spirit. (Session of the Assembled Constituents, 8 March 1947)

In the next section of this chapter I briefly present three contemporary sets of statements about women and the family. These are:

(1) the discussions in the Constituent Assembly on the Constitution;
(2) statements from the Italian Communist Party (PCI);
(3) statements from the Union of Italian Women (UDI).

Each of these occupies a very different terrain, comprises different aims and objects and assumes a radically different weight institutionally and politically. My aim in bringing them together is to testify to the ways and forms through which the variety of discourses about women and the family were commonly articulated in a vital period for postwar Italy. I suggest that the reliance on a set of understandings of the elision between women and the family and women and mothers is common to all three sets, that the tenacity of these accounts owes much to the strength of Catholicism and the legacy of facism, and that the task of legislating a different place for women is ultimately dependent on a biologism whose cultural effects act to constrain the official legal position of Italian women despite the activities of the women's emancipation movement and the workers' movements for much of the postwar period. The directions politically set in place during this time, the legal formulations role for Italian women as their special responsibility and expectation combine to establish some of the structuring conditions through which other massive postwar changes, e.g. emigration, have had their effects and are to be understood.

Aspirations towards formal equality conceal a multitude of problems in attempting a separate appeal to women as *first* women and *then* Italian citizens. The nationalist appeal gains strength through identification with other, taken-for-granted sources of emotional security and privilege.

THE CONSTITUENT ASSEMBLY

Elections for the Constituent Assembly, one of whose major tasks would be to draw up the constitution of the republic, were held in 1946. In these elections Christian democrats gained 35.2 per cent of the vote and the PCI–PSI combined, 39.6 per cent proportion to their overall elected numbers. Of the 20 women who had been elected to the Assembly four took part in the three sub-commissions set up to hammer out a form of wording for certain Articles, two communists, a socialist, and a Christian democrat.

This section refers to the substance of the discussions in the First and Third Sub-Commissions, respectively concerned with legal definitions of the family and marriage, and with state concern for the economic and social problems of the family. These Commissions met through the latter half of 1946, and their decisions were incorporated in Articles 3, 29, 31, 37 of the Constitution.[2] But it is the bases and presuppositions of these meetings that is of interest here. The final wording of the constitution establishes a series of norms that confirm a woman's place as mother as 'essential'. This directs many of the other issues, especially those with more direct policy implications, and serves to impede the other struggles for women's rights before the law in the subsequent period.

These meetings form a core of debates about how the family is to be understood and its institutional position guaranteed. The extent to which the family is seen as known and relatively unproblematic appears to depend on an absolute insistence on the role of women as mothers within it. It is not just that women are mothers first and foremost, it is that women *as* mothers may be seen as the guarantors of the family whether its timelessness and eternal aspects are being stressed or whether it is the family as an historically specific institution that is emphasised. There is little disagreement about the claims of motherhood and about women's primary familial location even when it is women workers that are the ostensible focus, or when equal treatment is being argued in conjunction with the idea that men and women have a different mission:

> The special and essential mission of woman is motherhood. This is a concept that must always be kept in the forefront. When there is concern for the working woman this is a concern above all for the fact of motherhood, for the tutelage of her condition before, during and after birth. What must be guaranteed to the working woman is being able to deal adequately with those special needs that surround maternity. (Terracini, in full session of the Assembled Constituents, 1947 p. 206)

This condensation of women's identity within the family is accompanied by a failure to recognise the complexity of state regulation of motherhood. For example, in the discussion on provision for mothers and for youth (Sessions of the Prima Sottocommissione, 7 November

1946 p. 372) the discussion never touches maternity; the appropriate forms of provision for the young are discussed but the one central provision concerning support for maternity is agreed in the First Commission without any discussion of its implications. Or in the Third Sub-Commission the discussion on the social function of motherhood, introduced by Teresa Noce (PCI) consistently adhered to the idea of the mother as the family despite discussion of irregular familial arrangements, such as unmarried mothers:

Protection for mothers means protection for society at its roots because around the mother, the family is established and through the mother, society's future is guaranteed. There is a need for insurance but also for welfare. Further, confirming the principle of the protection of the mother means attending to *all* children, including illegitimate ones. (Merlin, in the Session of the Prima Sottocommissione. 1946 p. 34)

Both this point and the discussion in the First Commission on state financial support for the family came up against Catholic belief about normal families and conservative restrictions on state support for the unworthy or the immoral, but the general point was unanimously accepted.

Togliatti (PCI) argues that women work both outside and inside the family, without prioritising one or the other, but still says that 'generally' women as mothers *are* the family. Moro (DC), concerned that women's entry into public life may lead to less weight being given to their familial roles, wants the constitution not only to guarantee certain things about the family but to structure and constrain women so as to ensure a continuation of their familial role and the primacy of their biological potential. (Sessions of the Prima Sottocommissione, 1946 p. 207).

Although the very themes that distinguish these debates testify to the framework of Catholic understandings that provide the discursive parameters here, there is little clear agreement about them, or about the policy implications that derive from them. However, the unanimity about women as the family is clear and indicates their central place in ensuring a healthy Italian nation.

The themes of these debates indicate the recognition that the modern state must assume responsibility and concern for areas that had been largely unattended to. Concern for the individual and for the private space of the family and its rights is also consistently put forward. The links between family, state and individual are seen as problematic and to be legislated in conformity with other emphases, the link between family and nation previously mentioned and the issue of whether the family is a natural association (a Catholic formulation).

To give two examples of the latter:

> There can be no doubts about the fact that the family is a natural society. (Sessions of the Prima Sottocommissione, 5 November 1946 p. 388; Sitting (11))

> Saying that the family is recognised by the state in so far as it is a natural society means allowing the possibility of that recognition even for families that are constituted outside the marital bond, families, that is, that are deprived of the crism of legality and the religious sacrament. In this sense concubinage would be recognised by the state. (ibid, 339)

The small degree of agreement on these issues is not surprising given the vast range of issues gathered under the rubric of the family: for example, the rights of and between married couples in relation to their children and the conditions in which state intervention can be countenanced; the relentless adherence to the metaphor of the health of the country as residing in the healthy family with indissolubility the only ultimate guarantee of this individual as well as national territorial stability; the family as bearer of the moral standards of a new society; the recognition that without certain external support, financial or otherwise, the family cannot fulfil its functions.

Throughout these debates the merging of the identity of woman with the family and with the new Italy is assumed. This acts to single women out as indispensible contributors to the forging of the new nation. Within the discussion of rights it also aims to extend a place to women as citizens, a place symbolised by the vote. But the retention of inegalitarian laws alongside the stress on the primacy of the family as women's place creates a set of difficult and restrictive norms from which to pursue women's parity with men.

THE ITALIAN COMMUNIST PARTY (PCI)

The Italian Communist Party had been founded in 1921 and under fascism existed underground or outside Italy. Party members were active organisers in the Resistance, participated in the committees of national liberation in the period after 1943, and collaborated in successive governments until their expulsion in May 1947, an expulsion which was tied to continued US support for reconstruction. In the PCI after 1944 its leader, Togliatti, saw reconstruction in terms of the establishment of a pluralist party system and the abandonment of working class opposition, in favour of collaboration with all democratic forces in the construction of a new 'demographic regime'. The continuity of PCI policy on this issue is fairly generally attested (Blackmer 1977; Napolitano 1977; Sassoon 1977). But it is its position on the family and its understanding of the 'woman question' that is of interest here.

The PCI's development of the 'woman question' in the postwar period is organised on an axis where poles are the family and its capacity for change on the one hand, and women's rights to waged work on the other. Theoretically and politically, the party combines the emphases of the international communist movement with the strength of cultural traditions that echo those of Catholicism.

Togliatti, leader of the PCI from his return from Moscow (1944) to his death in 1964, identified women as one of the major groups who would contribute to the reconstruction of Italy. Their centrality was a position shared neither by all party members nor all cadres, men or women. Togliatti's account encloses the specificity of the woman question in a set of Marxist categories that tie women's oppression to class oppression and to the need for a complete transformation of all existing social relations. But an elaboration of the woman question that engaged with its more problematic aspects is absent from PCI accounts. The importance of the family both for the Italian nation and for the health of all its citizens is continually insisted upon and the recourse to very traditional images of motherhood and femininity remain the central stamp of these accounts.

Unlike the Catholics, the communists do not dispute the supposed disruption of the bases of family life implied as following from women's waged work. They argue its necessity for the emancipatory process, but their position does not depend on a different evaluation of women's 'natural' role nor any challenge to their primary familial location. 'Today the family presents itself more than ever before as the original nucleus on which the citizens and the state must depend for the social and moral renewal of Italy (Rinascita 1 September 1946).

This article by Jotti sets out some of the considerations on the family that shape PCI statements in the period under study and well beyond. On the basis of the disruption and chaos occasioned by fascism, wartime conditions and the occupation, the family, given its traditional primacy in Italian life, is regarded as the obvious place from which to begin a reconstruction of the unity and solidarity that will be required to forge the nation anew: 'The state recognizes and attends to the family as the foundation of the material and moral prosperity of the nation' (Jotti 1946).

In conjunction with the party's emphasis on the moral position of the family it is the links between family, state and nation that provide the major orientation for the PCI's accounts for legislative reform. The latter sought to equalise the status of husbands and wives, to remove the anti-democratic features endorsed by fascism and to give the family those marks of serenity and dignity that would enable women to see marriage in a completely different way; through legal reform the family would become 'a font of joy and an aid for the development of the real personality of the wife':

> The woman acquires an independence (through right to work and other legal rights) that allows her to see marriage not as an expedient forced upon her as the only means of solving a difficult economic situation but as the satisfaction of a deep natural, moral and social need, as the means of her development and the crowning glory of her personality. (Jotti 1946)

In this account the links between marriage, the family and women's particular relation to it are as unproblematically tied together for the party as they are for the church. Despite the importance of the discourse of work for the communists they retain a conception of women's essential 'womanliness' that is not only linked to her familial locations but crucially dependent on it.

The PCI argues for state regulation through the introduction of welfare measures that will complement the necessary and desired work of women and will also provide the facilities for a different set of possibilities both in the family and in the more general relation between family and society. From the 1940s on, then, the PCI consistently support demands for state assistance and for the development of a network of health, education and social services that will provide an infrastructure of support enabling the Italian family to flourish and to provide the maximum possibilities for its members and for society.

Here the PCI may be seen as representing one wing of the modernising voices; their explicit commitment is to the need for state support and state intervention and an insistence that the modern family does not manage alone. But, in recognising the comprehensive and contradictory demands placed on the modern family, the PCI insists that it does not wish to deny the differences between men and women, or the privacy of the family; rather, its aim is to offer a different position to women in the family and a new position for the family in society, which, far from destroying the family, will safeguard and strengthen it.

UNIONE DONNE ITALIANE (UDI)

The Union of Italian Women (UDI) dates from September 1944. The initiative grew out of the groups for the defence of women that had grown up in the north towards the end of 1943 and groups in the centre and in Naples associated with the circulation of a clandestine news-sheet, *No. 1 Donne.*

Initial hopes for a united organisation were unsuccessful and Catholic women remained apart in their own separate organisation. The history of UDI, as it relates to a politics of and for women conducted within a commitment to socialist perspectives, is an important one both from the point of view of its gains and its losses. Its position is characterised particularly by a twofold orientation: firstly, an acknowledgement of the strength of Catholicism and a wish to avoid any challenge to it; and secondly, an account that sees the masses of Italian women trapped in traditional understandings, a situation encouraged and exaggerated by facism.

Within these perspectives UDI was committed to the link between family and nation and, in line with its strong links with the PCI, the link between the renewal of Italian society and women's emancipation. It aimed to provide a means for all Italian women to participate in the political and social life of the country.

As Mafai (1979: 37) points out, women in the Resistance are afterwards mobilised on two fronts. One of these was to provide assistance of various kinds to male combatants as well as providing support for families, children and so on. Although this was a traditional form of women's activity (both organised and unorganised), it was nonetheless important. The other, participation in military campaigns etc., was distinctively different. Both of these fronts need to be recognised and understood, as does the situation of the many women who remained outside either of them. The armed struggle was a mode of participation for both men and women for a far briefer time, but with this proviso: the major orientation in the post-liberation period was consistently towards traditional female tasks, combined with a commitment to full civil rights for women and the attempts to mobilise women workers.

The First Congress in October 1945 stressed the conquest of political rights and full participation for women in the life of the country; it especially stressed the right to work, demanded equal pay for equal work, improved working conditions, the provision of nurseries and the provision of training schools such as those that existed for men. It also stressed the need to guarantee women at home 'an adequate protection in law'. The conference argued for the education of women through the establishment of classes at work, evening classes, travelling libraries etc., all designed to begin to counteract the position of degradation and ignorance encouraged by fascism. These aims, together with the demand for legal reforms to ensure the removal of gross inequalities within families and the provision of welfare services, conform to traditional ways of effecting change in the practice of women's organisations.

In the sphere of response to the devastation of war, hunger and starvation, there is also the view of the family as an 'irreplaceable and fundamental nucleus', and a stress on the role of mother within it. This is not to underestimate the task in hand at that time but at this time one looks in vain to the specifically directed women's organisation for a recognition of some of the problems that pertain to the elision of women and the family.

In the pursuit of a politics for the new Republic it is again the family that is given pride of place, it is the family on which the new Nation depends, and it is the family that is seen as the thing to safeguard. The inappropriateness of putting other views and the directions taken then establish forms of accommodation that endure until the seventies. One looks in vain for the public voice of opposition.

When you have the will, there's time for everything; this is what those women who don't shut themselves egotistically in their own homes know. They understand that being mothers means that through their love for their own children they arrive at a love for all babies. In this way they recognise the imperative of working to construct a future of peace and well-being for all. (I Camino, 1945–6)

CONCLUSION

In this chapter I have suggested that the Italian Republic was concerned constitutionally to offer women an equality they had never had before. This had the support of the Communist Party and the Socialist Women's Organisation. How this was argued and presented reveals a basic set of assumptions that remain unchallenged in the period and for some considerable time after. In itself this may not have been so significant but for the generalised insistence on the appeal for distance and separation from the former regime.

The project of legislating and prescribing a different way of regulating women when the terms in which this is presented are almost identical, is one that is extremely daunting. There is considerable hesitation and distaste for the extremes of fascist demographic propaganda, but not sustained challenge to its assumptions. The constitutional aspirations co-exist perfectly well alongside the extensive commitment to Catholic concepts and alongside the laws that prescribe profoundly unequal parental and marital relations.

Motherhood in Italy has been idealised certainly, but the tenacity with which it was invoked in the period of reconstruction and the durability of these accounts was materially and legally supported by the new Italian state above all in defining a specific space for women in the construction of the new, and distinctively different, Italy. I have pointed to the difficulties for those postwar organisations committed to a politics of and for women by the initial inability to look beyond women's biological capacity.

NOTES

1. For an account of the fascist period, see L. Caldwell, 'Reproducers of the Nation', in D. Forgacs (ed.) *Rethinking Italian Fascism* (London: Lawrence & Wishart, 1986).
2. Article 3.
   All citizens are invested with equal social status and are equal before the law, without distinction as to sex, race, language, religion, political opinions, personal or social conditions.
   Article 29.
   The state recognises the family as a natural association founded on marriage.

Marriage is based on the moral and legal equality of husband and wife within the limits laid down by the law for ensuring family unity.
Article 31.
The republic facilitates, by means of economic and other provisions, the formation of the family and the fulfilment of the tasks connected therewith, with particular consideration for large families.

It safeguards maternity, infancy and youth, promoting and encouraging institutions necessary for such purposes.
Article 37.
Female labour enjoys equal rights and the same wages for the same work as male labour. Conditions of work must make it possible for them to fulfil their essential family duties and provide for the adequate protection of mothers and children.

The republic prescribes special measures for safeguarding juvenile labour and guarantees equal pay for equal work.

BIBLIOGRAPHY

Ballastrero, M.V. (1979) *Dalla tutela alla parita* (Bologna: Il Mulino).
Blackmer, D. (1977) 'Continuity and Change in Postwar Italian Communism', in D. Blackmer & S. Tarrow (eds) (1977).
Blackmer, D. & S. Tarrow (eds) (1977) *Communism in Italy and France* (Princeton University Press).
Caldwell, L. (1986) 'Reproducers of the Nation', in D. Forgacs (ed.) *Rethinking Italian Fascism* (London: Lawrence & Wishart).
Camino, Il in 'Internal Document of UDI' (Union of Italian Women), 1945.
Candeloro, G. (1953) *Il movimento cattolico in Italia* (Rome: Riuniti).
Jotti, N. (1946) 'La famiglia e lo stato', *Rinascita*, 1 September.
Mafai, M. (1979) *L'apprendistato della politica* (Rome: Editori Riuniti).
Michetti, M., M. Repetto and L. Viviani (1984) *UDI: Laboratorio di politica delle donne* (Rome: Cooperative libera stampa).
Napolitano, G. (1977) *The Italian Road to Socialism* (London: Journeyman Press).
Pavone, C. (1974) 'La continuita dello stato Instituzioni e uomini', in AAVV *Italia 1945–1948. Le origini della repubblica* (Turin: Giappicheli).
Poggi, G. (1972) 'The Church in Italian Politics 1945–1956', in S.J. Woolf (ed.) (1972).
Saraceno, C. 'Percorsi di vita femminile nella classe operaia. Tra famiglia e lavora durante il fascismo', *Memoria*, vol. 2 (October) 64–75.
Sassoon, D. (1977) 'The Ideology and Strategy of the Postwar Italian Communist Party', doctoral dissertation, London University.
Woolf, S.J. (ed.) (1972) *The Rebirth of Italy 1943–50* (London: Longman).

Official documents

Sessions of the Assembled Costituente, 1947. Full.
Sessions of the Prima Sottocommissione, 26 July–19 December 1946.
Sessions of the Terza Sottocommissione, 26 July–26 October 1946.

Index